Economics

Chris Brownless BA

GW00691164

Charles Letts & Co Ltd
London, Edinburgh & New York

First published 1989
by Charles Letts & Co Ltd
Diary House, Borough Road, London SE1 1DW

Text: © Chris Brownless 1989
Illustrations: Kevin Jones Associates © Charles Letts & Co Ltd 1989

British Library Cataloguing in Publication Data

Brownless, Chris
  Economics
  1. Economics
  I. Title
  330

ISBN 0 85097 852 1

Chris Brownless is Principal Lecturer in Economics at Staffordshire Polytechnic and head of their Economic Forecasting Service. He is co-author of *Basic Economics*, published by Butterworths, and has played a leading role in the development of the polytechnic's access schemes.

The author and publishers are grateful to the following organizations for their kind permission to reproduce questions from their past examination papers. (The model answers and answer plans are the author's own and have not been provided or approved by the examining bodies.)

The Chartered Association of Certified Accountants (*ACCA*)
The Chartered Institute of Bankers (*CIB*)
The Institute of Chartered Accountants in England and Wales (*ICA*)

Dedicated to Pauline, Annette and George

Printed and bound in Great Britain by
Charles Letts (Scotland) Ltd

Contents

1 Study skills

1.1 Introduction

Whether you find economics easy or a struggle, your results will be improved by paying attention to the points raised in this chapter. It is often assumed, by students and teachers alike, that appropriate study skills will have been acquired during secondary education. Anybody who has marked essays, projects or examination scripts knows that there is little evidence of this. So–to use the language of economists–if you want to maximize your marks you should allocate some of your scarce resource, time, to improving your study skills.

This chapter will teach you:

- how to approach study in higher education
- how to get the most out of lectures
- how to read textbooks and take notes from them
- how to write essays and reports
- how to revise for examinations
- how to perform as well as you can in examinations

1.2 The right approach to study

1.2.1 The importance of private study

Private study is very important in higher education. In contrast to GCSE and even A-level or equivalent courses, you will find that you are expected to work very much on your own. Students on business and social sciences courses are usually expected to spend about three hours in private study for every hour spent in class. The emphasis is on **you learning** rather than **you being taught**. This is only right, because for many of you this is the culmination of your formal education and the next step will be a responsible job where you will have to work on your own initiative.

Higher education aims to foster an enquiring approach and help students develop analytic and critical skills rather than encouraging the learning of 'chunks of knowledge' which rapidly become out of date. Rote learning will not take you very far–instead, you must concentrate on understanding ideas and ways of thinking. This approach emphasizes reading, thinking, writing and tackling problems and exercises, activities pursued almost entirely outside the classroom. Formal teaching is concerned with directing your study, answering your questions and helping you with problem areas, developing your communication skills and to some extent assessing your performance.

As private study is so important you need to be sure that your study skills are good enough to cope with the burden. No one will check whether you take notes in lectures, let alone whether you adopt the right approach.

1.2.2 School leavers, mature students and part-timers

If you have just completed 13 years of compulsory education at school you may feel that life seems to have been little more than writing essays and sitting examinations and that you have no more to learn about studying itself. Unfortunately, this is seldom true–there is a quantum leap beween school/college and higher education. It is not just that higher education places much more responsibility on the student; the type of answers expected in essays and examinations is different. This can be a particular problem with economics, where many students have studied the subject at A-level and believe, because the material is similar, that they have learnt enough to cope with a higher education course. If it is not appreciated that the subject matter will be studied in greater depth, familiarity can become a liability.

It is increasingly the case that students joining courses are returning to education after a gap of, sometimes, many years. If you are a mature student you may well feel apprehensive. Study skills like reading a textbook or writing an essay do become rusty after a time; but it is usually a straightforward matter to bring them back to a satisfactory standard, providing you recognize the problem and devote some time to tackling it. In spite of their lack of recent study practice, mature students often have an advantage over their younger colleagues: the experiences of working and bringing up a family often promote the self-discipline essential to private study.

Other readers will be studying courses on a part-time basis. You will have several extra difficulties: your job or family responsibilities will make great demands on your time. This means that it is even more important to make sure that your private study time is utilized efficiently. You will probably have less opportunity than full-time students to see your tutors and—equally important—you will probably not have the same chances to talk about the course with fellow students. These difficulties will be recognized by your tutors and they will attempt to compensate for them.

However, there are a number of steps you can take to ease your task. You will have to rely on textbooks more heavily than your full-time colleagues; so take time in choosing them and be prepared to spend generously. Make sure you tackle all self-test questions— this is a highly useful way of checking that you understand the material. Try to arrange to meet some other students on the course so that you can discuss topics together. Finally, if you are still having difficulties after reading your books and notes, arrange to see your tutor—a few minutes spent discussing a problem can sometimes save hours of anguish.

Whatever your background before coming into higher education, you cannot afford to neglect private study; time spent improving your study skills will be amply rewarded.

1.2.3 Getting into a routine

To study effectively, you need to be organized: the majority of your study will be done on your own outside the classroom. When and where this work is done is up to you. Essay deadlines will force you to do some work, but this alone will be insufficient. You may not think you have covered much new material in a particular subject in one week; but when you add up all the new material from all the subjects you are studying the amount will be significant. Two or three weeks of neglect will pose real difficulties as you struggle to make up a backlog while more new ideas are being introduced. It is harder and more time consuming to return to a topic after a gap of several weeks or months than it is to tackle it while it is being covered in class. The first topics you meet will be the basic building blocks of your subjects and if you fail to master these at the time, the rest of the course will be difficult or even impossible.

1.2.4 Relaxation

Despite what has been said so far a student's life should not be all work. The traditional non-academic activities of student life are an important part of the broad educational experience that higher education should provide. There is, in any case, a limit to the amount you can take in during any one study session. So when you plan your work schedule make sure you programme in short breaks in private study periods and distinct parts of the week, month and year when you relax and put work to one side.

Having preached the importance of study skills, it is now time to look at some of these skills more closely.

1.3 Lectures

1.3.1 Preparation

The lecture is an important teaching method in higher education. It may be formal, with an audience of several hundred, or more intimate, with only a few students present. However large or small the number on a course, a certain amount of class time will be spent with a lecturer conveying information to students who take notes. The role and limitations of this teaching method should be recognized.

A lecture is an efficient way of providing an overview of a course by indicating its scope and approach; it can therefore help direct your study. It can also be used to explain difficult subject areas. While this can be done in a lucid, motivating and entertaining way, you should not expect too much from lectures. They are useful for passing on information but it generally requires more time and effort on the part of the student to acquire real understanding. As a general rule nobody ever fully grasps ideas while they are being presented: a lecture is only a prelude to private study.

While most of the work associated with a lecture will take place afterwards, you should consider some previous preparation. You will probably have been given a list of lecture topics at the beginning of the course; failing this, the lecturer will indicate at the end of each lecture the subject matter of the next. This will allow you to do some preparatory reading. This should not be overdone in case you go off in the wrong direction; but a quick read through of a relevant chapter in a textbook will start you thinking and help you get more out of the lecture.

1.3.2 Taking notes

Taking notes in lectures is not easy. You need to listen to what the lecturer is saying, decide the important points and write them down in a form that will be of use later. Avoid extreme reactions to this task; do not unselectively write down as much as you can of what the lecturer is saying—you cannot, and should not, produce a verbatim account. The opposite extreme is to write down little or nothing, believing that attentive listening will suffice. It will not. Even an hour after the lecture, it is unlikely that you will be able to recall very much of what was said without the aid of notes.

You need to listen carefully and make notes of the main points. The lecturer should help by using the blackboard, overhead projector or some other mean of emphasis to indicate the principal headings, concepts and arguments.

The lecture should be a structured survey of a topic and your notes should reflect this structure. Use headings and subheadings labelled by letters and numbers to indicate the relative importance of points. Underlining and indentation help to distinguish the main points. This format will help you when you reread your notes. If you do not have time to write down all the points you can include the appropriate label and hope that a colleague (or the lecturer) will be able to fill the gap for you later.

In economics we make frequent use of diagrams, which are useful ways of summarizing analysis and argument. However, they can sometimes seem complicated and when you encounter a new diagram the significance of particular points or lines is not always immediately obvious. If you use different colours you will find diagrams easier to understand when you reread your notes. This is particularly useful where a diagram is built up by adding lines and points during the lecture—the different colours can correspond to stages in the argument. Do not make your diagrams too small as they will be much more difficult to decipher later.

In lectures the student role is at its most passive; this passivity can even turn to sleep. But you should not be misled—you need to work hard in lectures because you will be carrying out a number of tasks (listening, comprehending, evaluating and writing) simultaneously. If you are tired or hungry or preoccupied with other matters, you will get less out of your lectures.

1.3.3 After the lecture

The usefulness of a lecture largely depends on what you do afterwards. You should look at your notes very soon, preferably within hours. Add points or arguments that you can recall but did not have time to write down during the lecture. Rectify gaps in your notes by asking colleagues. It will generally be necessary to write up your lecture notes more neatly and clearly.

In most cases the lecture will have been an introduction and guide to a topic. Do not be surprised to find that there are parts of it you do not feel sure about. Take a lecture on production theory or international trade. Nobody has every fully understood those concepts simply by listening to a lecture: understanding requires reading, thinking and discussion. The lecture will have given you a framework to fill in by reading textbooks or articles and reinforce through exercises and seminar/tutorial discussion.

1.4 Tutorials and seminars

In addition to lectures, most courses provide a series of classes, tutorials or seminars where you are in small groups with a tutor. The form these take varies greatly between courses and institutions; but some general points are worth making.

This is your opportunity to raise questions about the areas of the subject which you are finding difficult. The format and the size of the lecture normally permits only an occasional question. It is important that you ask about points of difficulty at the appropriate stage in the course. This will allow you to make more sense of your reading and help you to grasp concepts that may be crucial to understanding later stages of the course. Do not feel embarrassed about raising difficulties—problems experienced by one student are usually shared by others. Do not forget that your tutor will be aware of those subject areas which cause problems and will have experience in helping students to understand them. So although you should always try to overcome difficulties yourself through your reading you should seek help when you get really stuck.

A second function of the tutorial or seminar is to provide an opportunity for student discussion. This is an important aspect of the learning process and of education in general. You should appreciate that there is debate and controversy over many areas of theory and policy and that there are different levels of understanding. Discussion promotes the greater confidence and understanding of ideas that it is the aim of higher education to develop.

A final and related point is the need for you to develop communication skills. In higher education much attention is rightly given to assessing a student's ability to present written arguments; but whatever job you eventually choose you will also need verbal skills. Your course may not build these into its assessment scheme, but you would be unwise to neglect something so important to your future career.

For all these reasons you should try to overcome any natural tendency to remain silent in these classes. Contributing to discussion will bring you short- and long-term benefits. Nor is it very fair to expect your tutor to answer a string of queries two weeks before the examination, if you have not taken advantage of opportunities to have them answered during the year.

If classes are to fulfil the roles we have outlined, it is essential that you prepare for them by appropriate reading; what you get out of these classes will depend on what you put into them!

1.5 Reading

Reading textbooks or articles is an essential part of the learning process and needs to be approached correctly. Do not expect to read a textbook in the same way you would a novel or a newspaper. You may well have to reread passages several times to understand them; to secure the greatest benefit from your reading you should take notes.

1.5.1 Reading a textbook

Your first task with any recommended reading should be to quickly survey it. Establish the outline and direction and do not worry about detail. Then read the chapter more slowly. You will probably find some passages particularly difficult and you may require several readings and a good deal of thinking before you feel able to make sense of them. Your first reading of the chapter should help you to decide where you really need to pause to understand a point and when ploughing on is a better option. Always be prepared to retrace your steps and accept that several readings of a chapter may be necessary. As we mentioned earlier, some economic concepts are not easy and you will certainly not understand them when you first come across them.

1.5.2 Note taking

Note taking is important for two reasons: it establishes that you have understood what you have read and it will help you recall the main points at a later stage (when revising or writing an essay for example).

You should take notes only when you are satisfied you have understood what you have read. If you are baffled by the original you will make even less sense later of any notes you take. Do not merely copy out sections of the text: if you cannot put the points into your own words then you have probably not understood the argument and you should reread the relevant parts. Sometimes the author's wording is the clearest and most succinct; but if you copy the author's own phrases or sentences you cannot be sure that you know how to express the ideas in your own language.

As with note taking in lectures, use a system of headings and subheadings, alphabetic and/or numerical labelling of points, indentations, colours and underlining. Always leave plenty of space between points. Remember that your main reason for taking notes is to have an economical means of recall, so your points must be neatly written with their relative importance clearly indicated.

1.6 Essay and report writing

1.6.1 Getting started

Writing an essay or report is only the tip of the iceberg—the main effort goes into the preparation and planning, so allow plenty of time for this. The obvious starting point is the question itself. Look at it very carefully—underline or section off different parts of it. Long questions often give many clues. Let us take a couple of examples from economics. (If you have not studied economics before, do not worry about the technical terms: they are fully explained later in the book. Our purpose here is to illustrate the approach rather than to explain the content.)

Consider the following essay question:

'Keynesian demand management policy failed because of poor timing, inaccurate forecasting and the inability to reconcile conflicting policy objectives.' Discuss.

The question immediately suggests a number of headings for the answer:

1 'Keynesian demand management policy'–explanation of

2 'poor timing'–problem of time lags

3 'inaccurate forecasting'–role of forecasting, problems of inaccurate forecasting

4 'reconcile conflicting policy objectives'–policy objectives and extent to which they conflict, problem in reconciling objectives

5 'Discuss'–assess the proposition: consider evidence, discuss different viewpoints

The essay already has taken a fairly firm shape before you begin reading. Other questions can be less helpful at the initial stage. For example:

'Assess the monetarist explanation of inflation.'

Even this tells you that you have to write about the monetarist explanation of inflation and alternative views of it. After only a few weeks of studying economics you should realize that economists are interested in empirical evidence as well as theoretical arguments; so the following headings should immediately suggest themselves:

1 inflation–brief explanation

2 monetarist explanation–theory, empirical evidence

3 alternative view(s)–theory, empirical evidence

4 assessment

You can draw up a preliminary framework simply by examining the question thoroughly. This should act as the starting point for your reading. Look through your lecture notes on the topic as these should give you some idea of the type and depth of approach that is expected of you; they may lead you to amend your original framework.

1.6.2 Reading

Do not rush into detailed reading–look around first. Survey the recommended texts and articles to get a rough idea what each one covers. If you do not have a reading list or if you wish to consult further sources, an initial survey is even more important. Use the contents page and index of books and their recommendations for further reading to lead you to other texts. Specialized bibliographies are available in libraries, but if you have not been introduced to these you would be well advised to ask the librarian for help. In this search you will obviously make use of headings and subheadings to form an impression of the topics covered. In economics diagrams are very often a quick way of judging the type and depth of coverage.

At this stage reconsider your essay/project title and the framework we discussed in the last section. You may already be in a position to amend or fill out your original ideas. Make a note of what seems the most promising reference for each of the main sections of the essay framework. When you have decided which text or article to start reading, approach it in the way suggested in section 1.5. You may well decide, wisely, that the work for an essay will be valuable preparation for examinations, and is in any case part of your general required reading. If this is so, the notes you take will have a more general usefulness than answering one particular essay question. However, always keep the essay title in mind and add important points to your framework as you discover them. For example, the framework for the inflation question referred to earlier might be enlarged through reading on 'monetarism' to look something like this:

Monetarism:

- theory–quantity theory
    –expectations–augmented Phillips curve
- empirical evidence–money supply, growth and inflation
    –Phillips curve (natural unemployment rate)

How much should you read? Your tutor will give you guidance on this, but you should always consult more than one reference to cover the topic adequately: understanding a subject invariably involves looking at it from more than one angle. You should consult widely because an important educational objective of essays and projects is to develop and assess your ability to use different sources to answer a problem.

But at what point do you decide not to read further? You cannot read everything – indeed, on a topic like inflation new material is probably being published faster than you can read it. Fortunately, economics itself gives us an excellent guide. You will discover that the law of diminishing returns applies to extended reading: the benefits from every additional half hour of reading get less. When the additional cost of reading (in terms of the time you sacrifice which could be spent on other activities) exceeds the extra benefits you gain, it is time to go on to the next stage! It is specially important that you allow sufficient time to write a detailed plan of your essay.

1.6.3 Essay or project plan

A plan is essential to successful essay and project writing. It ensures that your writing has a clear structure and that points are presented in a logical order. If you do not plan your answer, it will almost certainly appear muddled; you will increase the chance of missing out points and you may well waste time by rewriting parts of the essay when you realize you have allocated inappropriate space to various points or presented them in the wrong sequence. Part of what is being tested in an essay is your ability to present clear explanations and arguments.

If you follow the approach we have suggested you will probably find that the framework you jotted down when you first looked at the question has turned itself into a plan. Now is the time to take a further look at the question, the framework and your notes. Consider carefully the best order for the material. There is generally a large number of options, but some will be superior on logical grounds (e.g. present theoretical arguments before empirical evidence) and others will be preferably because they group related points together and avoid unnecessary repetition. In the end it is a matter of judgement which approach is best; but run through a number of options at the planning stage.

Your final plan should be fairly detailed, with the main and subsections listed. Key diagrams, tables and quotes should be included or clear cross-references made to your notes or books. Before writing, try a role reversal test: imagine you are a tutor about to mark an essay on the subject. What would you look for and how would you allocate marks?

1.6.4 Writing an essay and report

We now come to the tip of the iceberg – the writing stage. This is the visible part so it needs to be well presented. If you have a detailed plan then the main issues of content will be sorted out and you can concentrate on presentation. Your style should be serious but not ponderous. Do not try to be humorous – it is rarely effective – and avoid 'journalese'. Your main points should be clear to the reader. A carefully written introduction will highlight the structure. Do not be afraid to be explicit about how your answer relates to the question; the conclusion is a further and final opportunity to clarify this.

If you are writing a report you should provide a summary at the beginning. Sections and subsections should be indicated through some type of labelling: decimal numbering of the type used in this book is the most common approach. Consider the use of appendices for detailed data, technical notes and documentary evidence.

Essays and reports should contain a bibliography listing the articles and books that have been used. Where you quote from published material, use quotation marks and acknowledge the source. Carefully used quotations enhance an answer.

In economics essays and reports, tables, graphs and diagrams should be used where appropriate. Diagrams can be an economical and unambiguous way of making a point. Where data are available to back up an argument, use them rather than relying on a vague assertion. Try to use the language and terms of economists. The so-called jargon of the profession has been adopted because it is precise. It is better to say that the 'multiplier depends on the marginal propensity to consume' than to make some loose reference to consumers' spending habits.

Before handing in your work read it through and make any amendments. You should ideally leave your essay for a few days after you have finished it and then reread it. This short period will help distance you from what you have written and increase your chance of detecting passages that are not clearly or fully explained. There is no doubt that word processors are an enormous help in writing essays and reports: they make it easy to amend what you have written and produce clear copy. Most universities and polytechnics provide access to word processors and it is well worth spending the time to learn how to use them.

Finally, do not ignore your tutor's comments when your work is returned to you. Learn from your mistakes and if you do not understand or agree with the comments, discuss them with your tutor.

1.7 Examinations

1.7.1. Preparing for examinations

Most students dread examinations. They are anxious about the kind of questions they will be asked and they are afraid that their memory will fail them or that they will run out of time. Adequate preparation can drastically reduce the likelihood of problems. It is like an athletics match—of course the result depends on how well the athletes perform on the day of the race, but that in turn depends upon the quantity and quality of training.

Preparation for examinations should really start at the beginning of the course. Consistent work is one of the best safeguards of success in examinations. If you have worked consistently you will have done most of the necessary reading and have a set of notes from which to revise. There really is a limit to what can be read and understood in the few weeks before an examination. A further obvious point is to look at past examination papers. Consider any restrictions in the form of compulsory questions and the general structure of the paper as well as the type of questions asked.

1.7.2 Revision planning

Your time will not be best used by attempting to revise everything with equal emphasis: decide which topics you are going to concentrate on. If you are required to answer four questions in the examination, it will be a high-risk strategy to confine your revision to four topics. You may have your four favourites, but you need to revise at least a further two with almost equal intensity and then several more topics with decreasing emphasis. Review your notes (from lectures, classes and reading) on these topics and then plan how you are going to use your available time for revision. It is much easier to work effectively if you get into a routine and leave enough time to consolidate your revision by testing your recall. You should aim to reduce the main points of each topic (including key diagrams) to a summary that fits on one or two sheets of paper. Check your recall by seeing how many points you can write down from memory. Compare these with your summary and practise until you can recall all the headings. You should practise diagrams in the same way, but make sure you understand them, satisfying yourself that you can explain the significance of different lines and points as you draw them.

1.7.3 The examination

However much work you have done in preparation it is your performance in the examination room that will determine how effectively your revision is turned into marks. Weaknesses in examination technique invariably cost marks. The usual problem is a poor allocation of time which results in students writing too much and reading and thinking too little. Contrary to some myths, examination scripts are not weighed—it is quality not quantity that matters. This is why some short answers that are scribbled down in the last few minutes of an examination and amount to little more than an essay plan, can gain as many marks as a much longer answer. To understand this try a further role reversal test. If you were the examiner, what would you expect from particular questions and how would you allocate the marks in the marking scheme? There are often up to half a dozen key points which the examiner expects to find in an answer—if only two thirds of them are covered marks will be correspondingly limited. A complete skeleton of the main points will probably warrant a pass mark, with additional marks earned for putting flesh on the bones. It is always better to present an overall picture with limited elaboration of a part than a detailed exposition of one part only.

If you are going to allocate your time most effectively you must start by giving yourself sufficient opportunity to assess which questions you are going to answer. Make all your choices at the beginning. Do not postpone your decision: you will be thinking less clearly towards the end of the examination and it is a waste of time to make comparisons twice. Read the questions very carefully before reaching a decision and do not be distracted by key words. There may be a question on a topic you have revised in depth, but closer inspection may reveal that it is asking you to focus on a particular aspect that you are not so clear about or that it is linked to another topic.

It is important to plan your answers. It is best to plan them all before you tackle the first question. This will show up any mistakes in your selection of questions and you are likely to be calmer at the beginning of the examination than towards the end. If you know you have written a plan for later answers this will reassure you and allow you to concentrate on the answer in hand. If new points do occur later you can always add them.

You may use up to a quarter of your time for preparation and planning before starting to write. Careful planning is a sensible use of time. There are often signs in examination scripts of the rush into writing: paragraphs crossed out, points presented in the wrong order and even answers to questions abandoned after a page in favour of an alternative. A good plan should produce what examiners are looking for: the well-structured answer with points clearly made. Make sure you explicitly relate the material in your answer to the question. So often students seem to treat the question as an invitation to 'write down all you know about X' on the assumption that the examiner will pick out the relevant parts. The same basic material can often be used for a variety of questions; but good answers will direct that material towards the particular question. A few sentences and a clear conclusion can focus what you write and make all the diffrence.

You should try to allocate your time fairly evenly between answers. The temptation, which few can resist, is to spend much longer on the questions with which you feel more confident—but it is invariably a mistake. The extra marks you gain from the additional time on one answer are usually less than those you sacrifice by spending insufficient time on another.

Finally, some specific points on answering economics questions. As for essays, use diagrams where appropriate and try to use economists' terms. Your examination will include some questions asking you to explain and discuss economic theories; other questions will be problem/policy orientated and expect you to apply those theories. So ask yourself what the question is getting at and make sure your answer is analytical and uses the appropriate economic theory. It is both disappointing and surprising how often questions on, for example, the European Community or developing countries touch off xenophobia and produce a tirade reminiscent of an editorial in one of the tabloid newspapers, devoid of sound economic reasoning. Most questions will require discussion—they will involve you in considering alternative theories or evidence. Be prepared for this and if you find that your answer plan does not do this make absolutely sure you have understood the question.

1.8 Conclusion

You may feel that everything in this chapter is mere commonsense. It may be; but there is ample evidence in every pile of essays and examination scripts that it is often ignored. The most important point is to take the task of being a student seriously. Do not take study skills for granted: examine your own approach critically and ask yourself if you are adopting the best practices.

Studying hard and effectively brings its own rewards, not only in assessment and examination marks but in the satisfaction of understanding new ideas. In economics, in particular, you will discover that although we are surrounded by economic issues in our everyday lives, people are enormously ignorant about the subject. A small investment in effective studying will yield high returns in understanding.

2 Scope and method of economics

2.1 Introduction

This chapter aims to answer the question, 'What is economics?'. Whether you are starting economics for the first time, embarking on your revision or feeling confused in the middle of your course, the material in this chapter should help you understand the subject more fully. This in turn should give you a deeper appreciation of those parts of economics which are sometimes difficult to follow and seem remote from everyday problems.

The chapter will:

- give you information on the key features of the UK economy
- define economics
- explain the main subject areas of economics
- introduce you to the notation and the type of diagrams used by economists
- explain the method adopted by economists in studying economic problems

2.1.1 Examination guide

This topic is not always mentioned explicitly in exam questions and is often regarded as something to waffle about if desperate. This underestimates its importance. This type of approach, along with an indication of an overall grasp of the nature of economics, can produce top grade answers on a wide variety of topics. If there is an explicit question on the scope and method of economics, it should not be regarded as a question of last resort. An answer that is mere waffle, lacking ideas and structure, will receive few marks; but a serious attempt to address the topic and introduce the points covered in this chapter will be well received and suitably rewarded.

2.2 Some key economic issues

Economic issues abound in modern life—they influence the lives of individuals, affect the operations of business and lie at the centre of political debate. Economic problems are rarely absent from news bulletins and the front page of newspapers. In this section some of these main issues are introduced and are set in an historical perspective which should quickly give you an overall picture of the UK economy.

2.2.1 Unemployment

Throughout the 1980s opinion poll surveys have suggested that the public regard **unemployment** as the most serious problem facing British society. Figure 2.1 and Table

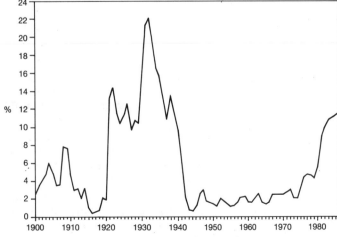

Fig. 2.1 UK unemployment rate 1900–86 (*The British Economy Key Statistics 1900-1970; London & Cambridge Economic Service*)

Table 2.1 Average unemployment 1950–86

	%
1950–59	1.7
1960–69	2.0
1970–79	3.4
1980–86	9.8

(*Economic Trends Annual Supplement*, 1987)

2.1 show why. During the 1980s the **unemployment rate** has risen towards the levels of the inter-war years. In sharp contrast with the 25 years following the Second World War, the number out of work in the mid-1980s was more than ten times greater than in the mid-1950s. There was a clear upward trend in unemployment in the 1970s, but the most dramatic rise occurred in 1980 and 1981 when the jobless doubled from 1.2 to 2.4 million in 18 months.

The two main reasons for concern about unemployment are, first, social—unemployment lowers the living standards of those out of work and tends to set up a vicious circle of deprivation—and second, that unemployment is a waste of resources—the unemployed could be producing much-needed output.

2.2.2 Inflation

Another problem that is a matter of widespread public concern is **inflation**—the rate of change in prices. This was the main problem of the 1970s and Table 2.2 illustrates this. At the inflationary peak, prices were rising by around 25 per cent per annum and at that rate the half-life (the time taken for the purchasing power of money to halve in value) of the pound was just over two years. Most of us have lived only in periods when prices are rising; but it has not always been like that, as Figure 2.2 shows—prices actually fell by around 2 per cent per annum in the early 1920s and in the last century spells of declining prices alternated with inflation.

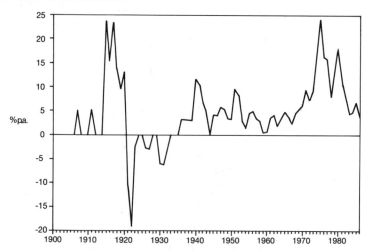

Fig. 2.2 UK inflation rate 1900–86 (*The British Economy Key Statistics 1900-1970; London & Cambridge Economic Service*)

Table 2.2 Average inflation rate 1950–86

	%
1950–59	4.3
1960–69	3.5
1970–79	12.6
1980–86	8.3

(*Economic Trends Annual Supplement*, 1987)

Why should **inflation** be a cause of concern? If people's **incomes** and **savings** do not keep pace with rising prices then they become worse off. People's ability to adjust to higher prices, and the speed at which they do so, varies and a **redistribution** of income and wealth between groups therefore takes place. This redistribution will neither necessarily conform to society's ideas of fairness, nor encourage economic efficiency. Businesses will be concerned if the UK **rate of inflation** is greater than that of other countries because this will threaten our **competitiveness**. Of particular concern to economists is the damage inflation can inflict on the way a market economy operates. **Prices** are important indicators, as we will see below: they fall when goods are relatively plentiful and rise when they are scarce. During periods of inflation, particularly when the inflation rate is fluctuating, it is difficult to read these price signals correctly.

2.2.3 Balance of payments

A further issue, which until the 1970s seemed to be one of the most pressing problems facing the UK, is the **balance of payments**. This is a record of a country's international transactions. Because about a quarter of UK exports (and roughly a fifth of imports) are services, a common measure of the balance of payments is the **current account,** which is the difference between the value of goods and services exported and those imported. Figure 2.3 shows the movement in the UK current account since 1970.

Oil has been an influential factor determining the fluctuations. The fourfold increase in oil prices in 1973–4 was partly responsible for the large current account deficit of the mid-1970s. When oil prices doubled in 1980 the UK had become an important oil producer and this led to record surpluses. North Sea oil has been largely responsible for reducing concern over the balance of payments in the last decade; but as oil supplies are used up UK trading performance will re-emerge as an important issue. One feature that should not be entirely overlooked is the long-term tendency for manufactured imports to grow faster than exports.

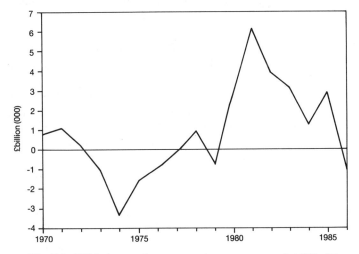

Fig. 2.3 UK balance of payments (current account) 1979–86
(*Economic Trends Annual Supplement,* 1987)

The **balance of payments** becomes a major problem when a country persistently spends more abroad than it receives in payments from foreign countries. In such circumstances total spending often has to be constrained to limit expenditure on imports. Such a constraint affects **growth** and **living standards**, at least in the short run.

2.2.4 Growth of living standards

This issue is of widespread interest. **Living standards,** as measured by the total output of the economy, the **Gross Domestic Product (GDP)** (see Figure 2.4), have never been higher

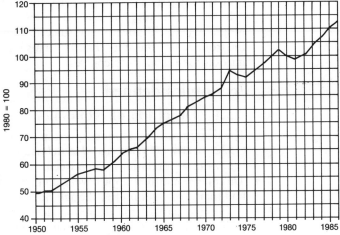

Fig. 2.4 UK GDP 1950–86 (average estimate) (*Economic Trends Annual Supplement,* 1987)

and yet economic growth has remained a constant source of concern for the UK. This is because the UK has grown more slowly than other major industrial countries. International comparisons of living standards are very difficult, but it is fairly clear that although the UK enjoyed one of the highest levels of income per head after the Second World War it has continually slipped down the league table since. However, all the major countries have experienced slower growth rates since the mid-1970s.

Table 2.3 Average UK growth rate (increase in GDP) 1950–86

	% pa
1950–59	2.4
1960–69	3.3
1970–79	2.1
1980–86	1.5

(*Economic Trends Annual Supplement,* 1987)

There are those who would question whether faster economic growth is desirable; but for many **increased economic growth** provides the means to enjoy more leisure as well as the opportunity to acquire more goods and spend more on services. Without the extra goods and services which result from growth, increased expenditure on some groups (e.g. the poor) or on certain basic needs (e.g. health) would require redistribution away from other groups and services.

2.2.5 Distribution of income and wealth

How society **distributes** its income and wealth has long been an important question for economists, politicians and the general public. Table 2.4 shows that income, and particularly wealth, are not equally distributed in the UK. This issue is one where views of what is a 'fair' or 'right' distribution tend to dominate debate and the economist cannot pass judgement on this. What the economist *can* do is to make a contribution to **measuring** how income and wealth are distributed (no easy matter) and consider the effects of a particular distribution on, say, the incentive to work and suggest the most **economically efficient** ways in which certain groups may be helped.

Table 2.4 Distribution of income and wealth

Population sector	Income (% or UK total) 1983	Wealth (% of UK total) 1982
Top 1%	6.0	20
Top 10%	28.3	54

(*Social Trends,* 1985)

2.2.6 Privatization and the role of the state

The last in our selection of key economic issues is the way in which activities are divided between the **private** and the **public sector** (**central** and **local government** and **nationalized industries**). Like the distribution of income and wealth this has long been the subject of economic and political debate.

Over the last hundred years the idea that the state should assume responsibility for a wide range of activities has been increasingly accepted and this is reflected in the growth of state spending as a proportion of total expenditure.

In the last decade, however, this view has been seriously challenged. The privatization programme of UK government since 1979 has been part of a policy designed to 'roll back the frontiers' of the state. **Public versus private provision** is an important theme of most introductory economics courses.

2.3 Economics defined

2.3.1 Definition of economics

The **definition** of economics given in most textbooks is the one used by Lionel Robbins (1932) nearly 60 years ago. He defined economics as 'the science which studies human behaviour as a relationship between ends and scarce means which have alternative uses'. This may not at first appear very illuminating; but if we look at it in more detail we will find that it offers a useful, though not fully comprehensive, definition.

The first part of the definition describes economics as a **social science**, i.e. it uses a **scientific method** to look at human problems. (This will be considered in more detail in section 2.4.) The second part indicates that the main problem is **scarcity**. Human wants exceed society's means of satisfying them (**resources**), creating a problem, **scarcity**. Since resources can be used for different ends (e.g. to build hospitals or roads or tanks), societies are faced with **choices** as to how best to **allocate** them. Economics studies the problem of **resource allocation**.

2.3.2 Resources and factors of production

Economists generally classify a society's resources into three types of **factors of production**.

1 Land is society's natural resource. In economics the term has a wider meaning than in everyday use and includes minerals, woodland, rivers, etc.

2 Labour is human intellectual and physical effort. (Entrepreneurship is sometimes distinguished as a fourth factor of production, but here we regard it as a type of labour.)

3 Capital is man-made aids to production, ranging in complexity from an axe to a computer-controlled assembly line. Care should be taken not to confuse this with money in bank accounts or stocks and shares (the everyday usage).

The production of goods and services which involves the use of these factors may be **labour-intensive** (e.g. farming in Bangladesh) or **capital-intensive** (UK or US agriculture).

2.3.3 Scarcity, choice and opportunity cost

Scarcity implies the need for **choices** and sacrifices. If resources are insufficient to meet all our needs, satisfying one need necessarily involves failing to satisfy another. This ideas is captured in an important economic concept–**opportunity cost**. The **opportunity cost** of a commodity is the alternative(s) that is sacrificed. When Goebbels suggested that Nazi Germany had to choose between guns and butter, he was saying that the **opportunity cost** of militarization would be a reduced output of food. Any individual firm, government or society will be familiar with the choices that have to be made over the use of resources. The economist's view that cost should be measured in terms of **alternative forgone**, as well as cost in pounds, is often neglected.

2.3.4 The production possibility curve

One way of clarifying the concepts outlined in the previous section is to give a schematized example of the production possibilities facing a society when all resources (land, labour and capital) are fully employed. Seven of these possibilities are shown in Table 2.5.

Table 2.5 Schema of a society's production possibilities

Production possibility	Guns (000)	Butter (million tons)
A	50	0
B	49	1
C	45	2
D	40	3
E	32	4
F	20	5
G	0	6

Possibility A devotes all resources to the production of guns; G is the opposite extreme, with five intermediate points in between. These positions can be shown on a diagram (Figure 2.5, overleaf) and the line joining these points is known as the **production possibility curve**. This curve shows the maximum output levels that this particular society can produce with given resources and technology.

Robbins's definition suggests that economics is the study of how societies decide where to locate themselves on the **production possibility curve** or, more simply, what to produce and how to produce it. The concept of opportunity cost can be simply illustrated. If a society were at point C (producing 45 thousand guns and 2 million tons of butter), then the opportunity cost of producing an extra million tons of butter (a move to point D) would be the production of 5000 guns. As resources are moved on to the farms, the output of armaments is lowered from 45 000 to 40 000.

The increase in living standards referred to in section 2.2.4 arose because societies have the ability to produce more of everything, rather than simply moving up or down the production possibility curve. **Improvements in technology** and **increases in factors of production** have presented a new set of production possibilities and a new curve.

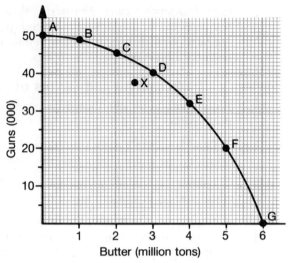

Fig. 2.5 A production possibility curve

Economic growth can be thought of as the rate at which a country's production possibility curve shifts outwards.

The explanation so far implies that a society is always operating on its **production frontier**; but this is often not the case. When Robbins wrote his definition (in the depth of the 1930s' slump) the UK was producing well inside its frontier, at a point like *X*. This has also been true throughout the 1980s. In such circumstances it is possible to increase output with zero opportunity cost (e.g. to move from *X* to *D*).

2.3.5 Micro- and macro-economics

It is common to draw a distinction between **micro-** and **macro-economics**.

2.3.5.1 Microeconomics

Microeconomics is concerned with the study of the behaviour of individuals and firms: microeconomics examines what factors influence the **employment decisions** of individuals and firms and what determines the **price** of particular products.

2.3.5.2 Macroeconomics

As the term suggests, **macroeconomics** is concerned with large rather than small matters: it examines **aggregate** or **total activity**. In contrast to microeconomics it investigates what determines total employment in the economy and the overall price level rather than what is happening at the level of firms or even an industry. Issues such as **inflation, mass unemployment** and the **balance of payments** are therefore macroeconomic problems.

2.3.6 Economic problems

To conclude this section we consider three broad types of problems that economists examine.

2.3.6.1 Allocation

One major area of study for economists is how societies tackle the problem of **allocating scarce resources**. As we will see in the next chapter, resources can be allocated by **planning** or by the **market**. **Allocation** includes the decisions of individuals, the choices of firms about what to sell and how to produce it and the intervention of governments, directly (via their own spending) or indirectly (through the use of **taxation**, their **monetary policy** and their influence on **expectations**) on the use of resources.

The view that all societies, even the richest, experience scarcity is widely accepted, though some economists, for example J.K. Galbraith, question whether this word accurately defines the relationship between wants and resources. This alternative view suggests that wants are generated by producers either indirectly, through the stimulus to demand that the existence of new products provides, or more directly, through large advertising expenditure. **Scarcity** is thus not an inherent and inevitable problem but one that derives from the nature of **socially generated wants**. In **centrally planned economies**, where there has not been the same drive to stimulate demand as in **market economies**, the authorities have been only too well aware of the problem of scarcity.

2.3.6.2 Distribution problems

Economics is concerned with the **distribution** of **income** and **wealth**, as well as with the **efficient allocation** of **resources**. It may not seem necessary to distinguish between **distribution** and **allocation** as both involve decisions about how resources are to be used. However, as Chapter 3 will make clearer, a country may be operating on the production frontier and allocating resources efficiently, yet that allocation may be widely regarded as unfair.

2.3.6.3 Stabilization

Some of the most pressing problems of recent years, such as unemployment, inflation and balance-of-payments difficulties, do not fit easily into the previous two categories. These macroeconomic issues are often referred to as **stabilization problems**. They are concerned with society's attempt to follow a **stable, inflation-free path** which avoids large imbalances in the balance of payments.

This threefold classification–**allocation, distribution** and **stabilization**–will be helpful when considering many economic topics. These headings often provide a way of organizing your material when you come to discuss the effects of some activity or policy and they will help you to avoid overlooking some important factors. For example, tax cuts can be expected to have implications for allocation (incentive effects), distribution of income and stabilization (effects on total spending and inflation).

2.4 Methodology of economics

Economics is a **social science**; but to what extent can it claim to be a **science** like physics? To answer this we need to briefly examine **scientific method** and then consider how economists go about the task of enquiring into economic problems. The section concludes with a case study which will illustrate some of the main points. (The next section on scientific method may go beyond the requirements of some courses and can be omitted.)

2.4.1 Scientific method

2.4.1.1 Induction

The popular idea of science can be summed up by saying that scientists are clever **observers of phenomena**–like space or molecules or plants–who discover through their observations the **underlying laws** of how the world works. This implies that the truth is hidden in the world around us and can be discovered through careful observation and correct interpretation. This popular view corresponds to an approach well known to philosophers of science: **the inductive method**.

This view of science has been seriously questioned both as a description of how scientists actually behave and on grounds of logic. It is not logically possible to arrive at general or universal laws from a finite number of observations. To use an often quoted example, it cannot be concluded that all swans are white from a given number, albeit a large number, of sightings of white swans. We cannot **prove** such general statements to be true even though we may be very confident about them when we have a great deal of supporting evidence.

2.4.1.2 Karl Popper and science

An alternative to the inductive approach has been suggested by **Karl Popper**, a philosopher of science who has been highly influential in this century in shaping our view of the scientific method. Popper has pointed out that although we cannot **verify** general statements and laws, we can **falsify** them. So the statement 'All swans are white' can never be proved correct, no matter how many white swans are observed: but one sighting of a black swan can disprove it. As scientific statements survive increasing attempts to refute them, so more confidence can be attached to them, though they remain **unproven**. The more rigorous attempts have been to falsify it the greater credence a scientific law or theory will carry.

Popper further argues that the scientific ideas which are so tested are not the direct result of **observations**, as the inductive approach suggests, but the product of human **imagination**. Scientists form conjectures or guesses as to how the world works. Their theories are **hypotheses** that have been tested and have not been falsified by confrontation with the observable world. In Popper's view observation and testing are very important, but they are not the origin of scientific laws but the means by which hypotheses survive or fail the falsification test.

This is quite different from the popular view of science and some people find it rather disturbing. It suggests that science does not study **true facts** about the world, but collects **conjectures** which are incapable of being verified, but to date have not been falsified. All knowledge is therefore tentative.

2.4.1.3 Science and non-science

The issue of **falsification** distinguishes science from other intellectual effort. Both science and non-science produce valuable insights into the world in which we live. Both are the product of human imagination; but scientific statements can be tested and falsified whereas novels, poetry and music cannot be. This idea enhances the status of scientists: they are not just good at observing but are highly creative.

2.4.1.4 Evolution or revolution of ideas?

Popper's ideas have attracted much support, though they have not gone unchallenged. **Thomas Kuhn,** for one, has suggested that Popper's views do not give a very accurate picture of the way, scientists actually behave. Kuhn argues that for most of the time scientists accept theories and approaches uncritically and that if experiments produce inconsistent results they are ignored. Anomalies may build up to such a point that there is a 'scientific revolution' when the old **paradigm** (standard way of approaching the problem) is overthrown and replaced. Popper's approach suggests that all theories are under threat all the time and that the weaker ones, which have been falsified, are rejected; for Kuhn theories are accepted for long periods, but are occasionally subject to major upheavals.

Despite the controversies surrounding the nature of science there is general agreement that it involves confronting scientific ideas with evidence–that is, **testing**.

2.4.2 Is economics a science?

Is it possible to apply a scientific method to the study of human behaviour?

2.4.2.1 Abstractions and the use of models

One obvious difficulty faced by economics (and other social sciences) is the complexity of the real world. At any moment billions of actions are taking place which might impinge on a particular event. We therefore need to be **selective** in trying to explain and examine economic problems. We use **models** which do not replicate the real world in detail but isolate the most important factors. This process is known as **abstraction**. We are all familiar with this approach in other contexts: the most obvious example is the use of maps. A street map of London is an **abstraction**–it has little physical resemblance to what we see when we walk or drive around. Students of economics commonly assert that **theories** or **models** are unrealistic, but **abstraction** is necessary if anything sensible is to be discovered about economic problems. If models were realistic they would be too complex and detailed; we would be unable to see the wood for the trees.

This process of abstraction can, however, become a licence to simplify the world so much that some important factors are excluded. How can we know whether we have departed too far from reality? There are no clear and commonly agreed rules and to some extent this rests with the experience and judgement of professional economists. One approach suggests that we should judge theories by their **predictive abilities**. If the **predictions** of a particular model are accurate then its degree of abstraction is justified and the theory on which it is based can be supported even if it seems to be very remote from reality.

But such models may tell us very little about the **chain of causation** and therefore provide only weak explanations of why events occur. Economists often investigate problems so that **policies** which change observed relationships may be devised and to do this information will be required about how factors interact. So the extent to which we are justified in simplifying the real world will to some extent depend on what we want of our theories.

2.4.2.2 Positive and normative economics

Our earlier discussion on scientific method introduced the idea of **testing theories against the evidence**. Most economists would stress the importance of this. **Positive economics** is the term used to describe testable statements and propositions in economics. This can be contrasted with **normative economics**, which involves value judgements and is concerned with what **ought** to be. As this type of economics involves personal beliefs about right and wrong, its statements are not testable. For example, a statement that 'the government ought to introduce policies to reduce unemployment' is normative–it reflects convictions and cannot be tested, whereas the proposition that 'tax cuts will reduce unemployment' is testable, that is we can collect evidence to verify or falsify it.

2.4.2.3 Non-laboratory science

Some people doubt whether it is possible to test economic theories because it is not possible to set up laboratory experiments. However, other accepted sciences, such as astronomy and meteorology, cannot set up experiments in a laboratory either. These **non-laboratory sciences** rely on **data** collected through **observations of the real world** to test theories and make predictions. A similar approach is adopted by economists. In fact, millions of 'experiments' are taking place all the time and many of these are recorded in the data collected by government departments, the Central Statistical Office and many private organizations. As these are not **controlled experiments** and as many things are changing simultaneously, it is not easy to be sure of the relationships between key **variables**. The use of **statistical techniques** and computers assist and there is a branch of economics, **econometrics**, which is concerned with developing and improving these techniques. Nevertheless it is more difficult than in some of the experimental sciences to test theories conclusively and the **interpretation** of evidence is an important source of debate.

2.4.2.4 Ideology

A further difference between social sciences and most natural sciences is that in the former humans are investigating their own behaviour, whereas in the natural sciences the subject of the study is non-human. Many observers will have strong views on the issues they are studying and this raises doubts about whether political ideology or religious beliefs can be excluded from scientific enquiry in the social sciences. It should be recognized that this is not altogether straightforward in the natural sciences either: ideological positions have influenced the acceptance or otherwise of theories on the motions of planets, chemical structures and the workings of the body.

We have already considered the distinction between **positive** and **normative economics**. Although this distinction is useful in stressing the need to separate testable statements from those based on value judgements it does not entirely resolve the problem. **Ideology** is likely to affect the issues economists choose to study and the way they approach their enquiries.

2.5 Case study: the Phillips curve

This case study is intended to illustrate the approach taken by economists. The main concern here is that you appreciate the way this economic problem is tackled rather than understanding the problem itself.

2.5.1 Phillips's hypothesis

After the Second World War the major political parties committed themselves to the policy objective of full employment. There were fears that this might generate inflation. This problem was investigated in the 1950s by **A.W. Phillips**, who examined the **relationship** between wage inflation and unemployment. Phillips's basic hypothesis was that wages would rise when the demand for labour (by employers) was greater than supply and that the greater the excess demand the faster wages would rise. Excess demand is not directly observable, but the hypothesis can be presented in a testable form by recognizing that as demand for labour increases, unemployment will tend to fall. A process of **deduction** has here led from an original hypothesis to a **testable prediction**, which, in algebraic notation, can be expressed

$$\frac{\Delta W}{W} = f(U)$$

The lefthand side of the equation stands for the proportionate change in wages. W denotes the level of wages and the symbol Δ (the Greek capital letter delta) is shorthand for 'change in', so ΔW represents the change in wages from one period to another (in this case the annual change). On the righthand side, U is the rate of unemployment. The $f(\ )$ means 'is a function of' and indicates a **relationship** between unemployment and the change in wages. The relationship may be simple or very complex; its exact form has to be determined by further theoretical analysis or empirical work, using data to find the association between the variables.

2.5.2 Testing the hypothesis

Phillips gathered data on unemployment and wage inflation for the period 1861 to 1913 and the relationship that best **fitted the data** was the curve shown in Figure 2.6. This highlights another function of **econometrics**, which is to **quantify relationships**, in this case the rate of wage increase likely to be associated with a given level of unemployment. In **applied economics** we are often interested in putting numbers to relationships.

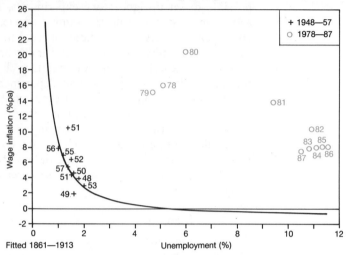

Fig. 2.6 The Phillips curve

The data points on unemployment and wage inflation for 1861–1913 lie quite close to the curve shown in the diagram, but the sensational feature of Phillips's work was that nearly all observations for the period 1948–57 also fitted the pre-First World War curve almost exactly. This was a remarkable finding, because the labour market of the 1950s was significantly different from the non-unionized market of the last half of the 19th century; this suggested a higher degree of stability in relationships than is normally obtained in economics. Phillips's **data** not only provided strong support for his **hypothesis** but seemed to contain some important and useful **policy implications**. Some economists calculated the level of unemployment which would produce a rate of wage increase consistent with zero inflation and advocated running the British economy with that amount of spare capacity. This is an example of the **normative** use of Phillips's work, because it rests upon value judgements about unemployment and inflation.

In recognition of Phillips's work the curve showing this relationship between wage (and more generally price) inflation and unemployment has been named after him. However, the term **Phillips curve** has remained more durable than the original numerical relationship. In the late 1960s, and particularly in the 1970s, there were some very large **predictive errors** and on some occasions rising inflation was associated with increases in unemployment. The theory was clearly falsified by experience. The reaction of many economists to this was not to reject the hypothesis outright but to seek to amend it to take account of what were felt to be missing factors.

Others argued that the Phillips curve ought to be rejected on the grounds that a number of changes had taken place in the period after the Second World War which made it no longer appropriate to regard the labour market as responsive to excess demand in the same way as the market for agricultural products. The difference in economists' responses to the failure of the Phillips curve has not been entirely unconnected with ideological positions. Some of those who favoured rejection were also sceptical about the effective working of the market system and felt that wage inflation was better controlled through **incomes policy** than regulation of demand pressure.

This approach of **hypothesizing, theoretical modelling** and **empirical testing** is typical of the one adopted by economists. There is argument among them about each of these stages, as you will see in the subsequent chapters.

3 Planned and market economies: an overview

3.1 Introduction

In this chapter we consider how economies tackle central economic problems. The emphasis is on **mixed market economies** of the type found in the UK, but there is some consideration of **planned economies**. A **market economy** is one where decision making is decentralized and resources are allocated according to the preferences of consumers and the decisions of firms. The framework for assessing the strengths and weaknesses of the **market mechanism** is particularly important. It provides an overall view of the workings of a **market economy** which should reduce the chance of you getting lost in the more detailed work of later chapters. The theme of this chapter is considered more rigorously in Chapter 19.

This chapter will:

- distinguish between allocative and technical efficiency
- consider the relationship between equity and efficiency
- examine how planned economies tackle the problems of allocation, stabilization and distribution
- explain the role of prices in allocating resources in market economies
- explain why market economies may fail to achieve an optimum allocation of resources

3.1.1 Examination guide

The issues raised in this chapter are basic to almost any economics course. There may be direct and explicit questions on the **price mechanism** and **market failure**; but if there are not, most courses will ask questions about the effectiveness of market solutions and the case for government intervention. These questions may be applied to a wide variety of areas (e.g. housing, health, education and training). There is a common approach to answering both types of question, which involves pointing out the strengths of the market approach (see section 3.4) and considering how far the **categories of market failure** (section 3.5) can be applied to the subject of the question.

3.2 Efficiency, equity and the optimum allocation of resources

All societies face a problem of **allocating scarce resources** and all hope to achieve an **optimum**, or best, **allocation**. But what is meant by an **optimum allocation of resources** and what factors do we need to take into account when considering whether a society has achieved it?

3.2.1 Technical efficiency

A useful starting point is the idea of **technical efficiency**. If a society operates within its **production possibility curve**, say at a point like X, in Figure 2.5, then it is not using its resources efficiently because some resources must be unused, or perhaps combined in an inefficient manner. **Technical efficiency** requires a society to be operating on its production possibility curve, producing an output combination which is the maximum possible, given its resources and technology. However, all points on the curve satisfy this condition and we cannot distinguish between A to G; yet society is not likely to be **indifferent** between these combinations. Some points will yield greater **satisfaction** than others, but we can determine this only if we known what society's preferences are.

3.2.2 Allocative efficiency

A way of representing society's preferences is by a community **indifference curve** or **social welfare function**. A set of these is shown in Figure 3.1. Each curve indicates combinations of Y and X which produce the same level of satisfaction or utility to society. On curve I, society is **indifferent** between the consumption patterns indicated by A and B. They produce the same **level of satisfaction** as C. To retain the same level of **utility**, a point which involves a lower consumption of *Y* (e.g. *A* compared with *B*) requires this to be compensated by more *X*. Curve II represents higher levels of satisfaction because it shows points of higher consumption combinations. (A more detailed discussion of **indifference curves** is to be found in Chapter 13.)

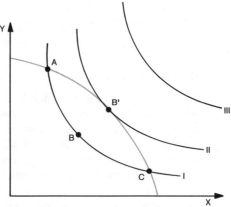

Fig. 3.1 Production possibility constraints

Society would clearly like to get on to the **highest community indifference curve** because in this way it would maximize its utility, that is, obtain the greatest amount of satisfaction. However, it will be constrained by the **production possibilities**. On Figure 3.1 we can see that point *B'* will be the preferred position—it is not possible to get on to a higher indifference curve (say III) because that involves combinations of *Y* and *X* that are beyond the production possibilities of this society and other positions offer lower levels of satisfaction. Points *A* and *C*, although technically efficient (on the production possibility curve), are on a lower indifference curve (curve I) and are therefore inferior to *B'*.

It follows, then, that if we were at *A* we could improve the **allocation of resources**, in terms of the satisfaction obtained by society, if we moved the production possibility curve round by shifting factors of production away from *Y* towards *X*. If we carried the process further and went beyond point *B'* then the level of satisfaction would start to decline as we moved on to lower indifference curves. Point *B'* represents an **optimum allocation of resources** given the preferences that society has and subject to the constraints embodied in the production possibility curve.

We can think of this point as one representing **allocative efficiency**, because other allocations produce inferior levels of satisfaction.

3.2.3 Equity

There may, however, be objections to a point of **allocative efficiency** of the type we have just shown because it may be associated with a highly **skewed distribution of income**, with a minority of the population receiving most of the income and abject poverty for the majority. Consider Figure 3.2 (a) which shows such a distribution, with many resources being used to produce yachts. A more equal distribution of income would produce a different set of preferences and indifference curves such as those shown in 3.2 (b). Each distribution produces its own point of allocative efficiency (B_1 and B_2) and further points would result if other distributions were considered. Can we say which one is preferable?

There is no scientific way of measuring the **satisfaction** one person gains from consumption compared with that enjoyed by another person—we cannot make **interpersonal comparisons of utility**. This means we cannot be sure that taking £100 from

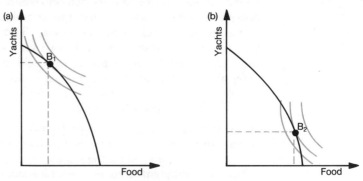

Fig. 3.2 Distribution alternatives

a rich person and giving it to a poor person will increase the overall level of **utility of society**. This does not mean that such redistributions are not justified but that the basis for them rests on ethical beliefs about what is a fair distribution of income. This is not to imply that the issue of distribution is unimportant: there is probably a near unanimous view that governments should intervene to affect the distribution of income, though there is far less agreement on the form and extent of such intervention.

3.2.4 Economic problems and economic systems

The preceding discussion has raised some important aspects of the economic problems confronting societies. Although **technical efficiency** means not wasting resources (that is, operating *on* the production possibility curve, not *inside* it) **allocative efficiency** requires society's preferences to be taken into account to determine the point on the production possibility curve which will produce the maximum satisfaction (or utility) for society. Changing the **distribution of income** will almost certainly alter society's preferences and therefore produce a different point of allocative efficiency.

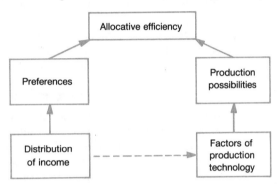

Fig. 3.3 Allocative efficiency

This is summarized in Figure 3.3. where **allocative efficiency** is seen to depend on society's preferences as well as production possibilities. Distribution of income is shown as an influence on preferences. The dotted line indicates that **distribution** may influence the supply of factors (and hence production possibilities) through its impact on **incentives**. This issue is considered further in 3.5.2.2.

There is one further type of economic problem that we identified in Chapter 2: **stabilization**. This is concerned with whether a society is operating with **unemployment**, **inflation** and **balance-of-payments** difficulties.

There are many approaches that societies can take towards these fundamental economic problems, but two extreme types are normally identified: **planned economies** and **market economies**. In the next two sections we explain in outline how these different systems work and we indicate some of the main strengths and weaknesses of each approach.

3.3 Planned approach

3.3.1 A simple view of a planned economy

If we take an extreme view of a **planned economy**, sometimes called a **command economy**, then decisions on the **allocation** and **distribution of resources** are taken by the planners. They decide the key questions of production: **what, how** and **for whom**. Individual enterprises receive commands in the form of **planning targets** and it is these rather than financial returns that motivate production. This may conjure up a picture of planners sitting around a table making decisions before issuing planning targets. While the key strategic choices will be made in this way, planning a modern industrial economy with its intricate interconnections is vastly more complicated than this: the informational requirements alone are enormous. In the USSR, millions of people are engaged in the exercise of planning itself.

3.3.2 Allocative efficiency

Given the size of the undertaking it would be surprising if **allocative efficiency** were achieved. Lack of proper coordination may well mean that inputs from certain enterprises are not produced in sufficient quantities so that labour and machinery are not fully utilized. The fear that input shortages may prevent planning targets from being met may lead production ministries to try to safeguard supplies by producing their own materials, sometimes in a most inefficient manner.

In an economy where plans are expressed in terms of quantities the **costs** of production are not likely to be clear or relevant to most enterprises. **Quantitative planning** may well result in poor quality goods unless targets are expressed clearly: for example, a vague target of 1000 tons of screws is likely to mean that enterprises meet this weight target in the easiest possible way irrespective of the size or quality of the product. This will to some extent by solved by specifying the type of screw; but if you consider how many different sorts of screws there are, you will appreciate why it is a gigantic undertaking to plan an economy in this manner. For all of these reasons it is almost impossible for a **planned economy** to achieve technical efficiency and it is therefore likely to operate within its production possibility curve.

The **preferences** of the general public are unlikely to be paramount, which is a further reason for doubting whether allocative efficiency can be achieved. In a **centrally planned economy** enterprises are concerned to meet their targets rather than directly meeting consumers' wishes: planners' preferences dominate. The planners may not reflect the preferences of the general public either because they deliberately decide to superimpose their own or because they make mistakes in estimating or interpreting what the public wants.

There are great difficulties in dealing with allocation problems through planning, as the volume of criticism in the Soviet press and the variety of suggested economic reforms, experiments and reorganizations indicate.

3.3.3 Static or dynamic efficiency

A very important qualification now needs to be made which may put the planning of the allocation of resources in a much more favourable light. We have suggested that planned economies will face severe difficulties in achieving allocative efficiency. But this is a **static** view which considers efficiency at one point in time. **Dynamic efficiency** takes a longer view and assesses how well an economy allocates resources over a number of years. By overriding consumer preferences planners may allocate resources in such a way that a faster growth rate is achieved; although their intervention results in short-term inefficiencies the long-term effect may be a higher output of goods and services.

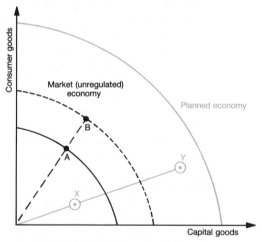

Fig. 3.4 Dynamic efficiency

This point can be illustrated (see Figure 3.4) using production possibility curves which show the maximum amounts of consumer goods (food, TVs, holidays, etc.) and capital goods (plant and machinery, roads, power stations, etc.) that can be produced. We can compare the paths of a planned and unregulated economy (e.g. a market economy) by considering a common starting point with both types of economy having the same initial production possibility curve, the solid curve nearest the origin. Suppose a planned economy is depicted by point X. This is inside the curve because of inefficiencies of planning and seems to compare unfavourably with an economy at point A, which is on the curve, and for the purposes of our illustration may be considered an unplanned or unregulated economy (e.g. market economy) alternatives. However, point X also indicates the ability of planners to devote more resources to capital goods than in the unplanned alternative. As it is generally accepted that a greater **investment in capital goods** is likely to produce a faster growth rate, the production possibility curve of the planned economy (outer curve) moves more than the curve of the high consumption unplanned economy (the dotted line). So after a number of years the planned economy may achieve a position such as Y where planning inefficiencies still mean it operates within the frontier—it is not experiencing **static efficiency**—but it is producing at an output level which is beyond the ability of the high consumption society (operating at B). The **planned economy** is inferior in terms of **static efficiency** but in terms of **dynamic efficiency** (viewing allocation of resources over time), its performance is superior.

3.3.4 Distribution

Planners have considerable opportunities to affect the **distribution** of **income and wealth**. They have the power to determine **wages** and can make extensive use of **price controls** by providing commodities and services like food, housing and transport at prices well below costs of production; this can have a significant effect on distribution. However, if planners do not have the power to direct labour **wage differentials** will be necessary to provide an incentive to people to undertake less desirable jobs. In highly bureaucratized systems there is also the danger that bureaucrats will reward themselves too generously.

We usually think of planning in the context of **socialist economies**. In these societies **private ownership** of the **means of production** is normally very limited, so wealth tends to be more evenly distributed, because it is publicly owned, than in the market economies. (Note that this is not necessarily true of income.)

3.3.5 Stabilization

Control over output, prices and trade tends to mean that the **stabilization problems** of unemployment, high inflation and balance of payments difficulties do not trouble planned economies in the same way as economies like those of the UK and USA. There may, however, be 'hidden' unemployment as a result of workers remaining idle or working unproductively because of planning inefficiencies. The absence of modern style balance-of-payments crises does not mean that planned economies do not face trade problems: it is often the case that high priority is given to directing resources into export activities because there is an urgent need to earn **foreign currency** to pay for much needed imports.

It is interesting to note that as the socialist economy of Yugoslavia has moved away from **central command planning** (of the type we have discussed here) towards **market socialism**, in which much more autonomy is given to enterprise, it has reduced some **allocative inefficiencies** but started to acquire the **stabilization** problems familiar in market economies.

3.4 The market economy

3.4.1 A simple view of the market economy

To grasp the most important features of a **market economy** it is helpful to think not of the UK but of some simple extreme case where there is no government to intervene. This immediately highlights a key point—**decentralized decision making**. Decisions are taken not by planners but by individual consumers, workers and firms. This may seem like a recipe for anarchy; but **control mechanisms** are operating.

Consumers express their **preferences** through their purchases in the goods market. The firms that produce goods and services use the receipts from these sales to bid for **land**, **labour** and **capital** in the **factor market**. When consumer preferences change demand for some goods rises, prices tend to go up and the profits for firms producing these goods will increase. These higher profits will act as an **incentive** to expand output and will attract new firms into the industry. The reverse will tend to happen to firms which are no longer favoured by consumers. They will contract or go out of business altogether. This will release **factors of production** which can be bought by expanding firms. In this way resources are allocated according to consumer wishes.

This is often referred to as **consumer sovereignty**—the consumer rules when it comes to determining the allocation of resources. The situation is even more consumer orientated than our picture suggests, because in the struggle to stay in business it is assumed that firms will pay close attention to quality, will strive to lower costs and will be continually trying to innovate and develop new products.

We have concentrated on the flow from consumer preferences through firms' activities to the allocation of resources; but there is also a need for **information** about production possibilities to be conveyed to consumers. This happens via **changes in prices**.

The consumer does not need to understand a new production technique or read trade papers to find out about it because pressure of competition should ensure that it is introduced and that prices fall to reflect the lower costs. The consumer can then adjust his expenditure patterns in the light of the lower price so that resources are reallocated.

3.4.2 The role of prices

At the centre of the operation of a market economy is the **price mechanism**. It is the movements of prices in goods and factor markets that regulate the economy in the market system, just as planners do in command economies. **Prices** carry out a number of functions simultaneously.

3.4.2.1 Rationing of scarce resources

The problem of **scarcity** means that **resources** have to be **rationed** in one way or another. In planned economies the planners make the decisions and under wartime rationing this is done by issuing coupons to the population; but in the **market system** it is **prices** that **ration scarce resources**: resources go to the highest bidder.

3.4.2.2 The transmission of information

Prices are a very economical way of transmitting **information**; we saw in the previous section that they can transmit information on costs and production possibilities. Changes in consumer preferences also tend to be reflected in price movements. Profits and factor prices all act as **price signals** that convey **information** about the state of the market.

3.4.2.3 Incentives

Prices have a further role—they provide a system of **incentives**. The increased prices that result from a change in consumer preferences not only inform producers of a change in tastes, they are also an **incentive** to firms to supply more of the commodity in question. Higher factor prices are an **incentive** to move factors to better paid uses or search for substitutes.

3.4.2.4 An illustration

An illustration should highlight the important role of prices. Suppose there were a significant reduction in the supply of oil due to some natural disaster or as a consequence of a Middle East war. The **price** of oil would rise as oil buyers competed more intensively; this would **ration** the reduced quantity. Although news of the state of the oil market might well be reported by the media, the most effective means of transmitting the information about scarcity would be through the rise in price. Consumers might not be aware of the extent to which some products were oil based, but they would not need to know, because price increases would reflect the extent to which any particular commodity was affected by the oil shortage.

The oil price increase would also have **incentive** effects: there would be an incentive to economize on oil and to consider alternative products. Planners would not need to issue revised planning targets for coal mines because raised consumer demand for coal as a substitute for oil and the incentive of higher sales and profits would encourage increased coal production, with miners' wages rising and providing an incentive to join the industry. The higher price of oil would also provide a powerful incentive to search for new sources of oil.

3.4.3 Optimum allocation of resources

We saw in the previous section that the **price mechanism** is an extremely powerful means of **allocating resources**. It reaches out to all relevant parts of the economy yet is highly economical in comparison with planning. But can the market economy achieve an **optimum allocation of resources**; that is, given society's preferences and production possibilities, can it achieve **allocative efficiency**?

It can be shown, though proof of this is beyond the scope of this chapter (but see Chapter 18), that under certain conditions this optimum may be achieved. This is a remarkable outcome given the **lack of coordination** of the market economy. It indicates the potential power of the market system. However, the conditions for realizing an optimum are not likely to be achieved in practice: there is **market failure**.

3.5 Market failure

The **failure** of the **market system** to achieve an optimum position can be considered under the familiar headings of **allocation, distribution** and **stabilization**. We will give particular attention here to **allocation**. (Stabilization aspects are considered more fully in Chapter 7 and while distribution is not an aspect of market failure in the technical sense, it is the cause of much criticism of unregulated market economies and the ground for a high degree of intervention.)

3.5.1 Allocation

3.5.1.1 Imperfect information

Consumers will not have **perfect information** about goods and services; their purchases may not reflect their true preferences. This may happen because they are ignorant or misled about the properties of their purchases. For example, the highly technical nature of many electrical and engineering products means that a consumer would need extensive test equipment to evaluate the goods on offer. Similarly, a medical qualification and a laboratory would be required to discover the true effects of medicines. Advertising does inform consumers, but there can be little doubt that in an unregulated market much effort is directed at misleading the public by making exaggerated or incorrect claims about products. Owners of factors of production may also suffer from **imperfect information**: workers may not be aware of job opportunities or may perceive wage levels incorrectly.

The result of **imperfect information** is a **misallocation** of **resources**: consumers buying products they do not really want or factors not moving in to uses that would maximize their returns. The market itself may respond to counteract this ignorance, as we see from consumers' associations with test reports and private employment agencies for workers. However, in many areas the possibility of disseminating **imperfect information** is regarded as strong grounds for **government intervention**, as in the regulation of drugs, legal establishment of safety standards and imposition of codes of conduct for advertising.

3.5.1.2 Monopoly and imperfect competition

The competitive situation, with its associated benefits of product improvement, cost reduction and attention to consumer wishes, may well not be realized in practice. Some firms may come to dominate an industry. **Monopoly** is strictly a situation where there is a sole seller, though the term is often used where one firm has a significant share of the market. There are other situations, known generally as **imperfect competition**, where competitive conditions do not exist and a group of firms **dominate** an industry or an area.

In these circumstances **consumer power** tends to be replaced by **producer power** and the incentives to reduce cost, innovate and provide the type of goods and services that consumers want are reduced. So **allocative inefficiency** occurs and resources are not used according to consumer preferences. High profits under these conditions will arise from the exploitation of a **monopoly** position, rather than from market signals which indicate a change in consumer preferences.

In many circumstances where a monopoly exists it is difficult for new firms to enter the industry so these high profits may not be competed away. **Profit** and the **lack of competition** will weaken the pressure to reduce costs and use resources efficiently. This is known as 'X-inefficiency' and is a situation where the maximum output is not being produced by existing resources (that is, a point within the production possibility curve) because they are not being used in the most efficient manner.

There are some industries which can be described as **natural monopolies**. With electricity and gas supply, for example, a competitive position, with the consumer being presented with the choice of several companies, each with their own wires or pipes, is unlikely to arise. In these cases and several others (telephone, water supply, sewage, railways) industries are either **state owned** or **private monopolies** with state regulation to safeguard the consumer.

3.5.1.3 Public goods

Some goods and services will never be provided by the market because, despite a demand by the public, no private firm will ever be able to produce them profitably. This happens because in some cases it is not possible to exclude non-payers from the benefits of products. Street lighting is a benefit enjoyed by all road users once it is provided; there is therefore a problem in persuading individuals to pay for the service. This is known as the **free rider** problem. Defence, law and order, lighthouses and radio and TV transmission (unless scramblers are used) are other examples.

The market system, in order to operate effectively, requires the **exclusion principle** to hold. This is where non-payers are **excluded** from enjoying the benefits. With **public goods** this breaks down completely; even the most ardent advocate of the market economy would accept that state intervention is required here, though it may be limited. Street lighting has to be financed by taxing the community: but it could be provided by local authorities inviting competitive bids from private street-lighting firms. In the case of TV viewers can be **free riders**, but the service may be financed by charging for advertisements, where the exclusion principle does work—if you do not pay, you cannot advertise. Of course it is necessary to entice viewers to switch on to persuade advertisers to pay and this is done by surrounding the advertisements with programmes that are given away free.

3.5.1.4 Externalities

The **exclusion principle** allows us to distinguish a **pure public good** (where the principle breaks down entirely) and a **pure private good** (where it holds completely). In between these two extremes are many examples where some benefits are enjoyed by non-payers, that is, there are some benefits external to the purchaser. These are called **externalities**. This situation may not be confined to benefits, but may exist with production, where there are external costs. These concepts can be clarified with a few examples.

On the benefit side, vaccinations are often quoted. These provide the person vaccinated with benefits; the **externalities** are the reduced incidence of the disease and the reduced chance of anybody catching it. Non-vaccinated people are therefore **free riders**; they gain from other people obtaining vaccination. A further example will show why **externalities** are a problem for **efficient resource allocation** (Table 3.1).

Table 3.1 Benefit and costs of draining a field (£)

	Cost	Benefit
Farm A	1000	700
Farm B	—	300
Farm C	—	200
Farm D	—	150
Total	1000	1350

In the example above the hypothetical **cost** of farm A draining its fields is £1000 and the estimated **benefits** are £700. Under these circumstances the farmer would clearly decide not to undertake the drainage work. But these are **private** costs and benefits. Where there are **externalities** the effects on society will be different: the social benefits and costs will differ from purely private ones. In our example, other farmers will benefit from the drainage scheme and the benefits to them might be sufficient to justify resources being employed to improve the land. In this case the extra benefits are estimated at £650 and so the **social benefits (private benefits plus externalities)** are £1350, which exceeds the total cost; the drainage scheme therefore seems to be justified.

External costs may be generated when production gives rise to noise, disease, pollution or other nuisance. A chemical firm which pollutes the atmophere and an adjacent river will cause costs to local householders (who have to repaint their houses more often because of the pollution in the atmosphere) and to firms such as brewers downstream, who have to incur extra costs to clean up the water.

When there are **externalities** resources will not be allocated in the best possible way when decisions are taken on private costs and benefits. In our farming example, the fields would not be drained on this basis. In the pollution example the price signals will be incorrect: chemicals will be sold at too low a price because the costs of **external** pollution will not be taken into account, whereas the price of beer will be too high because it is in effect paying part of the cost of chemical production by bearing the cost of cleaning the water. Consumers will tend to buy more chemicals and less beer than they would if prices reflected the **true costs of production**.

The activities of one generation may well have an important effect on another: production now may affect the quality of the environment for future generations. However, today's resources are likely to be allocated on the basis of the present generation and **future costs** seen as an **externality**. An **optimum allocation of resources over time** requires that account is taken of the wishes of future generations. However, the market cannot accommodate this, so resources may be **inefficiently allocated**.

3.5.1.5 Merit goods

There are certain goods and services known as **merit goods** which governments believe to be so important that more resources should be devoted to their production than an unregulated market economy would allow. Health, education, museums and housing are examples of **merit goods**.

Why are they regarded as **merit goods**? It is not because they are **public goods** because the exclusion principle generally operates—non-payers could be excluded from schools, hospitals and so on. In most cases **externalities** are associated with these services and **imperfect consumer information** is generally found in these areas. But this alone would not justify the separate categorization of these activities.

The argument for **merit goods** goes beyond the factors we have already isolated. It rests upon ethical principles and concepts of a civilized society. State intervention in education may be justified by a need for social cohesion; some see the principle of equality of opportunity as paramount. A paternalistic view may suggest that the state has a responsibility to ensure that children are brought up in a reasonable state of health, well educated and housed. The case for merit goods, though closely bound up with a concern for the poor, is not identical to the issue of distribution, but is really an argument that there should be collective provision of certain services. Society as a whole should take responsibility for certain matters and not leave them to individuals.

3.5.1.6 Dynamic efficiency

Dynamic efficiency, as we indicated earlier, is concerned with how well resources are allocated over time. Doubts have been raised about how dynamically efficient market economies can be. A comprehensive approach to allocating resources over time would involve a system of markets for commodities and services demanded and supplied in the future. In practice there are very few of these and the **price mechanism** is therefore better suited to achieving **static (present)** rather than **dynamic (future) efficiency**.

A second factor is that a market economy that relies upon individuals **maximizing benefits** may not allocate resources in a way that will produce the **growth rate** society wants. Even if higher growth depends upon reducing consumption now and raising expenditure on capital goods, individuals are unlikely to cut their consumption because what any one individual does has an insignificant impact on the growth rate; so each individual has an incentive to be a **free rider**. But if every individual took this view, then everybody would pursue higher present consumption in the hope that others were making sacrifices. Similarly, if high growth required the acceptance of technological change, with rapid alterations in industrial structure and the loss of traditional jobs, then individuals would understandably resist the costs but still want the benefits. Both these factors have been advanced as arguments for the necessity of **government intervention** in matters like raising the growth rate.

3.5.2 Distribution–market failure

3.5.2.1 The need for intervention?

Market failure refers to the inability of the market mechanism to achieve **allocative efficiency**. A highly **skewed distribution of income** with widespread poverty may be associated with allocative efficiency if the problems we referred to above are absent. Such an **unequal distribution** does not constitute **market failure** in a technical sense, but there is little doubt that the poverty that would occur in a totally unregulated market economy is unacceptable. While there is almost universal agreement on the need for some **redistribution**, the extent and form of help to the poor produces a heated debate. At one extreme there are those who accept government intervention only reluctantly and think that **private charity** should be the main means of alleviating poverty. There are others who believe that one of the main aims of governments should be to **redistribute resources equally** and that any departure from this principle needs justification.

Redistribution of income may come through a policy of **taxation** and **cash grants** to the less well off or it can result from providing goods and services at **subsidized** or **zero prices**. Free education and health services are worth much more, as a proportion of income, to the poor than to the better off. There are divisions over which means of redistribution are the most effective. Those who favour **market solutions** tend to stress the **cash grant approach** because it interferes least with the workings of the market economy: individuals retain the freedom to spend their income how they wish and services are provided at market rather than **subsidized** and **intervention prices**. Advocates of **redistribution** through expenditure are more sympathetic to collectivist approaches and tend to emphasize the importance of **merit goods**.

3.5.2.2 Equity or efficiency

The issues of **equity** and **efficiency** are rather more closely associated than our simplified discussion earlier in the chapter implied. As the market **allocates resources** it will simultaneously determine the **distribution of income**. It is the outcome of this process in an unregulated economy that is generally found to be unacceptable. But attempts to change it may have effects on the efficient workings of the system: if redistribution policies blunt incentives lower output will result. There is general agreement that some **differentials** in income are necessary, though considerable disagreement over whether the present system in the UK has disincentive effects.

3.5.3 Stabilization

We turn finally and briefly to stabilization issues. The general concern here is to what extent can the market be regarded as **self-regulating** or whether market failure requires **intervention**.

3.5.3.1 Unemployment

Given that the market economy is **decentralized** it would sccm astonishing if an unregulated system produced **full employment**. Yet many economists have held that it can. The Great Depression of the 1930s, which seemed to be a startling demonstration of market failure, produced what is known as the **Keynesian revolution**. This refers to **Keynes's** explanation that markets may fail to produce full employment and that government intervention is required if mass unemployment is to be avoided. Although this view has rapidly gained acceptance, it has been seriously challenged in the last 15 years by **monetarism**, which returns to earlier thinking by suggesting that government intervention is unnecessary and harmful.

3.5.3.2 Inflation

The split between the **Keynesians** and **monetarists** is mainly over the issue of **inflation**. **Monetarists** argue that **inflation** is caused by excess demand (a level of spending which is greater than output) which is the result of the government expanding the money in circulation at too rapid a rate. The **monetarist** remedy is to exercise strict control over the **money supply** to prevent unwanted **inflation**. **Keynesians** are much more sceptical and tend to argue that controlling spending in this way will affect output more than prices and that **high unemployment levels** may be necessary to control inflation. They tend to argue that inflation is the result of cost pressures (wage and import costs) rather than too much demand: so policy should be directed at controlling costs through **incomes policy**.

3.5.3.3 Balance of payments

The **balance of payments** is the difference between what a country **imports** and **exports**. As the state of the **balance of payments** will depend on the spending decisions of millions of people in this country and abroad, imbalances (deficits and surpluses) are likely to arise. Here again there is a division beween those who have faith in market solutions and those who are more inclined towards intervention. One important mechanism of control under modern conditions is the **exchange rate**. Those opposed to the unregulated market would suggest that foreign exchange markets are volatile and that some intervention is necessary. Some countries may suffer from deep-seated **structural problems** that produce **balance-of-payments** difficulties; government intervention will be necessary to correct this.

3.6 The mixed economy

There are deep divisions over the extent of market failure and the need for government intervention. It should be pointed out that even if **market failure** does occur, it does not necessarily follow that **government intervention** will improve matters. Governments often give rise to **monopolistic** and **bureaucratized structures** which are insensitive to consumers' wishes.

3.6.1 Growth of government in the UK

There has been a significant **growth** in **government intervention** in the economy since the turn of the century. This involvement has many aspects—legislation, state enterprises and expenditure, taxation and transfer payments (e.g. pensions, family allowances, student grants). Figure 3.5 shows the growth in government spending as a proportion of total output (GDP).

The reason for this growth can be traced back to the last century. At that time the dominant view was *laisser-faire*, which meant that the market economy should be left alone and government intervention should be kept to a minimum. This position was challenged as it became clear that 19th-century urbanization and industrialization produced problems (public health, transport, a poorly educated workforce) that required **intervention**. So the state gradually (predominantly through local government until the turn of the century) intervened in the allocation of resources.

State concern with **distribution** did not really arise until the beginning of this century, when the view that poverty was the result of personality deficiencies was gradually replaced by the recognition that poverty was a result of the workings of a market

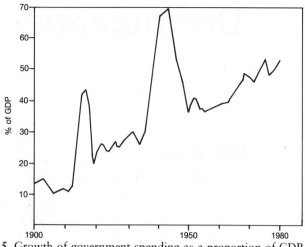

Fig. 3.5 Growth of government spending as a proportion of GDP 1900–86

economy. Since 1900 **redistribution** has been an important reason for the **growth** of **government spending and taxation**.

Laisser-faire in the area of stabilization lasted until the depression of the 1930s when it gave way to the Keynesian view that government intervention was necessary to achieve and maintain full employment.

3.6.3 International comparisons

Economies like the UK are **mixed economies**: while there is **private provisions** of many goods and services there is also a **large public sector** and significant **state intervention**. This is a feature of all modern market economies, as Table 3.2 shows, with government expenditure representing from a third to over a half of total spending. Table 3.2 shows the relative importance of **public goods** (here defined as defence and general public services), **merit goods** (education, health, housing and community and social services) and '**income maintenance**', which includes the **transfer payments** of pensions, sickness benefits, family allowance and unemployment pay. The 'other' category is a residual which includes **public debt interest** as well as expenditures that do not fall into previous categories.

Table 3.2 Government expenditure as a percentage of GDP in selected countries in 1981

Country	Total	Public goods	Merit goods	Income maintenance	Other
France	49.2	7.5	16.0	17.2	8.5
West Germany	49.3	6.8	14.3	16.7	11.5
Italy	51.2	7.0	14.0	15.8	14.4
Japan	34.5	4.2	12.5	6.9	10.9
UK	43.2	7.7	13.6	9.1	12.8
USA	32.8	8.4	10.2	7.8	6.4

(*OECD Economic Observer*, Jan/Feb, 1986)

3.6.4 The scope of the market–a continuing dispute

The debate over the proper role of the market and the state is a longstanding one in economics. It is an issue that will occur in nearly every chapter in this book. At the micro level there are arguments about state or market provision of goods and services such as electricity, water supply, health and education. In macroeconomic policy there is a debate over the need for and the role of government intervention.

We briefly traced the change in ideas on the role of the government in the economy in section 3.6.1; however, in concluding this chapter where we have considered **planned** and **market economies** we need to observe a shift in views that has taken place in recent years in many parts of the world. There has been growing support for market solutions in many areas of the economy, for example, the privatization and deregulation of industry. In the last decade this approach has been adopted in several countries and sometimes by socialist administrations. At the macro level, monetarist ideas have been more influential, and as we shall see in later chapters these challenge the Keynesian view that has been dominant for most of the period after the Second World War and which suggested that government intervention was necessary to ensure that market economies followed a stable path of low inflation and unemployment. The influence of these ideas is not confined to market economies. In the socialist economies, there has been a significant move towards decentralization and a greater role for prices in allocating resources.

4 Determination of prices

4.1 Introduction

It is often said that if you can teach a parrot to say 'demand and supply' you will have produced an economist. In spite of its rudeness, this comment is right about the central position that **demand and supply analysis** occupies in economics. This chapter concentrates upon the basic theory while the next considers a number of its applications.

The chapter will:

- explain what determines demand and supply
- explain the basic supply and demand diagram
- distinguish between what causes movement along and what causes shifts in the demand and supply schedule
- explain what determines prices
- explain elasticity

4.1.1 Examination guide

It is almost inconceivable that an economics course will not include **demand** and **supply**. It is one of the basic tools of economics and is likely to be examined indirectly in a range of questions. There is an increasing tendency to examine it directly through the use of multiple choice questions and questions requiring short answers. If this is not part of an examination it will almost certainly be included in coursework/assessment. Almost all courses will expect students to be familiar with **supply and demand diagrams** and show evidence of this in their answers. These diagrams are often a source of confusion, particularly in the early stages of a course; but with a little patience and a careful step-by-step approach they can easily be mastered. Always try to make sure you understand what is going on (do not simply learn the diagrams)–if you do not, retrace your steps. There is no substitute for practising drawing these diagrams yourself. As you do so, explain to yourself (or a friend) what each line and each stage means.

4.2 The role of supply and demand

The previous chapter explained the importance of **markets** and the **price mechanism** so here we merely summarize the key points.

Households own **factors of production** (**land, labour** and **capital**) and **supply** these to firms who demand them in order to make **goods** and **services**, which are produced to meet the **demands** of households. There is both a **demand for** and a **supply of** goods and services and it is the interaction of these two that determines **prices**. A similar situation is to be found in the **factor market** where **factor prices** (**wages, rents,** etc.) are determined; here **households** are the **suppliers** and **firms** give rise to the **demand** for factors.

4.2.1 The role of prices

As we observed in the last chapter, there is no central direction of the allocation of resources in a market economy. This function is performed by the **price mechanism. Prices ration scarce goods and factors,** convey **information** about the state of markets and provide **incentives** to buyers and sellers. The role of prices is an important one and this chapter explores how they are determined. (The discussion here concentrates on the market for goods and services; the factor market is considered further in Chapter 17.)

4.3 Demand

4.3.1 The demand function

At the outset, we need to clarify what is meant by **demand**. It is not the same as a person's wishes or aspirations–doubtless most of us have a demand for (a wish to purchase) a villa in the south of France; but few of us are in a position to turn this dream into a reality. More seriously, there is a need for food and housing for the world's poor and this may be described as a desperate 'demand' for essentials; but this is not a **demand** in the **marketplace**, because the wish or need to purchase is not supported by the **ability to pay**. **Demand** is defined as the quantities that buyers are willing **and able** to purchase.

It is important to recognize that we need to give a **demand** a **time dimension**. Consider a case where an individual's **demand** for beer is said to be 16 pints. We need to specify the **time period** that this **demand** refers to, otherwise the information is meaningless: the individual would be relatively abstemious if this were the annual demand or have a drink problem if this were a typical daily demand.

Economists speak of a **demand function** that relates the factors affecting demand to the **quantity** people wish to buy. We often refer to an individual's demand for a product or service; but there are many occasions when we are interested in the market or industry demand, i.e. an **aggregation** of individual demands for a product.

4.3.2 Determinants of demand

There are likely to be many factors which determine the **quantity** of a product that is demanded. We can classify them under five main headings (see below). The **demand function** for a product X can be summarized in mathematical notation as

$$Q_{dx} = f35f(P_x, P_o, Y, P_{ex}, Z)$$

where Q_{dx} is the quantity of x demanded, P_x is the price of x, P_o is other prices, Y is income, P_{ex} is the expected price of x and Z is taste and other factors.

4.3.2.1 The price of a product (P_x)

One obvious factor that is influential is the **price** of the product (P_x). Generally, the lower the price the more people will want to buy and vice versa.

4.3.2.2 Other prices (P_o)

Prices of **other goods** (P_o) will influence the demand for a commodity. For example, if the price of oranges falls the demand for apples is likely to be reduced. This is because oranges are a **substitute** for apples. Sometimes a different type of relationship may be found if we have what are known as **complementary goods** (goods which tend to be bought together). An example of this is gin and tonic water: when the price of gin falls—encouraging its consumption—we would expect the demand for tonic to rise.

4.3.2.3 Income (Y)

Another important factor determining the demand for a commodity is the level of **income**. A rise in income generally leads to an increase in demand.

4.3.2.4 Expected price of a product (P_e)

If the price of a product is **expected** to rise then this may encourage demand in **anticipation** of the increase (e.g. pre-budget spending on wines, spirits and tobacco).

4.3.2.5 Tastes (Z)

A category covering many other factors is generally called **tastes**. It covers such matters as personal tastes (e.g. whether a person is a beer drinker or not) but is also intended to incorporate **factors** such as the weather (hot summers increase beer consumption), demographic factors (beer drinking is particularly popular among the young), advertising and health campaigns.

4.3.3 The demand curve

The **demand curve** shows the relationship between the quantity demanded and the price of the product assuming other factors (prices of other products, income, expected price and tastes) do not change. (This does not mean that we think these factors are unlikely to alter or that these changes are unimportant. It is done solely to make the representation manageable.)

Table 4.1 (overleaf) shows a hypothetical relationship between price and quantity. This can be shown in a graph. In Figure 4.1 (overleaf) the points A to F in the table are plotted; the line joining these points is known as the demand curve.

The demand curve shows the **quantities** of X that consumers are willing to buy at different prices assuming that other factors are unchanged. If the price were £3 then the consumers would demand 20 units; but if the price fell to £2 they would demand 30.

Table 4.1 A demand schedule for *X*

	Price of *X* (£)	Demand for *X* (units)
A	0	50
B	1	40
C	2	30
D	3	20
E	4	10
F	5	0

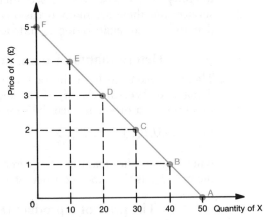

Fig. 4.1 A demand curve

Consumers' reactions to changes in the price of the product are shown by movements **along** the **demand curve**. If there are changes in other factors (income, other prices, etc.) then the **whole** demand curve will **shift** either outwards (to the right) or inwards (to the left) as in Figure 4.2.

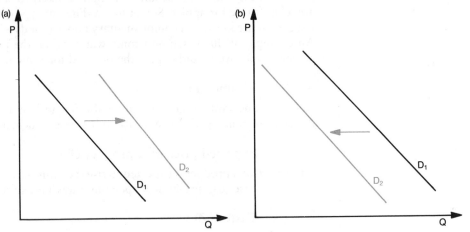

Fig. 4.2 Shifts in a demand curve

4.3.4   Shifts in demand

4.3.4.1   Other prices

The reaction of the consumer to a change in the price of other products depends on whether they are **substitute** or **complementary goods**. In the former case a rise in the price of a substitute will lead to an increase in the demand for *X* and the demand curve will shift out to the right. The demand curve shifts inwards if the price of a substitute falls. In the case of **complementary goods**, the demand shifts out when there is a fall in the price of the complement and vice versa. So when the price of computers falls the demand curve for disks shifts outwards.

4.3.4.2   **Changes in income**

We said earlier that with most goods the demand will increase when incomes rise; this can be represented by an outward shift of the demand curve. But this will not always be the case. Sometimes the quantity demanded will be unaffected by income changes. There will be examples of rises in income leading to lower spending, which causes the demand curve to shift inwards. When this occurs we say the products are **inferior goods**; cheap cuts of meat are generally cited as an illustration. **Normal goods** are those where demand increases (or is unaffected) by a rise in income.

4.3.4.3 Change in expectations

If the price of a product is **expected** to rise in the near future then consumers are likely to increase their purchases, so the demand curve will shift out.

4.3.4.4 Change in tastes

By now it should be clear that something which increases the consumers' preferences for a product will lead them to buy more of the product at any given price; the demand curve will then shift out to the right.

4.3.5 Shifts versus movements along the demand curve

Confusion between **shifts** of the demand and **movements along** it is a very common source of error in economics. A **change** in the **price** of the product involves a **movement along** the curve; **anything else** (assuming it has some effect) causes a **shift** of the schedule.

If you are considering a change in demand simply ask yourself what is causing it. If it is the **price** of the product, then a **movement along** the curve shows the effect; anything else, whether **price of other products, income, expectations** or **tastes**, causes the demand curve to **shift**.

4.4 Supply

4.4.1 Supply function

Just as we can have a demand function so we can have a **supply function**. This shows the factors that affect the **quantities** that sellers are prepared to **supply**. The concept of **supply** sometimes poses more difficulties than demand. This may be because we are all consumers; this gives us personal insights into demand which we may not have with supply. It is sometimes helpful to imagine that you are the owner of a firm or, in the illustrations we are going to use, a farmer.

4.4.2 Determinants of supply

4.4.2.1 Price of product (P_x)

We would expect the **price** of the product itself to affect the quantity supplied. Generally, the higher the price the greater the quantity that will be supplied. A farmer who is offered a high price for potatoes will plant a larger quantity than he or she would when offered a lower price.

4.4.2.2 Other prices (P_o)

The **price** of other products is likely to be influential because suppliers will give consideration to producing **alternative products**: the possibility of obtaining higher prices for swedes and turnips would probably persuade farmers to move away from potatoes.

4.4.2.3 Factor prices (P_f)

The quantity that will be supplied will be affected by the **price of factors of production**: lower factor costs will tend to encourage supply and vice versa.

4.4.2.4 Technology (T)

Technological innovations will be applied if they lower costs; this will tend to increase supply.

4.4.2.5 Other factors (Z)

There are a number of **other factors** that can affect **supply**. **Government policies** may impose restrictions which raise costs and therefore affect supply. For example, safety regulations may limit the type of production method used or require expenditure on safety equipment. The **objectives of firms** may influence supply. In economics we often assume that firms seek to **maximize profits**; but other objectives are recognized, such as **sales maximization**. Supply may be affected by **privatization**, depending on what requirements and responsibilities are placed on the new organization as compared with its nationalized predecessor. In the case of agricultural products **supply** can be affected by the weather and outbreaks of plant or animal disease.

4.4.3 The supply curve

We can draw a **supply curve** using an approach like the one adopted for demand. Table 4.2 shows a typical **supply schedule**, which is plotted in Figure 4.3.

Table 4.2 A supply schedule for X

	Price of X (£)	Quantity of X supplied (units)
A	1	0
B	2	10
C	3	20
D	4	30
E	5	40

Fig. 4.3 A typical supply schedule

This shows what sellers will be willing to supply at different prices, *ceteris paribus*—assuming other things (other prices, factor prices, technology etc.) are unchanged.

4.4.4 Shifts in supply

When these other factors change then the **supply curve** will shift outwards (to the right) o inwards (to the left), as in Figure 4.4. We will now briefly review some examples of **supply curve shifts.**

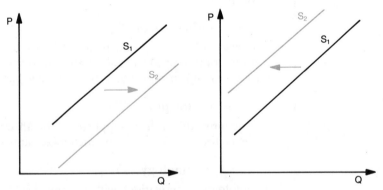

Fig. 4.4 Shifts in a supply curve

4.4.4.1 Changes in other product prices

A change in the prices of products which are **production alternatives** may shift the suppl curve. Using the example cited above, the potato farmer is likely to be attracted by th possibility of a higher price of swedes and turnips and will, therefore, plant fewe potatoes. The supply curve for potatoes shifts then inwards, with fewer being offered a any given price.

4.4.4.2 Changes in factor prices

An increase in the **price of factors**, *ceteris paribus*, will shift the supply curve inward because sellers will offer less at any given price. (It is sometimes more helpful to think o the supply shifting upwards rather than inwards.) Suppose there was an increase in the wages of farm workers; farmers would then require a higher price to make them willing to supply the same quantity e.g. they now want £4 instead of £3 and the supply curve shifts up. This is the equivalent of offering less at any given price, e.g. 10 instead of 20 at a price of £3.

4.4.4.3 Technology changes

Technological changes may influence costs, just as factor prices do. Suppose a **new technique** is developed for producing potatoes: an improved weedkiller, a higher yielding potato or better harvesting equipment. This will shift the supply curve out to the right because more will be offered at any given price. Again it may be more helpful to think in terms of an equivalent vertical shift. In this case the **innovation** which lowers the cost of producing a given quantity of potatoes means that suppliers will be prepared to supply the same quantity (20) at a lower price–say, £2 instead of £3.

4.4.4.4 Changes in other factors

A **range of other factors** may shift the supply curve: the introduction of new safety regulations may raise costs and shift the supply curve inwards and favourable weather conditions may produce a bumper harvest which shifts the supply curve outwards.

4.4.5 Summary

As in the case of demand, we issue a warning: take care to distinguish between factors that **shift** the **supply curve** and those which involve a **movement along** it. Again the rule is simple: if it is the **price** of the product that changes then the effects on supply are captured in the **movement along** the curve; if **anything else changes** then this will **shift** the **whole supply curve.**

4.5 Price determination

We have shown what quantity consumers are willing to buy at different prices (the **demand curve**) and the amounts that sellers will be prepared to supply (the **supply curve**) for a similar range of prices. We now use both demand and supply to show how **market prices are determined.**

4.5.1 Graphical representation of equilibrium price

If we bring together the **demand and supply curves** used earlier in the chapter and show them in Figure 4.5, we can see that the two curves **intersect** at a price of £3 and a quantity of 20. At this price the plans or wishes of buyers and sellers are in accord with each other: both are prepared to trade a quantity of 20 at the price of £3. This is known as the **equilibrium price** because at this price there is no need for change–buyer and sellers are mutually satisfied. This point is made clearer if we consider any other prices, where we will find **disequilibrium.**

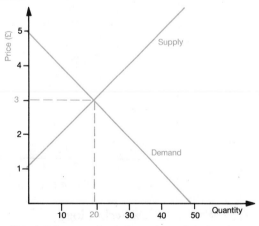

Fig. 4.5 Intersection of supply and demand curves

4.5.2 Disequilibrium: excess demand and supply

Disequilibrium arises when the wishes of buyers and sellers do not agree with each other. In our example, this happens at every price other than £3. At prices above the equilibrium we have **excess supply** (suppliers wish to sell more than consumers want to buy). When prices below the equilibrium point are considered we find we have **excess demand** (consumers wanting to purchase more goods and services than sellers are willing to supply). Neither type of position displays the settled conditions of equilibrium. If prices are free to move (we will consider cases where this is not so in the next chapter) we can expect them to change in response to disequilibrium.

Where there is excess demand prices will tend to rise because some demand will be unsatisfied and frustrated consumers will be willing to offer higher prices and sellers, aware of market conditions, will tend to raise prices. The situation is reversed when there is excess supply: sellers will cut prices to shift unsold goods and consumers, if they are aware of the state of the market, will seek discounts on prices. The position is summarized in Table 4.3.

Table 4.3 Equilibrium and disequilibrium

Price (£)	Quantity (units)		State of market		Direction of price change
	Demanded	Supplied	(D−S)		
1	40	0	+40	Excess demand	Up
2	30	10	+20	Excess demand	Up
3	20	20	0	Equilibrium	No change
4	10	30	−20	Excess supply	Down
5	0	40	−40	Excess supply	Down

There is a tendency in markets like the ones illustrated, where prices are free to move, for **prices** to move towards the **equilibrium**.

4.5.3 Equilibrium price and shifts in demand and supply

Shifts in demand and supply will change the **equilibrium price**. We consider two examples here: a change in consumers' preference and an improvement in technology.

4.5.3.1 Change in consumer preferences

If consumers increase their **preference** for a product this will cause the demand curve to shift out to the right (from D_1 to D_2 in Figure 4.6(a)). This will produce a position of **excess demand** (ED) at the original equilibrium price so prices will rise towards the **new equilibrium** at P_2. This provides a graphical illustration of the discussion in the previous chapter on the role prices perform in resource allocation. Price rises convey **information** about the state of the market and the higher prices act as an **incentive** to firms to produce more goods. The **new equilibrium** position is one where Q_2 goods are traded—the increase from Q_1 has involved shifting resources towards this product for which consumers have shown a greater preference.

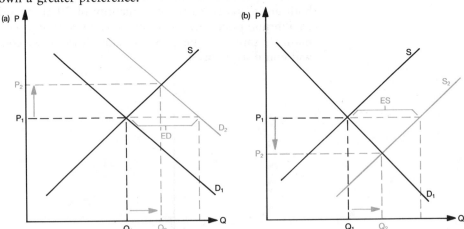

Fig. 4.6 Changes in supply and demand curves

4.5.3.2 New technology

A **technological** innovation which **lowers costs** per unit will shift the supply curve outwards (Figure 4.6(b)). This will produce **excess supply** (ES) at the original equilibrium price of P_1, causing prices to fall. The **new equilibrium** will be established at P_2 with a quantity of Q_2. The overall effect of the technological change is that consumers have been informed of it through lower prices and because of this buy more; the economy takes advantage of the new technology.

4.5.4 *Ex ante* and *ex post*

We complete this section with a technical point concerning the nature of **demand, supply** and **market transactions**. Demand and supply curves show the quantities that transactors are willing to buy or sell respectively. They are called *ex ante* concepts, by which we mean they show intentions or plans. These plans may not be realized.

Consider a typical demand curve like Figure 4.7. This shows the maximum amount a consumer wishes to buy at a given price and is in this sense a **boundary**. The **rational consumer** will not be found to the right of the demand curve– e.g. at point C; but he or she may be forced to purchase quantities within the demand curve, for example at point B. Similarly a supplier will not offer quantities to the right of the supply curve (e.g. point E) but may have to accept a point within the schedule, e.g. point A. What will push buyers and sellers within their demand and supply schedules is a **disequilibrium price**.

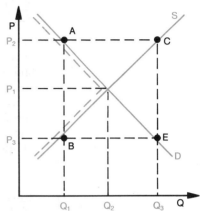

Fig. 4.7 Equilibrium and disequilibrium

At P_2, where there is excess supply, the actual quantity traded will be Q_1; suppliers are operating within their supply schedule and there are AD of unsold stock. At P_3 the positions are reversed; the consumer cannot buy all he or she would want (there is excess demand) and the actual quantity traded is Q_1.

The quantities traded will be at the '**short end of the market**', that is whichever is the lesser of the quantities demanded and supplied. This is shown by the dashed line. It shows the actual or realized quantities and these represent *ex post* measures. In an *ex post* sense demand will always equal supply because the quantities bought will always be the same as the quantity sold but, except at equilibrium, **intended** demand and **intended** supply will not be equal. It is these **intended** (or *ex ante*) concepts that economists are mainly concerned with because they give us the power to explain and predict events, while observations of the world are a record of **realized** (or *ex post*) values which are helpful in studying behaviour but are not direct evidence of it. This means that we have difficulty in identifying the nature of the demand curve from data; we discuss this further in Chapter 13.

4.6 Elasticity

4.6.1 Elasticity–a measure of responsiveness

A concept that is much used in economics is **elasticity**. This sometimes causes problems for students because undue consideration is given to learning formulae rather than understanding what the concept means. **Elasticity** is about **responsiveness**. As economists are interested in the interaction of a wide range of matters there are many occasions when they are interested in how responsive one variable is to changes in another–for example, the **interest elasticity** of investment, which measures the responsiveness of investment spending by firms to changes in interest rates.

In this chapter we concentrate on applying the concept to demand and supply. The quantity demanded is affected by several factors, as we explained earlier in the chapter, so we can consider several measures of **elasticity**, each relating the responsiveness of the quantity demanded to **changes** in different variables: **price, income** and the **price of other products**.

4.6.2 Price elasticity of demand (PED)

4.6.2.1 Formal definition

The **price elasticity of demand** (**PED**) shows the responsiveness of demand to changes in the price of the product. How do we measure it?

Suppose we were told that a cut of £1 in the price of a product led to an increase in the quantity demanded of 100. Does this tell us how responsive demand is? Of course not, because we do not know whether we can regard the price fall or quantity increase as large or small. We need to relate these changes to the prices charged and the quantities demanded. This is done by measuring **elasticity** in terms of **percentage** or **proportional changes**. So if the price cut was 20 per cent and the quantity change was 1 per cent, demand would not appear very responsive.

We measure **elasticity** formally in the following way:

$$\text{Price elasticity of demand (PED)} = \frac{\text{percentage change in quantity demanded}}{\text{percentage change in price}}$$

So in the example just given the **PED** would be

$$\frac{+1\%}{-20\%} = -0.05$$

The figure is **negative**, which is what we would normally expect with **PED** because cuts in prices will be associated with increases in quantity demanded and vice versa; but a widely observed convention omits the minus sign. So a **PED coefficient** of 0.05 is not the result of an unusual demand curve! We will follow this convention from now on. The **elasticity measure** we obtain in this way is an **average measure** which relates to the range of the demand curve we are considering by price and quantity changes. For this reason it is unwise to use too large a range because generally elasticity will vary along the schedule. Elasticity can also be measured at one point only.

4.6.2.2 A numerical example–different ways of measuring elasticity

Table 4.4 uses the demand curve we plotted earlier in the chapter to illustrate some aspects of elasticity.

Table 4.4 An illustration of elasticity

1	2	3	4	5	6	7
Price (£)	ΔP	Quantity	ΔQ	PED_1	PED_2	Total expenditure (£) ($P \times Q$)
0		50				0
	1		10	0	0.11	
1		40				40
	1		10	0.25	0.43	
2		30				60
	1		10	0.67	1.0	
3		20				60
	1		10	1.5	1.17	
4		10				40
	1		10	4.0	4.5	
5		0				0

Price elasticity coefficients are shown in column 5. To illustrate how they were calculated let us consider the price increase from £2 to £3. This represents a 50 per cent increase in price which will lead to a reduction of demand of one third from 30 to 20. We therefore calculate (to two decimal places) that **PED** will be 0.67.

$$PED = \frac{33.3\% \ (\text{change in } Q)}{50\% \ (\text{change in } P)} = 0.67$$

However, had we made the calculations in the same way but considered a cut in price rather than an increase, we would have obtained a different figure for the **PED**. Taking our previous example, if prices had fallen from £3 to £2 there would have been a 33.3 per cent change in prices and this would have led to an increase in quantity demanded of 10 from 20 to 30–a rise 50 per cent. This gives a **PED** of 1.5 (50 per cent divided by 33.3 per cent). The difference is a large one (0.67 compared with 1.5).

Our simple example exaggerates the matter because we are considering large changes (e.g. altering prices by one half or one third); but it is unsatisfactory to obtain different answers whether we move up or down the demand schedule.

The difference occurs because although changes in price and quantity are the same in both cases, the original prices and quantities on which we base our calculations of percentage changes are different. If we consider this closely, we can simplify our calculations and discover an alternative measure which will overcome the difficulty.

The **formula for calculating PED** is to **divide percentage change in quantity** by **percentage change in price**.

$$PED = \frac{\Delta Q \times 100}{Q} \bigg/ \frac{\Delta P \times 100}{P}$$

This can be simplified to: $\quad PED = \frac{\Delta Q}{Q} \bigg/ \frac{\Delta P}{P} = \frac{\Delta Q}{\Delta P} \times \frac{P}{Q}$

ΔQ is $(Q_1 - Q_2)$ where Q_1 is the original quantity and Q_2 the new quantity. The way the **PED** is normally calculated means that a more explicit statement would be:

$$PED = \frac{\Delta Q}{\Delta P} \times \frac{P_1}{Q_1}$$

(This is generally a much simpler way of calculating **PED** than working out percentage changes separately.)

An alternative way of calculating **PED** is to take the **average price** and **average quantity** instead of P_1 and Q_1; i.e. $(Q_1 + Q_2)/2$ for quantity and $(P_1 + P_2)/2$ for price. Again we can simplify expressions and obtain

$$PED = \frac{\Delta Q \times (P_1 + P_2)}{\Delta P \times (Q_1 + Q_2)}$$

The answers produced by this approach are shown in column 6 of Table 4.4. In the more specific case we were considering, a price change from £2 to £3, the **PED** calculated from this formula is 1; because we are taking the **average** of prices and quantities the answer will be the same whether we are moving up or down the demand curve.

4.6.2.3 Classifying elasticity

Whichever approach is adopted we are presented with a **range of PED coefficients**. How should these figures be interpreted and classified?

In some senses a **PED** of **1** provides a benchmark because this represents a position where the percentage change in quantity is the same as the percentage change in price. We call this **unit elasticity**. If the PED is **less than 1** then we are considering situations where demand is relatively unresponsive to price changes because the percentage change in quantity is less than that of price. In these cases we say that **demand is inelastic**. Where the PED is **greater than 1** and the quantity demanded is quite responsive to price changes then we say **demand is elastic**.

There are two extreme cases that we can identify. One is where quantity is completely unresponsive to price changes and the **PED is zero**. In these circumstances, demand is said to be **perfectly inelastic**.

The other extreme is where quantity is infinitely responsive to price changes. Here the **PED is infinity** and demand is said to be **perfectly elastic**. This last case may be difficult to comprehend but we make much use of it in economics (see Chapter 15); at this stage it is best regarded simply as an extreme case.

4.6.2.4 Total expenditure and elasticity

Elasticity has implications for total expenditure on products. If the PED is greater than 1 (i.e. **elastic**) then cuts in price will lead to an increase in total spending because the proportional increase in quantity is greater than the cut in price. Reductions in price when demand is **inelastic** will involve lower total expenditure, as quantity is less responsive to price changes. In the case of **unit elasticity**, total expenditure is unchanged when prices are altered because there are proportionally equal offsetting quantity changes.

These examples were illustrated in Table 4.4 where total expenditure was shown in column 7. The general relationship between expenditure and a straight-line demand curve is shown in Figure 4.8.

4.6.2.5 Shape of the demand curve and elasticity

There are some common misconceptions about the relationship between the shape of a demand curve and elasticity. So let us clarify what can and cannot be said about shape and elasticity.

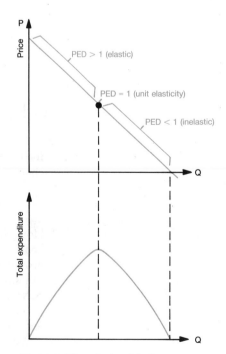

Fig. 4.8 The relationship between expenditure and a straight-line demand curve

Steep demand curves are not necessarily inelastic. A demand relationship can always be made to appear steep or shallow simply by altering the scales on the axes. As we see in Figure 4.8, straight-line demand curves do not have constant elasticity, except in the special cases discussed above.

We can now turn to more positive statements. A straight-line demand curve will have varying elasticity, as shown in Figure 4.8. We can explain why this is so by reference to our formula:

$$PED = \frac{\Delta Q}{\Delta P} \times \frac{P}{Q}$$

The first part of the expression on the righthand side will be a constant with a straight-line demand curve because it represents the slope of the line. The second term must decline in value as we move down the demand curve because as P (the numerator) gets smaller then Q (the denominator) gets larger.

The **variation of elasticity** as we move **along a demand curve** is an additional reason to be wary of making statements about elasticity from the appearance of a curve. However, there are three exceptional cases where shape does indicate elasticity (shown in Figure 4.9). The demand curve which has **unit elasticity** throughout its range has a special property: the area under every point is equal (this is described mathematically as a rectangular hyperbola). The area ($P \times Q$) is total expenditure, so the curve represents price/quantity combinations that show constant expenditure; we know this is a property of unit elasticity. A perfectly vertical demand curve indicates zero elasticity (perfect inelasticity) while a horizontal demand curve indicates perfect elasticity.

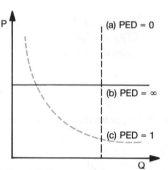

Fig. 4.9 Extreme cases of elasticity

4.6.2.6 PED: an overview

Price elasticity of demand shows the responsiveness of demand to price changes. It is an important concept that has many uses. Firms are interested in knowing the effect of price changes on quantity and, as households' expenditure is their revenue, the relationship between elasticity and expenditure. Governments are concerned about the impact of tax changes which affect prices on consumption. These main points are summarized in Table 4.5.

Table 4.5 Elasticity and demand

PED	Type of elasticity	Effect on total expenditure of cut in price
PED = 0	Perfectly inelastic (Demand curve = vertical line)	Fall
PED > 0 < 1	Inelastic	Fall
PED = 1	Unit elasticity (Demand curve = rectangular hyperbola)	No change
PED > 1	Elastic	Rise
PED = ∞	Perfectly elastic (Demand curve = horizontal line)	Rise

4.7 Other measures of elasticity

4.7.1 Income elasticity

Income elasticity of demand (IED) shows the responsiveness of demand to income changes. The approach to measuring it is similar to that adopted for PED.

$$IED = \frac{percentage\ change\ in\ quantity\ demanded}{percentage\ change\ in\ income}$$

How do we interpret the **IED coefficient**? Again we can use a coefficient of 1 as a benchmark. This coefficient shows a position where a change in income results in a proportionally equal change in the quantity demanded. If the figure is **greater than 1** we can say the demand is **income elastic**. Demand is **income inelastic** where the figure is between **zero and 1**–this will occur where demand is not very responsive. For example, an IED of 0.5 will indicate that a 10 per cent increase in income will be associated with a–5 per cent increase in the quantity demanded.

We need to consider the sign of the coefficient carefully when considering **IED**. If it is negative, the product is an inferior good because an increase in income leads to a reduction in quantity demanded. A normal good will have a positive sign (see earlier discussion in section 4.3.4.2).

The concept of **income elasticity** is useful, because where the IED is greater than 1 consumer demand is expanding faster than income, so this is likely to be a growth area in the economy. Leisure activities and tourism are a good example here; this has important implications for both private and public sectors.

4.7.2 Cross-elasticity of demand

Cross-elasticity of demand (CED) measures the responsiveness of demand to changes in the price of other products. The **CED** for a product X with respect to a change in the price of a product Y is calculated as follows:

$$CED = \frac{percentage\ change\ in\ quantity\ of\ X}{percentage\ change\ in\ price\ of\ Y}$$

For example, the **CED** for apples would be 2.0 if a 5 per cent fall in the price of oranges was associated with a 10 per cent fall in the quantity of apples demanded.

We again need to look closely at the sign of the coefficient. If the CED is positive the two products are substitutes, a negative sign is an indication that the two are complementary goods. A fall in the price of gin of 10 per cent (which we would expect to raise the quantity of gin demanded) will lead to an increase in demand for tonic of say 5 per cent. This will give a **CED coefficient** of -0.5. A **zero coefficient** indicates that there is no relationship between products.

4.7.3 Supply elasticity

Our main interest in the responsiveness of **supply** is in the sensitivity of quantity produced to price changes. The **price elasticity of supply (PES)** is measured as follows:

$$PES = \frac{percentage\ change\ in\ quantity\ supplied}{percentage\ change\ in\ price}$$

We can classify **PES** in a similar way to PED; a **PES coefficient of 1** represents **unit elasticity**; a figure **less than 1** indicates an **inelastic** (or relatively unresponsive) supply and a figure **greater than 1** indicates **elastic supply**.

Warnings must again be issued about the relationship between shape, slope and elasticity. Steep supply curves do not necessarily mean supply is inelastic. The only occasions when we can learn something about elasticity from the general appearance of the curve are shown in Figure 4.10. It should be noted that **any straight-line supply curve** that passes through the **origin** is one that has **unit elasticity**. A summary of PES is given in Table 4.6.

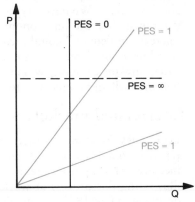

Fig. 4.10 Elasticity of supply

Table 4.6 Elasticity and supply

PES coefficient	Type of elasticity	Description of supply curve
PES = 0	Perfectly inelastic	Vertical straight line
PES > 0 < 1	Inelastic	
PES = 1	Unit elasticity	Straight line through the origin
PES > 1	Elastic	
PES = ∞	Perfectly elastic	Horizontal straight line

5 Applications of supply and demand

5.1 Introduction

The supply and demand analysis we developed in the last chapter offers insights into a wide variety of situations. All courses will expect students to be able to apply the theory to a selection of problems. It is not possible in a study guide to cover all the possible areas; but neither is it necessary to do so. If you learn how to use the analysis in some problems, you should be able to apply it elsewhere. We have selected certain aspects (e.g. interrelated markets, maximum and minimum prices, dynamics) that include most of the types of applications you are likely to encounter.

The chapter will:

- show you how to use supply and demand analysis to examine the interactions of markets
- explain and illustrate cases of markets with maximum prices
- explain and illustrate the effects of minimum price legislation
- show you how to illustrate and explain the imposition of a sales tax
- introduce you to the dynamic analysis of supply and demand
- illustrate some problems of agriculture using supply and demand and the concepts of elasticity

5.1.1 Examination guide

It would be an unusual economics course that did not in some way test your ability to use supply and demand analysis. This may be done in a number of ways: with multi-choice questions or questions requiring short answers or with essays which can be almost entirely based on supply and demand analysis or those where more advanced or additional theories are involved. For example, an essay question on **minimum wage legislation** or **rent controls** could require the use of material on **consumer theories** (see Chapter 13) or **distribution** (Chapter 17); nevertheless supply and demand analysis would be a useful starting point. Whatever type of answer, you should try to make extensive use of diagrams; they are an economical way of presenting points and avoid ambiguity: an 'increase in demand' could mean a movement down the demand curve or a shift of the schedule itself. You will not necessarily be given the benefit of the doubt in these situations—the examiner will be much more impressed by an answer where the student has had the skill and confidence to use the diagrams.

5.2 Interrelated markets

Economies are complex interrelated systems and changes in one area are likely to have repercussions elsewhere. There **price mechanism** transmits **information** and provides **incentives** for appropriate action. Supply and demand analysis is a useful way of illustrating this process at work. We have chosen an oil price increase of the type that occurred in late 1973 and again in 1979–80; but the approach can be applied to a wide variety of other problems and incidents.

5.2.1 Oil price increases

In late 1973 the major oil producers OPEC (Organization of Petroleum Exporting Countries) formed an effective **cartel** (a **producers' agreement to control prices or quantities**). By restricting the quantity supplied OPEC was able to raise prices significantly; the price of oil rose from around $2 to $10 a barrel. We can show this (in Figure 5.1(a)) by drawing a vertical section to the supply curve to represent the effective control OPEC had on the supply of oil which made the price increase (from P_1 to P_2) effective. Given the large **dependence** of industrial countries on oil and the **difficulty in substituting** alternative fuels, the price elasticity of demand for oil was low, so relatively small reductions in quantity were associated with a fivefold rise in prices. The market repercussions were profound. We show a few of these effects in the rest of Figure 5.1.

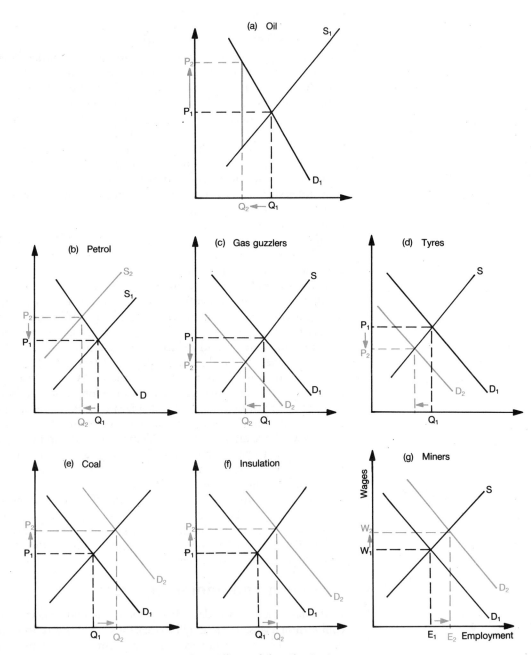

Fig. 5.1 Effects of the oil price increase

5.2.2 Complementary and substitute goods

Oil is a major input and cost in the production of petrol so the oil price rise caused the supply curve to shift outwards and the **equilibrium price rose**. Cars are a **complementary good** but some sections of the car market were particularly severly hit, especially the so-called 'gas guzzlers'—cars with a high petrol consumption. The demand curve for them shifted inwards. Tyres are a **complementary good** to cars, so their demand curve shifted inwards.

A rise in oil prices will lead consumers to **substitute alternative** fuels, so we can expect the demand for these substitute goods to shift out and their equilibrium price to rise. This was seen in the market for coal; but similar price increases occurred for other forms of energy. The rise in heating costs was an **incentive** to conserve energy and the demand for insulation also rose.

5.2.3 Derived demand

All **changes in demand** require a **reallocation of resources** and we can expect prices in the factor market to reflect this. The demand for factors is derived from the demand for products. In the coal industry, for example, there is a **derived demand** for miners which we would expect to shift out to the right if there were increased demand for coal. The large increase in miners' pay and the miners' strike in 1974 were in part the result of the increase in oil prices.

5.2.4 Partial and general equilibrium

As effects of higher oil prices work through the market they affect relative prices and provide information and incentives for adjustment in the allocation of resources. We have considered only a few of the many markets affected, but even if we had extended our approach the picture would still have been incomplete.

We have considered only the **first-round effects**; but the changes we have described will have **feedback effects** which in turn have further consequences. Our analysis of individual markets has assumed that everything else remains the same, or to use the term that is frequently employed in economics, *ceteris paribus*. The demand for oil was drawn on assumption that the price of other products was unchanged; but when the price of substitutes such as coal rises this revises the demand for oil. A full examination requires a more powerful analysis which is able to cope with the complexity of the situation. **General equilibrium analysis** studies the interactions of markets, whereas the approach we have so far adopted involves describing points of **partial equilibrium**. This will in many cases give quite acceptable results and the large amount of extra time that would be spent coping with more complex analysis would not be worthwhile.

In the example we are considering the analysis of supply and demand, which has highlighted changes in relative prices and resources allocation, needs to be supplemented to take account of the **macroeconomic effects**. Oil is such an important commodity, and the price changes we are considering so large, that there were significant effects on **total demand, employment** and **inflation**. (These aspects are considered further in Chapter 7.) This underlines the need in many problems to use both micro and macro analysis.

Another reason why our analysis of the OPEC price rise is incomplete is that we have considered only the **short-run effects**. In the **long run** (and in this case we are considering years rather than months) high oil prices will have **powerful incentive effects**. They will spur the development of energy-saving devices and the development of alternative power sources will have an impact on the demand for oil. On the supply side the long-run supply curve is likely to be much more elastic than the short-run curve. Hitherto unprofitable oil fields will be exploited and exploration for new oil sources will eventually lead to additional supplies.

In the decade after 1974 these incentive effects encouraged many new suppliers of oil. For the UK it justified the exploration and exploitation of marginal fields in the North Sea—so much so that by the time of the second hike in oil prices in 1979–80 the UK was a major oil producer. The increase in supply weakened the OPEC cartel and this led to the 1985–86 collapse of oil prices.

5.3 Maximum and minimum prices

In the last chapter we described why we would expect **prices** to move towards their **equilibrium levels**. There may be occasions when this is prevented from happening. This is often the outcome of government intervention but it may result, as our first example shows, from the pricing policy of a firm or institution.

5.3.1 Cup Final tickets

The capacity of Wembley stadium determines the quantity of tickets supplied for the Cup Final and the FA fixes the prices. This gives a rectangular supply curve, as shown in Figure 5.2. There is normally **excess demand** for tickets at the official prices. The FA, having decided that rationing tickets on the basis of price would be unfair, uses an alternative method—allocating blocks of tickets to the clubs of the finalists and other bodies. In turn

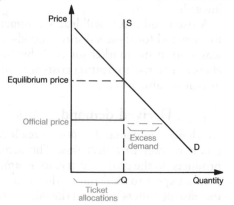

Fig. 5.2 Cup Final tickets

the clubs use some **rationing techniques** (often coupons collected from the programmes of matches held earlier in the season). This is an example of imposing a **maximum price**. Where price is held below equilibrium, excess demand means unsatisfied buyers and there is a strong likelihood that a **black** (or **unofficial**) **market** will arise (witness Cup Final ticket touts).

5.3.2 Wartime rationing

Maximum price legislation was widely used during the Second World War. The supply of civilian goods was restricted because of the need to divert resources to military use. This might have led to sharp price rises (the market system's way of rationing scarce supplies). This was not felt to be fair or appropriate in wartime conditions so a rationing system was introduced, with **maximum prices** imposed. Ration books were issued with coupons that entitled each holder to an equal quantity of rationed goods.

As with Cup Final tickets, **black markets** grew up in response to the **excess demand**. Harold Wilson, who was President of the Board of Trade in the post-war Labour Government made use of the black markets in deciding when to remove clothes rationing in the late 1940s. He knew that the reduction of rationing would be welcomed only if prices did not shoot up. He used his training as an economist and sent out officials to discover the level of black market prices. When it was apparent that they differed very little from official prices, he concluded that there was little excess demand and that it was therefore safe to remove rationing.

5.3.3 Rent controls

Our final example of **maximum price legislation** is **rent controls**. These were introduced to help those on low incomes who would otherwise find it difficult to pay market (i.e. **equilibrium**) rents. However, lower rents reduce the return on property to landlords and act as a **disincentive to supply** rented property: so as compared to the situation in an unregulated market the quantity of rented property will decline (from Q_1 to Q_2 in Figure 5.3).

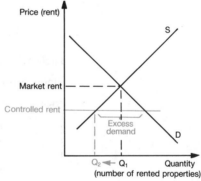

Fig. 5.3 The effect of rent controls

5.3.4 Minimum prices: minimum wage legislation

Intervention in the market is not confined to imposing maximum prices. **Minimum wage legislation** is designed to raise wages above the equilibrium level. We illustrate this in Figure 5.4 where the demand for labour (by firms) and supply of labour determine the **equilibrium wage** (W_e) and **employment** (E_1). The **minimum wage** is shown by the

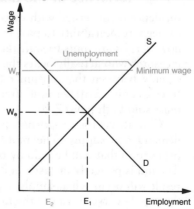

Fig. 5.4 The effect of minimum wage legislation

horizontal line drawn at W_m. Our analysis suggests that although the wages of the low paid may be raised it will be at the cost of the number of jobs: employment falls from E_1 to E_2 as firms demand a lower number of workers. (The increased unemployment is shown by the bracket.) The actual impact of **minimum wage legislation** is likely to be somewhat more complicated than this in real life but our supply and demand analysis does highlight some serious problems associated with this form of help to the low paid that require further consideration.

5.4 Taxation and subsidies

5.4.1 Effect of a sales tax on supply

Our analysis can be used to show the impact of a **sales tax**. Suppose a tax of £1 per unit were imposed. Producers would then require a price £1 higher to supply the same quantity (this is shown in Table 5.1). In graphical terms, the supply curve shifts up by the amount of the tax–see Figure 5.5–from S_1 to S_2.

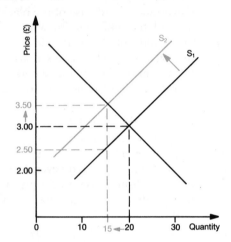

Fig. 5.5 The effect of sales tax

Table 5.1 Effect of a sales tax on supply

Supply before tax		Supply with tax	
Price	Quantity	Price	Quantity
1	0	2	0
2	10	3	10
3	20	4	20
4	30	5	30
5	40	6	40

However, the **market price** does not rise by the amount of the tax because attempts to sell the same quantity at a higher price will be unsuccessful unless the demand curve is perfectly inelastic. In our illustration the **market price rises** by 50p from £3 to £3.50 and the quantity traded will decline from 20 to 15. The **tax revenue** received by the government is therefore £15 (15 units times the £1 tax).

5.4.2 Incidence of the tax

Incidence is concerned with who pays a tax. The **formal incidence rests** with whoever has the legal responsibility to pay. In our example this will be the retailer or seller. There will, however, be attempts to shift the burden of taxation on to others. The **effective incidence** measures who actually bears the burden. In our example, the **effective incidence** is shared equally between the consumer (price rises from £3 to £3.50) and the **seller** who now receives only £2.50 per unit after the tax is paid. In terms of total tax payments on the 15 units sold both pay £7.50.

What affects the proportion paid by the consumer? This depends on the **elasticities of demand and supply**. The more inelastic the demand, *ceteris paribus*, the greater the proportion that will be paid by the consumer. This can be seen in the extreme case where demand is perfectly inelastic and the whole of the tax is paid by the consumer. The same result will occur when supply is perfectly elastic because, *ceteris paribus*, the more elastic the supply curve the more the tax will be passed on to the consumer. **Effective incidence**, then, depends upon the **relative elasticities of demand and supply**.

5.4.3 Subsidies

Subsidies can be regarded as **negative taxes**. A subsidy will shift the supply downwards by the amount of the subsidy. We would normally expect this to lower equilibrium prices and increase the quantity traded.

5.5 Dynamic analysis

5.5.1 Static and dynamic analysis

The type of approach taken so far is known as **comparative static analysis**: it compares one equilibrium position with **another**. For many purposes this is quite satisfactory; but it does not tell us **how long** it takes to move to the new equilibrium position, nor does it show **the path taken**. In Figure 5.6 we illustrate three possible ways in which a new equilibrium position may be approached after a shift in demand. Path (a) shows a more rapid response than (b), whereas path (c) shows **overshooting** of the equilibrium price and a **cyclical movement** around the new price before equilibrium is achieved. It will sometimes be important to know how markets respond over time to some event that disturbs an equilibrium position. **Dynamic analysis** incorporates time and attempts to answer these questions.

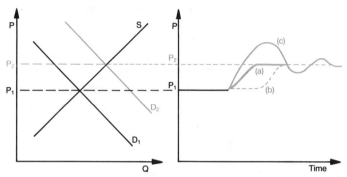

Fig. 5.6 Comparative statics and dynamics

5.5.2 Time lags

Dynamic analysis is a recognition that most markets do not respond immediately to changes–there are **time lags** between one variable changing and another being affected. One convenient way to approach this is to divide time up into discrete periods–months, quarters, years etc.–and use some notation to distinguish different periods (see Table 5.2).

Table 5.2 Time notation

Variable X with time subscript	X_{t-3}	X_{t-2}	X_{t-1}	X_t	$X_{t+1}\ldots$
Time period	$t-3$	$t-2$	$t-1$	t	$t+1\ldots$
Quarters	I	II	III	IV	I $\ldots$
Years	1989				1990

Here X_t refers to the value of X at a particular time, for example the fourth quarter of 1989. X_{t-2} refers to its value two quarters before that (that is, the second quarter of 1989) and X_{t+1} is the value in the next quarter. This allows us to explicitly **introduce time** into our analysis. So we can replace the expression $Qs = f(P)$, which states that quantity supplied is a function of price, with the **dynamic equivalent**

$$Qs_t = f(P_{t-1})$$

This means that the **quantity supplied** in a particular **period** is a **function of price in the previous period**. We will now use this example in a simple dynamic model of agriculture.

5.5.3 Simple dynamic model: the cobweb

5.5.3.1 The model

Agriculture is a good example of **time lags** and **dynamic analysis**. The length of the growing period means that supply cannot respond immediately to price changes. In many cases there is a **time lag** of about a year between planting and harvesting; and this can be longer with crops like fruit trees and livestock. Let us consider cases where decisions are made in the autumn of one year and the crops harvested a year later. If we assume that the quantity supplied is influenced by the price at the time the crop is planted then the supply relationship is

$$Qs_t = f(P_{t-1})$$

indicating the one-year time lag involved. Demand is not affected by time lags in the same way, because if we go to the supermarket and find that one food product is relatively expensive we can **substitute** another straight away. This can be represented as follows:

$$Qd_t = f(P_t)$$

Market prices will be determined by **demand and supply**:

$$Qd_t = Qs_t$$

To see how this model works consider the situation depicted in Figure 5.7 where the equilibrium price is £2 and the quantity traded is 200. If this were disturbed by, say, a bad harvest which reduced the quantity supplied to 50, then the price would rise to £3. This is the price that would clear the market of excess demand. If there were no further disturbances, then our **static analyses** would suggest there would be a **return** to the original equilibrium price and quantity.

However, the **dynamic model** indicates that matters are not so straightforward. Responding to the relatively high price of £3, farmers plan to supply a quantity of 300 for the following year. Assuming their plans were achieved this would produce excess supply at a price of £3 and prices would fall to £1.30. This price would make the crop appear unattractive and a smaller quantity, 130, would be planned for the following year, which would push prices up. And so the process would continue.

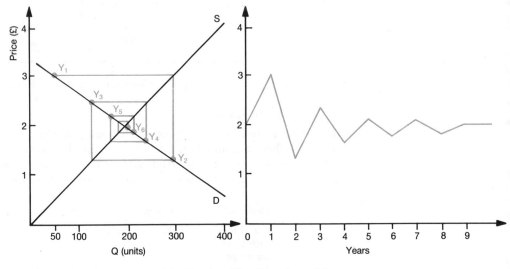

Fig. 5.7 The cobweb model

It is characteristic of this type of model that **oscillations** in output and prices occur when an **equilibrium position** is disturbed. In the example we have been considering the cycle is dampened, i.e. the fluctuations diminish over time and equilibrium values are approached. The path followed is traced out in the figure and it is easy to see why this has been called the **cobweb model**. The outcome could have been more dramatic, with the fluctuations getting larger, producing a divergent (as opposed to a convergent) cobweb. It is the relative slopes of the demand and supply curves that affect the pattern of the cycle. Try for yourself a similar exercise to the one described above, but use a demand curve with a steeper slope than this. The fluctuations should increase over time. You will find the same result if the supply curve is more elastic.

5.6 Agriculture: a further illustration of supply and demand

Supply and demand is well suited to the analysis of agriculture. This is a sector of the economy where there is a large number of independent producers and market prices are highly flexible. We shall now consider the much greater fluctuations in agricultural prices compared with manufactured goods and services and conclude by looking at some aspects of **government intervention** in agriculture.

5.6.1 Agricultural prices

Table 5.3 below shows the unreversed rise in the price of manufactured goods that might be expected in a period of high inflation. The prices of potatoes and carrots display a high degree of volatility: there is a nearly fourfold rise in potato prices between 1973 and 1975, which then double in 1976 to be followed by two successive years in which prices halve.

Table 5.3 Indexed prices 1973–78 (1975 = 100)

	1973	1974	1975	1976	1977	1978
All manufactured products	66	82	100	117	141	153
Potatoes	27	34	100	230	93	51
Carrots	44	67	100	113	136	75

(*Annual Abstract of Statistics*, various years)

5.6.2 Reasons for price fluctuations

5.6.2.1 Supply shifts: climate and disease

One obvious reason for **price fluctuations** is variation in supply induced by the weather or outbreaks of disease. This can be seen in Figure 5.8(a) where Q_1 and Q_2 represent the output of a bad and a good harvest respectively. We have shown this by two short-run supply curves S_B and S_G representing bad and good harvest respectively. Prices fluctuate between P_1 and P_2.

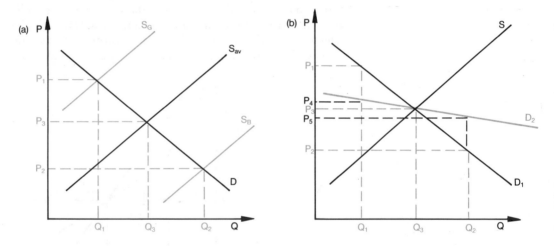

Fig. 5.8 Variations in supply in agriculture

5.6.2.2 Elasticities

The variation in prices will be greater the more inelastic the demand curve. In Figure 5.8(b) D_2 is a more elastic demand, and whereas prices varied between P_1 and P_2 with relatively inelastic demand, D_1, they only range between P_4 and P_5 with demand D_2. The **price elasticity in demand** for agricultural products tends to be low, so this is an additional reason for fairly large price fluctuations.

5.6.2.3 Cobweb

The **cobweb model** described in section 5.5.3.1 also helps to explain oscillations in agricultural prices. The model was first developed in the context of agriculture to explain fluctuations in pig prices. An uncoordinated agricultural market with many thousands of producers each having to make individual judgements about prices, may well result in large variations in supply.

5.6.2.4 Effects on farmers' incomes

How will these wide price variations affect farmers' incomes? It will depend on the **price elasticity of demand**. If the PED were 1 then incomes would be unaffected because price multiplied by quantity would always be the same. However, if the demand curve is inelastic then bad harvests (producing low quantities) will improve farm incomes and bumper crops will depress incomes. As it is unlikely that the demand curve has **unit elasticity** then the behaviour of prices means fluctuating farm incomes.

5.6.3 Government intervention

Government intervention in agriculture is a common feature in **market economies**. Apart from the difficulties arising from fluctuations in prices and incomes there is the problem of **low incomes**. Agriculture is declining relative to the rest of the economy and the market signals to reallocate resources involve low payments to factors. The UK experienced major agricultural readjustments many decades ago but employment in agriculture has fallen by two thirds in the last 30 years. For other European countries this is a more acute problem as agriculture is a larger employer. After the war around a quarter of the workforce was employed in agriculture compared with 5 per cent in the UK. There are many ways in which governments can intervene in agriculture and the details of any particular scheme are often complicated. We consider three types of scheme in principle.

5.6.3.1 Price stabilization schemes

One way governments can tackle the problems of fluctuating prices is by **controlling the supply**. If they can **coordinate** the thousands of producers and **forecast demand** accurately they can **stabilize prices**. However, as no one can accurately predict the weather this approach is not appropriate to this source of price fluctuation. An alternative approach is to **buy up excess supplies** in bumper harvest years and release these stocks in periods when there are poor harvests. In terms of Figure 5.9 and Table 5.4 this means buying Q_3Q_2 in when there are good harvests and selling Q_1Q_3 in poor years. While this would **stabilize** prices it would still mean that farmers' incomes fluctuated sharply: they would get only the same price in bad as well as good years. This could be overcome by **intervening** to ensure that farmers always received the same income by allowing prices to fluctuate by an amount that would occur if the demand curve had unit elasticity (e.g. buying Q_5Q_2 and selling Q_1Q_4). The dashed line D_u is a hypothetical demand curve with unit elasticity. In the case illustrated, price fluctuations would be reduced and farmers' incomes stabilized.

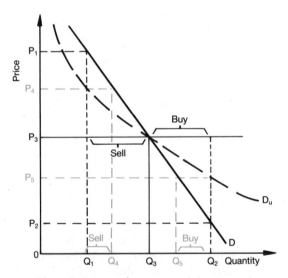

Fig. 5.9 Price and income stabilization schemes

Table 5.4 Price and income stabilization

Type of harvest	Price – no intervention	Price stabilization		Income stabilization	
		Intervention	Price	Intervention	Price
Bad Q_1	P_1	Sell $Q_3 - Q_1$	P_3	Sell $Q_4 - Q_1$	P_4
Average Q_3	P_3	None	P_3	None	P_3
Good Q_2	P_2	Buy $Q_2 - Q_3$	P_3	Buy $Q_2 - Q_5$	P_5

5.6.3.2 Deficiency payments

One approach to supporting agriculture that was used in the UK is a scheme of **deficiency payments**. This is really a **subsidy** paid to farmers and we can examine it by means of the analysis used in section 5.4. In Figure 5.10(a) D_d and S_d refer to the domestic demand and supply curves for food and P_w indicates the world price. In an **unregulated market** Q_1 would be the domestic supply and Q_1Q_2 the volume of imports. To prevent agriculture shrinking to that size the government could introduce a system of **subsidies**, or **deficiency payments**; this is shown on the figure by the dotted line supply curve S_s, with the subsidy

54

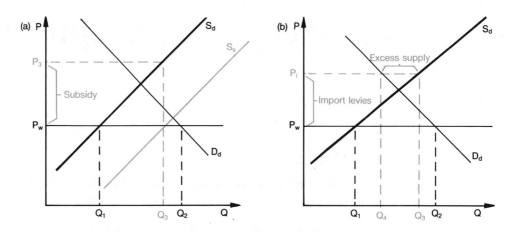

Fig. 5.10 Deficit payments and import levies

marked. The domestic supply is now Q_3 and imports are Q_3Q_2. This scheme allows consumers to buy at world prices but requires the imposition of taxes to raise the revenue for the **subsidies**.

5.6.3.3 Import levies

We conclude by considering an approach similar to the CAP (Common Agricultural Policy) scheme in the EC. **Import duties** are levied on agricultural products to ensure that they trade an **intervention price** P_i on the diagram Figure 5.10(b). The **levy** is marked on the diagram. At the **intervention price** shown there will be support for the farming sector; but there is clearly a tendency for stocks to increase (butter mountains and wine lakes). This is partly offset by **export subsidies**, known as **restitution payments**, which allow farmers to sell on world markets at prices below those they would charge domestically.

6 Measuring output and prices

6.1 Introduction

Unemployment, inflation and **growth in living standards** are central issues of our time. In the next few chapters we consider economists' explanations of these problems and the policy prescriptions for improving an economy's performance in these areas. This chapter introduces some key concepts and explains how they are measured. In the course of it you will become acquainted with some important UK macroeconomic statistics. These will be helpful when you study policy problems later—courses in economics increasingly expect a familiarity with **data**. This partly reflects a tendency for courses to become more applied and problem-orientated and partly a growing recognition that **economic data** can be an aid to decision making. Understanding the sources, meaning and limitations of these **data** can contribute to other parts of business studies and social science courses as well as to your subsequent career. This chapter concentrates on **general macroeconomic data**; later chapters cover consumption, investment, the balance of payments and money and banking.

This chapter will:

- explain the different ways of measuring national income
- indicate the problems involved in measuring national income
- distinguish between net and gross product, national and domestic product and factor cost and market price measures
- distinguish between constant and current price measures of national income and explain the meaning of the GDP deflator
- explain the Laspeyre and Paasche indices
- explain how the Retail Price Index is constructed
- outline other measures of prices

6.1.1 Examination guide

Most essay questions on this topic are directed at the difficulties that are encountered in measuring **national income** or require a discussion of the limitations of **GDP** as an indicator of economic welfare. Many courses now include questions that require short answers. **National income accounts** and measures of prices lend themselves to this type of question. In this case you need to be clear about the key definitions of the terms used in this area and be able to perform simple calculations designed to test your understanding of these terms.

6.2 National income accounts

6.2.1 Measuring national income

6.2.1.1 What is national income?

National income is essentially a measure of total income or output of a country. It is the **money value** of the flow of goods and services that arise from the economic activity of a nation. Many terms are used in **national income accounting** and this is generally a source of confusion to newcomers to the subject. What, for example, is the distinction between **Net National Product at factor cost in constant prices** and **Gross Domestic Product** (expenditure measure) **at market prices in current prices**? The next subsection will begin to explain these terms.

6.2.1.2 Three measures of national income

To understand some of the principles of **national income accounting** we will introduce a simplified way of looking at an economy: the **circular flow of income**. Figure 6.1 is the simplest representation; we assume there is no government or foreign trade. The economy has two types of institutions: **households**, *H*, and **firms**, *F*. **Households** are owners and suppliers of factors of production to **firms** who are producers of goods and services. These represent **real flows** in an economy and are shown by the coloured lines in the figure. Associated with these real flows are **money flows** as income (wages and salaries, profits, rent and interest) is paid to households for factor services and expenditure flows from households to firms in payment for goods and services. These money flows are shown in black.

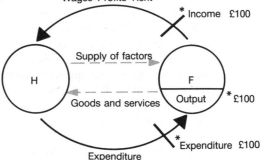

Fig. 6.1 Circular flow of income

The national income of an economy can be measured in three ways: by **output, income** and **expenditure**. This can be seen in our circular flow diagram where the different points of measuring economic activity are shown by an asterisk. Each approach should given an identical value. It does so in our illustration because the value of **output** (£100) is paid to households as factor **incomes** (£100) and as all **income** is spent then **expenditure** (£100) will be the same as **output**. This **identity** applies throughout national income accounting because it is assumed that the value of output is income to some factor, that all income is spent and that all output is bought by somebody. It is easy to see this in our illustration but there are many cases when this is less obvious: households might save some of their income (we consider such as case in section 6.2.2). However the identity still holds in these situations. If an activity is counted as output it is equally regarded as income and expenditure.

It is important to recognize that national income accounts measure **actual** or **realized values** of output, expenditure and income and therefore tell us nothing directly about the intentions or plans of economic agents with which economic theory is concerned. Indeed, it will be an important feature of the **Keynesian theory** we develop in the next chapter that **planned aggregate expenditure** may be less than **planned output**. In this case a recession may occur as firms respond to unsold production by cutting back on output. The national income accountant cannot know what plans people had; he merely records what actually occurred.

6.2.1.3 Problems of national income accounting

Two types of problems face the national income accountant: conceptual and compilation.

1 Conceptual problems concern what should be counted as **production**. The boundary between economic activities which are counted as output and those which are excluded is blurred. For example, do-it-yourself painting, gardening and housework is not counted as production, whereas the output of a firm of decorators, landscapers or domestic servants would be. In principle we could **impute a value** to the output of these activities for which payment is not normally made when carried out by households. In practice it would be difficult and it is not done.

There is one major exception to this and that is the case of owner-occupied housing. The country's stock of houses produces a flow of housing services, which in the case of rented property generates a clearly identifiable payment, rent, which is included in the national income accounts. Owner-occupied housing does not produce a similar payment even though a clearly similar flow of services is provided. The national income accountant **imputes** (that is, assigns an amount as though payment had been made) **a rent**. The identity of income, expenditure and output is maintained as the imputed rent is counted as income (to the owner occupier) as well as expenditure and the same value is counted as part of the country's output of goods and services. A similar approach is taken in the case of own- produced food by farmers and payment in kind to certain groups, such as the armed forces.

2 The second type of problem is **compilation**: there are difficulties surrounding the collection and preparation of statistics. Millions of households receive income and are engaged in spending money on a wide variety of goods and services. Output is produced by tens of thousands of firms. It is not surprising, therefore, that there are major difficulties in accounting for all these money flows. The data that are collected will be **inaccurate** (e.g. because incorrect returns on income and output have been made by individuals and firms respectively) and **incomplete** (some groups or individuals may not be covered so estimates have to be made). The so-called **black economy** is an example of the former problem and though estimates are made to make allowances for it there is no way of knowing how accurate these adjustments are.

Estimates of GDP are revised as new information comes to light. Those covering the most recent period are particularly subject to revision but even accounts for GDP 10 years earlier may be revised. An indication of the size of likely revision is shown by the Central Statistical Office when quarterly GDP figures are published. For example, in July 1988 the growth of real GDP for the year to the first quarter was estimated to have been 4 per cent; but if the magnitude of past revisions is maintained then growth for this period will lie in the range of 3.75 to 5.5 per cent. In a third of cases the size of the revision will be even larger.

A further illustration of compilation difficulties is seen in the differences between the three measures of national income. Although by definition they are equal, in practice, because the data are drawn from different sources the output, expenditure and income measures produce different totals. Figure 6.2 shows the divergence of the three measures in 1981 and 1982. Notice that in the last quarter the output measure of GDP rose while the income measure fell and expenditure remained essentially unchanged. While such a confusing picture is unusual it is by no means unique and the differences in the other seven quarters often show divergence in direction and rate of change as well as level of GDP.

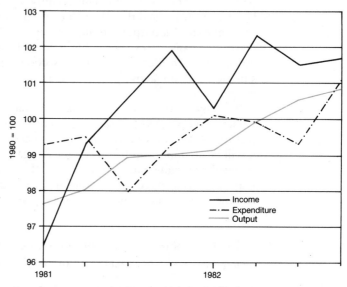

Fig. 6.2 Three measures of GDP 1981–82

These differences clearly pose problems for economists, government and companies wishing to understand recent movements in the economy. It is common to use an **average measure** of GDP which is a simple average of the three measures, though the **output measure** is often considered the most reliable indicator of short-term movements in GDP. As far as the national income accounts are concerned the three approaches should yield the same total, with discrepancies representing measurement errors; so a residual error is added to two of the three measures. In the UK other measures are made equal to the expenditure measure, not because this is deemed any more accurate than other measures but simply by convention to maintain the identity.

6.2.1.4   The problem of double counting

Measuring the output of an economy is not simply a matter of adding the output of individual firms. To do so would produce an inflated measure of production because the **output** of many firms are the **inputs** of others. A simple example will illustrate the point and show how a more satisfactory measure can be obtained. Suppose we have an economy which produces only skirts, with production consisting of three stages (Figure 6.3): wool (A), cloth (B) and skirts (C). The wool producers sell their output for £40 to the cloth manufacturers who in turn sell £60 of cloth to skirt firms whose output is sold to consumers for £100. If the value of output of these three stages is added together, total output would be £200 (£40 + £60 + £100); but this exaggerates the output of the economy because it involves **double counting**. The value of wool is counted in its own right as output as well as part of the input into cloth. Similarly cloth is counted twice: in the value of skirts and as output of the cloth manufacturers.

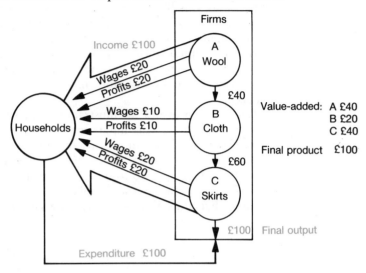

Fig. 6.3 A simple three-stage economy

This can be clearly seen if we consider the effect of a new production technique which introduces a new stage in the manufacturing process. Suppose the wool is processed before being sold to the cloth manufacturers for £50; this would make the value of aggregate output £250 instead of £200. But the country is not able to consume any more and is in no sense any better off. What we have introduced is a further **intermediate** stage in the manufacture of skirts. To avoid double counting, we really need to count **final ouput** only—in our example £100 of skirts—and ignore **intermediate products**. In practice it is not easy to identify final output because the same product may be **intermediate** and **final** depending on the purpose of the purchase. For example, coal is a final product when bought by households for heating; but when it is sold to power stations it is an intermediate product. Fortunately there is a fairly straightforward way of avoiding counting intermediate products and this is by taking the **value-added** at each stage. Figure 6.3 and Table 6.1 illustrate the **value-added method**.

Table 6.1 The value-added method

	Sales	Value-added
A	£40	+£40
B	£60	+£20
C	£100	+£40
		£100

We assume that firm *A* does not buy in any products from other firms so the full amount of its sales, £40, is value-added. However with firm *B* we must deduct £40 of bought-in products from its sales of £60 to obtain the value-added of £20. The value-added by firm *C* is £40 and total value-added is £100. This approach avoids counting intermediate products and therefore gives us the same answer as just counting final output. We can also see that it will give the same result as the income approach. The value-added is income to factors which, for convenience, we have assumed in our example is divided equally between wages and profits.

There are several other types of transactions that need to be excluded if we are to avoid an inflated and misleading impression of national income. **Transactions in second-hand goods** (for example, cars, houses, antiques) should be excluded because they do not constitute an additional flow of goods and services that are available to the economy. Similarly **dealings in financial assets** are excluded. However, the payment for services provided by dealers (and represented in their value-added) should be counted as output and income of an economy. **Transfer earnings** which involve the transfer of income from one group to another (e.g. pensions, student grants, unemployment benefits) are not included in national income because their inclusion would clearly involve double counting.

6.2.2 Savings and investment

6.2.2.1 Investment, savings and the circular flow of income

In the previous section we dealt with the simplest of cases of the circular flow where all expenditure was by households on **consumption**. However, economies use part of their production of goods for **investment** purposes as well as consumption. **Expenditure** on **capital goods** (plant, machinery, infrastructure and housing) is known as **fixed investment**. Part of the **capital stock** is in the form of **inventories** or stocks of finished, semi-finished goods or raw materials and changes in the holdings of these inventories are regarded as investment in stocks and work in progress. This can be negative when inventories are reduced.

Figure 6.4 provides an illustration of a simplified case where there is saving and investment. Firm *A* sells inputs for Firm *B*, which produces investment goods, and for Firm *C* which manufactures consumer goods. **Final output** consists of £75 of consumer goods and £25 of capital goods. Value-added is equal to £100 (*A*: +£10; *B*: +£20; *C*: +£70) which is equal to income. Households do not spend all of their income but save £25. For convenience and simplicity we show only saving by households (**personal savings**); but firms also save (**corporate saving**).

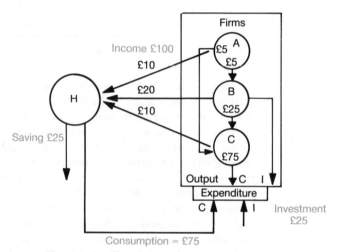

Fig. 6.4 An illustration of saving and investment

6.2.2.2 Identities and equilibrium conditions

In our example savings and investment are equal. In a two-sector economy (where there are only two sectors, households and firms) this will always be the case. Yet in the next chapter we will explain an important feature of **Keynesian macroeconomics: planned savings** and **planned investment** need not be equal. How can both statements be true? The key to understanding how they can be reconciled is to recognize that national income accounts are concerned with *ex post* (actual or realized) values, whereas economic theory is principally involved with *ex ante* concepts, that is the plans or intentions of economic agents (people or institutions). As plans are not always realized the two values need not be the same.

We can demonstrate this difference for a two-sector economy. The basic national income identity states that income (*Y*), expenditure (*E*) and output (*O*) are the same:

$$Y \equiv E \equiv O$$

As income can be spent either on consumption (*C*) or saved (*S*) we have a further identity:

$$Y \equiv C + S$$

Expenditure in a two-sector economy can be of two types only: consumer (*C*) and investment (*I*). So

$$E \equiv C + I$$

It therefore follows that

$$Y \equiv C + I \quad \text{and} \quad I \equiv S$$

that is, **investment** is always the same as **savings**. But this is only true in an *ex post* sense, as a numerical illustration will show.

Table 6.2 Investment and savings

		Case 1 (£)	Case 2 (£)
Y	Income	100	100
S	Saving	25	30
C	Consumption	75	70
I	Investment	25	25
	Change in stock	0	+5

Case 1 is illustrated in Figure 6.4; saving and investment are equal to £25. Let us assume that planned saving and investment are equal to £25, so that plans are being realized. This is an **equilibrium position** because the economy is producing an output of £100 and planned expenditure (consumption plus investment) is equal to £100. (This is more fully discussed in Chapter 7.) Consider case 2, where we assume that households decide to consume less and increase their savings to £30. If output is still £100 and planned investment is £25, then planned savings will exceed planned investment and intended expenditure will be less than output. This is a **disequilibrium position** because there will be a deficiency of spending (or demand) and unsold output. This will cause an increase in value of stock of £25. As this change in stock is counted as investment we find that measured investment is £30 and is equal to saving. Measured expenditure will be (and always will be) equal to output; but if planned spending is less than output we can expect firms to react to the unintended build up of stocks by cutting output. This is the type of insight that theory gives us; but the national income accountant cannot know what people intended so he or she can merely record what has actually happend. If the increase in stocks had been intended then case 2 would represent an equilibrium position; but there is no way of deducing intentions from the recorded figures.

We can summarize the argument more formally. The identity we derived can be written as:

$$S \equiv I \equiv I_i + I_u$$

where I_i is **intended investment** and I_u is **unintended investment**. *Ex post* (measured or recorded) investment has two parts, the **intended** and the **unintended**, which are indistinguishable to the national income accountant. Equilibrium is where intended investment and saving are equal and unintended investment is zero:

$$S \equiv I_i \quad \text{and} \quad I_u = 0$$

6.2.2.3 Gross and net concepts

Each year part of the **capital stock** will need replacing because it has ceased to function properly or become obsolete. This is known as **capital consumption** or **depreciation**. It is, therefore, necessary to engage in a certain amount of **replacement investment** each year simply to maintain the capital stock. Investment that exceeds the replacement level is **net investment** and this raises the capital stock and productive potential of the economy. **Gross investment** is net investment plus replacement investment. This leads us to distinguish between **Net** and **Gross National Product**:

Net National Product = Gross National Product − Capital consumption

Net National Product is the flow of goods and services after provision has been made for worn out capital stock. In many ways the net concept is more appealing because every nation in the long run must replace its obsolete or broken down capital in order to survive; net product therefore gives us a better idea of the standard of living we can enjoy. However, obtaining a reliable measure of capital consumption is extremely difficult: in practice it is almost impossible to distinguish between replacement and net investment so data on capital consumption must be treated with a certain amount of scepticism.

6.2.3 Government and national income

6.2.3.1 General government final consumption

We can now extend our explanation of national income accounts to include **government**. Care needs to be taken here to avoid double counting by including **transfer payments** such as grants, subsidies and debt interest. Around half of total government spending in the mid-1980s was **transfer payments**. We include those expenditures that involve a direct demand for goods and services (for example, NHS drugs, school textbooks) including the services of government employees (nurses, teachers, civil servants, etc.). **Capital expenditure** by the government is included in **gross domestic fixed capital formation**, which shows the **gross investment spending** of the public and private sectors. General government final consumption excludes capital expenditure as well as transfer payments. In 1987 it accounted for half of total government spending.

6.2.3.2 Factor cost and market prices

Governments impose **indirect taxes** such as VAT and excise duties but may also **subsidize** certain goods and services. Hence market prices do not entirely reflect the costs of production and the income received by factors will not be the same as the expenditure on goods and services. We can rectify this if we deduct indirect taxes and add in subsidies. This is known as the **adjustment to factor cost**. We therefore obtain two measures of **Gross Domestic Product**: at **market prices** and **factor cost**.

GDP at factor cost = GDP at market prices − Indirect taxes + Subsidies

6.2.4 National income accounts and an open economy

6.2.4.1 Imports and exports

In an **open economy** some expenditure will be on **imported goods** while some of the spending that affects output will be by people overseas on our **exports**. We can see how this is treated in the national income accounts by distinguishing between different measures of expenditure. **Total domestic expenditure** (*TDE*) is total spending by UK residents:

TDE = C + I + G + Δ STOCKS

That is, it is the sum of consumption (*C*), gross fixed capital formation (*I*), government final consumption (*G*), and stockbuilding (Δ STOCKS). The last item is the change in stocks or inventories held known as stockbuilding. It is negative when stocks are being run down.

We can extend *TDE* to include the expenditure by people and firms overseas on UK output by adding in exports (*X*); this gives **total final expenditure** (*TFE*). So

TFE = TDE + X

TDE and *TFE* include expenditure on imports which clearly affects other countries' output but not that of the UK. If we deduct imports (*M*) from *TFE* we obtain **Gross Domestic Product (GDP)**:

GDP = TFE − M = C + I + G + Δ STOCKS + X − M

6.2.4.2 National and domestic products

Some of the income of UK residents arises from assets owned by them but located abroad. Similarly some of the income generated in the UK will be received by overseas owners of UK assets. The addition of this income from abroad and the deduction of income received by overseas owners of UK assets is known as net property income. Its inclusion converts Gross Domestic Product into **Gross National Product (GNP)**:

GNP = GDP + Net property income from abroad

Table 6.3 The expenditure approach to national income accounts

	£ billion
Consumers' expenditure	258.4
General government final consumption	85.8
Gross fixed investment	70.8
Value of physical increase in stocks	0.6
Total domestic expenditure	415.6
Exports of goods and services	107.5
Total final expenditure at market prices	523.1
less Imports of goods and services	−112.0
Gross Domestic Product at market prices	411.1
less Taxes on expenditure	−68.0
Subsidies	5.8
Gross Domestic Product at factor cost	348.9
Net property income from abroad	5.5
Gross National Product at factor cost	354.4
less Capital consumption	−48.2
National income	306.1

(*National Income and Expenditure*, 1988)

6.2.5 The UK national income accounts

The expenditure approach (Table 6.3) illustrates the points made in the previous two sections. **Gross Domestic Product at market prices** is obtained by subtracting imports from total final expenditure. Subtracting indirect taxes and adding in subsidies (factor cost adjustment) gives **GDP at factor cost. Gross National Product** is obtained by adding net property income from abroad. Finally, the deduction of capital consumption produces national income which is **Net National Product** at factor cost.

The **income** approach is illustrated in Table 6.4. Most of the items are self-explanatory so we confine our comments to those that require clarification. (Slight discrepancies in the totals are due to rounding errors.) The imputed change for consumption of non-trading capital, which is a relatively small item, is an imputed income for the owner-occupation of property by government and non-profit-making bodies.

Table 6.4 The income approach to national income accounts

	£ billion
Income from employment	226.3
Income from self-employment	33.0
Gross trading profits of companies	65.6
Gross trading surplus of public corporations	6.6
Gross trading surplus of general government enterprises	−0.2
Rent	24.8
Imputed charge for consumption of non-trading capital	3.3
Total domestic income	359.4
less Stock appreciation	−4.9
Residual error	−5.6
Gross Domestic Product at factor cost (Expenditure)	348.9
Net property income from abroad	5.5
Gross National Product at factor cost	354.4
less Capital consumption	−48.2
National income	306.1

(*National Income and Expenditure*, 1988)

An increase in the value of stocks (or inventories) is treated as profits by businesses; but this can give a misleading measure of national income. There may have been no increase in the physical volume of stocks; but rapidly rising prices would cause domestic income to be inflated even though the country were no better off. **Stock appreciation** is a measure of the increase in the value of stocks arising from increased prices. It is deducted from domestic income to avoid an exaggerated measure of income (when stock prices are rising). The **residual error** is included to make the GDP obtained from the income measure equal to that measured by the expenditure approach. Recall that we said that income, output and expenditure are defined to be equal. In practice they are measured from different sources of data and, not surprisingly, the measured totals are not the same. The identity is maintained by including a residual error in the income and output measures. This is not meant to imply that the expenditure measure is more accurate than the other two.

The output measure (Table 6.5) shows the output of goods and services in the economy measured by the value-added method. The adjustment for financial services relates net interest receipts of the financial sector. It is shown here in summary form; more detailed presentations are published in the UK National Income Accounts. The output measure represents the production of the main sectors of the economy in index number form; so its main use is a measure of change in output. The table shows that, according to the output measure, GDP in 1987 had risen 7.7 per cent since 1985 in real terms.

Table 6.5 The output approach to national income accounts, 1987 (1985 = 100)

Agriculture, forestry and fishing	99.4
Production:	
Energy and water supply	105.0
Manufacturing	106.6
Total production	106.1
Construction	108.7
Service industries:	
Distribution, hotels and catering; repairs	110.2
Transport and communication	110.9
Other	107.9
Total services	108.8
Gross domestic product (output-based)	107.7

(*National Income and Expenditure*, 1988)

6.2.6 National income and economic welfare

How good a measure is national income of economic welfare? In other words, if GNP rises by 5 per cent in real terms is society 5 per cent better off in terms of **utility** or **satisfaction**? There is no way we can ever answer the last question because it involves comparing the utility of millions of people. There is no doubt that the national income accounts include many of the goods and services that give people pleasure. It should be equally clear, though, that it is far from being a perfect measure. We have already indicated that a number of activities (such as housework and DIY) are not included in GNP, which therefore underestimates the income and output of a country. There are also grounds for believing that GNP overestimates the benefits. We can illustrate this with a simple scheme for an alternative measure.

If we use the term **net social welfare** (NSW) to represent an alternative measure we can start by recognizing that there are benefits that are not counted by the national income accountant and therefore need to be added to NNP. These should not only include the type of activities we mentioned earlier but leisure and such benefits as the reduced infant mortality rate associated with rising living and health standards. These benefits are extremely difficult, or in some cases impossible, to measure; but we can recognize that they exist.

We also need to build into our framework a recognition of the evils associated with economic activity that are not properly accounted for in NNP. Amenity loss will occur where the air or waterways become polluted and beautiful countryside is destroyed. This should be regarded as capital consumption and deducted in our measure of NSW. We limit amenity loss by devoting resources to clearing up the environment or rectifying spoiled amenities. However, it would be wrong to treat this economic activity as something positive which increases NSW so it ought to be deducted from NNP. We call this item growth costs. A society that spends very little on these is likely to find its amenity loss significant. Conversely, if amenity loss is to be prevented then growth costs will be high and in both cases NSW will be reduced (compared with NNP), though quantifying the reduction is fraught with problems.

6.3 Prices

6.3.1 Current and constant price measures

National income accounts are measured in **current** and **constant prices**. The **current price** measure simply means we value everything in terms of current prevailing prices. It can be formally expressed as

$$P_1^t Q_1^t + P_2^t Q_2^t \ldots \ldots \ldots + P_n^t Q_n^t$$

where P is the price
          Q is the quantity
          t refers to the current period
          $1 \ldots n$ refers to 1 to n commodities

The **constant price** measure values output in the prices of a base year. At present this is 1985 prices for the UK accounts. We can express this as

$$P_1^0 Q_1^t + P_2^0 Q_2^t \ldots \ldots \ldots + P_n^0 Q_n^t$$

where 0 refers to the base time period.

    Constant price (or **real**) measures of GDP, consumer expenditure, investment, etc. are more frequently used by economists than the **current price** (or **nominal**) equivalents because they give a clearer picture of what is happening to the economy than the inflation-affected current price measures. Our theories (for example theories of consumer expenditure and investment) are generally developed in real terms.

6.3.2 GDP deflator

If we have a measure of current and constant price GDP we can calculate the implied change in price. The **GDP deflator** can be measured by dividing GDP at current factor cost by GDP at constant factor cost and multiplying by 100 to express the result as an index number:

$$GDP \; deflator = \frac{GDP \; current \; factor \; cost}{GDP \; constant \; factor \; cost} \times 100$$

e.g. $GDP \; deflator \; (1987) = \dfrac{£348.9}{£324.0} \times 100 = 107.7$

We calculate the **inflation rate** suggested by the GDP deflator by taking the **percentage change** in the index. As the GDP deflator in 1986 was 102.6 the inflation rate in 1987 was 5 per cent.

This measure is often known as an **implicit deflator** because the price change is implied rather than explicitly indicated. A number of national account deflators can be obtained by using the same approach. (In 6.3.5 we refer to a **consumer expenditure deflator**.)

6.3.3 Paasche and Laspeyre indices

It is a relatively straightforward matter to measure what has happened over time to the price of a single product (though even here difficulties may arise if the quality of the product has changed over the period). It is much more challenging to obtain a measure of how prices have changed **overall**. It would not make much sense to take a simple average because that would give the same weight to a box of matches as to a motor car. A more sensible approach is to weight prices according to their importance in total expenditure. But then we have to decide to take either the current weighting or that of some base period. This, essentially, is the distinction between the **Paasche** and **Laspeyre indices**.

The **Laspeyre index** uses base periods weights of quantities. We can represent it formally as

$$\frac{P_1^t Q_1^0 + P_2^t Q_2^0 \ldots\ldots + P_n^t Q_n^0}{P_1^0 Q_1^0 + P_2^0 Q_2^0 \ldots\ldots + P_n^0 Q_n^0}$$

This approach is adopted when constructing the **Retail Price Index** (**RPI**). In contrast, the **Paasche index** uses current weights of quantities as the GDP deflator does. The **Laspeyre index** will tend to overestimate inflation because by using base quantities it does not allow for the reduction in quantities that occur when prices rise. The reverse is true for the Paasche index.

6.3.4 Retail Price Index

The **Retail Price Index** (**RPI**) measures the change in the cost of a representative **basket** of goods and services bought by a typical household. The weights attached to the items in the basket are obtained from the **Family Expenditure Survey** which is conducted every year to discover the spending pattern of a sample of households. The general index of retail prices is meant to be broadly representative of most households, but two groups are excluded. Neither high income households (defined for the first half of 1987 as those earning more than £600 per week–approximately 4 per cent of households) nor pensioner households, where more than 75 per cent of income is derived from state pensions or supplementary benefit, are included. Two separate **pensioner price indices** for one- and two-person households are published.

The weights (out of 1000) for 1988 were:

Food	163	Household services	41
Catering	50	Clothing and footwear	72
Alcoholic drink	78	Personal goods and services	37
Tobacco	36	Motoring expenditure	132
Housing	160	Fares and other travel costs	23
Fuel and Light	55	Leisure goods	50
Household goods	74	Leisure services	29

These are the broad categories. Some 350 items are measured each month. Prices are checked in different parts of the country and in different types of retail outlet. In total some 150 000 price changes are measured.

6.3.5 Other measures of prices

The RPI is the best known measure of price changes; but there are several others. We have already mentioned the GDP deflator. We can obtain a consumer expenditure deflator in a similar way. This is the **Consumer Price Index**. It differs from the RPI in a number of respects. It covers all consumer expenditure so it will include the top income groups and uses current weights for expenditure rather than the base weights of the RPI. Finally, its measure of owner-occupied housing costs is the imputed rent, whereas the RPI uses mortgage interest payment. This means that the RPI will rise faster, other things being equal, when interest rates are rising and more slowly when rates are falling.

7 The Keynesian revolution

7.1 Introduction

In this chapter we consider a core element of most courses: **Keynesian macroeconomics**. You will discover that **macroeconomics** is a more controversial subject than microeconomics. In addition to the basic theory a number of applications are considered.

The chapter will:

- explain the circular flow of income
- explain withdrawals and injections
- outline the classical model
- explain the key features of the Keynesian revolution
- define endogenous and exogenous variables
- explain equilibrium in the Keynesian income–expenditure model
- show how equilibrium may be represented graphically
- define marginal and average propensity to consume and save
- explain the multiplier
- explain and illustrate inflationary and deflationary gaps
- explain and illustrate the paradox of thrift
- apply the income–expenditure model to the problems of unemployment and oil price changes

7.1.1 Examination guide

The Keynesian income expenditure model is part of the core analysis of economics and, unless you are following a course which avoids macroeconomics completely, you can expect to be tested on it. Essay questions may ask directly for an explanation of the model (perhaps contrasting it with the classical model) or may require you to apply the model to a particular problem. You may also encounter questions requiring short answers, for example drawing or completing a diagram or solving a numerical problem. All of these questions will require you to have mastered the basic model so that you can explain and illustrate an equilibrium level of income. In addition, you should be able to discuss why income changes and explain the workings of the multiplier. Essential preparation for this is practice in drawing the diagrams and attempting the type of numerical problems found in the question and answer section for this chapter at the end of the book.

7.2 The circular flow of income

The **circular flow of income**, as described in the previous chapter (section 6.2.1.2 and Figure 6.1) is part of the basic theoretical framework of macroeconomics. This simple model does not suggest there will be problems at a **macro-** or **aggregate level**. If firms produced £100 billion of goods and services, the value of this would be received as **income** in the form of **wages, salaries, rents, dividends** and **interest** by **households**; if they in turn spent all of this income on consumption then the total amount of spending in the economy would equal the total value of goods and services produced. In these circumstances there would be neither over- nor under-production at the aggregate level and the income level could be regarded as being in equilibrium. However, as we saw in Chapter 6, this picture is still too simple: other withdrawals and injections must be taken into account.

Household saving can be seen as a **withdrawal** or **leakage** from the **circular flow of income**—it is part of the flow that is not passed on to the next stage. Just as there can be a **withdrawal** from the circular flow so there can be an **injection** into it: **investment spending** by firms on plant and machinery is an item of total expenditure on goods in addition to spending on consumption by households and is therefore an **injection** into the circular flow.

When **government** and **foreign trade** are introduced, other **withdrawals** and **injections** can be recognized. **Government expenditure** is another additional item of expenditure which purchases part of the output of goods and services and is therefore an **injection**. On the other hand, **tax revenue** is a **withdrawal**: some consumer spending goes to the government as **VAT payments** and **excise duties** and some income is not received by households but is paid as **income tax**. Expenditure on **imports** is a **withdrawal** as that part of spending is not received by a country's firms but **leaks** out of the circular flow and is part of the demand for a foreign country's output. **Exports** produce an **injection** into a country's circular flow. Figure 7.1 lists all the injections and withdrawals, shown for convenience at a single point.

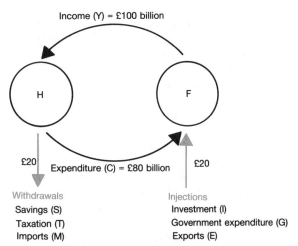

Fig. 7.1 Injections and withdrawals to the circular flow of income

The notion of **macroeconomic equilibrium** can now be reconsidered. If **total spending** from all sources—households, firms, government and overseas (on exports)—is to exactly match the output of firms, then **total withdrawals** from the circular flow must be exactly balanced by **injections**. In these circumstances there is an **equilibrium level** of income and output. An alternative way of defining **equilibrium output level** is where total expenditure (consumption plus injections) equals aggregate income; total spending will then exactly match output. Figure 7.1 shows an equilibrium situation.

If, instead of the position illustrated, households spent only half of their income on consumption of the country's goods and services—£50 billion—then withdrawals would be greater than injections, and expenditure would be £80 billion, which would be less than income. This is a **disequilibrium position**, as firms are producing an output of £100 billion, yet only £80 billion is being purchased. Such a situation cannot persist: some reactions and changes are inevitable, otherwise warehouses would overflow with unsold goods.

How likely is it that an equilibrium level of income will be achieved and are there **market forces** that operate to move an economy towards such a state? On the face of it, it seems highly unlikely that equilibrium can exist or even be approached in a decentralized market economy; total spending in the economy is the result of the decisions of tens of millions of households and thousands of firms, as well as millions of people in other countries. It would be fortuitous if aggregate expenditure were to equal total income or output, or if income and withdrawals were to equal injections.

We are now in a position to answer some basic questions about the operation of modern economies. Are there **market mechanisms** to ensure that injections and withdrawals are equal? If they are not equal, what are the consequences? If they are equal, and the economy is in equilibrium and all production is bought, will the output level be sufficiently great to give **full employment**? Economists have tended to disagree over the answers to these questions; we now consider the **classical** and **Keynesian** responses.

7.3 The classical view

The **classical** view was the one which dominated thinking on macroeconomic issues up to the 1930s. (**Classical** was the term used by Keynes.) In some ways this is an unfortunate use of the term because it is usually associated with the classical political economists who wrote in the late 18th and early 19th centuries. Keynes was particularly criticizing later writers, including some of his contemporaries. These are now more normally referred to as **neoclassical economists**. The **neoclassical** period began around 1870 and is responsible for much modern marginal microeconomic analysis. However, there are elements of classical thinking in the neoclassical view, e.g. Say's law, referred to below. It is a mark of

Keynes's influence that the term **classical economists** that he employed is the one that is normally used today.

Classical economists held that market economies were self-regulating—they tended towards an equilibrium at full employment without the need for government intervention. Two theoretical propositions were important in reaching this conclusion: one was **Say's law** and the other concerned the **labour market**.

7.3.1 Say's law

Say's law, named after the 18th-century French political economist **Jean Baptiste Say,** states that 'supply creates its own demand'—there will always be sufficient demand to purchase output. It is easy to accept this view in a simple barter economy, where people either produce all their own needs or supply goods to the market only when they demand some other type of good in return; but can it apply to a modern market economy with extensive **division of labour**? The **classical economists** thought so. Suppose we have a **closed economy** (no foreign trade) from which, for the time being, we exclude the government sector. There is one **withdrawal**—saving—and one **injection**—investment. To uphold Say's law we require a mechanism to ensure that savings and investment are equal; if they are not, savings may be greater than investment and there will be deficiency in demand.

The **interest rate mechanism** fulfils this role. Its operation is simple and seemingly plausible. **Savings,** the classical economists argued, would be loaned out because this would earn interest, whereas holding on to savings as money would mean forgoing interest payments. **Savings,** therefore, are a supply of **loanable funds** which, though affected by many factors, are likely to increase as the interest rate rises. Demand for **loanable funds** arises from the need of firms to finance their **investment expenditure**. This, too, is likely to be affected by **interest rates** (as well as other factors), with lower interest rates making additional investment projects profitable and increasing the amount of money firms wish to borrow. This view of **savings** and **investment**, as a demand for and supply of, **loanable funds**, is shown in Figure 7.2.

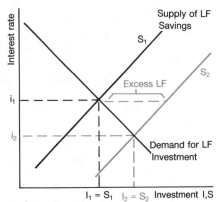

Fig. 7.2 The classical view of the interest rate mechanism

The plans of millions of savers, who refrain from consumption for a wide variety of motives, are unlikely to exactly match the investment intentions of thousands of firms; but **interest rate movements** should reconcile divergences. If saving is greater than investment, there will be an excess supply of loanable funds and the interest rate will fall. This will discourage saving and act as a stimulus to investment, which will in turn lead firms to wish to borrow more. The **equilibrium interest rate** will be a point where planned savings and investment are equal.

This mechanism can cope with all types of changes and shocks. For example, if households become more thrifty, then the savings schedule shifts out to the right (see dotted line on Figure 7.2). There is now an excess supply of loanable funds at i_1, and interest rates drop and re-establish an equality of investment and savings at the new equilibrium interest rate of i_2. Shifts in the investment schedule would similarly change the equilibrium rate.

If the **interest rate** behaves in this way, any tendency for a deficiency in demand will be corrected and **Say's law** holds. It should be stressed that no government intervention is required and the result is achieved by agents pursuing selfish interests—savers and investing firms seeking the best deals for themselves. Extending the model to include **foreign trade** brings us to another market mechanism which **classical economists** believed could be relied upon to balance the withdrawal, imports, with the injection, exports. The gold standard mechanism, explained briefly in Chapter 20, performed the same role for imports and exports as the interest rate did for savings and investment; so equilibrium still held. If **market forces** could be relied upon to ensure that there was sufficient demand to purchase output, then there was no need for government to intervene in this area. Indeed, the state's responsibility was confined to the **allocative** and **distributive functions** referred to in Chapter 3 and at the macro level it had only to raise sufficient tax revenue to finance its expenditure and balance its budget.

7.3.2 Classical view of the labour market

There remains a potential problem in the **classical** position. Even though there will be sufficient demand to purchase output, will output be high enough to employ the whole labour force? In the classical view **unemployment** is an excess supply of labour, which occurs when the wage rate is above the equilibrium level (see Figure 7.3).

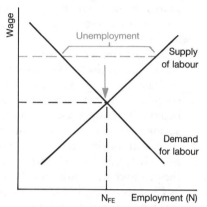

Fig. 7.3 The classical view of the labour market

The **labour market mechanism** operates to eliminate **unemployment**—excess supply will lower wages and this will lead firms to move down their demand curves, resulting in more employment until equilibrium is reached and **full employment** is achieved. **Demographic changes** which shift the supply schedule, and **changes in technology** or **capital stock** which shift the demand schedule, will be accommodated by adjustments in the wage rate and full employment will be maintained.

7.3.3 Classical view and government policy

This view justified *laisser-faire* macro-policy prescriptions. Despite periodic trade depressions in the 19th century the classical view could be supported by data from the period before the First World War if allowance were made for the time it took for market forces to work through the economy. Periods when many were out of work alternated with periods of low unemployment. The same could not be said of the interwar period, when unemployment never really fell below 10 per cent and rose to 23 per cent in 1931.

This experience shattered faith in the classical view. Yet at the depths of the Great Depression there was no widely accepted alternative view and governments obeyed the same policy prescription that had been adopted for decades: **balance the budget**. As the slump lowered tax revenues and created a budget deficit, government policy in the early 1930s was directed towards raising taxes and cutting expenditure.

This was exactly the opposite of the recommendations of one eminent economist, **John Maynard Keynes**; but Keynes's new theoretical approach had to be accepted before government policy could change and increases in government spending and tax cuts could be regarded as an appropriate way of reducing unemployment. Keynes produced the most complete statement of his alternative to the classical position in the *General Theory of Employment, Interest and Money*, which was published in 1936.

7.4 The Keynesian revolution

Keynes brought about a revolution in economic thinking. He inverted Say's law: rather than supply creating its own demand, he suggested that **demand determined supply or output**. Market forces failed to deal with deficiencies in demand; indeed the market system acted to magnify such problems. **Mass unemployment** was not the result of too high a level of wages, but of too little demand; cuts in wages would not increase employment and might even worsen the unemployment problem. Keynesian policy recommendations suggested the end of *laisser-faire* in macroeconomics and made a powerful case for

intervention. In explaining these radical ideas, we will start by considering Keynes's rejection of **Say's law.**

7.4.1 Keynes and Say's law

Recall the classical view of the **interest rate mechanism.** The institutional arrangements for this loanable funds market consist of a number of interconnected financial institutions; the one that most obviously brings together firms wishing to borrow money for investment and lenders of funds is the **Stock Exchange**, which Keynes described as a casino: far from being the well-ordered market implied by the classical view, it was dominated by **speculative buying** and **selling.** This presents a different picture of the **savings–investment relationship.** In the classical view all savings would be loaned out, as it would be irrational to retain them as money and forgo interest payments. But in Keynes's view it was quite sensible to use savings to increase holdings of money if loaning it out meant acquiring shares or bonds whose prices were likely to fall. Keynes introduced the **speculative motive** for holding money—which is more fully explained in Chapter 10—and which provides an alternative use for savings.

This alternative use for savings may prevent the **classical interest rate mechanism** from working effectively. To take an extreme case to illustrate the point: if there were an increase in savings and none of the extra savings were loaned out but the total was held as **speculative money** because of fears of capital losses on shares and bonds, then there would be no fall in interest rates and no increase in investment to compensate for the increased savings (and reduced consumption). A deficiency in demand would result. In fact, Keynes did *not* argue that interest rates would not fall but only that the fall would not be sufficient to accomplish the task required by the classical view. Lower interest rates would reduce the demand for bonds and shares and lead to an increased preference for holding money, as Chapter 10 explains. The essential point is the same as in the extreme case. This view of savings and investment means, contrary to Say's law, that a deficiency in demand may emerge.

This is just the start of the problem. The **deficiency in demand** leads to a fall in output, as Keynesians argue that firms will not continue to produce goods that cannot be sold. The cutbacks in output reduce the number of jobs and incomes fall. This in turn leads to further reductions in demand, reducing output, employment and income even further and so on. This is a radically different view of the way market economies operate: not only does the **interest rate mechanism** fail to correct an imbalance between savings and investment, but the disturbance is amplified by the system's reaction to the initial deficiency in demand. This amplification process is known as the **multiplier** and is considered more fully in section 7.5.4.

It may seem that there is no end to the decline in output; however, with the fall in incomes there will be a reduction in saving and this will eventually restore the equality between saving and investment, as illustrated in Figure 7.4.

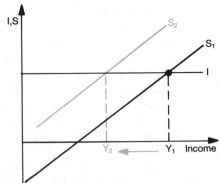

Fig. 7.4 The Keynesian model of savings and investment

With an initial equilibrium at Y_1 the increase in savings referred to earlier is depicted by an upward shift of the savings schedule (S_1 to S_2). The deficiency in demand that this produces leads to a decline in output and income and a movement down the savings schedule, as the volume of savings is related to income. A new equilibrium is established at Y_2, where all output is demanded but where there will be unemployment.

7.4.2 The Keynesian view of the labour market

At this point in the classical system adjustments in the labour market would start to reduce the dole queues. The Keynesian view is again radically different. Recall that in our example the departure from full employment occurred because of a decline in demand following the increase in saving. No mention was made of any changes in **wage rates**. Indeed, we may assume that the level of wages is still the one that obtained equilibrium at full employment. The situation can be shown as a movement from *A* to *B* in Figure 7.5, with the distance *AB* representing **involuntary unemployment**. (This should be contrasted with the classical representation of unemployment in Figure 7.3.)

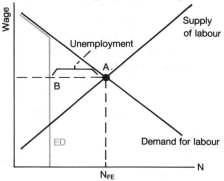

Fig. 7.5 The Keynesian model of the labour market

But though **high wages** are not the cause of unemployment, will a cut in wage rates not improve job prospects? Not in these circumstances. Firms have been forced off their original demand curve for labour, *D*, by lack of sales, and there is now an effective demand curve, *ED*, passing through *B*. A cut in wage rates, though presumably welcome to firms, will not lead to a revision of employment decisions which were prompted by the level of demand, not by wage levels. The **redistribution of income** from wage earners to profit recipients may reduce total demand further if the cuts in spending by workers are greater than the increases by other, generally better off, income groups.

The explanation of the **Keynesian view** of the **labour market** we have given here is one that is associated with a reinterpretation of Keynes's work that took place in the early 1970s. Prior to that the explanation of unemployment in the Keynesian model was in terms of **wage rigidity**–that the labour market failed to respond to excess supply. This did not credit Keynes's work with a theoretical breakthrough though it did give him recognition for clarifying the implications of **wage rigidity**. There is still much disagreement on the matter but the interpretation we have presented underlines the importance of the Keynesian revolution.

The conclusion is a bleak one for an **unregulated market system**. An equilibrium, with withdrawals equal to injections, has been established by means of unemployment and no forces seem to be working for its removal. This is **market failure** at the macro level. In the 1930s Keynes offered this analysis to explain the market failure embodied in the groups of unemployed standing at street corners. During the Depression some of the unemployed were so poor that they could not afford shoes. Some of these may well have been shoe workers who were out of work because there was a lack of demand for the goods they produced. Shoe manufacturers with idle capacity would have willingly employed them had there been the demand and had the workers had jobs they would have been able to afford shoes. The **market system** was failing to transmit the correct signals.

7.4.3 The policy revolution

Keynes not only explained how **unemployment** could emerge and persist in market economies, he showed how the problem could be overcome. It was necessary to inject **extra spending** into the economy to raise demand. This could be done by **increased government spending** or through **tax cuts** which would reduce withdrawals from the circular flow and mean that households had more to spend. The **multiplier process** would assist this explanation of the economy. An increase in **government spending** on road building would increase **employment** in the construction industry and these workers would in turn be able to spend more, say on shoes, which would put some shoe workers back to work and so on.

Notice that the **Keynesian policy prescription** is exactly the opposite of the policy actually pursued in the early 1930s: it involved overthrowing decades of adherence to the idea of a **balanced budget**. Such was the anxiety to find a solution to **mass unemployment**, particularly among politicians, that Keynes's view was accepted, despite its radical message, with remarkable speed. The first Keynesian budget in the UK was in 1941, barely five years after the publication of the *General Theory*. The White Paper on employment,

1944, gave formal recognition to a policy revolution and indicated a consensus among the major political parties on the conduct of post-war macroeconomic policy. This consensus was to last 30 years.

7.5 Income-expenditure: a two-sector model

7.5.1 Macro-modelling

We turn now to a more formal presentation of the Keynesian model and begin by considering some general features of **macro-models**.

At the outset it is usually helpful to define concepts through **identities**. These are truisms–true by definition–and are therefore indisputable, though how worthwhile they are depends on how useful they are in establishing the framework for examining a problem. In this section we will develop a two-sector model (households and firms) providing two straightforward illustrations of an **identity**. The first,

$$E \equiv C + I$$

defines the two components of expenditure (E) as consumption (C) and investment (I). The other,

$$Y \equiv C + S$$

states that income (Y) can either be spent on consumption or saved.

Equations are a vital part of any model. **Behavioural equations** try to capture the behaviour of some sections of the economy. An important illustration in Keynesian economics is the **consumption function**,

$$C = f(Y)$$

which is the hypothesis that consumer expenditure is related to the level of income. **Technical equations** feature in many models and these represent some technological or institutional relationship. An example from a three-sector model (one that includes the government sector) is

$$T = f(Y)$$

which relates tax revenue to income.

Equations may be **endogenous** or **exogenous**. **Endogenous** equations are solved within the model. Our model to determine equilibrium income will simultaneously determine the level of consumer spending. The values of **exogenous** variables are determined outside the model. This may be because they are non-economic (for example, climatic factors in models of agricultural production) or because they are not considered crucial for modelling the particular project in hand. In our basic macro-model investment will be an exogenous variable and this is depicted by placing a bar over the variable:

$$I = \bar{I}$$

Given the task of developing a simple model it is reasonable to treat investment in this way. However, there may be occasions when it is more appropriate to incorporate investment within the model in which case, of course, it becomes an **endogenous variable**. (See the paradox of thrift at the end of this chapter and the IS–LM model in Chapter 10.)

Finally, there are **equilibrium conditions**. As the term suggests these state what is required for **equilibrium**. In the Keynesian models they may be expressed in either of two ways:

$Y = E$ (income equals expenditure)

$W = J$ (withdrawals equal injections)

These are *ex ante* concepts in that they relate to intentions or plans of people and institutions in the economy. A disequilibrium will arise if planned withdrawals are greater than planned injections.

In a two-sector model this means

$$Y = C + I \quad and \quad S = I$$

We will now consider a diagrammatic representation and solution to a two-sector model.

7.5.2 Consumption and saving

Consumption is a function of income–higher income is associated with increased consumer expenditure. If we represent this relationship by a **linear function** (one that is graphically a straight line) it will have the following type of equation:

$$C = a + bY$$

Here the a is a constant: it is the level of consumer expenditure when income is zero and graphically is the intercept of the consumption function with the vertical axis (marked on Figure 7.6 by the brackets). The way consumption responds to income is determined by the value of b and it is represented by the slope of the function. The higher the value of b, the steeper the slope, and the more consumption responds to income changes.

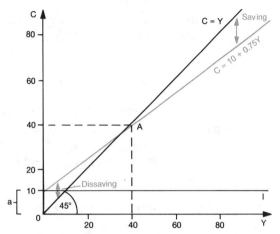

Fig. 7.6 Consumption, income and saving

In the example here we will let $a = 10$ and $b = 0.75$: $C = 10 + 0.75\,Y$.

Table 7.1 Consumption, saving and income given $C = 10 + 0.75\,Y$

Income (Y)	Consumption (C)	Saving (S)	APC (C/Y)	MPC (ΔC/ΔY)	MPS (ΔS/ΔY)
0	10	−10			
				0.75	0.25
20	25	−5	1.25		
				0.75	0.25
40	40	0	1.00		
				0.75	0.25
60	55	5	0.92		
				0.75	0.25
80	70	10	0.88		
				0.75	0.25
100	85	15	0.85		

In a two-sector model saving is the difference between income and consumer expenditure; it can therefore be easily calculated and is shown in column 3. The negative figures indicate what economists call **dissaving**, where consumption is greater than income. The relationship is shown graphically in Figure 7.6. The 45° line shows points where expenditure, in this case consumer expenditure (shown on the vertical axis), is equal to income, shown on the horizontal axis. (But note that the line is at 45° only when the scales on the axes are the same, as they are here.)

When an income level is 40 (A) all income is spent on consumption; this is the point where the **consumption function** crosses the 45° line and savings are, therefore, zero. At income levels above 40 there is positive saving; this is indicated by the vertical distance between the consumption function and the 45° line.

Two concepts relating to the consumption function should now be noted. The first is the **average propensity to consume (APC)**. This indicates the proportion of income that is spent on consumption and is measured by dividing consumption by income:

$$APC = \frac{C}{Y}$$

The values for our illustrative consumption function are shown in the **APC** column of Table 7.1.

A second, more widely used concept is **marginal propensity to consume (MPC)**. This shows how consumption changes as income changes and is measured by the equation:

$$MPC = \frac{\Delta C}{\Delta Y}$$

In terms of the graph, the **MPC** is the slope of the **consumption function** (see Figure 7.6), b in our linear consumption function $C = a + bY$, which in our numerical example is 0.75. There is a corresponding **propensity to save function**. The **average propensity to save** (**APS**) is the ratio of savings to income (S/Y) and the **marginal propensity to save** (**MPS**) is the proportion of any change in income that is saved ($\Delta S / \Delta Y$) and is the slope of the savings schedule (in our numerical example this is 0.25).

7.5.3 Investment

Investment can be dealt with very briefly in the basic model. It is an **exogenous variable** and in our numerical example is equal to 10:

$$I = \bar{I} = 10$$

In Figure 7.6 the **investment function** is a horizontal line because it is always equal to 10.

7.5.4 Equilibrium in a two-sector model

We are now in a position to bring together these different elements and to determine the **equilibrium level of income**.
Recall that the condition for equilibrium is

$$Y = E$$

or, alternatively, in terms of withdrawals and injections,

$$W = J$$

The 45° line in Figure 7.7 shows points where $Y = E$, the equilibrium condition. Points to the left and above the 45° line are where expenditure is greater than income and the reverse is true below the 45° line. The **equilibrium income** is shown as Y_E in Figure 7.7. It is determined graphically by plotting the **consumption function** and adding to it the value of **investment** to give an **expenditure** (E) **schedule** which is therefore equal to $C + I$. The equilibrium income is where the expenditure schedule crosses the 45° line; in this case it is at an income of 80. An alternative way of deriving the equilibrium is to plot savings and draw the investment schedule to represent spending of 10; the two cross (i.e. $S = I$) at equilibrium because this is where withdrawals and injections are equal (Figure 7.8).

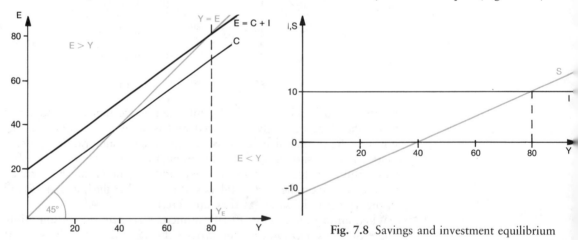

Fig. 7.7 Expenditure and income

Fig. 7.8 Savings and investment equilibrium

We can now see why other income levels do not represent an equilibrium and how the economy is likely to change in these **disequilibrium** circumstances. Below an income of 80 the expenditure schedule is above the 45° line: expenditure is greater than income and injections into the circular flow are greater than withdrawals. Sales are therefore exceeding output, stocks are being run down and order books are lengthening. Providing there are spare resources, which we assume to be the case at this stage, output and income will expand. At income levels above 80, the reverse is true with expenditure less than income and firms unable to sell all of their output. This is a disequilibrium situation and there will be cuts in output and income will fall. Only at the equilibrium level will there be no tendency for output and income to change. Of course some individual firms will be overproducing and some underproducing, but this is a microeconomic problem which will resolve itself in the way described in Chapter 3; at the macro level we have balance or equilibrium in the economy.

7.5.4 The multiplier in a two-sector economy

The **multiplier** played an important part in Keynes's analysis and we can now see more clearly how it is determined. Suppose investment increases from 10 to 20; equilibrium income will then rise from 80 to 120 (see Figure 7.9). A change in investment of 10 has resulted in an increase of income of 40—the **multiplier** is 4.

$$\textit{Investment multiplier} = \frac{\Delta Y}{\Delta I} = \frac{40}{10} = 4$$

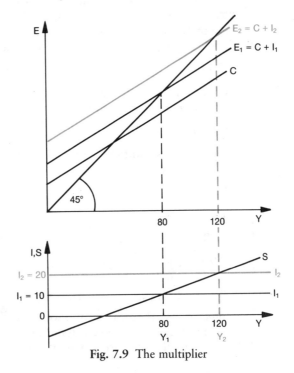

Fig. 7.9 The multiplier

The **multiplier** effect occurs because the intial increase in spending (in this case investment) raises output and income and the recipients of this extra income increase their own spending. The **size** of the multiplier depends on how much extra consumer spending results from the increase in income: in other words it is determined by the **marginal propensity to consume (MPC)**. The **multiplier** is formally expressed as:

$$\frac{1}{1 - MPC}$$

In the extreme case where MPC is zero (i.e. households do not increase their consumer spending at all in response to extra income) the **multiplier** is 1 and national income and output rise by only the amount of the extra investment. We would normally expect MPC to lie between 0 and 1; in this case there will be a **multiplier effect** and the higher the MPC the larger it will be.

An alternative way of measuring the **multiplier** is to concentrate on what part of an increase in income is not spent, that is, what is withdrawn from the circular flow. We can define **marginal propensity to withdraw (MPW)** as the ratio of change in withdrawals (ΔW) to the change in income (ΔY), i.e.

$$MPW = \frac{\Delta W}{\Delta Y}$$

In basic Keynesian models the **multiplier** is the reciprocal of the **marginal propensity to withdraw**:

$$\textit{Multiplier} = \frac{1}{MPW}$$

In a two-sector model there is only one withdrawal (savings), so the investment multiplier is the reciprocal of the marginal propensity to save:

$$\frac{\Delta Y}{\Delta I} = \frac{1}{MPS} = \frac{1}{0.25} = 4$$

The greater the **marginal propensity to withdraw**, the smaller the **multiplier**.

7.6 Three- and four-sector models

The basic model can now be extended to include **government** and **foreign trade**. The extension is fairly straightforward because we have already established the main principles.

7.6.1 The government sector

Introducing **government** involves incorporating **taxation** and **government expenditure**. **Tax revenue** is likely to be related to the level of national income because as income rises not only will more income tax be paid, but there will be a higher level of spending: indirect tax receipts (VAT, excise duties) will therefore be greater. Formally,

$$T = f(Y)$$

where T is **tax revenue**.

Government expenditure is regarded in the basic model as an **exogenous variable**:

$$G = \bar{G}$$

Equilibrium conditions have to be modified to take account of **government expenditure** and **tax revenue**:

$$Y = E$$

$$Y = C + I + G$$

$$W = J$$

$$S + T = I + G$$

7.6.2 Overseas sector

Imports, like the other **withdrawals**, will be related to the level of income. As national income rises expenditure will increase and that will include spending on **imported goods**. Thus, **imports** (M) are function of income:

$$M = f(Y)$$

Exports (X) depend on a number of factors which are not included in a basic model so they are treated as **exogenous**:

$$X = \bar{X}$$

7.6.3 Equilibrium in a four-sector model

The conditions for equilibrium involve carefully extending the basic conditions ($Y = E$ and $W = J$) encountered earlier in the chapter to a model with four sectors. Taking the income–expenditure approach the condition is

$$Y = E$$

$$Y = C + I + G + X - M$$

The term on the righthand side is the total of expenditure of the four sectors ($C + I + G + X$) less the expenditure on imports. The final item is necessary because it is only spending on a country's output that will affect its national income, therefore spending on imports must be deducted from total spending which includes the purchase of imported as well as domestically produced goods.

In terms of withdrawals and injections the condition for equilibrium is

$$W = J$$

$$S + T + M = I + G + X$$

Figure 7.10 shows equilibrium using the two approaches.

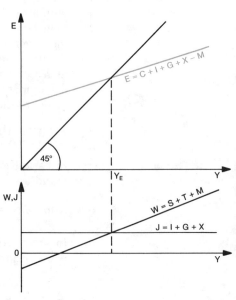

Fig. 7.10 Two representations of equilibrium in a four-sector model

7.6.4 The multiplier

The size of multiplier, which depends on the **marginal propensity to withdraw**, will be affected by the **marginal propensities to save** ($\Delta S/\Delta Y$), **tax** ($\Delta T/\Delta Y$) and **import** ($\Delta M/\Delta Y$). So an increase in the basic rate of income tax will reduce the size of the **multiplier**. The alternative way of viewing the **multiplier** in terms of the **marginal propensity to consume** needs to be interpreted with a little care. It will be the marginal propensity to consume domestic output (i.e. after deducting the import content) at factor cost (with indirect taxes deducted and any subsidies added back in) that will determine the size of the multiplier.

7.6.5 The multiplier in the UK

The **multiplier** in the type of model we have considered in this chapter will be subject to a number of **leakages**; but by examining the national income accounts we can obtain some idea of the size of these.

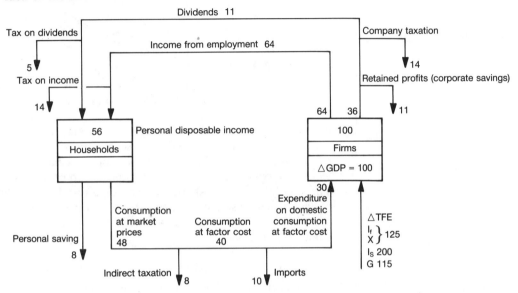

Fig. 7.11 An illustration of leakages

Figure 7.11 shows that for an increase in an injection which raises output or GDP by £100 only £56 is received by households as personal disposable income. Of the original income of £100, £11 is retained by firms (this is a form of savings—corporate saving) and £33 is leaked as taxation (income and corporation tax). There are then leakages of personal savings, imports and indirect taxation. Only £30 is retained in the circular flow—this is the consumption on domestic output at factor cost referred to in the last section. On this basis, which is only approximate since it uses **average** rather than **marginal** propensities, the multiplier in the UK would be less than 1.5. Given the **openness** of the economy and the **extent of taxation** this magnitude is not surprising.

7.7 Applications of the income–expenditure model

We conclude this chapter by considering some applications of the basic Keynesian model.

7.7.1 The 1930s recession

The Keynesian model was formulated in response to the slump of the 1930s and it was first used to analyse the recession and suggest remedies. In Figure 7.12 (overleaf) the top graph shows the **income–expenditure model** with an original equilibrium at Y_1 with expenditure at E_1. The lower graph shows the position of the budget deficit at different income levels. Tax revenue (T) is a function of income and so too is government expenditure (G), though this declines as income rises. The shape of the government expenditure schedule shows that some components, such as unemployment pay, rise as output and incomes fall. At the original income level, Y_1, the budget is balanced.

The world depression of the 1930s involved a collapse in world trade and the UK's exports fell by a half between 1929 and 1932. We show this **reduced aggregate demand** in Figure 7.12 by a downward shift of the expenditure schedule from E_1 to E_2. This resulted in a large budget deficit as tax revenue fell and dole payments simultaneously increased. The government's reaction was to try to **balance the budget** by expenditure cuts and tax

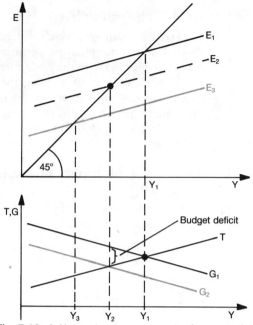

Fig. 7.12 A Keynesian income–expenditure model

increases. (To prevent the graph becoming over-complicated we show only the expenditure cuts.) The effect of these measures was to further depress demand so that expenditure fell from E_2 to E_3: the attempt to balance the budget was unsuccessful. The **Keynesian remedy** was to reverse this policy: to raise government spending and cut taxes. This would raise the expenditure schedule to offset the slump in exports. The resulting budget deficit was seen as justifiable since it prevented mass unemployment; as we have seen, balancing the budget only made the problem worse and did not even succeed in eliminating the deficit.

7.7.2 Paradox of thrift

It is a fairly natural tendency for households to increase **savings** when the economy becomes depressed and unemployment threatens; **thrift** is frequently presented as a virtue. However, in times of recession **increased savings** are not helpful to the economy. We can see this by using a two-sector model in which we slightly modify the investment function by allowing spending on plant and machinery to be influenced by the level of output and income in the economy (Figure 7.13).

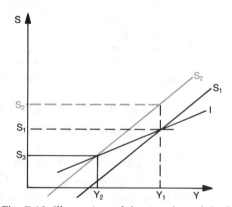

Fig. 7.13 Illustration of the paradox of thrift

The original equilibrium income is Y_1 the level of saving is S_1. The increase in thriftiness is shown by an upward shift in the savings schedule to S_2. With the community now saving S_2, withdrawals are greater than injections and national income contracts to a new equilibrium of Y_2. This has increased unemployment but had the paradoxical result that the attempt to save more has resulted in less being saved (S_3). Whatever its merits for the individual, increased saving is not beneficial for the community in times of recession. Keynes appreciated this and made radio broadcasts appealing to the housewives of Britain to go out and spend; but this could be no substitute for an expansionary government policy.

7.7.3 Inflationary and deflationary gaps

By the time Keynes's ideas had become sufficiently influential for the government to act upon them the nature of the problem had changed. The outbreak of war meant that there was too much demand in the economy, as increased military requirements as well as civilian needs made heavy demands on limited resources. Keynes showed that his analysis could be used to suggest remedies to this type of problem too. The general Keynesian message was that it would be fortuitous if the aggregation of demand in the economy exactly coincided with the output a full employment economy was capable of producing; **excess demand** was as possible as demand deficiency. We can see this by looking at Figure 7.14. The vertical line at an income Y_F indicates the income that is associated with full employment output. If expenditure in the economy is E_1 there is an equilibrium at full employment; but for the reasons suggested earlier in the chapter total spending may be less than this, say E_2, in which case there is a shortfall of demand at the full employment level, AB, and this is known as the **deflationary gap** (DG). This is the gap, for example, that would have to be filled by an increase in government expenditure if full employment were to be achieved. The wartime problem was that given all the demands on resources, spending was tending towards a position like E_3 in the diagram. In these circumstances there was an **inflationary gap** (*IG*), BC. Equilibrium is at a level of real output which exceeds full employment output. Attempts to spend more in real terms than the economy can produce lead to rising prices. (This is explored further in Chapter 11 where we discuss aggregate supply.) The task of government policy is to remove, or at least reduce, this gap. This was done in the 1940s by high rates of taxation with the wartime standard rate of income tax rising to 50 per cent. The nub of Keynesian policy for achieving full employment is to try to estimate whether there is a **deflationary** or **inflationary gap** and to introduce the appropriate remedy: **reflation** (expansion of demand) in the former case and **deflation** (reduction in demand) in the latter.

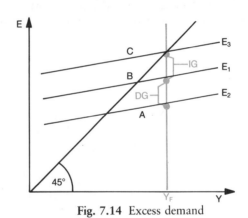

Fig. 7.14 Excess demand

7.7.4 OPEC oil price increases

In Chapter 5 we considered the microeconomic effects of the **oil price increases** of the mid- and late 1970s. Here we look at the **macro economic effects** which were no less dramatic. OPEC raised prices by a factor of 4 in late 1973, transferring a large amount of purchasing power or demand from the oil consuming countries (including the UK at that time) to oil producers. The increase was so large that OPEC members were unable to spend it all, in the short run at least. So world **aggregate demand fell** and produced the worst recession since the Second World War.

The effects for oil consuming countries are shown in Figure 7.15 (overleaf). The withdrawals schedule shifts up (W_1 to W_2) as the import bill rises because of the oil price increases: this lowers national income. The effect of this in other countries **depressed world trade** and exports tended to fall, shifting the injections schedule downwards (J_1 to J_2). The effect on employment might have been offset had governments introduced reflationary policies but in fact most of them **deflated** demand further, shifting the injections schedule down from J_2 to J_3.

There are two reason why such an apparently perverse policy was pursued. The **balance of payments position** had deteriorated following the oil price rise and the conventional response to this type of problem was to reduce spending. The state of the **balance of payments** is influenced by the level of income in the economy so deficits can be reduced by deflation. However, the success of this remedy for any one country depends on the policies of other countries. It is impossible for *all* countries to improve their balance of payments

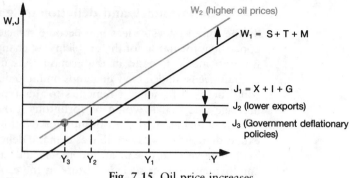

Fig. 7.15 Oil price increases

simultaneously—the counterpart of the OPEC surpluses was deficits for oil consumers. In these circumstances deflation was largely a matter of trying to pass the deficit on to another oil consumer; the only way in which *all* oil consumers could have avoided a worsening of their balance of payments position was to reduce the demand for oil to such a level that OPEC never acquired increased revenues; but that would have meant an unthinkable fall in industrial production.

The second reason for demand reducing policies was **inflation**. The OPEC oil price increases were inflationary as well as deflationary. This significant upward boost to prices occurred at a time when most countries were already concerned about rising **inflation**. The conventional policy response to inflation is to reduce demand. Government policy as a whole generally aggravated the unemployment produced by the OPEC price rises.

This last section has indicated that Keynesian macro-policy to manage demand has to take account of problems other than unemployment. This is a more difficult matter than may have been implied earlier in the chapter. The next chapter explores some of these difficulties. In the 1970s support for the Keynesian view was starting to crumble and concern over **inflation** led to **monetarism** and reawakened the debate of the 1930s.

8 Extension to the Keynesian model

8.1 Introduction

This chapter extends the basic **Keynesian macro-model** introduced in Chapter 7. We take a closer look at **consumption** and **investment** spending. The introduction of **time** allows some **simple dynamic models** to be developed so that we can start to understand the fluctuations in an economy's output. An important feature of Keynesian demand management policy was the use of **macroeconomic forecasts** and while support for Keynesian policy waned in the late 1970s, interest in **macro-forecasting** did not and today a wide range of forecasts are published. The basis for these forecasts, which are increasingly used by businesses, is explained in section 8.5. We conclude by extending the discussion of **Keynesian stabilization policy** begun in the previous chapter.

This chapter will:

- give you information on consumer expenditure in the UK
- introduce you to theories of consumption
- consider the main factors affecting investment spending
- explain the accelerator theory of investment
- provide an introduction to the simple dynamics of income determination including the multiplier–accelerator model
- explain how macroeconomic forecasts are made
- examine the interrelationship of policy objectives with illustrations from the UK
- explain some of the problems of conducting a Keynesian macro-policy

8.1.1 Examination guide

There is a wide variation between courses over the requirements concerning the material covered in this chapter. While most courses require a basic understanding of the main features of **consumer expenditure** and **investment**, many may not expect students to consider the theoretical development (e.g. **permanent income hypothesis** and **accelerator theory**) surveyed in this chapter. You should be guided by the syllabus and your tutor on the depth of treatment. Similarly most courses will consider the problems of **macroeconomic policy** but may not cover the topic of **macroeconomic forecasting**.

Given this diversity it is difficult to give specific guidance. However, a general point which will apply to most courses can be made. Many answers are improved by relating theory to the UK economy; but avoid taking an entirely descriptive approach. Most introductory courses involve applying theory to economic problems but the approach in answers should be analytical rather than descriptive.

8.2 Consumption

8.2.1 A closer look at consumption

8.2.1.1 Consumption as a function of disposable income

In the last chapter we suggested that consumer spending was related to income. As a broad generalization this is correct, however, even in an introductory course we need to look a little more closely at the concepts of **consumption** and **income**.

The income measure that is most relevant to households in determining their consumer spending is their **disposable income**, i.e. income after income tax and national insurance contributions have been paid. As we normally consider the relationship in real terms (i.e. at constant prices, by removing the effects of inflation) it is **real personal disposable income (RPDI)** that is the appropriate measure. Figure 8.1 (overleaf) shows that there is a close relationship between **annual consumer expenditure** and **RPDI** for the period 1950–86. The line that best fits those observations has an equation

$C = 11\,536 + 0.8RPDI$

which suggests that over the period as a whole 0.8 of the increase in RPDI was spend on consumer goods. The close fits is not surprising because consumption is a major component of aggregate demand and affects output and incomes. Nevertheless, no one seriously disputes that **disposable income** is an important influence on consumer spending, though the relationship is likely to be more complex than we have so far recognized. Both the notions of consumption and income and the way they are measured warrant further examination.

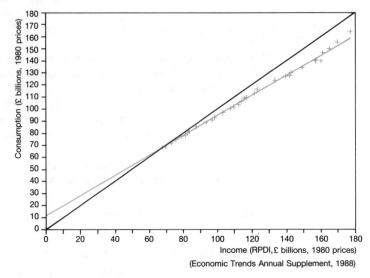

Fig. 8.1 Consumption function (1950–86; $C = 11\,536 + 0.8RPDI$, £1980)

8.2.1.2 Durable and non-durable consumption

A major part of consumer spending is directed at **goods** and **services** which are enjoyed or consumed at the time of purchase or soon afterwards. However, about 10–12 per cent of consumer spending in the UK is on **durable goods** such as cars, electric goods and furniture which last for several years; so the consumption of the benefits or services from these goods does not closely correspond to recorded expenditure. For example, the family that replaces its TV every five years does not 'consume' all the benefits of a TV in the first year of purchase but enjoys them in the intervening years as well. In this sense, published data on consumer durable expenditure, which records purchases, is not necessarily an accurate measure of the consumption of these goods.

The relationship between income and purchase of durables is likely to be different from that affecting expenditure on **consumer non-durables**. Many **durable items** such as cars and suites of furniture involve the outlay of large sums of money which is often financed by **credit**; the **cost** and **availability** of **credit** are therefore influential factors in determining spending. Households' timing of the replacement of durable goods is much more flexible than their purchase of food or electricity. For these reasons **durable goods expenditure** is much more volatile than that of consumption as a whole (see Figure 8.2).

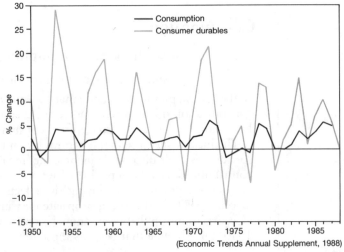

Fig. 8.2 Consumer expenditure (1950–87, annual percentage change)

8.2.1.3 Savings ratio

A topic that has attracted considerable interest since the mid-1970s, and which is related to the consumption function, is the **savings ratio**. This is the ratio of personal savings to real personal disposable income. It is an *ex post* (i.e. measured or realized) concept where **personal savings** are the difference between measured income and measured consumption. Its rise in the mid-1970s was largely unexpected and led to an overprediction of consumer expenditure. It became generally accepted that the behaviour of the **savings ratio** is associated with the **inflation rate**; a decline in the latter–as in the early 1980s–has usually caused a fall in the savings ratio. The most favoured explanation for this is the erosion by **inflation** of the real value of liquid financial assets fixed in money terms. When the **inflation rate** rises the erosion effect increases and households increase savings (reduce consumption) in relation to income in order to maintain the real value of their assets. The reverse happens when inflation falls (see Figure 8.3).

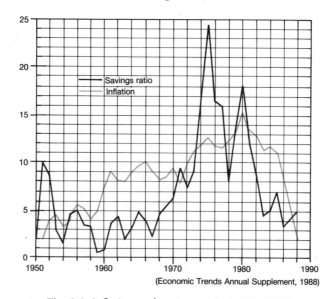

(Economic Trends Annual Supplement, 1988)

Fig. 8.3 Inflation and savings ratio (1950–1986)

So **consumer expenditure** is affected by the inflation rate as well as by income and, in the case of durables, by the rate of interest and the availability of credit. The relationship between consumption and disposable income is more complex than was indicated earlier. We now turn to the theoretical arguments underlying this relationship.

8.2.2 Theories of the consumption function

8.2.2.1 Absolute and relative income hypotheses

So far we have suggested that consumer expenditure is related to currently received income. Even if we were to introduce a **lag** to allow consumers time to adjust to a new income level, this would still suggest that past income levels and **expected future income** were not relevant in determining behaviour. This does not seem very plausible and a number of post-war theoretical developments have sought to analyse the relationship between income and expenditure more precisely. One early development was the suggestion that it is not **absolute income**–the current level of income viewed in isolation– but **relative income** (current income related to some other income level) that is important in determining consumer spending. The term **relative income** is used in two senses.

Current income is related to past peaks in income: the effects of decreases and increases in income are not regarded as symmetrical. Households may spend a certain proportion of income on consumption, say 0.8, as incomes increase over time; but if incomes were to decline they would try to maintain the level of expenditure associated with the previous peak and so the proportion spent might rise temporarily while incomes were depressed. When recovery occurred and income returned to the previous level the earlier proportion would be restored.

The second interpretation of **relative income** concerns the effect of **distribution** of income on consumer spending patterns. The evidence on consumer spending suggests that the average and marginal propensity to consume of the better off is lower than that of the poor. If absolute income determined behaviour then we might expect the poor to adopt the spending patterns of the rich, as incomes increased over time. This does not seem to be the case, so it is suggested that it is people's **relative** income position that is important. So, to take the simplest illustration, if everyone's income doubled, *ceteris paribus* the **proportion of income** spent by different groups would not change.

8.2.2.2 Life-cycle and permanent income hypothesis

A different approach that has commanded widespread support is the suggestion that consumption is determined by **expected lifetime income**. This shifts the attention from actual or absolute income to what Milton Friedman has called **permanent income**. The idea can be simply illustrated by considering the consumption–income relationship of monthly salary earners. Although income is received on only 12 days in the year, consumption will not be confined to pay days. Consumer expenditure will occur on most days in the month, determined by the income that individuals **expect to receive**.

The time horizon of consumers goes far beyond deciding today's consumption on the basis of today's income. But how far does that horizon extend? In principle over a **lifetime**, which is the emphasis of a similar approach, the **life-cycle hypothesis**, put forward by Professor Modigliani and others. Individuals survey their **expected lifetime earnings**, which for most of us will have a pattern similar to the one illustrated in Figure 8.4, and form an idea of **normal** or **permanent income**.

According to the hypothesis we are discussing, it is this type of income that determines consumer spending. This does not necessarily mean that **consumer expenditure** will be the same as **permanent income** because households may choose to spend more at various stages of their lives. However, suppose this is what households decide to do. In the early years, when income is relatively low (period *A* on the graph) it would be necessary to borrow against future income, whereas in period *B* debts could be repaid and assets acquired which could be used later to supplement the relatively low retirement income in period *C*. This illustration also shows that calculating **permanent income** is

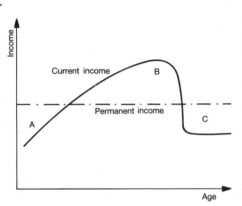

Fig. 8.4 Illustration of permanent and current income

not simply a matter of averaging the actual income received over a lifetime, but involves **discounting future income** using a rate of interest (see section 8.3.1 for an explanation of discounting).

The **permanent income/life-cycle hypotheses** provide some important insights into consumer behaviour. However, our simplified picture needs some modification to take account of the practical difficulties confronting households. First, there are limitations on the ability to borrow against future earnings. Most students discover that their expected (hoped for) high incomes after graduation are not fully reflected in the overdraft facilities available to them. This may be related to a second difficulty: **uncertainty of future income**. While the general shape of the income curve in Figure 8.4 may be accepted, the steepness of slope and position of the curve may be the subject of much uncertainty. Both of these are likely to mean that consumption is more closely related to current income than the hypotheses suggest—in the first case because borrowing power is limited and in the second because, in the absence of firm information on the future, current or recently received income heavily influence expectations.

8.2.3 Consumption function in the UK

In the large macroeconomic models of the UK it is common to distinguish between consumption of non-durables and durables. These equations reflect the **permanent income/life-cycle hypotheses** outlined above and include the **inflation rate** which, when it rises, depresses consumption because the **savings ratio** increases. Durable consumption equations have additional variables, such as the interest rate, and credit variables (e.g. bank lending, HP debt). Most macro consumption functions failed to fully predict the strength of the consumer boom of 1986 to 1988. Subsequent work has given emphasis to consumer credit. Some economists stress the influence of demographic factors: it is suggested that the decline in the proportion of 45 to 65 year olds, typically net savers (area B on Figure 8.4), contributed to the fall in the savings ratio.

We ought finally to consider the effect of what we have discussed on economic policy.

An important implication of the permanent income/life-cycle hypotheses is that the impact of **fiscal policy** is less than our simple view of the consumption function would suggest. This is because consumption is affected only if permanent income changes; for example, tax cuts which increase current disposable income only raise consumer expenditure to the extent that they lead households to revise their estimates of permanent income.

To Keynesians, the essential message of Keynes's consumption function is not lost. Although subsequent thinking has stressed notions other than absolute income, uncertainty about future income and limited borrowing power means that currently received income is an important influence on consumer spending and that recession does constrain the spending powers of the unemployed which in turn has a **multiplier effect**. However both **relative** and **permanent income theories** suggest that the fall in consumption in recessions will be less than the absolute income hypothesis would predict.

We turn now to a more complex and less predictable item of aggregate demand: **investment**.

8.3 Investment

Investment is expenditure on man-made aids to production such as plant, machinery, dwellings and infrastructure such as roads. **Investment** is a **flow concept** which measures the spending on these items over a period of time (e.g. a year); it should not be confused with the **capital stock**, which is the value of the stock of these goods, and reflects the **investment spending of many periods. Investment** resists simple attempts to explain it. In part this is because of the diversity of spending that it covers. We need to distinguish between **private** and **public sector expenditure** because their objectives are not necessarily the same. Around a fifth of all investment is in dwellings and the factors affecting this are likely to be different from those determining expenditure on plant or machinery. Similarly, **replacement investment** may be dominated by different influences and pressures from those associated with expanding output.

A profile of some of the features of **investment spending** in the UK is given in Table 8.1.

Table 8.1 Investment in the UK 1980–87 (£ billion in 1980 prices, averages 1980–87; % of total investment in brackets) (*Economic Trends Annual Supplement, 1988*)

Investment by sector		
Private	31.1	(74)
General government	5.0	(12)
Public corporations	6.0	(14)
Investment by asset		
Dwellings	8.1	(19)
of which		
private sector	6.0 (14)	
public sector	2.1 (5)	
Other new building	14.6	(35)
Vehicles, ships and aircraft	4.1	(10)
Plant and machinery	15.2	(36)

Gross fixed investment as percentage of GDP 20

In addition to total fixed investment (**gross domestic fixed capital formation**), which is a fifth of Gross Domestic Product, there is investment in stocks or inventories. **Stockbuilding** may be negative (running down stocks) as well as positive (accumulation). It is not a particularly large item–on average 3 per cent of fixed investment and just over 0.5 per cent of GDP. However, it is a volatile item and has varied from −£2.8 billion, in 1980 (nearly 1.5 per cent of GDP) to +£0.6 billion in 1985 (0.3 per cent of GDP).

8.3.1 Theories of investment

Several theories attempt to explain investment but most of them are in some way related to the two approaches we consider below.

8.3.1.1 Neoclassical marginalist theory

One longstanding approach which we referred to in the last chapter, is the view that **investment** is inversely related to **interest rates**. We can enlarge on this by considering the investment decisions of firms. We assume they wish to maximize their profits, so they will undertake investment projects that offer a return in excess of costs. The calculation is not entirely straightforward because the outlay on the investment will precede the returns, which are likely to be spread over a number of years. This means that those returns have to be forecast and these forecasts are likely to be very sensitive to **expectations**. We need to recognize that a pound received next year is worth less than a pound received today–the difference is accounted for by the rate of interest.

To illustrate this consider what a sum of money (P_0) we have today would be worth in a year's time. This is shown below, where i is the rate of interest and in the numerical example equals 10 per cent.

$$P_1 = P_0 (1+i) \text{ e.g. } £110 = £100 (1+0.1)$$

After two years the same sum is worth:

$$P_2 = P_1 (1+i) = P_0 (1+i)^2 \text{ e.g. } £121 = £100 (1+0.1)^2$$

We can reverse the way of looking at this by considering what a sum of money received in two years time would be worth today. This is represented by the following expression:

$$P_0 = \frac{P_n}{(1+i)^n}$$

where $n = 2$.

So, when interest rates are 10 per cent, £121 received in the two years time would be worth £100 today.

We can now use this approach to evaluate an investment project. We can calculate the **present value** (**PV**) of an expected flow of **net returns** (**R**)–i.e. revenue less operating costs–on an investment project in the following way:

$$PV = \frac{R_1}{(1+i)} + \frac{R_2}{(1+i)^2} + \frac{R_3}{(1+i)^3} \cdots + \frac{R_n}{(1+i)^n}$$

We can then compare the **present value** (**PV**) of these returns with the **cost** of the machine (C) and if $PV > C$ then the project is profitable.

A similar approach is to calculate the rate of return (often known as the **internal rate of return** (**IRR**)) that would be necessary to discount expected net returns back to the cost price of the machine:

$$C = \frac{R_1}{(1+r)} + \frac{R_2}{(1+r)^2} + \frac{R_3}{(1+r)^3} \cdots + \frac{R_n}{(1+r)^n}$$

where $r = $ IRR.

In this case investment would be profitable if $r > i$.

These calculations are easily performed on a calculator or a computer; but providing reliable data is more difficult. In practice there may be some uncertainty over the cost of the investment project and there will be doubts about future interest rates. But the greatest problems surround the estimates of **the rate of return** because this involves projections of future revenues and costs associated with the investment. These estimates will be based on forecasts of demand and assumptions concerning the performance of the machinery, labour, fuel and raw material costs. The estimated PV or IRR will therefore have **margins** attached to them to take account of this uncertainty.

We can now explain downward sloping investment schedules (of the type seen in Figure 7.2) in two stages. First, firms have a range of possible investment projects which could be ranked in terms of their profitability: a larger capital stock will be associated with a lower IRR or **marginal efficiency of capital**, as it is often called. So a lower interest rate will increase the amount of capital firms want because this will raise PV and means that the interest rate is below the present IRR. The second stage is the investment expenditure necessary to raise the capital stock to the desired level. The attempt by all firms to do this is likely to encounter supply constraints in the capital goods industry which will tend to push up the prices of plant and machinery. This will affect the amount of investment that takes place (and the slope of the schedule) and hence the time it takes to achieve the desired new capital stock.

This approach suggests that a lower interest rate is likely to lead to higher investment i.e. a move down the schedule. However, as our earlier discussion indicated, the calculations on the most profitable capital stock depends upon expected profits and costs. This makes **investment** highly susceptible to **changes in expectations** and these will shift the schedule to the right (more optimistic) or to the left (less optimistic expectations). Indeed for around thirty years after the war the influence of interest rates on investment was generally felt to be small; but there has been a shift in opinion recently and greater emphasis has been put on interest rates. One factor that is likely to influence expectations is the growth in output and this is a determinant that is stressed by the **accelerator theory**.

8.3.1.2 The accelerator

The **simple** (sometimes called **naive**) **accelerator** is easily explained. Suppose the capital stock (K) is related to output (Y) in the following way:

$$K = vY$$

where v is the capital–output ratio; it then follows if v is assumed fixed that changes in the capital stock are related to changes in output:

$$\Delta K = v \, \Delta Y$$

As a change in the capital stock is net investment (In) then, using time subscripts, we can write the relationship as follows:

$$In_t = v(Y_t - Y_{t-1})$$

so **investment** is a function of changes in output.

The **accelerator** has some interesting properties that are best illustrated numerically. In our example we assume that the actual capital stock is always equal to the desired capital stock. In Table 8.2 we show the response of investment to fluctuations in income.

Table 8.2 Relationship of investment to income

Year	Output (Y)	Capital stock (K)	Change in output (ΔY)	Net (In)	Replacement (R)	Gross (Ig)
1	100	300	0	0	30	30
2	100	300	0	0	30	30
3	110	330	10	30	30	60
4	120	360	10	30	30	60
5	125	375	5	15	30	45
6	125	375	0	30	30	30
7	115	345	−10	−30	30	0
8	105	315	−10	−30	30	0
9	100	300	−5	−15	30	15
10	100	300	0	0	30	30

Capital output ratio (v) = 3
Replacement = 30 per annum

The capital–output ratio is assumed to be 3, so the desired capital stock in years 1 and 2 will be 300. The **accelerator** principle explains only **net investment** (changes in the capital stock); but each year a certain amount of capital will wear out and require replacing. In our illustration we have assumed this figure to be 30 a year. **Gross investment** is the total of **net** and **replacement investment** and is equal to 30 in years 1 and 2 because there is no wish to increase the capital stock. In year 3 an increase of 10 in output leads to net investment of 30 (given the capital–output ratio of 3). This rise in output (10 per cent) has an **accelerated effect** on investment which increases by 100 per cent. In the following year a further rise of 10 in output is associated with a levelling off in investment.

This arises because investment is a function of **changes** in output; if output changes by a constant amount then investment remains constant. For investment to increase a **greater change** in output is necessary. This point is vividly illustrated in year 5. Although output is still rising, investment starts to decline because the **change** in output is less than it was: it has declined from +10 (year 4) to +5 (year 5). For the same reason a steady output level of 125 in year 6 is associated with a further decline in investment.

In years 7 to 9 the decline in output requires a reduction in the capital stock—that is, negative net investment. This is achieved in years 7 and 8 by not replacing worn out machinery. Notice that investment rises in year 9 despite the fall in output. Because output declines by a smaller amount the desired fall in the capital stock is less and, given the replacement demand, gross investment rises from 0 to 15. A similar explanation can be given for year 10 when a stationary output level is associated with a further rise in investment.

Our illustration shows an important feature of the **accelerator theory**: fluctuations in investment are greater than those of income (hence the term **accelerator**). This is in accord with our experience of the cyclical behaviour of the capital goods industry and the accelerator is one of the leading suggested explanations. Figure 8.5 shows the relationship between changes in output (lagged by one year) and investment in manufacturing industry. This gives some support to the simple accelerator, though the relationship is not a close one. This is not too surprising because the basic accelerator is rather crude.

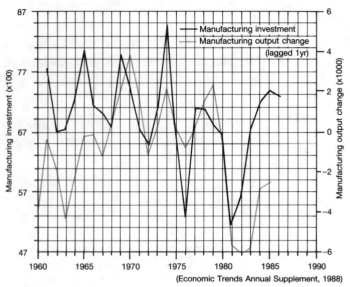

Fig. 8.5 Manufacturing investment and output change
(change in manufacturing output lagged one year)

(Economic Trends Annual Supplement, 1988)

A number of criticisms can be made of the **simple accelerator.**

1 Capacity utilization—the theory implies that firms are working at **full capacity.** If firms have spare capacity then output may be raised without increasing the capital stock. The notion of **full capacity** is not necessarily rigid in practice, so even at high utilization levels firms may prefer to squeeze out some extra output through overtime rather than by raising investment. This would apply particularly if increase demand was expected to be temporary.

2 Expectations—firms will adjust their capital stock to the level of **expected output.** When a change in output is expected to be short-lived firms will let order books lengthen or work existing capacity more fully (see 1). Firms may form their **expectations adaptively** (i.e. adjust their **expectations** in the light of experience), in which case they will respond to recent changes in demand for output (though their approach is likely to be more sophisticated than our simple equation suggests).

3 Variable capital–output ratio—in our illustration the **capital–output ratio** v was assumed **constant.** It will in reality be affected by a number of factors which mean that it is likely to change. For example, interest rates (see previous section), the wage rate and technological changes are likely to cause planned alterations in the **capital output ratio.**

4 Capital goods industry capacity—the **accelerator** relationship we have examined is in effect a demand for capital goods. The **capacity** of the capital goods industry may give rise to **supply constraints.** So there may be lags before the investment takes place.

5 Finance and other supply constraints—in a similar way, investment projects will require **other factors**—e.g. skilled labour—and shortages of these may delay or curtail investment. A major constraint may be the **availability of finance.** We consider this further in the next section.

Our simple accelerator needs to be modified to take account of these criticisms. The result is a **flexible accelerator** which has various lags and adjustments built in which recognize that firms will not necessarily react mechanically to increases in demand and that moves towards a new optimal capital stock level will take time.

8.3.2 The investment function

We have now discovered that **investment** is likely to be affected by a number of factors such as interest rates and changes in output and is heavily influenced by entrepreneurs' expectations. There is one further factor that we have touched upon—**the financing of investment**—which is sufficiently important to warrant further discussion: indeed, separate theories have been proposed with the **finance of investment** at the centre. The basis of most of these is that investment is largely financed from **retained profits**, either through preference or because of limited access to external finance. It is argued that it is the level of profits which determines the volume of investment spending. There is certainly a fairly close correlation between private sector investment and profits (see Figure 8.6) though both, along with several other influences or investment, move in line with the general cycle of business activity so that disentangling cause and effect is not easy.

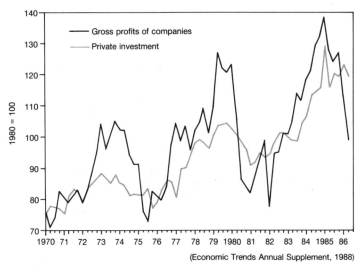

(Economic Trends Annual Supplement, 1988)

Fig. 8.6 Private sector investment and profits (1980–87)

Modelling and **forecasting** investment expenditure is not easy either. If we look at large macro-models of the UK we find not one investment function but several, reflecting the types of investment categories we referred to in section 8.3. Some types of **investment** are treated **exogenously** in recognition of the difficulty in forecasting them or in preference for forecasts based on published plans (e.g. some public sector categories) or investment intentions surveys. The equations for the other categories reflect the relative importance of different factors. **Investment in dwellings** is affected by interest rates, house prices relative to general prices and the flow of funds into building societies. The investment functions for **private sector manufacturing** and other industries tend to involve a **flexible accelerator relationship** (sometimes with a **capacity utilization** variable) and interest rate and cash flow (profits) variables.

8.4 The simple dynamic of income determination

8.4.1 Lags in the income–expenditure model

8.4.1.1 The nature of lags

We introduced time lags into the simple supply and demand model in Chapter 5 to explain the movement of prices. In this section we take a similar approach to the basic macro-model. Our earlier discussion of the income expenditure model was **comparative static**: it compared one equilibrium point with another. The simple **dynamic models** developed here introduce **time** and show the path from one equilibrium to another. We can identify three types of lag.

The **expenditure lag** is the time lag between changes in income and expenditure (see next section) and the **output lag** is the time taken for output to respond to changes in expenditure or demand. There may also be a delay between output being produced and the income it generates being received (e.g. dividend payments); however, we ignore this **income lag** in the discussion below.

8.4.1.2 Expenditure lag and the dynamic multiplier

The simplest illustration of a **dynamic macro-model** introduces a **lag** into the consumption function so this period's consumption is determined by last period's income:

$C_t = f(Y_{t-1})$

Other lags are ignored, so output responds without delay to expenditure changes. The properties of this model are best demonstrated through a numerical example. Table 8.3 (overleaf) shows the effects of an increase in government expenditure of 10 (from 10 to 20) on consumption and income. The original equilibrium level of income in this closed economy model (where $Y = C + I + G$) is 100. Consumption, which is a function of the previous years' income ($C_t = 10 + 0.5Y_{t-1}$) is 60. When government expenditure rises in year 2 output and income increases by the same amount. As income increases by 10 in period 2, this affects consumption in the following period, causing it to rise by 5 to 65, which means that period 3 income is equal to 115. In turn this will affect consumption in the following period and so on. You can follow the example for the remaining periods as it converges on an income of 120. This is the equilibrium income we would expect from our comparative static analysis.

Table 8.3 Expenditure lag

Year	Income (Y)[1]	Consumption (C)[2]	Investment (I)	Government expenditure (G)
0	100.0	60.0	30.0	10.0
1	100.0	60.0	30.0	10.0
2	110.0	60.0	30.0	20.0
3	115.0	65.0	30.0	20.0
4	117.5	67.5	30.0	20.0
5	118.8	68.8	30.0	20.0
6	119.4	69.4	30.0	20.0
7	119.7	69.7	30.0	20.0
8	119.8	69.8	30.0	20.0
9	119.9	69.9	30.0	20.0
10	120.0	70.0	30.0	20.0
11	120.0	70.0	30.0	20.0
12	120.0	70.0	30.0	20.0

[1] $Y = C + I + G$; [2] $C_t = 10 + 0.5\,Y_{t-1}$.

What we are seeing here is the workings of the **multiplier**, as an initial increase in spending (government expenditure) raises incomes by a larger amount. This **dynamic multiplier** shows the path the economy would follow. It is a fairly smooth one, with income increasing by ever diminishing increments, so that most of the rise is achieved after 6 periods. In a quarterly model this would mean that the **multiplier** would take just over a year for the bulk of its effects to be felt.

8.4.1.3 Output lags and inventory adjustments

Another type of lag that is likely to be important is an **output lag**. Firms are not necessarily able or willing to adjust output to changes in demand and expenditure immediately. They will hold **stocks** or **inventories** to act as a **buffer** between demand and output changes. This does not just mean that this period's demand becomes next period's output, because attempts to maintain stocks will have additional effects on output. So an increase in demand which is initially met by running down stocks will then give rise to a subsequent demand on output if firms wish to maintain a constant stock–output ratio. The **accelerator model** discussed earlier would seem a useful starting point to explaining adjustment in inventories. However, other factors such as interest rates, tax treatment of stocks and computerization of stock control will affect the desired stock–output ratio.

8.4.2 The multiplier–accelerator model and business cycles

A feature of all market economies is the tendency for periods of boom to be followed by recession **business cycles**. Evidence of this runs through most macroeconomic data series, as we will see in section 8.6. If we combine the properties of the **accelerator** and the **dynamic multiplier** discussed earlier we can consider one of the main explanations of cyclical movements. The **basic multiplier–accelerator model** is outlined in Figure 8.7 and Table 8.4. The accelerator is slightly different from the one we considered earlier. An extra lag has been introduced and the autonomous investment of 30 reflects replacement and other non-accelerator influences. The numerical illustration shows the effect of an increase in government spending of 10 on the original equilibrium of 100. The values of the *MPC* (of 0.5) and *v*, the capital–output ratio (1.0), have been chosen for simplicity rather than realism, so it should be quite easy to follow.

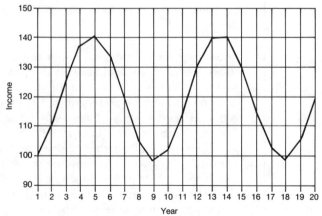

Fig. 8.7 Multiplier–accelerator model $(C_t = 10 + 0.5\,Y_{t-1};\ I_t = 30 + 1.0(Y_{t-1} - Y_{t-2}))$

Table 8.4 Basic multiplier–accelerator model

Year	Income (Y)	Consumption (C)[1]	Change in income (ΔY)	Investment (I)[2]	Government expenditure (G)
0	100.0	60.0	0.0	30.0	10.0
1	100.0	60.0	0.0	30.0	10.0
2	110.0	60.0	10.0	30.0	20.0
3	125.0	65.0	15.0	40.0	20.0
4	137.5	72.5	12.5	45.0	20.0
5	141.3	78.8	3.8	42.5	20.0
6	134.4	80.6	−6.9	33.8	20.0
7	120.3	77.2	−14.1	23.1	20.0
8	106.1	70.2	−14.2	15.9	20.0
9	98.8	63.0	−7.3	15.8	20.0
10	102.1	59.4	3.3	22.7	20.0
11	114.4	61.1	12.2	33.3	20.0
12	129.4	67.2	15.0	42.2	20.0
13	139.8	74.7	10.3	45.0	20.0
14	140.2	79.9	0.4	40.3	20.0
15	130.5	80.1	−9.7	30.4	20.0
16	115.6	75.3	−14.9	20.3	20.0
17	102.9	67.8	−12.7	15.1	20.0
18	98.7	61.4	−4.2	17.3	20.0
19	105.2	59.3	6.5	25.8	20.0
20	119.1	62.6	13.9	36.5	20.0
21	133.4	69.5	14.4	43.9	20.0
22	141.1	76.7	7.7	44.4	20.0
23	138.2	80.5	−2.9	37.7	20.0
24	126.2	79.1	−12.0	27.1	20.0
25	111.1	73.1	−15.1	18.0	20.0
26	100.5	65.6	−10.6	14.9	20.0
27	99.6	60.2	−0.9	19.4	20.0

[1] $C_t = 10 + 0.5\,Y_{t-1};$ [2] $I_t = 30 + 1.0(Y_{t-1} - Y_{t-2}).$

You can see that the effect of the increase in government spending is more dramatic than in the case of the dynamic multiplier. Instead of moving towards an equilibrium of 120, income fluctuates around that level. The reason for this can be seen if we examine the first few periods of the example. The increase in government expenditure raises national income and produces **multiplier effects** but the inclusion of the **accelerator** means that this income increase induces extra investment spending. So the income level of 120 is **overshot**. Why should income not rise indefinitely? In our example, the increase in income slows down so that in period 4 it rises by only 12.5 compared with 15 in the previous period. This causes a fall in investment in the following period which in turn slows the growth of the economy further, so that by period 6 the boom is over and a decline in income is under way. The **accelerator** magnifies this downturn, just as it gave an extra boost to the multiplier effect in earlier periods; but it also provides the reason for the recovery in investment spending which finally brings the recession to an end.

In this particular example the **cycles** generated will continue indefinitely; but this is only one possible outcome of a model of this type. If **cycles** are produced they may be **dampened** (i.e. shrink and converge on a new equilibrium) or **explosive** (i.e. increase in size). It is also possible that there may be no cycles at all–income could carry on increasing or it could gently move towards an equilibrium (as in our example in Table 8.3). The outcome is determined by the relative size of the *MPC* and *v* (capital–output ratio). The lower the value of *v* the smaller will be the accelerator effects on investment and this will reduce the impact on income. In the extreme case where $v = 0$ we obtain the result shown in Table 8.3. The size of *MPC* also influences the outcome. The larger the *MPC* the greater the **multiplier effect** which will in turn stimulate the **accelerator effect**. In our illustration, if either *v* or *MPC* were increased, the cycles would become explosive and if either were reduced, the fluctuations would become dampened.

The **multiplier–accelerator** provides an explanation of cyclical behaviour. In the form we have described it is rather crude; a more advanced treatment would involve incorporating the modifications to the consumption function and the accelerator we discussed earlier in the chapter. There are other aspects of **cyclical behaviour** (e.g. interest rates and prices) that also need to be considered.

There are other possible accounts of the **business cycle**–monetarists, for example, would tend to explain it in terms of the effects of the government's **monetary policy**. It has also been suggested that there is a **political business cycle** which is the result of governments managing the economy so that they will get re-elected. Economies are expanded in the run up to an election and tougher deflationary action to deal with problems like inflation and the balance of payments is put off until after the election. These theories explain cycles of just a few years; but recently there has been a reawakening of interest in **long-run cycles** which may last for some fifty years from peak to peak. This has been prompted by the slow down in growth in the last decade which has come after 25 years of rapid expansion after the Second World War. Various explanations have been put forward, of which **Schumpeter's** is the best known. He suggested that major **innovations** (e.g. steam, internal combustion engine) give rise to expansionary waves of activity which are followed by periods of low profits and recession as these opportunities are exploited.

8.5 Macroeconomic forecasting

One of the major applications of macroeconomics is the construction of large models to produce **forecasts** of the main macro-variables, such as GDP, consumption, investment, unemployment and inflation. We will now consider the approach and accuracy of such models.

8.5.1 The approach to macroeconomic forecasts

8.5.1.1 A simple illustration

Macroeconomic forecasting is best understood through a simple illustration. The model here is like the one we encountered in the last chapter, except that consumption (C) is a function of disposable income ($Y_d = Y - T$) and tax revenue (T) depends upon income (Y) and the tax rate (t). Imports (M) are a function of income. Government expenditure (G), investment (I) and exports (X) are exogenous.

$$Y = C + I + G + X - M$$

$$C = a + bY_d$$

$$T = tY$$

$$M = mY$$

To use this model for forecasting purposes we need to estimate the values of a, b and m. This is done by using **past data** and **statistical techniques** to estimate the **coefficients**. We obtained the regression equation $C = 11\,536 + 0.8\,Y$ at the beginning of the chapter simply by seeing what produced the best straight line fit for observations of consumption and disposable income (RPDI). In practice the estimation stage is far from straightforward and calls for much skill in considering the specification of the model in the light of the evidence and in examining the structure of time lags. Once estimated, the model can be used for forecasting.

8.5.1.2 Using the forecasting model

Before a forecast can be generated three further stages are involved. We first need to make **assumptions** about government policy. In our example this involves assumptions about government expenditure and tax rates (t). We can base assumptions about government expenditure on announced spending plans, though we may adjust these if government spending has systematically departed from plans e.g. if there has been persistent overspending. The normal practice of forecasters is to assume unchanged policies, which always used to be interpreted as no change in tax rates. However, in the mid-1980s, when the government's declared policy was to aim for tax cuts, some reduction in the basic rate was often assumed.

The second step is to provide **values** for the other **exogenous variables**, in our case investment and exports. Variables may be exogenous because they are difficult or expensive to model and it may consequently be more reliable to use the results of an investment intentions survey to provide a figure for investment spending. One of the main determinants of exports is the growth in world trade and in this case a good deal of expensive modelling of the world economy may be avoided by making an assumption based on other (e.g. OECD) published forecasts.

Assumptions may also have to be made about other events e.g. the likelihood of a Middle East war, major strikes, the outcome of US or other elections. Once decisions have been made a forecast can be generated by solving the model. In our example this is fairly straightforward because we can solve the model and provide a single equation solution for national income. In large macro-models with more complicated equations such an approach is not possible and computers are needed to solve the model, through an iterative process, and produce values for income and consumption, etc.

The description so far suggests that the process is rather mechanical. In reality there is art as well as science in forecasting and the **judgement** of the forecasters plays an important role. This can be crucial when events, like the miners' strike in 1984, the hike in oil prices, the abolition of investment allowances and the imposition of an incomes policy make reliance on model equations unreasonable. In such cases the forecasters' judgement will override the values derived from the equations. There is another more general application of judgement that is perhaps less obvious. The estimated equations may not fit the data exactly; for example, the consumption equation ought to be

$$C = a + bY + u$$

where u is the **error term** or **residual**. **Errors** should be **random**, but sometimes forecasting equations develop **systematic patterns** in the residuals so that they consistently over- or under-predict. Our estimated consumption function performs very badly, consistently overpredicting for the period 1973–82 and then underpredicting for the following period. We know from our discussion of the permanent income hypothesis and the impact of inflation on the savings ratio that we could **respecify** the equation and improve its performance; but this remedy may not be open to us. We may not be sure how to **respecify** the equation or it may be too expensive to do so. In this case it is sensible to take account of the systematic over- or under-prediction and make **adjustments**. This process of constant or residual adjustment may be mechanical (e.g. taking an average of the errors) or it may rely more heavily on the judgement of the forecasters.

Before the final forecast is published several computer runs may be necessary to satisfy the forecasters that a consistent and plausible result has been obtained. A summary of the stages we have discussed is shown below.

1 Model specification

2 Estimation

3 Assumptions–policy
          –exogenous variables
          –other events (e.g. strikes, wars)

4 Model solution/Residual adjustments/Judgement

5 Forecast

8.5.1.3 Sources of error

Given all the difficulties and uncertainties it is not surprising that forecasts are not entirely accurate. The reasons for errors can be classified as follows.

1 **Model error**–a **poorly specified** or **wrongly estimated** model will produce errors even if all the other information is correct.

2 **Exogenous variable error**–if the estimates of the **exogenous variables** were incorrect then forecast errors would result.

3 **Unforeseen events**–there are some events that economists cannot predict (e.g. wars and the weather). Economists should not be blamed for the inability of political scientists and metereologists to make accurate forecasts, so these occurrences can be regarded as **unforeseen events**.

4 **Data revision**–in large macroeconomic models with many time lags published data on variables like GNP or consumption will be used. However, most of these data will be subsequently **revised**. In the meantime, they may have been partly responsible for causing errors in forecasting.

5 **Judgemental errors**–as the forecasters' **judgement** is an important element in the forecasting process, they may exercise this incorrectly and produce inaccurate forecasts.

8.5.2 Macroeconomic forecasting in the UK

8.5.2.1 The Treasury and other models

With the use of **Keynesian demand management policies** after the war it became important to know the direction the economy was taking so that the appropriate adjustments to aggregate demand could be made. For about twenty-five years the models used for **macroeconomic forecasting** were small and relied heavily on judgement. By 1970 two factors had stimulated the development of more sophisticated models: the availability of relatively **cheap** and **reliable computers** and sufficient **post-war macro-data** to estimate equations.

Forecasting has not been confined to the **Treasury**. In 1959 the **National Institute for Economic and Social Research** was set up, partly with Treasury money, and has since then produced regular forecasts. Another major forecaster, the **London Business School**, started publishing forecasts in the mid-1960s. In more recent years there has been a considerable growth in the production and use of these forecasting models. They are an important aid to business planning, providing forecasts of GDP, its major components and wage and price inflation.

The **Treasury model** is currently the largest of the major macro-models. It has over 700 equations and 1275 variables. Despite this, it is still largely based on the type of income–expenditure model we discussed earlier. The large number of variables in this and other forecasting models is a result of the high degree of **disaggregation** that has been developed.

8.5.2.2 Accuracy of forecasts

It is not an entirely straightforward matter to assess the **accuracy of forecasts**. We may be as interested in advanced knowledge of turning points in the **business cycle** as we are in year by year changes; or we may judge forecasts that are capable of avoiding very large errors to be more successful than those that do not, even if the latter make fewer mistakes. We may be interested in the source of the error and judge forecasts less favourably when inaccuracy is the result of model error than when it is due to data revisions or unforeseen events such as wars. It is important to know whether forecasters' judgemental adjustments improve performance or whether models would have been better left alone.

We do not always get clear unequivocal answers. Models sometimes perform well on one criterion for certain types of variables and yet do not do so at different periods or for different variables. There does not seem to have been a marked improvement in accuracy over the last 15 years, despite much intellectual effort and greater model sophistication. Yet again it is difficult to assess whether this is a mark of success or failure because this period has been one of major oil price shocks, record post-war inflation rates and great variability in most economic indicators. Table 8.5 shows the average absolute errors (ignoring signs, so that negative errors do not cancel out positive errors) of the Treasury and London Business School forecasts of selected variables.

Table 8.5 Forecasting errors
(average absolute error, percentage points)

Forecasts made in the first quarter

	Treasury	LBS
Gross Domestic Product	1	0.8
Consumer expenditure	1	0.9
Fixed investment	2.5	2.0
Exports	2.5	1.9
Imports	0.75	3.0
Inflation	1	1.0

(*Financial Statement and Budget Report*, March 1988;
LBS, *Economic Outlook*, February 1988)

8.6 Keynesian stabilization policy

We conclude this chapter by considering some general problems of **Keynesian demand management**. In the last chapter we suggested that the Keynesian solution for unemployment was for the government to raise aggregate demand by increasing expenditure or reducing taxes. This is not so simple a remedy in practice when other factors such as **inflation** and the **balance of payments** have to be taken into account and when this type of policy involves **fine tuning** a level of **aggregate demand** which is fluctuating because the cyclical movement of the economy.

8.6.1 Conflicting objectives

8.6.1.1 The interrelationship of policy objectives

It is generally considered that governments have four main macroeconomic objectives of policy:

- full employment
- price stability or low inflation
- sustainable balance of payments position
- rapid economic growth

Problems arise when these objectives conflict with one another. We will now consider briefly the consequences of raising aggregate demand to reduce unemployment.

1 Full employment and inflation–in the *General Theory*, Keynes was largely concerned with suggesting how unemployment might arise and how it might be cured. However, it was recognized that reducing unemployment could give rise to other difficulties, principally inflation. This interrelationship was captured in the **Phillips curve** (see Chapter 2). Although there has been a considerable controversy over the nature of the Phillips curve, it is probably fair to say that most economists (and all governments) accept the view that, at least beyond a certain point when unemployment is low, raising aggregate demand will tend to exacerbate the problems of **inflation**.

2 Balance of payments constraint? The **balance of payments** is likely to deteriorate as unemployment is reduced. Two factors can cause this: first, if the exchange rate is fixed (or relatively fixed) the higher inflation rate, *ceteris paribus*, will make a country's goods less competitive. Second, higher national income and spending will increase the volume of imports. At some point a balance of payments deficit may act as a constraint on the growth of demand.

3 Full employment and growth–will the **growth rate** suffer as we approach full employment or will it be raised? It is tempting to suppose the latter because relatively large increases in output will be necessary to move an economy towards full employment; but this is not necessarily so. The growth of an economy depends upon the rate at which productive capacity is increasing, i.e. the extent to which the production possibility curve is shifting out to the right. Whether and how this is affected by the degree of **capacity utilization** (or the proximity to the **production frontier**) is a matter of some debate. Many economists would argue that high levels of activity often produce conditions conducive to **high growth rates**: high investment expenditure results from buoyant profits and demand and a greater willingness by labour to accept new working practices because there are plenty of job opportunities. However, there are those who would argue that high levels of demand encourage **inefficient practices**. It is quite possible to argue that, at least over a range of capacity utilization, the growth of capacity is unaffected. Post-war policy seems to reflect these opposing views. In the early 1960s and 1970s two attempts to break out of the slow UK growth rate were associated with expansionary policies, whereas in the early 1980s, highly deflationary policies were pursued during recession, with the aim of reducing inflation and changing attitudes and practices to provide the conditions for faster growth.

8.6.1.2 Tinbergen's rule

If the major macroeconomic objectives conflict then it will not be sufficient to use one policy instrument, such as fiscal policy, to alter aggregate demand. **Jan Tinbergen,** a Dutch economist, suggested that successful Keynesian type policies required as many policy instruments as there were objectives. This subsequently became known as **Tinbergen's rule**. Table 8.6 gives one possible example:

Table 8.6 An illustration of Tinbergen's rule

Instrument	Objective
Fiscal policy	Full employment
Incomes policy	Inflation
Exchange rate	Balance of payments
Monetary policy	Growth

This implies that setting various policy instruments with particular objectives in mind will allow an economy to perform better in each. However matters are not so straightforward. There is considerable debate over which instrument should be assigned to which objective–this is known as the **assignment problem**. To complicate matters, the effects of one instrument are not confined to one objective: devaluing the exchange rate to improve the balance of payments will almost certainly worsen the inflation rate. We must add to this the uncertainty both of effect and timing of policy instruments.

8.6.2 Fine tuning aggregate demand

Given the cyclical nature of the economy, a Keynesian demand management policy requires boosts to aggregate demand when the economy is depressed and the opposite in a boom. This is known as **fine tuning**. Apart from the difficulty of trying to reconcile conflicting objectives, Keynesian policy makers have to cope with a further set of problems concerning the accurate manipulation of aggregate demand.

8.6.2.1 Fiscal marksmanship

Chancellors need to know exactly the amount by which they should change taxes and expenditure if they are to achieve desired targets. Our knowledge of the economy is unfortunately not sufficient to allow us to give precise answers to questions about the extent and timing of policy changes. Even if accuracy were possible the ability of the government to regulate its own expenditure and tax revenues to achieve recommended levels is in some doubt. This is sometimes referred to as **poor fiscal marksmanship**.

8.6.2.2 The problem of time lags

Time lags in identifying problems and in responding to them produce difficulties for **fine tuning**. In Figure 8.8, suppose the line marked tt is the chosen target level of income and the solid line shows the cyclical movement of national income around that chosen path. A **counter-cyclical policy** requires a flattening out of these fluctuations. At t_1 it has become apparent that the economy is becoming over-heated, but it takes some time for the remedial deflationary policy to be introduced at t_2. It might, for example, be some months to the annual budget. A further **time lag** occurs before the policy changes start to have their main effect on the economy, say at t_3. By this time the nature of the problem has changed as the economy is entering a recession and the effect of policy is to intensify the slump. This suggests that policy may be **destabilizing**, i.e. it may aggravate the fluctuations rather than reduce them.

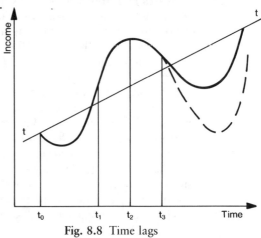

Fig. 8.8 Time lags

8.6.2.3 The need for forecasting

Macro-forecasts are a means of overcoming time lag problems. If governments know in advance of problems that will affect the economy they can introduce policies in time to rectify them. So if in our example a forecast had been made at t_0 then policies would be introduced in sufficient time. The problem with relying on forecasts is that they are never entirely accurate, as our discussion in 8.5.2.2 made clear.

8.6.3 Demand management in the UK

Keynesian demand management policies were followed in the UK after the Second World War until the late 1970s. How successful were they and to what extent were they troubled by the difficulties we outlined above?

The pursuit of these policies broadly coincided with a period of high growth and low unemployment for the UK economy from 1945 to the mid-1970s. It is not clear how much credit Keynesian policies can take for this; many factors, such as the **liberalization of trade** and **underinvestment** during the war and the 1930s, were conducive to high growth rates; but it is probably the case that government commitment to high employment policies had a beneficial effect on **expectations**. Although Keynesian policies did not get all the credit for post-war success they did get some criticism for the deterioration in the economy's performance after 1974. This contributed towards the rejection of Keynesian policy making and its replacement by what was generally known as **monetarism**. (We consider this in more detail in Chapter 11.)

A number of investigations from the mid-1960s onwards assessed the more specific charge that **fine tuning policy** had been **destabilizing**. Attempts were made to assess what path the economy would have followed in the absence of policy changes to see whether governments had made matters worse. The results were not entirely conclusive nor were they free from controversy; nevertheless several of them did suggest that policy *had* been destabilizing–a disturbing finding for advocates of Keynesian policy.

Michael Kennedy of Manchester University compared the actual path of the economy with an estimate of the one the government had planned. **Planned output**, expressed as a proportion of potential output, was derived from budget speeches and other sources before 1968 and from the *Financial Statement and Budget Report* since at that time Treasury forecasts adjusted for budget policy changes were a reasonable representation of the government's target output. Actual and planned (or target) output broadly corresponded. There were large forecasting errors around the early 1960s and again in 1974; but we might generally conclude that the main failures of fine tuning policy were technical. The government largely got what it seemed to want.

A second important conclusion is that the government did not aim for a stable level of output in relation to capacity: it planned **instability**. Why should it do so? There are two main explanations. One is that this is evidence of a planned **political cycle**, with governments deliberately expanding the economy before a general election and dealing with the effects of overexpansion afterwards. There is some evidence that governments tend to become expansionary near an election; but this is not convincing as a complete explanation. A second and more persuasive explanation is that the planned instability is a reflection of the inability to reconcile conflicting objectives. So a 'stop go' policy is pursued as governments expand the economy to reduce unemployment; they are then forced to plan a recession to deal with inflation and balance of payments problems. Two major planned expansions (the Barber boom of the early 1970s and a similar expansion a decade earlier) were associated with attempts to push the UK growth rate on to a higher path.

We return to **Keynesian policy** as an alternative to **monetarism** in Chapter 11; but our conclusion at this stage is that while there are many serious technical difficulties in pursuing a successful fine tuning policy, the evidence does not suggest that it has failed badly: the recession and booms have been more a result of planning than accident. This highlights the unresolved difficulty of trying to reconcile conflicting objectives, particularly full employment and low inflation.

9 Money and banking

9.1 Introduction

In earlier chapters we discussed money flows of income and expenditure but so far we have said nothing explicitly about what **money** is or what determines its **supply**. As you will discover, defining **money** is no straightforward matter. However, as any definition must involve the **liabilities of banks**, we will here examine the nature of the banking system. We conclude the chapter by discussing the government's control of the **money supply**.

The chapter will:

- explain the principles of banking and deposit creation
- explain the functions of money
- consider the problems in defining money
- examine UK definitions of the money supply
- provide an explanation of the role and interrelationship of the main financial institutions in the UK
- examine the means and difficulties of government control of the money supply
- explain the interrelationship of fiscal and monetary policy by examining the relationship between the Public Sector Borrowing Requirement (PSBR) and the growth of the money supply

9.1.1 Examination guide

Most courses will require you to understand the basic principles of **money** and **banking**. Students' explanations of **deposit creation** in essays and examinations often reveal confusion and mistakes, so make sure you really understand this topic. Courses will vary in how much you will be expected to know about financial institutions. Try to avoid being too descriptive and make sure you appreciate the role performed by different institutions and how they fit into the overall picture of money and **capital markets**. How detailed and rigorous your understanding of the **control of the money supply** needs to be will also vary among courses. In section 9.5 we have tried to satisfy varying needs by presenting simple as well as more theoretically demanding explanations. If your course expects you to understand the basis of macroeconomic policy in the last decade you will certainly need to be familiar with the ideas covered in this section.

9.2 Principles of banking

Bank deposits dominate in almost every definition of **money supply** and so in this section we consider the determination of these deposits. We will concentrate on the principles of banking, so our account is rather simplified: for example, it ignores the distinction between **sight** and **time deposits** and restricts the number of banks' assets. This approach will allow you to grasp the main points and we will later (in section 9.4.6) drop the simplifications and present an actual **balance sheet** of UK banks (Table 9.8).

9.2.1 History of banking

One of the simplest ways to understand banking is to consider its development from the days of the goldsmiths when people needed a secure place for their gold coins. If £100 of gold coin were deposited with the goldsmith then his balance sheet would appear as in Table 9.1.

Table 9.1

Liabilities		Assets	
Deposit notes	£100	Gold	£100
	£100		£100

The gold in his vaults is clearly an **asset** to the goldsmith, but this is matched by a **liability**: a promise to repay £100 of gold to the depositor. We will call this promise a **deposit note**. As people gained confidence in goldsmiths it became acceptable to pay for goods by transferring the **deposit note** (i.e. the right to withdraw gold); the modern equivalent is paying by cheque. Deposit notes saved the tedious and sometimes risky task of physically withdrawing and transferring the gold. These deposit notes became **customary money** (i.e. they were accepted as money). As the practice developed, the goldsmiths found that much of their gold was never withdrawn and they realized that they could profitably **loan** some of it out. A more typical balance sheet might then look like Table 9.2.

Table 9.2

Liabilities		Assets	
Deposit notes	£1000	Gold	£100
		Loans	£900
	£1000		£1000

Loans are **assets** to the goldsmith because they are promises by the borrower to repay. Loans would not necessarily involve the withdrawal of gold because of the widespread acceptance of deposit notes as a means of payment; so the goldsmith, in making the loan, would issue an equivalent amount of deposit notes which would give the borrower an option to use these or withdraw gold. In either case, of course, the total liabilities would be equal to assets.

The situation above is one where the gold in the vaults is only 10 per cent of the potential claims (deposit notes) on it. In this illustration we assume that this represents a prudent position which experience has established is sufficient to meet the day-to-day demands for the withdrawal of gold. There is always the temptation to grant more loans because these are profitable, as interest is charged on them, whereas gold in the vaults is not. This illustrates the age old conflict of bankers: **liquidity versus profitability**. To be highly liquid (in our case to hold large gold balances) involves forgoing profitable opportunities, whereas too much emphasis on profit-generating loans may place the institution in a situation where it is unable to pay depositors. Experience should suggest a balance between the desire for profitability and the need for liquidity, though the pre-20th-century UK experience is littered with bank failures when banks overstretched themselves through greed, bad judgement or occasionally misfortune.

The goldsmiths in our illustration have really become bankers—they have moved beyond the stage of merely taking care of people's gold to one where they are producing **financial instruments: deposit notes**. These were increasingly accepted and became known as **bank notes**. Various Bank Acts discouraged this and the Bank Charter Act of 1844 restricted the issue of private bank notes; today their issue is confined to the Bank of England and selected Scottish banks. This stimulated growth in the use of **cheques**, the means by which bank deposits are transferred from purchaser to seller.

9.2.2 Banking: deposit creation

Modern banking bears a strong resemblance to the practices of its goldsmith predecessors. In the simplified balance sheet below **cash** (**notes** and **coins**—and we could include **operational balances** held at a central bank, like the Bank of England, which can be converted into **cash on demand**)—has replaced gold and **bank deposits** are to be found instead of deposit notes (see Table 9.3).

Table 9.3

Liabilities		Assets	
Deposits	£1000	Cash	£100
		Loans	£900
	£1000		£1000

Notice that cash is only 10 per cent of deposits. This is for the reason we described earlier: day-to-day demands for cash are relatively limited because bank deposits (cheques) are being used to make purchases. This is known as **fractional reserve banking**. The reserves, **cash**, are a fraction of the **deposits**—we will refer to this as the **reserve asset ratio** (**RAR**) which in this case is 0.1 or 10 per cent. This allows banks—like goldsmiths when reserves were gold—to **create money** through a **deposit creation process**. An illustration will demonstrate how this is done.

In order to highlight the main features of this process we will assume that there is only one bank in the economy—the multi-bank case is considered briefly below. Now suppose that an extra £100 is deposited with the bank. This will appear on a balance sheet as shown in Table 9.4.

Table 9.4

Liabilities		Assets	
Deposits	£1000	Cash	£100
	+£100		+£100
		Loans	£900
	£1100		£1100

$$\text{Reserve asset ratio } (RAR) = \frac{£200 \ cash}{£1100 \ deposits} = 18.2\%$$

If we assume that an RAR of 10 per cent is regarded as sufficiently prudent to meet demands for the withdrawal of cash, then the position above is not an equilibrium one for the bank. It is not maximizing its profits because it is too liquid: the RAR is 18.2 per cent. There is an opportunity to make some loans which will raise its profits without damaging its ability to meet demands for cash. With £1100 of deposits it is only necessary to keep £110 in cash, so for illustrative purposes let us suppose our bank makes a loan of £90. Two extreme possibilities are illustrated in Table 9.5.

Table 9.5

Case A: total cash drain

Liabilities		Assets		
Deposits	£1100	Cash	£200	
			−£90 = £110	
		Loans	£900	
			+£90	
	£1100		£1100	RAR = 10%

Case B: zero cash drain

Liabilities		Assets		
Deposits	£1100	Cash	£200	
		Loans	£900	
	+£90		+£90	
	£1190		£1190	RAR = 16.8%

In case A all of the loan is withdrawn in cash and the RAR falls to 10 per cent. In case B the borrower does not withdraw cash but makes his purchase by bank deposit (by use of a cheque) and although the borrower's account is reduced by the amount of the purchase, the seller's account increases by the same amount. As no cash has actually been withdrawn the RAR is 16.8 per cent, well above the 10 per cent target level.

Which of these cases is more likely? We can be fairly certain that it is *not* case A. We know that bank deposits are regarded as **customary money**, so it would be untypical for all of the loans to be withdrawn in cash. Case B is more representative of what really happens as it reflects the overwhelming importance of **bank deposits** as a **means of payment**. It is certainly an extreme position and in practice some cash drain can be expected. We will retain the assumption that no cash is withdrawn because this allows us to conclude our illustration without tortuous arithmetic and so offers a type of example that could reasonably be produced in an examination. The bank would be able to make further loans until it retained the position shown in Table 9.6.

Table 9.6

Liabilities		Assets		
Deposits	£2000	Cash	£200	
		Loans	£1800	
	£2000		£2000	RAR = 10%

The process could go no further because this would push the RAR below 10 per cent, while if it were halted before this point profitable loan opportunities would be sacrificed.

At this stage it is useful to summarize the position. Cash to the value of £100 has been deposited with the bank and this has resulted in deposits rising by £1000 because of the loans that have been made. When a bank makes a loan, which is an asset to a bank, it simultaneously creates a liability, a bank deposit. In creating these deposits the banks have increased the money supply. It is in this sense that it is said that banks can **create money**, as bank deposits are regarded as part of the money supply.

9.2.3 Deposit creation multiplier

The process whereby an extra £1 of cash (or reserves) deposited with a bank leads to a larger increase in bank deposits (and hence the money supply) is known as the **deposit creation multiplier**. It is sometimes referred to as the **credit creation multiplier**; this description focuses on the loans created which appear on the asset side of the balance sheet. In our simple illustration this depends entirely on the **reserve asset ratio**, which we will call r. So:

$$RAR = r = \frac{R\ Reserves}{D\ Deposits}$$

therefore

$$D = \frac{R}{r}$$

If we assume that banks stick rigidly to their RAR then the increase in deposits will equal the increase in reserves (or cash in our example) multiplied by the reciprocal of the RAR. The **deposit creation multiplier** is

$$\frac{\Delta D}{\Delta R} = \frac{1}{r}$$

which in our illustration is 10. The multiplier process can explain a multiple contraction of bank deposits as well as an expansion, as a loss of reserves will push the RAR below required levels so that banks will have to reduce loans which in turn will cause a fall in deposits.

In reality the **deposit creation process** and **multiplier** are not as simple or mechanical as our account suggests. Some cash drain during an expansion of deposits can be expected, so the overall effect on deposits will not be quite as large as we have stated. The increase in deposits will not be as great if the public and firms do not wish to take out loans. In these circumstances banks may be forced to remain more liquid than they would prefer and the multiplier impact will be diminished. The process we have described implies that banks react mechanically to charges on their reserves. However, banks have more control over their business than this. They can stimulate the demand for loans when they are relatively liquid and in the reverse circumstances they can borrow in money markets by creating **certificates of deposits**.

We finally need to consider what the effect is if we drop our simplifying asumption of a single-bank system. Clearly the picture becomes more complex because in our example above a loan made by Bank A may be used to purchase goods from a shop that has an account with Bank B. So Bank A's deposits do not rise in line with the extra loans and settling the indebtedness between the banks would involve a transfer of reserves (in our case cash) between the two. However, as Bank B is in a more liquid position because of the rise in its reserves, it can expand loans and deposits. So if there were no cash drain from the banking system as a whole, and providing each bank expanded loans and deposits if its RAR rose above the desired level, then the overall effect would be the same as in our earlier example. Unless you are specifically asked to consider a multi-bank position, you would be well advised to illustrate the principle of **deposit creation** through a single-bank system or, which amounts to the same thing, state that you are showing the consolidated balance sheet of a multi-bank system where all banks are assumed to operate on their RARs.

9.3 What is money?

9.3.1 Legal and customary money

What is **money**? The answer would seem to be straightforward—it is **coins and notes**. These are certainly legal tender and are obviously used to make many purchases. Although notes and coins have a legal status as money (we will call this **legal money**), the majority of purchases by value are made by other means—by the use of **bank deposits**. When an item is bought by **cheque**, this transfers part of the purchaser's bank deposit to that of the seller. As there is widespread acceptance of this means of payment, even though it is not obligatory to accept cheques, we call this **customary money**—in other words, by custom bank deposits have come to be accepted as money. Before we consider how these notions of **legal** and **customary money** are reflected in the measures of the money supply, it is important to be aware of the different functions of money.

9.3.2 Functions of money

It is generally recognized that money has three functions, of which the first two are the most important.

9.3.2.1 Medium of exchange

Money is an acceptable means of payment—it acts as a **medium of exchange**. Without it we would have to rely on barter and on the exchange of one good for another. This is inconceivable in modern society because the success of a barter system depends upon the double coincidence of wants, so that, for example, a chicken farmer who wanted a pair of boots would have to find a cobbler with a demand for chickens. This type of problem might be surmountable, though time consuming, in a society where people engaged in little trade because they were largely self-sufficient. But in an economy like ours where there is extensive division of labour and most people produce only a fraction of their day-to-day needs, productive activity would grind to a halt without a **medium of exchange**.

9.3.2.2 Store of value

Money acts as a **store of value**—indeed, it must do this if it is to be acceptable as a **medium of exchange**. The lack of synchronization between receipts and expenditure which gives rise to a need for a medium of exchange implies that money is acting as a store of value. If it did not hold value then money would not be acceptable. This is demonstrated during periods of very rapid inflation. In the hyperinflation in Germany in 1923 when prices were doubling in a matter of hours, legal tender, the mark, became unacceptable because the **store of value function** had become seriously impaired.

There is a broader and more important sense in which money acts as a **store of value**. Money is one of the ways in which we can hold our wealth. Compared with property, antiques, stocks and shares, it is a highly liquid asset which can be used to purchase goods and services directly. Recognition of this function is important when we consider, in the next chapter, the factors that affect the demand for money.

9.3.2.3 Unit of account

Money acts as a unit of account—without a common unit, comparisons between sales of products and calculations of profits and costs would be impossible. Money also acts as a **standard of deferred payment**. It allows a convenient way of scheduling repayment of a loan over a period of time. It is obviously more acceptable to enter into a contract to repay £30 a week for a car than to state the contract in terms of parts of the vehicle.

9.3.3 Measures of the money supply

We said at the beginning of the chapter that money could be regarded as **bank deposits** as well as **notes and coins**. However, there are several types of bank deposits and many other financial assets which resemble bank deposits. This gives rise to difficulties in deciding how to measure the money supply. For this reason, the UK and most other countries have a number of different measures ranging from narrow definitions where most types of deposits are excluded to broader measures which include these other assets. **Financial innovation**, for example the growth of banking services by the building societies, means that periodic changes in definition are required if the measures are not to appear dated. Such a revision was made in May 1987 and we present the main measures with an indication of their relative size in Table 9.7. In addition to the five main measures, M1 to M5, we show M0, the monetary base, which we will consider later.

9.3.3.1 M1

M1 consists of **notes and coins in circulation** and **sight deposits** (more generally referred to as **current accounts**). This would seem to correspond to our notion of money, as it includes both **legal tender** and **bank deposits** (**customary money**) on which cheques can be drawn. However, there are two reservations about M1.

Table 9.7 Measures of the money supply, Quarter 3 1987 (£ billion)

M0			
1 Notes and coins	13.2		
UK sight deposits			
2 Non-interest-bearing	31.6 →	1 + 2	44.8
3 Interest-bearing	44.5	Retail deposits	
4 **M1**	89.3	(parts of 3 and 5)	46.8
		Building society retail deposits	88.9
		National Savings ordinary	
5 UK time deposits	87.3	deposits	1.6
		M2	182.2
6 **M3**	176.6		
7 Building society shares and deposits	128.1		
less			
8 Building society holdings of M3	−12.1	→ M3	176.6
		Deposits in other currencies	30.4
9 **M4**	292.6	**M3c**	207.0
10 Private sector holdings of			
money market instruments	4.6		
11 National Savings deposits	10.3		
12 **M5**	307.6		

(Central Statistical Office, *Financial Statistics*, April 1988)

First, it might be regarded as too narrow a definition because it excludes time deposits (more commonly called **deposit accounts**) in banks and other financial assets (for example **building society deposits**), which can easily be converted into cash or sight deposits. If we are concerned with influences on spending power then there is a strong argument for including these other liquid assets. The measures M3 and M5 represent a broader set of **monetary aggregates**. It should be emphasized that there is no logical point at which this broadening process should stop because there is a spectrum of financial assets and, whichever we include and call 'money', there will always be some arbitrary exclusions.

Our second concern over the suitability of M1 is that included in **interest-bearing sight deposits** are very short-term (e.g. overnight deposits) by companies and financial institutions which probably represent money that is destined for long-term financial assets and are not closely related in the short term to spending.

9.3.3.2 **M2**

M2, introduced in 1982, is a recognition of these difficulties and is an attempt to measure the balances that the private sector has available for spending on goods and services. These are referred to as **transactions balances**. In addition to **notes and coins** and **non-interest-bearing sight deposits**, M2 includes **retail interest-bearing bank deposits, retail shares** and **deposits with building societies** and **National Savings Bank ordinary accounts**. Retail interest-bearing bank deposits include all deposits (sight and time) on which cheques and standing orders may be drawn and deposits under £100 000 which require less than one month's notice of withdrawal without significant penalty in terms of loss of interest. This is designed to exclude large corporate deposits which are not likely to finance purchases of goods and services, at least in the short run. Building society deposits are treated in a similar way, so only those deposits that are likely to be drawn upon to finance transactions are included.

9.3.3.3 **M3**

M3 is a broader money supply measure than M1. It includes **time deposits** and **certificates of deposits–CD**. A CD is issued by a financial institution and is a form of borrowing large sums (usually in excess of £50 000). The certificate shows the period of the deposit with the borrower (normally less than one year) and the interest to be paid. There is a **secondary market in CDs** which means that the holder may sell the CD at any time, making it highly liquid.

The **M3** measure used to be known as **sterling M3** because the deposits were all in sterling and this distinguished it from a similar measure which included foreign currency deposits. Since 1987 the latter has been referred to as **M3c**.

9.3.3.4 **M4**

M4 broadens M3 to include building society deposits that are similar to those of banks, though the societies' holdings of M3 (i.e. bank deposits) are deducted to avoid double counting.

9.3.5.5 M5

The broadest of the UK monetary aggregates is **M5** (formerly known as **PSL 2**) which represents an extension of M4 to include **National Savings Deposits** and **private sector holdings of money market instruments**. The latter refers to financial instruments such as **Treasury** and **Bank bills** (see section 9.4) which are a means of short-term borrowing (three months) by government and companies. There is a market in these bills so they are highly liquid. This category also includes short-term borrowing by local authorities in the form of bills and the equivalent of time deposits with councils.

9.3.3.6 M0

Finally, we turn to **M0** or the 'wide monetary base'. This comprises **notes and coins** held by the public or the banks in their tills and the **banks' operational balances** with the Bank of England. The latter, which is only about one to two per cent of notes and coins, can be converted into cash on demand. **M0** is the monetary base (or very nearly so) of the financial system. This has a particular importance to some economists, as we will see in section 9.5.

Let us now try to summarize what must appear a complex and perhaps confusing picture. The main point is straightforward: there is no agreed measure of money. What does exist is a spectrum of financial assets ranging from cash, through sight and time deposits, certificates of deposit, deposits with building societies, to Treasury and Bank bills. Beyond this there are other financial instruments with similar characteristics. Where we draw the dividing line between money and what might be called **near money** is somewhat arbitrary: there are always competing arguments for widening and narrowing most definitions.

The seven measures (M0 to M5, which include two M3 measures) reflect this difficulty, which is also shown by the shifting emphasis of interest and targets by government since the mid-1970s when they first became concerned with the rate of growth of the money supply.

9.4 Financial institutions and banking in the UK

9.4.1 Financial institutions: an overview

Banking forms only part of a large **financial sector** in the UK. Banking, finance and insurance accounted for about 18 per cent of value added in 1985, (about three-quarters the sum of manufacturing industry). In the decade to 1985 output grew faster than in any other sector except energy and fuel and in terms of employment growth it was the clear leader. The **financial sector** encompasses **pension funds, finance houses** and **insurance companies** as well as those institutions we have already mentioned: **banks** and **building societies**. It involves a number of markets: the **capital market**, including the **Stock Exchange**, the **money market** and **foreign exchange market** (we consider this in Chapter 20).

The main functions of the financial system are:

1 Payments—the system provides, mainly through the banking sector, a means of payment through the use of deposits as we have discussed above.

2 Credit—the system provides a wide variety of sources of credit for individuals, firms and public sector bodies.

3 Savings—just as most people need to borrow at various points in their lives, so do they wish to save. Financial institutions offer a wide selection of outlets for **savings**. Of course this function is connected with the previous one of **lending** to those seeking credit. The process of channelling savings into funds for borrowing is known as **financial intermediation** and is discussed below.

4 Insurance—part of the financial system, insurance companies, provide cover for a wide variety of risks from personal insurance to satellite failure.

5 Advice and consultancy—as the financial system has grown in size and complexity there has been an increasing demand for advice and guidance, and a need for specialist information on what is available.

9.4.2 Financial intermediation

Financial institutions carry out an important role of **financial intermediation** by channelling savings into loans. In this process they carry out a number of functions that make them attractive to both lenders and borrowers.

9.4.2.1 Aggregation

It would be difficult for large borrowers to find individuals with sufficient savings available to lend, as typically many individuals set aside small amounts as savings every week or month. **Financial intermediaries** are able to aggregate these small amounts into large sums.

9.4.2.2 Risk transformation

As well as **aggregation** there can be a **pooling of risks**. Some borrowers will default, which could ruin individual savers and would therefore make lending unattractive. **Financial intermediaries** can generally offer **little** or **no risk** to savers and can withstand a certain proportion of bankruptcies and non-payers among their borrowers. In this way **risk** has been transformed for the individual saver.

9.4.2.3 Maturity transformation

There is generally a greater requirement for long-term borrowing than long-term saving. For example, most people wish to borrow for 20 to 25 years when they purchase a house, yet few would wish to commit their savings for this period. Financial intermediaries can **transform short-term savings** into **long-term loans** because they can regulate the number of new long-term commitments they enter into according to flow of new short-term savings that are deposited with them.

9.4.2.4 Specialization and economies of scale

There are clearly many benefits of specialization, particularly in gathering information and acquiring expertise on making loans to different sectors of the economy. This means there are significant economies of scale and that it will often be cheaper for an individual to use a financial intermediary than to acquire this information personally.

9.4.3 Capital market

The **capital market** is the market used for **long-term borrowing**. Firms will often have a need for external funds (as opposed to retained profits) to finance their investment expenditure on plant and machinery. They may raise this in a variety of ways: by **issuing shares** (equities), **borrowing from banks,** by **debentures** (fixed term loans) and **mortgages**. Governments need to borrow on a long-term basis and they do this by selling **bonds or gilt-edged securities** (often referred to as **gilts**) which have a fixed term before they are due for repayment and a fixed rate of interest. For example, Treasury stock 10 per cent 2004 will pay £10 per year for every £100 of stock and will be repaid in 2004. Finally, individuals borrow long-term when they take out mortgages for houses.

The **Stock Exchange** is not only a place where newly issued shares and bonds can be sold; more importantly it provides a **secondary market** for existing **securities**. This means that holders of long-term debt are always able to sell it and this clearly increases the attractiveness of these financial instruments. Individuals participate directly in Stock Exchange dealings but the market tends to be dominated by **institutional investors**. These are **pension funds, insurance companies** and **unit trusts**, which are important **financial intermediaries** that channel savings of individuals and businesses into long-term lending.

9.4.4 Money markets

The **money markets** are concerned with **short-term financial instruments** ranging from overnight deposits to those of several months maturity. **Discount houses** form a traditional and important element of the money markets and we discuss their role in the next section, but there are a number of so called **parallel markets** which we consider first.

1 The **interbank market** is the largest of these markets and is a means of banks lending and borrowing from one another. The market produces a set of interest rates (depending on maturity) known as **LIBOR (London Interbank Offer Rate)** which determines the base rates and interest charges to large customers.

2 The **market for certificates of deposit** has already been referred to. Its advantage as a financial asset is the existence of a secondary market which means that holders can always sell.

3 Finance house market–finance houses which provide **credit to households and companies** on a short and medium basis also provide an outlet to lenders (mainly banks) as they seek deposits to finance their activities.

4 Local authority market–local authorities require **short-term finance** through deposits and the issue of bills.

5 Intercompany market: large companies may lend to one another. This is an example of **disintermediation** because it bypasses financial institutions.

6 Sterling commercial paper market–large companies with net assets above £50 million who are quoted on the **International Stock Exchange** have, since 1986, had the opportunity to issue short-term (7-364 days) **debt securities in sterling**. This is an alternative to the use of commercial bills which we consider in next section.

9.4.5 The discount houses

The **discount houses market**, which in March 1986 comprised nine discount houses, plays an important role in the UK monetary system. It provides a market in **private and public sector bills**; it acts as a buffer between the banks and the Bank of England and it is an important vehicle for conducting the government's monetary policy.

Bills are a means of short-term borrowing. The government uses this method by selling Treasury bills. These are 91-day bills which are repaid after 91 days. They are sold at a discount and the difference between this and the redemption price amounts to the interest paid. For example, Treasury bills with a par value of £10 000 which were bought for £9700 when issued would provide a gain of £300 over a period of three months, an annual rate of interest of approximately 12 per cent. There is an active market in these bills so it is not necessary to hold them for the full period and as there is also a weekly issue of Treasury bills there is always a range of maturities on offer. **Local authority bills** are a way of financing short-term borrowing by councils.

It is not only the public sector that borrows in this way: companies may obtain short-term finance through **commercial** or **trade bills**. The willingness of the market to hold and trade in bills is increased if they are **accepted** by a reputable bank. This provides a guarantee of repayment by the bank. Eligible bank bills are those that have been accepted by banks designated as **eligible** by the Bank of England. To help maintain and foster the bill market the bank has increased the number of eligible banks.

In addition to providing a market for bills, in which bank or commercial bills dominate Treasury bills, **discount houses** also hold large amounts of CDs.

The **discount houses** act as a buffer between the banks and the Bank of England. Most of the money with which the **discount houses** buy bills comes from banks on a very short-term basis. Indeed, nearly all is lent at call or overnight and so is liable to immediate repayment. This means that banks can easily respond to liquidity shortages; but this transfers the difficulty to the discount houses, who have **borrowed short** but **lent long**. However, they can turn to the Bank of England which is always willing to lend as **the lender of last resort**. In practice the Bank intervenes daily to smooth out liquidity difficulties by the purchase and sale of bills from the **discount houses**. Government finances are also assisted by an arrangement that involves discount houses agreeing to bid for all the Treasury bills on offer each week; many of these bills will subsequently be bought by the banks. So the **discount houses** stand between the banks and the Bank of England and effectively sort out the system's liquidity difficulties.

This relationship is useful to the government in conducting its **monetary policy**. The government can influence short-term interest rates by determining the rates at which it will lend to **discount houses** or, which amounts to the same thing, the price it will pay for bills which it purchases to ease liquidity difficulties in money markets. It can use open-market operations (see section 9.5.1) if it wishes to make sure that the **discount houses** are forced to borrow from the Bank.

9.4.6 Retail banks in the UK

Table 9.8 shows the balance sheet of UK retail banks. Most of the items have been discussed at various points in this chapter. On the liabilities side, 'other currency deposits' refers to deposits held in non-sterling currencies and 'other liabilities' covers such items as share capital, reserves and loans in transmission. The asset structure reflects the twin but conflicting objectives of **liquidity** and **profitability**. In addition to notes and coins and balances with the Bank of England, banks hold several highly liquid assets and market loans, which include the lending to the discount market referred to above, as well as loans to other parts of the money market. Bills, mainly eligible bank bills, are also liquid assets.

Table 9.8 Balance sheet of retail banks, 30 December 1988 (£ millions)

Liabilities	
Sight deposits	90 686
Time deposits	88 635
Certificates of deposit	11 965
Other currency deposits	43 016
Other liabilities	48 270
Total	282 572

Assets	
Notes and coins	3 375
Balances with Bank of England	749
Market loans	31 371
Bills	8 087
Advances	154 862
Investments	8 670
Other currency assets	54 634
Miscellaneous assets	20 824
Total	282 572

(*Bank of England Quarterly Bulletin*, February 1989)

By far the largest single asset is 'advances to persons and companies'. Investments are the banks holdings of gilt-edged securities and long-term assets. Overseas assets (i.e. foreign currency) are a large item, with advances accounting for about a quarter of this.

9.4.7 The Bank of England

All countries have a central bank and in the UK it is the Bank of England. It has a number of functions.

1 Government's bank–the government uses its account with the Bank of England to make payments and to receive income. The Bank of England borrows on the government's behalf through the sale of Treasury bills and gilt-edged securities. It has responsibility for managing the national debt.

2 The bankers' bank–banks hold balances at the central bank and these provide a means of settling net indebtedness between themselves.

3 Manager of exchange equalization account–it manages the holdings of the country's stock of gold and foreign currencies (known as the **exchange equalization account**). This is described more fully in Chapter 20; it involves intervention in the foreign exchange market by selling or buying sterling.

4 Conduct of monetary policy–the Bank of England plays an important role in conducting monetary policy through its activities in the money, gilt-edged and foreign exchange markets.

5 Supervisory–the Bank of England has a supervisory role over the behaviour of financial institutions in general and the banking system in particular.

6 Note issuer–the Bank of England is the principal issuer of bank notes in the UK.

9.5 Control over the money supply

9.5.1 The money supply and the PSBR

Since the mid-1970s governments have tried, with varying degrees of commitment, to **control the money supply**. The policy of Labour administrations in the late 1970s included measures which tried to control deposits directly by imposing a **corset** on their growth by penalizing increases in excess of specified targets. In the 1980s control has been carried out via the **Public Sector Borrowing Requirements** targets and **interest rate policy**.

The interconnection between fiscal and monetary policy is relatively easy to grasp in outline. **Government spending,** by itself, tends to raise the money supply, whereas **taxation** produces a flow in the opposite direction as money is paid to the government by households and firms. This suggests that if the budget is balanced the net effect on the money supply is zero. It implies, too, that if there is a budget deficit with tax revenue less than government spending, there is a tendency for the **money supply** to increase. We can show this idea through a bank's balance sheet (Table 9.9, overleaf).

Government expenditure of £100 raises bank deposits as the sellers of goods and services pay in the cheque from the government. It also increases the bank's balances at the

Table 9.9 Interrelationship between fiscal policy and money supply

Liabilities		Assets	
Deposits	£2000	Cash and balances with Bank of England	£200
Government expenditure	+£100		+£100
Taxation	−£50		−£50
		Loans	£1800
	£2050		£2050

Bank of England when the cheque is cleared and the net indebtedness between the government's bank (the Bank of England) and the banks is settled. (Tax payments of £50 reduce both bank deposits and balances with the Bank of England by £50). This leaves the bank with increased reserves of £50 and the potential to increase deposits further through the **deposit creation process** we discussed earlier.

However, the government has a deficit of £50 and the way it finances this is important in determining the impact on the money supply. If it were to borrow from the banking system then the level of bank deposits would not be directly affected. For example, the sale of Treasury bills would simply alter the asset side of the bank's balance sheet as it used its extra balances at the Bank of England to make loans to the discount market or hold more Treasury bills. So the banks would find the increase in bank deposits resulting from the budget deficit undiminished and they would have acquired extra highly liquid assets, compared with a pre-deficit position. Budget deficits financed by borrowing from the banking system have the potential to increase the money supply.

However, the government may choose to finance its deficit in another way which would not stimulate money supply growth: it may **borrow from the public**. If the Bank of England, on behalf of the government, sells gilt-edged securities to the bank public the effect is shown in Table 9.10.

Table 9.10 Interrelationship between fiscal policy and money supply

Liabilities		Assets	
Deposits	£2000	Cash and balances with Bank of England	£200
Government expenditure	+£100		+£100
Taxation	−£50		−£50
Bond sales	−£50		−£50
		Loans	£1800
	£2000		£2000

The public's payment for £50 of gilts reduces their bank deposits by this amount and when the cheque is cleared the bank's balances with the Bank of England are debited by that amount. The overall effect on bank deposits of a budget deficit where the PSBR is financed by selling long-term debt to the non-bank public is zero. However, to persuade people to hold extra gilt-edged securities, deficit interest rates will have to be pushed up compared with what they might otherwise have been; so the budget deficit will tend to raise either the **money supply** or **interest rates** depending on how it is financed. We return to this issue when we consider the government's monetary policy in Chapter 11.

This reminds us that the relationship between **budget deficits** or the **PSBR** and the **growth of the money supply** is not a simple one: large deficits may be associated with low or zero rises in the money supply if the government is prepared to borrow heavily. There are further qualifications which we introduce below. Before considering these, it should be said that the government is likely to be heavily involved in selling gilts whether or not it has a budget deficit. Each year a number of gilts will be due for redemption and the government has to decide whether to issue new ones and keep the level of the national debt the same, replace the long-term debt by short-term instruments or allow the amount of outstanding debt to change. The process of covering the PSBR by the issue of long-term debt is known as **funding**. If the government decides to **overfund** the deficit—sell more gilts than the PSBR and redemption of old gilts require—then they will tend to reduce the level of bank deposits and therefore the money supply. This will tend to put pressure on liquidity in the system as banks' balances with the Bank of England fall. Dealing in marketable securities in this way is known as **open-market operations**.

We can summarize the position for a closed economy (i.e. no foreign trade) as follows:

$$\text{Money supply growth} = \text{PSBR} \quad - \quad \begin{array}{l}\textit{Net sales} \\ \textit{of debt to} \\ \textit{non-bank} \\ \textit{public}\end{array} \quad + \quad \begin{array}{l}\textit{Bank} \\ \textit{lending} \\ \textit{to private} \\ \textit{sector}\end{array}$$

So the **growth in the money supply** will depend on the extent to which the PSBR is financed by government borrowing from the public and by the amount of bank lending to the households and firms. It shows that fiscal policy and monetary policy are related to each other, but not in any rigid way. It is quite possible for a **budget surplus** (**a negative PSBR**) to be associated with a fairly sharp increase in the money supply. Such a situation occurred in 1988 when the surplus (or **PSDR, Public Sector Debt Repayment**) was used to repay some public sector debt (so reducing the national debt which is the stock of outstanding debt) and high growth in spending led to sharp growth in bank lending.

9.5.2   The money supply in an open economy

In an **open economy** the **money supply** can be affected by the effects of payments to and receipts from abroad. Again, a useful way of illustrating this is through the impact on the banks' balance sheet. We will assume that the person or firm abroad makes and requires payment in their own currency and that UK transactors convert to or from sterling. We will also assume that the foreign currency required by UK traders is obtained from the Bank of England via their own bank and that all foreign currency acquired by UK exporters is paid into their own bank, which in turn pays it into the Bank of England in return for sterling which is credited to banks' balances with the Bank. This long list of assumptions reflects the many variables concerning the monetary effects of international transactions. It is a useful exercise to consider the implications of dropping one or more of these assumptions.

Payments abroad for imports (and the acquisition of foreign assets) will reduce the level of bank deposits in the UK but increase deposits abroad. Payments for UK exports (and the purchase of UK assets by those abroad) will increase bank deposits in this country. The net effect of a deficit on the balance of payments will be a decrease in bank deposits and, therefore, the money supply. There will be a further consequence, given our assumptions, because the Bank of England will be acquiring sterling as it runs down its reserves of foreign currency and it can use this to buy gilt-edged securities. In this way a balance of payments deficit can help finance a budget deficit. The money supply in an open economy is likely to be influenced by the balance of payments, a factor that needs to be taken into account when devising monetary policy.

Our summary at the end of the previous section now needs amending to take account of external influences:

$$\text{Money supply growth} = \text{PSBR} \quad - \quad \begin{array}{l}\textit{Net sales} \\ \textit{of debt to} \\ \textit{non-bank} \\ \textit{public}\end{array} \quad + \quad \begin{array}{l}\textit{Bank} \\ \textit{lending} \\ \textit{to private} \\ \textit{sector}\end{array} \quad + \quad \begin{array}{l}\textit{External} \\ \textit{currency} \\ \textit{flows}\end{array}$$

9.5.3   Methods of controlling the money supply

The government, or the monetary authorities on its behalf, have a number of ways of controlling the money supply. Basically they can use either **quantitative** or **price controls**. Our summary of the factors affecting the money supply (see end of previous two sections) can be used as a framework to understand how these controls may be used.

9.5.3.1   Direct controls

Bank lending may be controlled by introducing **quantity controls** by issuing directives or a milder control, requests, to banks to stay within **stated target levels** or **growth rates**. This approach was used fairly extensively in the early post-war period. In the 1970s (1973–80) there was a scheme to control the growth in bank deposits. The **supplementary special deposit scheme** (or 'corset') laid down targets for the growth in bank deposits and provided a set of penalties for failing to meet them. Under these penalties banks which exceeded targets were required to make deposits, on which no interest was paid, with the Bank of England. These **supplementary deposits** varied from five to fifty per cent of the excess growth depending on how far the target was exceeded; they were therefore significant.

This type of control is generally fairly successful in regulating targeted variables, such as bank deposits; however it has a number of severe drawbacks. There will normally be successful attempts to circumvent the controls. Banks unable to lend because they are operating on or close to their targets may arrange loans for their customers with institutions not subject to these controls; or borrowers may go directly to unregulated institutions. This process is known as **disintermediation**. A further disadvantage results from the impact of this type of control on the efficiency of the financial system. For the regulated institutions, a system of controls will weaken incentives for efficiency and reduce the drive to compete because targets limit the amount of business it is worthwhile acquiring.

9.5.3.2 Interest rate policy

An approach that has found much more favour in the 1980s is the use of **interest rates** to affect the **price of loans**. The demand for loans is assumed to be responsive to interest rates, so raising interest rates will lower the demand for loans and hence reduce the growth in the bank deposits and the money supply. There are a number of difficulties with this approach. A major problem concerns the **stability** of the demand for loans. If it is not stable and the authorities are not able to predict it then the effects of interest changes are likely to be uncertain. There are likely to be time lags between interest rate changes and alterations in the demand for loans and the associated spending. It is highly likely that in the short run **interest elasticity** is very low. There may be some undesirable side effects to interest rate changes, particularly on **investment** and house building, which are likely to be more **interest elastic** than many other items of expenditure.

9.5.3.3 Open market operations

Ceteris paribus, the money supply can be affected by the **volume of sales of government debt** to the non-banking sector (see section 9.5.1). Buying and selling these securities (e.g. gilts) is known as **open-market operations**. One difficulty with this approach is that it may involve accepting large fluctuations in interest rates. For example, if the authorities wish to sell gilts on a **falling market** when buyers are reluctant to purchase, high interest rates may be necessary.

9.5.3.4 PSBR

The size of the **PSBR**, *ceteris paribus*, can influence the growth in the money supply, as we explained in section 9.5.1. So reducing the PSBR by tax increases or government spending cuts can help exert a downward pressure on monetary growth.

9.5.3.5 External flows

The government may seek to influence **external monetary flows** by intervention in foreign exchange markets and through an exchange rate policy.

9.5.3.6 Monetary base control

One approach to controlling the money supply which has found favour with a number of monetarists is **monetary base control**. We consider this more fully in the next section.

9.6 Monetary base control

We now consider an approach advocated by some economists as the best way of controlling the money supply. The **monetary base**, or what is sometimes called **high powered money**, can be thought of as cash held by the public and the reserves of the banks which are their balances (those that can be withdrawn on demand) with the central bank plus the cash that they have in their tills. It is suggested that by controlling this base the government can control the money supply. The underlying rationale can be seen by the manipulation of two identities which define the monetary base (H) and the money supply (M):

$$M = C + D$$
$$H = C + R$$

where C = cash held by public
D = bank deposits
R = reserves of the banking system

Dividing M by H gives

$$\frac{M}{H} = \frac{C+D}{C+R} = \frac{C/D+1}{C/D+R/D}$$

So

$$M = \frac{c+1}{c+r} H$$

where $c = C/D$, public's cash to deposit ratio and
$r = R/D$, banks' reserve asset ratio.

This suggests that the money supply is related to the monetary base by two ratios: c, the public's **cash to deposit ratio** and r, the **banks' reserve asset ratio**. If both of these are stable and predictable then changes in H will have a **multiplier effect** on M. So if both c and r were 0.1 (or 10 per cent) then a £100 increase in H would increase the money supply by £550.

It is further suggested by advocates of monetary base control that the government can affect the size of the monetary base relatively easily and accurately. It certainly has the monopoly of printing cash, though in practice in the UK the authorities do not seek to control this directly and allow it to change according to the public's needs. The government does have the potential power to affect the reserves of the banking system through open-market operations and in this way it may control the money supply.

A number of serious reservations arise about the effectiveness of monetary base control:

1 Stability of c and r—These ratios reflect the behaviour of the public and banks. Behaviour is likely to be influenced by a number of factors, including interest rates, so the ratios will certainly not be fixed in any way and it is doubtful how stable they are for control purposes. The r ratio may well respond to the demand of the public for advances. For example, if the monetary base were increased and the banks were not able to expand deposits because the public were unwilling to take out loans then the reserve asset ratio, r, would rise.

2 Difficulty in controlling H—even if these ratios were stable, there could be great difficulties in controlling the monetary base. The base will be affected by numerous factors, some of which are directly under the government's control though others are not. Even those the government can control, such as tax revenue and government expenditure, are not susceptible to accurate targeting because they will be affected by many factors such as the level of activity in the economy. Others pose greater difficulties: as we suggested in the last section the reserves of the banking system may be affected by the balance of payments and most of these flows are not directly controllable.

3 Interest rate implications—despite all of these difficulties it could be argued that an active open-market operation could still exert a control over the reserves of the banking system. However, this may well mean selling gilts when the market is unwilling to buy and squeezing the liquidity of the banking system when there is great need for it. In these circumstances interest rates may have to go to very high levels. Monetary base control may involve large fluctuations in interest rates, particularly if the policy permits little variation from the targets.

4 Financial innovation—any policy of control may well be frustrated by the ability of financial institutions to innovate by introducing new financial instruments or practices or even by the ability of institutions to evade the controls.

10 The role of money

10.1 Introduction

In the previous chapter we considered the **money supply** but said nothing about the **demand for money**. We remedy this in this chapter and in doing so we examine the different views on the **role of money**.

In the last 20 years the rise of **monetarism** has revived an interest in money which had been largely lost in the earlier post-war period. This aspect of **monetarism** is founded on a long-established view: the **quantity theory of money**. The Keynesians adopted a somewhat different approach to money. Most courses will cover this material, though only a minority are likely to consider the **IS–LM** model, which involves integrating the money market with the income–expenditure model. We use the **IS–LM** model to derive the **aggregate demand curve**. A simplified approach to aggregate demand is used in the next chapter for those courses which omit **IS–LM** analysis.

This chapter will:

- explain the quantity theory of money
- explain the assumptions behind this theory
- examine the behaviour of the money supply in the UK
- explain the demand for money
- provide a model of income determination
- explain fiscal policy and crowding out
- explain the Keynesian view of money and its relationship to employment
- outline post-war monetary policy in the UK
- explain the IS–LM model

10.1.1 Examination guide

Questions on the **role of money** will generally require an explanation of the **quantity theory of money** and the **Keynesian alternative** and an assessment of each. We argue in the chapter that disagreements between the advocates of each approach have tended to diminish in recent years. So avoid overstating the divide; nevertheless you would probably be wise to adopt the approach we have taken in the chapter of simplifying the positions in order to clarify the main features of each approach.

Some questions on **monetarism** or the relationship between **money supply** and **inflation** will require use of material covered in the next chapter. For those whose course includes the **IS–LM model,** you should be prepared to use the analysis and diagrams in answers to questions even though specific mention is not made of this approach. Questions on **monetary** and **fiscal policy** will clearly benefit from using this model.

10.2 The quantity theory

10.2.1 The quantity of money identity

The most useful starting point for understanding the **quantity theory** is the following identity:

$$MV \equiv PT$$

i.e. value of money spent $\equiv$ value of goods and services bought, where

M = money supply
V = velocity
P = average price
T = number of transactions

This is true by definition: it states that the value of goods and services bought is equal to the amount of money spent.

The **velocity of circulation** is the average number of times a unit of money is spent in a period of time. As it is not possible to keep track of every pound of cash and bank deposit the only way it can be measured is by dividing the value of goods and services bought by the money stock:

$$V \equiv \frac{PT}{M}$$

So if £300 billion worth of goods and services were bought in a year when the money supply was £100 billion, the **velocity of circulation** would have been 3. This identity is indisputable—what turns it into a controversial theory are the assumptions and hypotheses that are made about it.

10.2.2   The quantity theory of money

There are three assumptions/hypotheses associated with the **traditional quantity theory.**

10.2.2.1   Velocity (V)

The **velocity of circulation** is stable. This does not mean that it is fixed, only that its behaviour is predictable.

10.2.2.2   Exogeneity of the money supply (M)

The assumption that the **money supply is exogenous** means that it is determined outside the model—so it is not determined by V, P or T. The importance of this, as we shall see, is that it establishes a causality between the money supply and other variables. The normal view is that **government controls the money supply.**

10.2.2.3   Fully employed resources (T)

The view that the economy is operating at **full employment** is less stringently adhered to, particularly in the short run (see for example, **modern monetarists**). The **full employment assumption** normally rests upon the view that economies are self-regulating and that market forces tend to eliminate unemployment.

Combining these together gives us the famous prediction that increases in the money supply cause inflation:

$$MV = PT$$

As the **velocity** is stable (to simplify the illustration we shall treat it as a constant) an increase in the money supply leads to an increase in spending. The assumption that resources are fully employed means output and the number of transactions (T) cannot rise so the increase in spending causes prices to rise. In the numerical example below a doubling of the money supply from £100 to £200 leads to a twofold increase in spending (£800 to £1600) and a doubling of prices.

$$MV \quad\ = PT$$
$$£200 \times 4 = £1.00 \times 800$$
$$£400 \times 4 = £2.00 \times 800$$

It seems an obvious step from explaining inflation in these terms to advocating control of the money supply as a means of regulating inflation. In our example, if there had been only a 10 per cent increase in the money supply then price increases would have been limited to the same amount. However, no one suggests that the control of inflation is quite so straightforward. Apart from difficulties in achieving **monetary targets** (see previous chapter), **quantity theorists** would accept that various **rigidities** and **lags** prevent the relationship from holding exactly at every point in time. There are more fundamental objections to this interpretation which we consider in section 10.3.3.

10.2.2.4   Time lags, rigidities and the quantity theory

The response of **prices** to changes in the **money supply** is not likely to be instantaneous. Spending may not respond immediately to an increase in the money supply and a further delay may be expected before prices adjust. This raises the role played by **expectations, time lags** and **adjustment processes.** We explore these more fully in the next two chapters. **Milton Friedman,** who has been particularly associated with the revival of the **quantity theory,** suggests that variable (and unpredictable) time lags of around 6 to 24 months may occur between changes in the money supply and inflation.

10.2.3 The behaviour of the money supply, velocity and inflation in the UK

10.2.3.1 Money supply and inflation

Figure 10.1, which shows the growth of M3 and inflation, does not reveal a high correlation between the two. However, if there is a **time lag** of around two years between changes in the money supply and inflation, the evidence is more consistent with the **quantity theory**. Increases in the money supply of around 25 per cent in 1972–3 were followed by accelerating inflation which reached a similar figure in 1975. A similar rise in monetary growth preceded the increase in inflation rates in 1979 and 1980. The pattern in the 1980s does not seem to fit the two-year lag interpretation. If allowances are made for special factors (the removal of the **corset** arrangement which was a government imposed constraint on the growth of bank deposits) which caused some sharp increases in M3 in 1981, then the lag seems to have disappeared. Indeed, the data could be interpreted as representing a **lag** of **monetary growth behind inflation.**

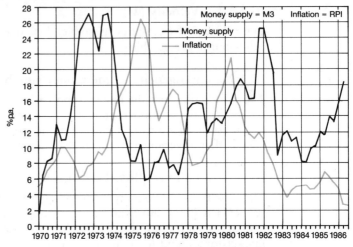

(Economic Trends Annual Supplement, 1988)

Fig. 10.1 Money supply growth and inflation (1970–87)

This does not necessarily mean that the evidence is inconsistent with the quantity theory because one monetarist position which we discuss in Chapter 12 predicts that such a lag may occur. However, as we have noted, this would seem to require one explanation of the evidence for the 1970s and another for the 1980s. Of course, there are many special factors, apart from the one we have mentioned, which both advocates and critics of the quantity theory would argue should be taken into account. We will see later that some economists explain the path of inflation in this period with little, or in some cases no, reference to the growth of the money supply.

10.2.3.2 Velocity

The **velocity of circulation** cannot be measured in the way it was defined at the beginning of the chapter because we do not have data on the money value of all transactions (PT). We do have information on **money** or **nominal GDP,** which is GDP measured in current prices. This differs from PT because it excludes transfer payments and intermediate transactions–it also includes some non-cash transactions e.g. imputed earnings.

However, if we are prepared to assume that PT and money GDP are highly correlated then the latter provides a useful indication of movements in velocity. Using this approach, **velocity** is measured by dividing money GDP (Y) by the money supply (M):

$$V = \frac{Y}{M}$$

This gives as many measures of velocity as there are measures of the money supply. The **velocity** of M3 is shown in Figure 10.2 revealing quite considerable movements over the period. It should be emphasized that the **quantity theory** does not require the velocity to be constant, but merely predictable. However, in the case of M3 the government's abandonment of targets may be regarded as a sign that velocity could not be accurately predicted. **M1 velocity** displays a strong upward trend until 1980 when, like M3, it declines. From the mid-1970s the velocity of M4 rises too, but its decline in the 1980s has been steadier. The most consistent of the velocity measures is M0, which has shown a relatively small variation around a strong upward trend.

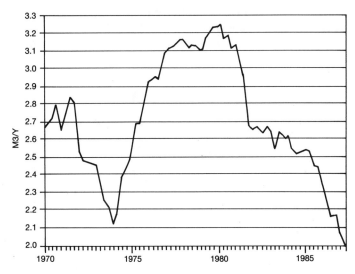

(OECD Economic Observer, various years)

Fig. 10.2 M3 velocity (1970–87)

Long-term velocity movements reflect institutional changes such as payments habits. For example, a reduced use of cash for purchases and a trend to pay workers by cheque will tend to increase the M0 velocity. Shorter-term changes may result from several factors. It may reflect **interest rate changes** which lead people to alter their holdings of money in relation to income. So high interest rates may lead people to economize on their holdings of sight deposits in favour of some interest-bearing non-monetary asset. **Adjustment lags** may be responsible for velocity changes. For instance, if there is a sudden increase in the money supply it may take some time before spending and national income are affected, and consequently the velocity will be temporarily depressed.

10.2.4   The demand for money

In the traditional **quantity theory** the demand of money (M_d) is a function (k) of **nominal income** (Y). **Nominal income** is income measured in current prices; it is the same as the price level (P) times real income or output (O):

$$M_d = kY \equiv kPO$$

It is assumed that the **amount** of money, as a proportion of income, that people wish to hold is fairly stable, so k does not vary in an unsystematic way. The **equilibrium condition** is where the demand for money is equal to supply:

$$M_d = M_s$$

We can see the relationship of V to the demand for money if we adopt the approach discussed in the previous section and write the quantity theory as:

$$M_s V = Y = PO$$

Substituting M_d for M_s (because in equilibrium $M_d = M_s$) and rearranging (by dividing both sides by V) we obtain

$$M_d = \frac{1}{V} Y$$

which can be compared with our original expression for the demand for money, $M_d = kY$. In effect k is the reciprocal of V. So we can see that the argument that V is stable and predictable rests on the view the demand for money is stable. We return to the issue of the stability of the demand for money in section 10.3.3.

10.2.5   A model of income determination

We can use the $MV = PO$ form of the **quantity theory**—which is the approach we shall adopt in the rest of the book—to illustrate an alternative to the Keynesian model of income determination. In Figure 10.3 (overleaf) the demand for money (M_d) is shown as a function of nominal income (Y) and the money supply (M_s) is exogenous, assumed to be determined by the government. With the money supply equal to M_{s1} the equilibrium ($M_d = M_s$) is at Y_1. Below Y_1, say at Y_2, the supply of money exceeds the demand for it and expenditure increases, which will raise Y towards Y_1. Above Y_1 the money supply is less than the money people wish to hold, so expenditure will be cut in an attempt to increase money balances. **Equilibrium** will occur only when Y falls to Y_1. If the money supply is increased from M_{s1} to M_{s2} this will mean there is an excess supply of money at Y_1 which raises expenditure and income until the new equilibrium income at Y_3 is achieved.

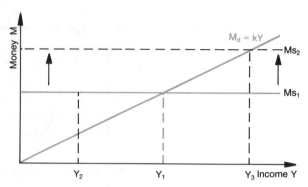

Fig. 10.3 Demand for money

This approach can be contrasted to the Keynesian view where **autonomous expenditures** are the driving force behind income changes. However, we should note that the **Keynesian model** we developed earlier was one which analysed the determination of **real** income whereas this **quantity theory model** refers to **nominal** income. The detailed matter of how far expenditure changes affect real income or prices is considered in the next chapter.

10.2.6 Fiscal policy and crowding out

There are implications in the models we have just considered for the relative effectiveness of **fiscal** and **monetary policy**. The **quantity theory** suggests that if there is no change in the money supply, and velocity is constant, then there can be no change in national income. This implies that an **expansionary fiscal policy** (say an increase in government expenditure) will not increase national income if money supply is unaltered. If this is correct then total demand has not been raised so the increase in public expenditure must be offset by reductions elsewhere. This phenomenon is known as **crowding out**.

Several explanations have been put forward to suggest why it might occur but we will consider only one at this stage (but see section 10.5.2 and Chapter 11). If an expansionary fiscal policy is not financed by expanding the money supply then it may well be funded by increased government borrowing which pushes up interest rates. This could well **crowd out** some private sector expenditure by reducing investment and consumer spending. The **quantity theory view** can be summarized below. (As we are exploring the implications of unchanged income we can ignore the fact that one is a model of **nominal income** and the other **real income**.)

$$\text{Crowding out}$$
$$\downarrow \quad \downarrow \quad \uparrow$$
$$MV = Y = \quad E = C + I + G + X - M$$

Quantity   Keynesian income–
theory   expenditure model

This suggests that **fiscal policy** is not the powerful policy tool that most post-war Keynesians had argued and that governments had assumed when they made budgetary changes to control the economy. It points to **monetary policy** as a more important policy weapon.

Empirical work has not generally supported an extreme view of **crowding out** where **fiscal policy** has no impact on output (and where the government expenditure multiplier $\Delta Y/\Delta G$ is zero). Many large macro-models do not display total **crowding out**— government expenditure multipliers are often around 1, although in the Treasury model the multiplier becomes zero after five years, when M0 is fixed, and after only two years when M3 is not allowed to rise.

The debate over crowding out, which was prominent in the 1970s, did raise doubts about the efficacy of **fiscal policy** and helped reawaken an interest in **monetary policy**. It focused attention on financial factors which may limit fiscal multipliers even in a Keynesian framework. We explore this more fully in the final section of this chapter.

10.3 The Keynesian view of money

10.3.1 The demand for money

Keynesians normally distinguish three motives for holding money:

10.3.1.1 The transactions demand

Money is a medium of exchange and people therefore hold it to finance transactions. This is essentially the same as the quantity theory. We can think of the transactions demand (M_{dT}) as a function of nominal income (Y):

$$M_{dT} = f(Y)$$

It may also be related to **interest rates** because high interest rates will provide incentive to economize on transaction balances. However, we can afford to ignore this in a simplified account because, as we will see, interest rates will be included in the factors affecting total demand for money.

10.3.1.2 Precautionary demand

In addition to holding money for day-to-day transactions people may want some money balances as **precaution** against **unforeseen events**. This demand is likely to be related to income levels (and perhaps interest rates too) so for explanatory purposes we can include it with the transactions demand.

10.3.1.3 Speculative demand

One of Keynes's major criticisms of the **classical quantity theory** was its apparent failure to recognize that money is a means of holding wealth, so that there is a demand for it as a **financial asset** over and above the transactions demand. The great advantage of money is its liquidity—other financial assets and physical assets (property, paintings, etc.) have to be **sold** in order to acquire money to buy goods and services whereas money, as the medium of exchange, does not. We can understand Keynes's ideas if we take a simplified example where there are only two financial assets, money (cash and sight deposits) and bonds. We assume that people and firms have made their decision on the amount of financial wealth they wish to hold, but need to decide in what form (**money or bonds**) to hold it.

As **bonds** pay a rate of interest and money (in our example) does not, it would appear an easy decision—however, bond prices vary so capital loss is possible. In comparison, money's nominal value does not change. We can summarize this in Table 10.1.

Table 10.1

Money	Bonds
No interest paid	Interest paid
Certainty of nominal value	Uncertainty of nominal value

The decision on whether to hold **bonds** or **money** will depend upon the **expectations** of bond prices.

Bond prices will vary inversely with interest rates. We illustrate this by considering the case of 2½ per cent consul. This is an irredeemable fixed interest government stock which will pay £2.50 per annum for each £100 (nominal value) stock in perpetuity. If market rates of interest were 2½ per cent a bond holder could expect to sell a consul for £100. However, if market interest rates were to rise to 5 per cent then the price of consuls would fall to £50. This would represent a yield of 5 per cent: £2.50 interest payment on the £50 purchase price. Any higher price would involve receiving a yield below the market rates payable on other bonds. In our example, a doubling of interest rates leads to a halving of consul prices. The situation with other bonds where the redemption payment has to be taken into account is a little more complicated, but the general rule still applies: rising interest rates are associated with falling bond prices.

With the aid of Figure 10.4 (overleaf) we are now in a position to complete our explanation of the **speculative demand for money**. People will have some **expectations** concerning interest rates and if i^* represents the expected rate it follows that if the market rate (i) is below the expected rate (i^*) there will be **expectation** that interest rates will rise and bond prices (BP) fall (because of the inverse relationship between bond prices and interest rates). To avoid incurring capital losses financial wealth will be held as **money** rather than **bonds**. The reverse will apply when $i > i^*$.

This view gives a step-like shape to the speculative demand for money. If we assume that **interest rate expectations** differ over the market between i_1 and i_2 in Figure 10.4(b) then aggregating individuals' demands gives the curve shown in the diagram. Above i_2,

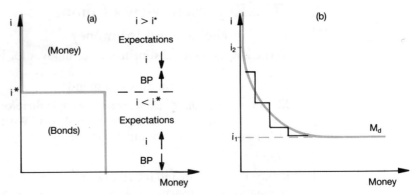

Fig. 10.4 Speculative demand for money

everyone believes interest rates will fall and the demand for speculative balances is zero. The opposite occurs when interest rates fall to i_1 and the demand for speculative balances becomes perfectly elastic–this is known as the **liquidity trap**. Widespread changes in expectations of interest rates will shift the schedule and this is a potential source of **instability** for the **demand for money**.

A modern alternative to Keynes's view of the **speculative demand** can be explained briefly. The more bonds that are held in a financial portfolio, compared with holding money, the greater the risk of capital loss but the greater the return on assets. As most people will enjoy interest payments but wish to avoid risks, they will decide on the best balance for their portfolio given their preferences. Those who are highly **risk averse** will hold a relatively small proportion of bonds. Note that people will generally hold a **mixed portfolio** of money and bonds, whereas the Keynes approach suggested **all or nothing** behaviour. If interest rates were to rise, this would lead people to hold more bonds and less money, as the increased interest would compensate them for taking a higher risk. As with the earlier explanation of the speculative motive, the demand for money is likely to be inversely related to interest rates: $M_{ds} = f(i)$.

10.3.2 Money supply changes and the effect on output

We can now bring together the demand for and supply of money to explain the **Keynesian view of the role of money**. In Figure 10.5(a) the money supply is assumed to be exogenous and fixed by the government. The **demand for money** reflects the factors we discussed in the previous section. There will be an interest rate, i_1, where demand equals supply and the money market is in **equilibrium**.

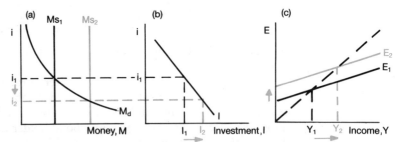

Fig 10.5 Illustration of the effects of change in money supply

If the money supply is increased then there is an excess supply. This leads to an increased expenditure on financial assets, bonds, which raises their price and lowers interest rates (recall the inverse relationship between bond prices and interest rates). When interest rates fall to i_2 then people are willing to hold the increased money supply. In contrast to the simple **quantity theory** in which expenditure on goods and services responds to money supply changes, the Keynesian approach stresses the impact on financial markets. This does not mean that output is unaffected because interest rate changes are likely to affect some items of expenditure. We can see this in Figure 10.5(b) and (c). In Figure 10.5(b) the lower interest rate encourages investment which in turn increases aggregate expenditure (Figure 10.5(c)) from E_1 to E_2 and raises income and output from Y_1 to Y_2. We can summarize:

$$M \rightarrow \Delta i \rightarrow \Delta I \rightarrow \Delta Y$$

Many **Keynesians** have tended to be sceptical about the impact of money supply changes on income. They have argued that money supply changes may not have a large effect upon interest rates because there are a large number of money substitutes. So an excess supply of money will spill over into the amount of liquid (non-money) assets held but may have relatively little effect on bonds and interest rates. In these circumstances, the demand for money is highly interest elastic.

A second reason for doubting the efficacy of monetary policy concerns the **lack of sensitivity of expenditure** to interest rate changes. If investment or other expenditure is interest inelastic, money supply changes will have little impact on output, even if large interest rate changes occur.

The Keynesian belief that both of these links in the transmission chain (from **money** to **income**) were weak led to the conclusion that policy makers would do better trying to directly influence aggregate demand through **fiscal policy**.

10.3.3 Keynesian objections to the quantity theory

The three assumptions we considered at the beginning of the chapter which turn the quantity of money identity into a theory have been challenged by Keynesians.

10.3.3.1 Stable velocity

We have seen that this assumption rests on the view that there is a **stable demand for money**. Keynesians are less inclined to believe in this stability. The widespread availability of **money substitutes** weakens the link between money and spending. So a tight control of some aggregate that is designated as '**money**' would lead to the use of some other financial instrument. The ability of institutions to innovate means that the authorities are always likely to be 'one step behind'. This point was vividly made by Lord Kaldor, who, after remarking on the close correlation between cash in circulation and spending, argued that if the authorities were to restrict cash withdrawals close to Christmas it would be most unlikely to stop festive spending as both sellers and purchasers would find an alternative means of payment.

The extreme case of this argument can be summarized as follows:

$$\overset{\uparrow\downarrow}{M}V = PO$$

i.e. $\Delta M \rightarrow \Delta V$

10.3.3.2 Exogeneity of money—the issue of causality

Kaldor's example can be used to illustrate a second criticism which focuses on the issue of **causality**. In the **quantity theory view**, the money supply is exogenous: it determines spending, not vice versa. However, Kaldor pointed out that Christmas spending is not caused by an increase of cash in circulation, but by the desire to spend.

The causality in the **quantity theory** may run from right to left rather than the direction suggested by the quantity theorists. This position is illustrated below.

$$\overset{\uparrow \longleftarrow \overset{\uparrow}{} \overset{\uparrow}{}}{M V = P\ O}$$

External   Wage
changes   pressures   Expenditure

i.e. $\Delta P \rightarrow \Delta M$, $\Delta O \rightarrow \Delta M$

Here, both prices (*P*) and output (*O*) are treated as **exogenous**. Output may be determined, in the Keynesian manner, by aggregate demand or expenditure, while prices are influenced by wage settlements and external factors such as oil prices and exchange rate movements. When the value of goods and services bought increases, because of inflationary or real pressures, this causes the money supply to increase.

This view of the **quantity theory** explains why many Keynesians are unimpressed by a high correlation between inflation and monetary growth. As always, correlation tells us nothing about causality and in this case it supports two different explanations of the role of money. Some indirect support for the Keynesian view comes from advocates of the quantity theory who have in the past criticized governments for adopting a passive monetary policy which allowed the money supply to expand to accommodate inflationary pressures. They argued that the causality could be reversed and that a tight monetary policy would lead to a decline in inflation rates. But this leads us to a third criticism of the quantity theory.

10.3.3.3 Full employment? The unemployment cost of anti-inflation policy

The traditional quantity theory assumed that the economy operates at **full employment** so increases in spending, caused by a rise in the money supply, cause prices to rise. Keynesians would argue that **full employment** cannot be assumed and the **unemployment costs** of a tight monetary policy may be severe and prolonged. This can be summarized:

$$\text{MV} = \begin{array}{c} \downarrow \xrightarrow{\hspace{1cm}} \downarrow \\ P \quad . \quad O \\ \uparrow \quad \downarrow \\ W \leftarrow U \end{array}$$

To concentrate on the essentials of this argument we have ignored or rejected earlier objections and have accepted that a reduction in the money supply, with V constant, will affect spending. But the impact of the policy is on **output** and **unemployment**. The tight monetary policy reduces spending and as firms cut back on output, workers are laid off and **unemployment** increases. This may exert a downward pressure on wages which can then feed through into prices. However, the Keynesian view of the trade off between unemployment and wage inflation suggests that large unemployment increases may be necessary to secure a modest reduction in wage increases. (We explore this further in Chapter 12.) Keynesians would also argue that self-regulating forces cannot be relied upon to return the economy to full employment; a slump in output might persist.

Many **modern monetarists** accept that there are short-run unemployment costs in an **inflation-reducing monetary policy**; but they argue that these are temporary. In the long run, they suggest, the traditional quantity theory is correct: money supply changes affect prices, not real variables like output and unemployment. (This is discussed more fully in the next chapter.)

10.3.4 Monetarists versus Keynesians—how large is the divide?

We have presented some significantly diverging views on the role of **money** which probably exaggerate the extent of the divisions among economists. Most monetarist economists would not stick rigidly to the **traditional quantity theory** in the short run. Milton Friedman's restatement of the quantity theory in the mid-1950s suggested a demand for money function that embraced Keynesian thinking by recognizing that money was a way of holding wealth and was not just demanded for transaction purposes. The experience of the last decade in the UK, with persistent high unemployment and reservations being expressed about the stability in the demand for money, may have swelled the ranks of the so called **pragmatic monetarists**.

The Keynesian position has tended to shift over the post-war period. The view that 'money doesn't matter at all' because velocity is highly variable and unpredictable, is now a minority one (held by a group known as **extreme Keynesians**). Although many would accept that governments should pay attention to the **rate of monetary growth**, they would not advocate that a policy to reduce inflation should be based entirely on monetary control because, as we explained in the previous section, the **unemployment costs** would be extremely high. While some still hold extreme monetarist and Keynesian views, the two viewpoints have moved closer together over the influence of money on spending (the lefthand side of the quantity theory). Most debate in recent years has been over the **impact of monetary policy on unemployment**–the righthand side of the equation.

10.4 UK monetary policy

10.4.1 An outline of post-war monetary policy

The widespread acceptance of Keynesian ideas after the Second World War meant that **quantity theory views** were set aside and **monetary policy** played a secondary role to **fiscal policy**. There were no attempts to control the money supply. **Monetary policy** was directed at controlling credit through directives limiting bank advances and hire purchase controls. By the early 1970s there was concern that the banks were unduly restricted by this approach. The introduction in 1971 of **Competition and Credit Control** was designed to encourage competition between banks and to rely upon interest rates rather than direct restriction to control credit. A massive expansion in banks' deposits followed and by the end of 1973 some hire purchase controls had been returned and the '**corset**' arrangement designed to control the growth in bank deposits had been introduced.

The deterioration in economic performance during the 1970s, particularly the sharp rise in inflation rates, led to a search for an alternative approach to managing economies. Monetarist ideas gradually gained support among leading institutions and governments. **Monetary targets** were introduced in many countries. In the UK there had been a growing interest in **monetary aggregates** throughout the 1970s, though the first publicly announced money supply target did not occur until 1976. This certainly did not mark a complete conversion to the quantity theory. **Incomes policy** at that time played a more prominent role in the attempt to reduce inflation and the government were still **fine tuning aggregate demand** in the Keynesian manner.

10.4.2 Monetary policy in the 1980s

It was the election of the Thatcher government in 1979 that formally marked a significant shift in approach to macro-policy. It made the **reduction in inflation** through the control of the **money supply** its major objective. We discuss this policy more fully in Chapter 13 but we now outline its main features.

A **medium-term financial strategy (MTFS)** was introduced with M3 (or sterling M3 as it was then known) money supply target ranges for a period of four years. These targets were accompanied by PSBR plans which were intended to minimize the pressure on interest rates that reducing the rate of monetary growth might have produced. The underlying relationship is the one we discussed in the previous chapter and can be summarized as:

Money supply growth = PSBR −	Sales of	+	Bank	+	External
	debt to		lending to		currency
	non-bank		private		flows
	public		sector		

If a large PSBR had persisted then meeting MTFS targets would have involved, *ceteris paribus*, large sales of debt (mainly gilts) to the public and this would have put upward pressure on interest rates. So an **appropriate fiscal stance** was regarded as crucial to meeting the government's money supply targets.

The government abolished a number of restrictions which affected the operation of money markets: **exchange controls** (1979), the **corset** (1980) and **reserve asset ratio** (1981). At the same time it ensured that an **active bill market** could be maintained by increasing the number of eligible banks and requiring them to hold a minimum of 4 per cent of their liabilities with the discount houses. The suspension of **MLR** (**minimum lending rate**) was designed to increase the ability of the authorities, through intervention in the money markets, to influence short-term interest rates.

It was through the **PSBR** and **interest rates** that the authorities tried to control the money supply; but they were not highly successful in meeting targets. Much of this difficulty arose because of the behaviour of bank lending to the private sector: it did not seem very responsive to changes in interest rates. There were some attempts to control its growth by overfunding the deficit (selling more gilts than the PSBR) but this was stopped in 1985. Growing doubt about M3 as a target and indicator led to increased attention to other monetary aggregates and the introduction of M0 targets. The practice of setting four-year targets for M3 was dropped in 1986. There was a gradual but noticeable shift in emphasis in the MTFS away from **money supply control** to **fiscal policy** and **PSBR targets** during the 1980s.

10.5 The IS–LM model

10.5.1 The IS–LM model

10.5.1.1 Interaction of the goods and money markets

In section 10.3.2 we saw that changes in the **money supply** can affect output by the effects of interest rate changes on aggregate demand:

$$\Delta M \to \Delta i \to \Delta I \to \Delta Y$$

This does not give the complete picture because income changes will affect the demand for money e.g. higher income will raise the transaction demand and if the money supply is fixed this will cause interest rates to rise. This can be summarized as:

$$\Delta Y \to \Delta M_d \to \Delta i \ldots$$

This will affect demand and income and have further feedback effects on the demand for money.

What we are observing is two markets which interact with each other. There is the '**goods market**' in which real output is determined by aggregate demand. This is the **Keynesian income–expenditure model** where the condition for equilibrium is that income equals expenditure ($Y = E$). There is also the **money market** in which equilibrium occurs where the demand for money is equal to the supply of money ($M_d = M_s$). The two markets interact, as we have shown, through **interest rates** (which affect aggregate demand) and **income** (which affects the demand for money).

The **IS–LM** model allows us to find a position where both markets are simultaneously in equilibrium. This is achieved by considering for each market the **income–interest rate combinations** that produce an equilibrium. This is most clearly understood through a diagrammatic approach that produces IS and **LM schedules.**

10.5.1.2   The IS schedule

The **IS schedule** shows points of equilibrium in the goods market for a combination of income levels and interest rates. To illustrate how an **IS schedule** is derived we will use a very simple income–expenditure model, the **goods market**, where consumption (C) is a function of income (Y), investment (I) is a function of interest rates (i) and government expenditure (G) is exogenous.

$$C = f(Y)$$

$$I = f(i)$$

$$G = \overline{G}$$

$$Y = E = C + I + G \text{ (equilibrium condition)}$$

In Figure 10.6 we have the familiar income–expenditure diagram which we will assume is in equilibrium initially at Y_1. We need to know the interest rate to establish an equilibrium income because investment, a component of aggregate expenditure (E), is sensitive to interest rates. We have assumed that the initial interest rate is i_1. We have an interest rate–income combination (Y_1 i_1) that is consistent with equilibrium and we can mark this as point A in the diagram. Now, let us consider the implication of a lower interest rate, i_2. Investment will rise to I_2 and this will raise aggregate expenditure (from E_1 to E_2), which will increase the equilibrium income level from Y_1 to Y_2. We now have another income–interest rate combination (Y_2, i_2) which can be shown as point B. A similar procedure for an interest rate of i_3 will produce point C. If we join points A to C (and clearly we could have generated many similar points by the same process) we have an **IS schedule.** Every point on this schedule represents **goods market equilibrium.**

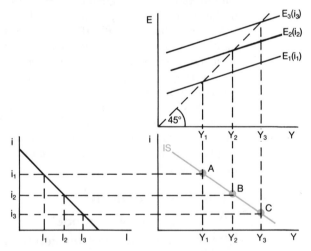

Fig 10.6 Derivation of an IS schedule

IS schedules can be derived easily for more complicated models. We would generally expect them to look similar to the one we have derived. If expenditure is inversely related to interest rates it will behave in the manner we have described. The slope of the IS schedule will depend upon:

1 The **interest elasticity of expenditure**–the lower this is, the smaller will be the effect on aggregate expenditure and therefore income so the IS will be relatively steep.

2 The **marginal propensity to withdraw**–the higher the marginal propensity to withdraw the smaller the impact of expenditure changes on income; so interest rate changes have a small effect on equilibrium income thus giving a relatively steep IS schedule.

10.5.1.3   The LM schedule

The **LM schedule** shows points of equilibrium in the **money market** for combinations of income and interest rate. We derive it in Figure 10.7. Part (a) is the same money market diagram we used in section 10.3.2 (Fig 10.5(a)). Recall that demand for money is a function of income and interest rate and the money supply (M_s) is exogenous.

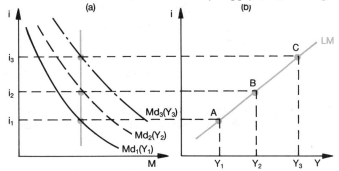

Fig 10.7 Derivation of the LM schedule

$M_d = f(Y, i)$

$M_s = \overline{M}_s$

$M_d = M_s$ *(equilibrium condition)*

We need to know the level of income before we can draw the demand for money; let us suppose it is Y_1. Figure 10.7(a) shows us that the money market is in equilibrium at i_1 and we can therefore derive the income–interest rate combination A in 10.7(b). If we take a higher income level, say, Y_2, then this raises the **transaction demand for money** (at any given interest rate) and shifts the demand for money schedule outwards to M_{d2} where the new equilibrium is at interest rate i_2. This allows us to derive point B in Figure 10.7(b). By a similar process we can derive point C. Joining these points gives the **LM schedule**. It shows **money market equilibrium** for a given money supply.

The **LM schedule** is normally drawn with a positive slope as in our illustration. Its slope will depend upon:

1 Income elasticity of the **demand for money**–the higher the income elasticity the steeper the slope of the LM schedule.

2 Interest elasticity of the demand for money–the lower the interest elasticity the steeper the slope of the LM schedule.

10.5.1.4 Equilibrium in the IS–LM model

We can determine a point of **general equilibrium** (i.e. where both money and goods markets are simultaneously in equilibrium) by bringing the two schedules together. This is done in Figure 10.8. Remember that the **IS** shows points of equilibrium in the **goods market** and the **LM** shows equilibrium points in the **money market**. So the point where they cross (A) is the only income–interest rate combination where they are both in equilibrium. All other points mark **disequilibrium**–the nature of the disequilibrium is marked on the figure.

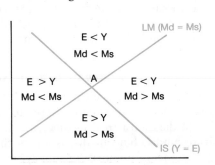

Fig. 10.8 LM and IS equilibrium

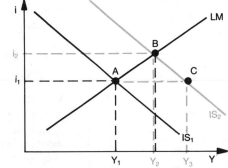

Fig. 10.9 Shift in IS schedule

The equilibrium will alter if the IS and/or LM schedule shifts. In Figure 10.9 we show the effect of a rightward shift of the IS schedule which, for example, would occur if government expenditure was increased. The equilibrium income rises from Y_1 to Y_2 and interest rates increase from i_1 to i_2. Expenditure multipliers will generally be less in an IS–LM model. In the illustration the IS schedule shifts out by a distance AC ($= Y_1Y_3$). Point C represents a goods market equilibrium if interest rates remain at i_1 but the effects of this expansion in income on the money market will not allow interest rates to stay the same. Increased income means higher transactions demand for money and if the money supply is unaltered then interest rates must rise, as the upward sloping LM schedule shows. So the overall change in income Y_1 to Y_2 is less than if interest rates remained the same. The distance $Y_2 Y_3$ relative to $Y_1 Y_3$ (the constant interest rate case) is sometimes taken as a measure of **crowding out**. It is an indicator of how far a fiscal policy not accompanied by an expansion in the money supply is effective in increasing income.

10.5.2 Application of the IS–LM model

10.5.2.1 Monetary and fiscal policy

The **IS–LM model** is well suited to examining the relative strengths of **fiscal** and **monetary policy**. In Figure 10.10(a) we can compare the impact of an expansionary fiscal policy under three monetary conditions which for convenience we represent on one LM schedule. The horizontal range in the LM schedule results from a perfectly elastic demand for money or 'liquidity trap', as described in section 10.3.1.3. It may be thought of as an **extreme Keynesian position**. In contrast the vertical part of the LM schedule is where the demand for money has zero interest elasticity. This would occur with the quantity theory where the demand for money is only a function of income. In this range **fiscal policy** is totally ineffective in changing income; there is total **crowding out**. At the other extreme fiscal policy is at its most effective. Figure 10.10(b) allows us to consider the effectiveness of **monetary policy**. It shows the effect of an increase in the money supply which causes a rightward shift in the LM schedule (because at a given rate of interest money market equilibrium is associated with a higher income level). **Monetary policy** causes the largest effects on income in the quantity theory range of the LM schedule. By contrast in a liquidity trap interest rates do not fall so income is unaffected.

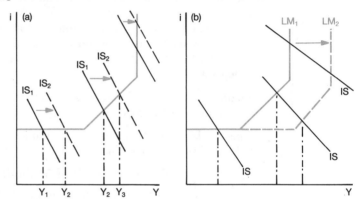

Fig. 10.10 Fiscal and monetary policy

Differing views about the **interest elasticity** of the demand for money and the responsiveness of aggregate expenditure to interest rates (which refers to the slope of the IS schedule—not illustrated here) have been the source of debate over the relative efficacy of monetary and fiscal policy in the past. The IS–LM model can be used to illustrate these arguments and also to show the effect of an expansionary fiscal policy financed by an expansion in the money supply (both IS and LM schedules shift to the right) in contrast to one that is funded by selling gilts to prevent an increase in the money supply (only the IS schedule shifts).

10.5.2.2 Derivation of the aggregate demand schedule

We turn finally to the effect of price changes on the IS–LM model. This requires us to clarify a matter that we have conveniently chosen to ignore until now. The income on the Y axis of the IS–LM diagram is real income, which is the appropriate measure for the **income–expenditure model**; but our discussion of the demand for money so far in the chapter has been in terms of nominal (or money) income. Fortunately we can reconcile this difference in approach comparatively easily. We can relate the demand for money to real income; but we must recognize that this will be a demand for real money balances (M/P). Money market equilibrium requires that this demand be equal to the real money supply.

A fall in the price level, *ceteris paribus*, will raise the real money supply (M/P) and shift the LM schedule out to the right. (We can alternatively view this as a downward shift of the LM schedule showing that money market equilibrium at a given income level is now associated with a lower interest rate following the fall in prices.) This is sometimes known as the **Keynes effect**.

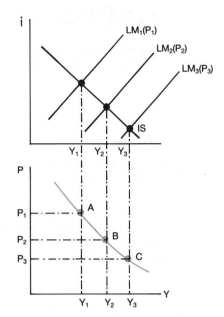

Fig. 10.11 Aggregate demand schedule

We can now derive an **aggregate demand schedule** to show what the various sectors of the economy (households, firms, government and the overseas sector) are prepared to buy at different price levels. In Figure 10.11 at price level P_1 the IS–LM equilibrium is at Y_1; this allows us to derive point A in the bottom diagram. A lower price (P_2) will shift the LM schedule out to the right and produce the new equilibrium Y_2; this gives point B in the price–real income diagram below. By a similar process other points such as C may be derived. The resulting line joining these points is the **aggregate demand schedule**. We use this in the next chapter, along with aggregate supply, to consider further aspects of macro-policy and the controversies surrounding it.

11 Aggregate demand, supply and growth

11.1 Introduction

The macroeconomic analysis so far has centred on aggregate demand and ignored **aggregate supply**. In this chapter we will look at the short- and long-run aspects of aggregate supply and consider the different approaches of **Keynesians** and **monetarists**. The **monetarist** approach is generally used to show the ineffectiveness of demand policies and to indicate the role of **supply-side policies** which we discuss in section 11.5. The long-run aspect of aggregate supply involves a consideration of the factors which determine a country's growth rate. We conclude by briefly discussing why the UK has had a relatively poor growth rate since the Second World War.

The chapter will:

- explain how an aggregate demand curve (showing the relationship between price and output) is derived
- explain the derivation of the aggregate supply curve
- discuss the different monetarist and Keynesian views on the shape of the aggregate supply schedule
- illustrate output determination in the aggregate demand and supply model
- discuss the effectiveness of monetary and fiscal policies using the aggregate demand–supply model
- explain what is meant by supply-side policies
- outline two basic theories of growth
- consider the reasons for the slow growth of the UK economy

11.1.1 Examination guide

This chapter covers a number of topics that may arise in examination questions, though the coverage will vary with the course. Most courses will require you to be aware of the debate over the **effectiveness of demand management** policies. The aggregate demand and supply model provides a suitable framework for considering this topic. An alternative approach is provided by the **Phillips curve**, which is discussed in the next chapter. The **aggregate demand and supply** model can be used to analyse a wide variety of problems, for example, the macroeconomic effects of tax cuts and oil price increases. You should consider whether it is a more fruitful approach than the **income–expenditure model**. In the two examples cited there are advantages in using aggregate demand and supply because in the case of tax cuts both demand- and supply-side effects can be illustrated and with oil price increases it is an approach that allows both the deflationary effect on output and the inflationary consequences for prices to be shown.

Supply-side policies have become increasingly popular with governments and this is reflected in many examination papers. If the question is a general one, which it is likely to be on introductory courses, then you should make sure that you cover all the main aspects of this approach (see section 11.5).

Economic growth invites two types of questions. Firstly, the main emphasis may be on exploring the **theories of growth**. Many courses, particularly those leading to professional qualifications, place more emphasis on the second area, the causes of growth, which are often considered in an applied manner and related to the issue of slow growth in the UK. Do not attempt to learn reams of figures but concentrate on the main arguments and conclusions.

11.2 Aggregate demand

11.2.1 Derivation of the aggregate demand schedule

In Chapters 7 and 8, where we developed the basic Keynesian model, we tended to call the expenditure schedule **aggregate demand**. This term is used in many introductory courses. However, it is also used to describe something which more obviously resembles a demand curve: a schedule showing the demand for an economy's output or real national income, (Y), and the price level, (P).

The derivation of this aggregate demand curve is shown in Figure 11.1. We start with the familiar income–expenditure model in the top diagram showing an equilibrium at Y_1. If the prevailing price level is P_1, we can mark a point, A, showing the equilibrium in the bottom diagram which plots income (Y) against the price level (P). If prices fall we can expect aggregate expenditure to increase (say to E_2) for two main reasons. First, lower prices, with a fixed nominal money supply, will mean that real money balances increase. As these are part of the wealth of households this will tend to stimulate consumer spending. Secondly, interest rates will fall as a result of the larger real money supply and this will increase spending. So a lower price level of P_2 is associated with a new equilibrium income of Y_2. This is shown in point B in the lower diagram. Other similar points can be derived and these form an **aggregate demand schedule**. The greater the wealth effects and the more interest elastic spending, the more responsive aggregate demand will be to changes in the price level.

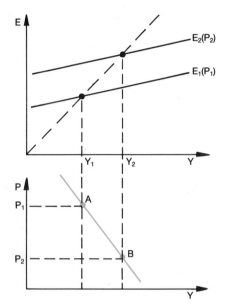

Fig. 11.1 Aggregate demand curve

For those of you who cover the **IS–LM** model in your course a derivation from that model was shown at the end of the last chapter. (The derivation did not include the wealth effect on consumption, but that can be added by recognizing that it would shift the IS curve out and make the aggregate demand schedule flatter.)

11.2.2 Shifts in the demand schedule

Any change which causes the aggregate expenditure schedule to shift upwards will cause the aggregate demand schedule to shift outwards (to the right): an increase in investment expenditure, exports or autonomous consumption will all move the aggregate demand schedule out to the right. The same effect will result from an expansionary fiscal policy which raises government spending and cuts taxes.

Increases in the nominal money supply will lower interest rates and stimulate spending so it will shift the demand schedule outwards. Changes in the exchange rate, *ceteris paribus*, will affect aggregate demand. A depreciation of sterling (which, *ceteris paribus*, improves the UK's competitiveness) will shift aggregate demand to the right as more is exported and less imported.

11.3 Aggregate supply and output

11.3.1 Aggregate supply

Aggregate supply shows the total output that will be supplied at different price levels. We concentrate upon the short-run supply curve where the stock of capital is fixed and employment, (N), is variable. In these circumstances the behaviour of the labour market will determine employment and hence output. We distinguish between different views of how the labour market operates and varying approaches to aggregate supply. This has significant implications for output determination.

11.3.2 The classical view

A convenient starting point is the **classical view of aggregate supply** which Figure 11.2 will help us understand. Figure 11.2(c) shows the **labour market,** with demand for and supply of labour as a function of the real wage. The real wage (W/P) is the money (or nominal) wage deflated by the price level. It is suggested that the demand for workers by firms will depend on the money wage that has to be paid in relation to the price the firm can expect to obtain for its product. So if money, wages and prices increase by 10 per cent the **real wage** is unaltered and employment will not change because labour is no more expensive, in real terms, than it was. It is similarly assumed that workers, in determining the amount of labour to supply, will be influenced by the real wage.

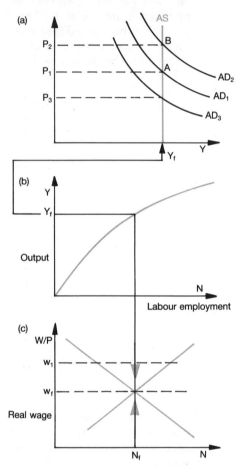

Fig. 11.2 Classical view of aggregate supply

If we assume that the **labour market always clears**—excess demand and supply are rapidly eliminated by alterations in the real wage—then employment will be N_f. We can regard this as full employment. (Some unemployment will be associated with this point but we can defer discussion of this until section 11.5). As we know the level of employment we can work out output from the production function. The production function relates output, (Y), to factor inputs:

$$Y = f(K, N)$$

As we are assuming that capital (K) is fixed in the short run, output varies with employment of labour (N). If employment is N_f then output is Y_f.

Aggregate supply will be a vertical line at Y_f (see Figure 11.2(a)). It does not vary with changes in the price level because of our assumption that the labour market clears. **Equilibrium income** is determined where aggregate demand equals aggregate supply. With demand curve AD_1 this will be at point A. If aggregate demand increases to AD_2 then a new equilibrium point will be at B and price level P_2. Notice that output is unaffected and remains at Y_f. The reason for this is that the rise in prices, with a given money wage, would depress real wages and create excess demand for labour. This in turn increases wages. The market will clear with real wages unchanged at w_f; but money wages and prices will have increased in the same proportion. The reverse will occur if demand declines, e.g. falls from AD_1 to AD_3, with money wages and prices both declining but real variables such as output and real wages being unaffected. This model has profound policy implications. It shows that demand management policy will not affect output and employment: it can only affect prices. This also suggests that the only way to raise output is through shifts of the aggregate supply schedule.

11.3.3 The Keynesian view

The **Keynesian view** implied by the simple income–expenditure model is illustrated in Figure 11.3(a). This shows that the schedule is perfectly elastic up to the full employment income (Y_f). So increases in aggregate demand (e.g. AD_1 to AD_2) raise output until Y_f is reached, without affecting prices. After that further increases in demand (e.g. AD_2 to AD_3) raise prices (P_1 to P_2) but do not affect output.

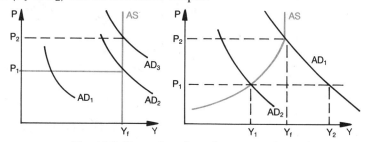

Fig. 11.3 Keynesian view of aggregate demand

This approach, which is often described as **extreme Keynesianism**, makes the assumptions that non-competitive firms set prices according to costs and that a unionized labour market, with negotiated settlements, makes wages inflexible in the short run so that reductions in money wages are resisted. Downward rigidity in money wages is also assumed in an **alternative Keynesian view** of aggregate supply. In Figure 11.3(b) a reduction in aggregate demand from AD_1 to AD_2 will cause prices to fall but as historically given money wages do not fall, the real wage rises and employment and output decline as firms move up their demand curves. This is reversed if aggregate demand rises from AD_2 to AD_1: both output and prices rise, from Y_1 to Y_f and P_1 to P_2 respectively. However, when full employment is achieved further increases in aggregate demand do not raise output but cause prices and wages to rise.

Whether the **aggregate supply** is an inverted L shape or upward sloping, it is clear that increases in aggregate demand can raise output and employment (providing there are unemployed resources–that is if output is below Y_f).

The **multiplier effects** of an expansionary policy will differ according to which aggregate supply curve we choose. With an upward sloping supply curve multiplier effects will be less than in the model from which the aggregate demand schedule was derived (i.e. the **income–expenditure** model or **IS–LM**). This reduced impact is the effect of rising prices on real money balances. Rising prices reduce real money balances (given an unchanged nominal money supply), which in turn raises interest rates and reduces expenditure. This is reinforced by wealth effects which cause lower consumption. The differences can be seen in Figure 11.3(b) where the outward shift of aggregate demand, at a given price level, shows what the multiplier effect would be in the basic income–expenditure model (or IS–LM model). So income would rise from Y_1 to Y_2 if prices were constant. However, the increase in prices confines the income change to Y_1 to Y_f.

11.3.4 Monetarist aggregate supply

All **monetarists** accept that the **long-run aggregate supply schedule** will be vertical, for the same reasons outlined above: the labour market will clear at the equilibrium real wage. However, there are differences over the short-run position. We consider the two views: the **gradualist monetarist** and the **new classical monetarist**.

11.3.4.1 Gradualist monetarists

Milton Friedman, who has been a leading figure in the growth of monetarism, has been very much associated with what we are describing as a **gradualist monetarist position.** He argues that in the long run increases in the money supply will affect only nominal variables, such as prices, and leave real variables, like output and employment, unaffected. However, in the short run, output *will* be affected. This means that while the long-run supply curve is vertical, the short-run schedules are upward sloping. An illustration will help clarify this. In Figure 11.4(a) (overleaf) we start at an equilibrium position at A; the associated equilibrium in the labour market is X (Figure 11.4(b)).

Expectations play an important role in this model. We assume that initial price and wage levels are what is expected. If there is an increase in aggregate demand (from AD_1 to

AD_2) this will be perceived by individual firms as an opportunity to raise prices. As wages will not be expected to increase firms believe that real wages will fall so they move down their demand curve for labour, from X to Z in Figure 11.4(b). But the workers' view of the situation is very different. They interpret the tighter conditions in the labour market as presenting an opportunity for money wages to rise. As they expect prices to remain at P_1 their **expectation** is that real wages will increase so they move up their supply curve from X to Y.

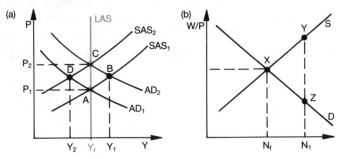

Fig 11.4 Equilibrium and expectations

This diametrically opposed interpretation of what is happening (and is likely to happen) by firms and workers allows employment and output to rise. We move along an upward sloping short-run aggregate supply curve SAS_1 from A to B. This situation can only be temporary because it is based upon misconceptions about wages and prices. Firms have based their expectations of wages on the levels paid in the past; so as increased demand in the labour market raises money wages they **adapt their expectations** to what they experience. Similarly, workers who thought prices would remain unchanged **adapt their expectations** as prices rise. The effect of this is that firms move back up their demand curve for labour as they realize that real wages have not declined and workers move back down their supply curves as they learn that prices as well as wages have risen and their expectation that real wages would rise was incorrect. Employment and output will fall and the short-run aggregate supply curve will shift to the left. Long-run equilibrium is restored when output returns to the original level and the labour market is operating at the original real wage. Although real variables have not changed, money wages and prices are higher. In terms of Figure 11.4(a), the new long-run equilibrium is C—it is a point on the new short-run curve (SAS_2) and on the vertical long-run supply curve (LAS).

We will always be on the **long-run supply curve** (LAS) as long as expectations of nominal variables such as prices are correct (see points A and C where this is the case); but false perceptions will cause movements up or down the **short-run supply curve** (SAS). If prices are above those expected then output will be above Y_f (as we have seen in our illustration); but if they are less than expected their output will be below Y_f. We can see this if we trace the effects of a fall in demand from AD_2 to AD_1. Prices fall from P_2 but the expected price level is initially still equal to P_2. Employment and output are reduced as we move towards point D. Expectations start to adapt in the face of lower prices and the supply curve shifts downwards. Eventually equilibrium is restored at point A when the lower price of P_1 is expected and the short-run aggregate supply curve is SAS_1. Notice that we have a different short-run supply curve for each expected price level.

We develop this model further when we consider the **interrelationship** between **inflation and unemployment** in Chapter 12. It is from the policy implications for the control of inflation that the term **'gradualist'** is derived. We saw in our last illustration that there are short-run implications for employment when demand is reduced; monetarists like Friedman stress there are short-run unemployment costs in reducing inflation because it takes **time** for **expectations to adapt**. The faster governments try to bring inflation down, the greater the cost: so they are advised to adopt a **gradualist approach** and tighten demand conditions slowly.

The gradualist approach is known as **adaptive expectations**. This suggests that people form their **expectations** on what they have become used to and **adapt** them in the light of experience. This appears to be a rather backward looking view and has the rather implausible implication that expectations could be systematically wrong. For example, in our earlier illustration, successive demand increases would have left people consistently underestimating the price level. This does not appear to be rational behaviour, so many monetarists take a different view, known as **rational expectations**. This approach is not exclusive to monetarists, but we will discuss it in the context of what has sometimes been described as extreme monetarism—the **new classical school**.

11.3.4.2 New classical monetarists

The **new classical school** has two important characteristics: it uses **rational expectations** and it assumes **rapid market clearing**. The **rational expectations** approach assumes that best use is made of all available information to form expectations: economic agents (firms, workers, etc.) will use this information to generate forecasts. Using an earlier illustration, forecasts of the price level would use an aggregate demand–supply model (if this was the best that was available) and feed in information on policies and events that would be likely to affect aggregate demand. So if, for example, the government raised aggregate demand from AD_1 to AD_2 (Figure 11.4), this would be incorporated in the forecast. If, for the moment, we assume that the forecast accurately predicted a price level of P_2, this would be used by firms and workers to set prices and wages. The misinterpretations we discussed earlier need not occur.

Here we need to introduce the second (and distinctive) characteristic of the new classical school: its assumption of **rapid market clearing**. This implies that prices (including wages) are highly flexible and will respond rapidly to increase in demand so that the short-run aggregate supply curve will be vertical. (In our example the economy will move straight from point A to C without a detour towards a point like B. This takes us back to the classical view. It suggests that demand management policies are totally ineffective in changing real variables such as output and employment.

In our illustration we used the simplifying assumption that the price level was accurately forecast; but this assumption is not part of the **rational expectations hypothesis**: there will generally be **forecast errors**. These will arise because of unforeseen policy changes as well as model errors and the type of factors we discussed in Chapter 8 (section 8.5.1.3). However, these errors cannot have a systematic pattern, because if they did this information could be used to improve forecasts. We are left with a random forecast error (u) that will affect output in an unsystematic way:

$$Y = Y_f + u$$

So demand management policies are still unable to affect output–except unpredictably.

Shifts in aggregate demand do affect prices and one implication of the **new classical position** is that inflation may be reduced with little cost. So if we were at point C in Figure 11.4(a) a reduction in aggregate demand from AD_2 to AD_1 would lead to a move from C to A, with prices falling from P_2 to P_1. A combination of **rational expectations** and **rapid market clearing** would affect output and employment. This argument is sometimes used to support a policy of **immediacy**, as opposed to **gradualism**, in eliminating inflation.

The **new classical school** has attracted a good deal of criticism, which we discuss in Chapter 12.

11.3.4.3 Eclectic monetarists

Finally we can identify a group that might be described as **eclectic monetarists**. This group would accept that some markets clear rather slowly–particularly the labour market: the short-run supply curve will be upward sloping. Some of this group of economists are very close to the Keynesian position, at least in their analysis of the short-run situation.

11.3.5 The implication for demand management policy

The monetarist analysis has important implications for macroeconomic policy, so it may be helpful to summarize the main points:

1 Generally, **expansionary demand policies** will raise the price level and this will tend to reduce the **multiplier effect** of these policies. However, **extreme Keynesians** argue that the aggregate supply curve is horizontal while there is a spare capacity, and in this case extra output can be secured without raising prices.

2 **Monetarists** argue that in the long run demand management policy is ineffective in changing output and employment. It affects only nominal variables such as prices and money wages, not real variables.

3 Many **monetarists** suggest that in the short run demand management policy can affect output because of misperceptions (resulting from **adaptive expectations**) and /or inflexible prices and slowly clearing markets. However, this effect is only temporary and in the long run output will not be affected.

4 **New classical monetarists** argue that a combination of **rational expectations** and **rapidly clearing markets** means that even in the short run output and other real variables will not be affected.

5 The **monetarist attack** on demand management policies does not leave the government totally powerless to affect output but it does mean the emphasis should be on **supply-side policies**, designed to shift the aggregate supply curve out to the right.

11.4 A closer look at the labour market

So far in our discussion of the **labour market** we have said relatively little about **unemployment**. We can now consider what factors affect the degree of unemployment associated with **labour market equilibrium** and we introduce a concept that is much used by monetarists: the **natural rate of unemployment**.

11.4.1 Types of unemployment

While an **equilibrium position** in the labour market represents a point where demand and supply of labour are equal this does not imply that unemployment is zero. In Figure 11.5 the line EE plots employment against the real wage. At the equilibrium real wage, OW, employment is L_1, not L_2 (which is how we showed it in our simpler accounts earlier in the chapter). So although there are L_2 jobs available, only L_1 will be filled. L_1L_2 ($= AB$) represents the **frictional unemployment** which results from imperfections in the operation of the labour market which prevent synchronization between demand and supply.

There will be a number of reasons for this. In a dynamic labour market some people will be unemployed because they are between jobs. Poor information may mean that workers who are in demand are unaware of job vacancies. There may be an occupational mismatch between the jobs available and the skills of the workers seeking work. Finally, there may be a geographical mismatch between vacancies in one part of the country and the unemployed in another area.

Sometimes the occupational and geographical mismatch is associated with a changing industrial structure and the resulting unemployment is known as **structural unemployment**. Keynesians would want to add a further explanation of the unemployment AB by arguing that the position of the EE schedule is affected by the pressure of demand in the economy and that a low level of spending can give rise to **demand-deficient unemployment**.

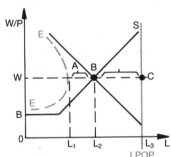

Fig. 11.5 Unemployment

Unemployment may be voluntary—some people may not actively seek work. In Figure 11.5 the vertical line $LPOP$ represents the total working population and as the supply curve, S, indicates those who are effectively seeking work, the difference BC ($=L_2L_3$) is **voluntary unemployment**. This will arise because some people have formally or effectively taken early retirement, for example women (or occasionally men) who stay at home to bring up children, the ill and incapacitated and those for whom state benefits are higher than available wage rates. The position of supply curve S will be affected by income tax rates, which determine the proportion of income retained, and by the value of state benefits. In the diagram, OB represents the basic benefit level and it is assumed that the supply curve becomes perfectly elastic at that point.

Total unemployment is represented by the distance AC. However, this will not necessarily correspond to the registered unemployed to which published figures refer. Registration rules will determine how much of AC appears in the official unemployment count.

11.4.2 The natural rate of unemployment

We are now in a position to define a term that has been much used by monetarists in recent years: the **natural rate of unemployment**. It is the rate of unemployment that occurs when the labour market is in equilibrium: AC, in our illustration. The natural rate is the amount of unemployment we would get when the economy was at Y_f in Figure 11.4. Market clearing will take us towards this rate and it should be clear from our discussion in section 11.3.4 that it cannot be affected by demand management policies, at least in the long run. It is, however susceptible to **supply-side policies**.

11.5 Supply-side policies

Supply-side policies are designed to shift the aggregate supply curve to the right. These policies encompass a variety of measures, some of which command widespread support while others are highly controversial.

11.5.1 Reducing frictional unemployment

11.5.1.1 Information

It has been recognized since the beginning of the century, when labour exchanges were introduced, that employment can be increased if **information flows** in the labour market can be improved.

11.5.1.2 Training

Occupational mismatch can be improved through training. There are differences in opinion over the extent to which the market can be relied upon to provide adequate training. The more general the skills required the more likely that government intervention will be appropriate because there is likely to be underprovision by the private sector as firms try to be **free riders** and rely on others to provide training.

11.5.1.3 Housing policy and geographical mobility

Geographical mismatch may be improved by better information to both sides of the labour market and financial assistance to workers seeking jobs. Some advocates of **supply-side policies** highlight difficulties in the housing market as a cause of geographical immobility. It is not easy for a council house tenant to give up a house in one area and obtain another elsewhere. The private rented sector is relatively small, so in general mobility is confined to owner occupiers. It is suggested that greater incentives for private landlords (e.g. the removal of rent controls) would expand the rented sector and that sales of council houses make former tenants more mobile.

11.5.2 Reduction in real benefit payments

A controversial proposal which is suggested by some economists as part of supply-side package, is a **reduction** in **real benefits payments**. This would make being unemployed more unattractive and act as incentive to work. In Figure 11.5, *OB* indicates the basic benefit level. If this were reduced the supply curve would shift down and to the right, reducing voluntary unemployment *BC*.

This policy is designed to alter the **replacement ratio** (the ratio of benefits to net income from work). This ratio has changed relatively little in the last twenty years and so it seems unlikely that it has been a major cause of the general rise in unemployment over the period. Of course, this does not necessarily prevent benefits cuts from reducing unemployment. There is evidence that a more relaxed application of the work test for claimants may have put them under less pressure to seek work.

The benefit cuts proposals have attracted much criticism, particularly from those who believe that this category of voluntary unemployment is relatively small and that benefit cuts will lower the living standards of a group that is already relatively poor.

11.5.3 Reduction in marginal income tax rates

The incentive to work for the unemployed could be increased if the **denominator of the replacement ratio**, net income from work, could be raised. This could be achieved in many cases through **income tax cuts**. This proposal has a much wider application and the emphasis is often directed towards the higher marginal tax rates of high-income earners. Cutting these rates, it is suggested, will encourage entrepreneurial and managerial effort and raise output. It will also raise the net income on savings so that more finance will be available for investment. More generally, tax cuts may encourage overtime working. If there is an **incentive effect** from the tax cuts, the labour supply curve will move to the right so employment and output will be raised. Income tax cuts need not necessarily reduce tax revenue, as a number of supply siders have been keen to point out.

If the **incentive effect** is sufficiently strong the expansion of the tax base (income) will be sufficient to compensate for the lost revenue resulting from a lower tax rate. The point is illustrated in Figure 11.6 (overleaf) in what is known as the **Laffer curve**. It shows that tax revenue will increase with higher tax rates up to t_1 and then start to decline as the rate becomes a disincentive to work. In the region above t_1, cuts in tax rates will increase tax

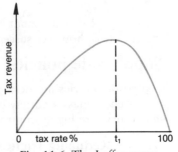
Fig. 11.6 The Laffer curve

revenue. High tax rates will also encourage tax avoidance schemes—as the rates fall there is less incentive to avoid the tax.

There can be little dispute over the approximate shape of the **Laffer curve** because there will be no tax revenue when there is a zero tax rate, and if the tax rate were 100 per cent no one would work. Over a certain range tax revenue must rise; it will then decline. There is, however, considerable dispute over where the UK and other countries are in relation to t_1. The evidence is difficult to interpret as it is unclear how far an output expansion following a tax cut is due to the cut or some other factors.

Those sceptical about the ability of this supply-side policy to raise output would point out that tax cuts may reduce effort and labour supply. This is because the increase in income will tend to encourage people to take more leisure (and therefore work less). This tendency, known as the **income effect**, contrasts with the view underlying our earlier discussion. There we assumed that people would substitute more work (which is now better rewarded because of the tax cut) for less leisure—this is known as the **substitution effect**. The overall effect of a tax cut will clearly depend upon the relative strengths of the two effects.

11.5.4 Reduction in trade union mark up

Another argument with **supply-side implications**, which has been put forward strongly by Professor **Patrick Minford**, among others, is that curtailing trade union powers can reduce unemployment and raise output. The argument can be simply put: trade unions raise wages above the competitive level (this is known as the **trade union mark up**) and in doing so they reduce employment. If the trade union mark up can be reduced, for example through **legislation** which limits the powers of trade unions, then employment and output can be raised and the aggregate supply can be shifted to the right.

11.5.5 Privatization

Milton Friedman has frequently argued that services are more efficiently provided by the private than the public sector. This view is shared by advocates of **privatization**. If correct it means that by selling off nationalized industries we can release resources to be used elsewhere in the economy and so raise output generally. Like many of the other policies we have discussed here this one attracts a certain amount of opposition. We discuss **privatization** in Chapter 16; but we can point out at this stage that in many cases nationalized industries are monopolies and it is doubtful whether there will be efficiency gains if **privatization** occurs without suitable **regulatory control**.

11.5.6 Supply-side policies in the UK

The use of the term **supply-side policy** in the macro-policy debate has very much accompanied the attack on **demand-side policy**. It is frequently used to argue for a change in emphasis away from the use of macro-demand management to affect output and employment, towards micro-policies of the type outlined in the previous sections. Demand policies (control of **PSBR** and **monetary targets**) are, according to this view, to be directed towards **controlling inflation**.

This approach to policy was broadly adopted by the Conservative government in 1979 in the USA the Reagan administration (1980–88) similarly laid stress on **supply-side policies** as a means of raising growth and employment. Several other governments have followed this lead. The evidence on various aspects of the policy is not conclusive, as we indicated in earlier sections. We will consider the impact of UK policy in the next chapter along with our assessment of anti-inflation policy. Whatever the limitations and doubt about the type of **supply-side policies** we have been discussing, it should be recognized that they have raised some questions about the operation of **labour markets** that had previously been somewhat neglected.

However, it would be wrong to suppose that post-war **Keynesian policy makers** were exclusively concerned with manipulating aggregate demand. It was certainly the case that immediately after the war the main concern was to prevent a recession: but by the mid-1950s a decade of extremely low unemployment and a recognition that the UK economy was growing more slowly than those of our major competitors led policy makers to look for ways of increasing the **supply-side** potential of the economy. There were tax concessions to encourage investment and restrictions on bank loans were generally directed at personal rather than corporate borrowers. The first half of the 1960s saw two attempts, one by Harold Macmillan's Conservative administration and the other by the Labour government elected in 1964, to introduce **indicative planning** to raise the growth rate. This was loosely based on what was regarded as a successful approach to planning in France. It involved leading industrialists, in principle, revealing their plans for the next four years, identifying inconsistencies and adopting policies in cooperation with the government to provide a coherent programme for rapid growth. The French method had its limitations, but British attempts to adopt the approach were rather rushed and insufficiently prepared. Labour's National Plan was effectively aborted by a sterling crisis within a year of its publication.

While these were not particularly successful attempts to increase the growth of potential output, they demonstrate a concern to do so. There were other approaches too: the Labour government introduced the selective employment tax designed to raise productivity in the economy through a shake out of labour from the service industries toward manufacturing. The **Barber boom** of the early 1970s was intended to be more than simply an attempt to reduce unemployment through higher demand. It was hoped it would increase aggregate supply at a faster rate, so allowing the UK to enjoy a virtuous circle of high growth and productivity combined with low inflation and a surplus on the balance of payments.

11.6 Economic growth

11.6.1 Long- and short-run growth

Economic growth in the long run depends on the **growth of aggregate supply** or productive potential. In terms of a diagram we have used before, economic growth can be represented by the outward shift of the **production possibility curve** (see Figure 11.7). The study of growth is about explaining such a movement. In the short run the change in output may be greater or smaller than growth in productive potential or capacity, depending on whether capacity utilization is increasing or decreasing. For example, the movement from A to C in Figure 11.7 involves an increase in output which is greater than the growth in capacity (B to C); but as C is on the production frontier, subsequent output increases are confined to growth in capacity.

The distinction between a **rise in capacity** (shift of the production possibility frontier) and an **increase in capacity utilization** (operating nearer to the frontier) is an important one. Arguments that centre on the inefficient operation of an economy are probably directed at capacity utilization rather than the growth of capacity itself and therefore offer only shortterm gains in output rather than the long-term ones that are associated with movements of the frontier. The growth of economies is of longstanding interest to economists; we begin our account by looking at the **Harrod–Domar growth model**.

11.6.2 The Harrod–Domar growth model

Within a few years of the publication of Keynes' *General Theory* economists were exploring the long-run implications of the Keynesian model. The so called Harrod–Domar model is one outcome. **Domar** pointed out that **investment expenditure** has a dual role: an income and a capacity effect. The first is the familiar **Keynesian relationship** that investment generates income, via the **multiplier**. The **capacity effect** arises because investment will increase the capital stock and therefore the potential output of the economy. Maintaining full employment will require a growth in demand to match the increase in supply potential. In Figure 11.8 (overleaf), Yf_1 represents an initial full employment level of output and in this simple two-sector model (where we assume there is no government or foreign trade) equilibrium will require an investment spending of I_1, given the savings behaviour of households as shown by the savings schedule ($S = sY$, where S is the value of savings per period of time and s is the marginal propensity to save). If we assume that this represents net investment (i.e. capital stock is increased), then the capacity of the economy is raised and full employment output will rise, say to Yf_2. This means that in the next period, if full employment is to be maintained, that investment will have to rise to I_2. We can put this more formally: the change in equilibrium income (ΔY)

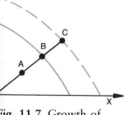

Fig. 11.7 Growth of aggregate supply

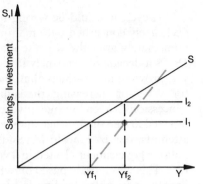

Fig. 11.8 Harrod–Domar growth model

will be equal to the change in investment times the multiplier, which in this type of model is equal to the reciprocal of the marginal propensity to save (s):

$$\Delta Y = \frac{1}{s}\Delta I$$

The increase in capacity or full employment income, (Y_f) is assumed to be related to investment:

$$\Delta Y_f = \sigma I$$

where σ is the marginal capital–output ratio (i.e. the ratio of the change in output to the change in the capital stock). If full employment income is to be maintained then ΔY must be equal to ΔY_f. Setting the two expressions equal and rearranging we obtain

$$\frac{\Delta I}{I} = \sigma s$$

indicating the required growth of investment depends upon the marginal propensity to save and the marginal output capital ratio—an increase in either will raise the growth rate.

While Domar was concerned to explore the conditions for full employment to be maintained, **Harrod** considered whether it was likely to be achieved. Harrod uses a simple two-sector model in which equilibrium is where $S = I$; but he introduces an **accelerator investment equation**:

$$S = sY \qquad \text{savings}$$
$$I = v\Delta Y \qquad \text{investment}$$
$$S = I \qquad \text{equilibrium}$$
$$\text{So } sY = v\Delta Y \qquad \text{and}$$

$$G_w = \frac{\Delta Y}{Y} = \frac{s}{v} \qquad \text{desired or warranted growth } (G_w)$$

The **equilibrium growth path** (or what Harrod called the **warranted growth rate**, G_w) is equal to the ratio of the marginal propensity to save (s) and the accelerator coefficient, or capital–output ratio, v. This is an equilibrium growth rate which would fulfil the plans of households and firms. However, there are two important points to consider. First, there is no certainty it will be achieved; and second, there is no guarantee that if it is achieved it will be consistent with full employment.

The first difficulty is known as the **stability problem**. It arises because investment will depend on the expected growth of output and if businessmen do not correctly predict the

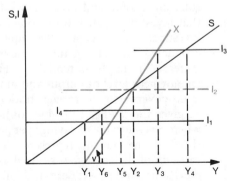

Fig. 11.9 Warranted growth path

warranted rate, it is not likely to be achieved. We can see this with the aid of a diagram. In Figure 11.9 the initial equilibrium is at Y_1 with investment I_1. The slope of solid line Y_1X represents the accelerator coefficient. So if firms believe output will rise to Y_2 it will indicate the amount they wish to invest, which in this case will be I_2. If they do so they will fulfil their expectations. This is the **warranted growth path**. What happens if they expect some other output? If they expect a growth rate higher than the warranted, for example, Y_3, the accelerator relationship will indicate that invesment should be I_3; but with that level of spending output will be Y_4. So although firms have overestimated the warranted rate they believe they have underestimated (because the expected Y_3 is less than Y_4), so they will revise their expectations upwards. This will take them further from the equilibrium warranted rate. The reverse happens if they underestimate the warranted rate. Suppose they expect an output of Y_5: the Y_1X line shows they will wish to invest I_4. In doing so, a lower output level will be achieved than they predicted (Y_6 instead of Y_5), so the expected growth rate will be revised downwards and they will move further away from the warranted rate. The warranted rate is the only one where expectations are fulfilled and offers the prospects of a steady path. However, if there is a departure from it, then the actual growth rate is likely to diverge from the warranted path.

The second main difficulty that Harrod pointed out was the **uniqueness problem**. This refers to the likelihood that the warranted growth rate (G_w) will not be compatible with the rate required for full employment. The latter Harrod called the **natural rate of growth** (G_n). It will be equal to the growth of the labour supply (n) and the growth of output per head resulting from new techniques (t):

$$G_n = n + t$$

Overall, steady growth at full employment requires the warranted and natural rates to be equal:

$$G_w = G_n \quad \text{i.e.} \ \frac{s}{v} = n + t$$

The difficulty arises because the four variables, s, v, n and t, are regarded as independently determined and it will therefore be fortuitous if G_w and G_n are equal.

The **Harrod model** is in keeping with the **Keynesian view** that market economies are inherently unstable and cannot be relied upon to achieve full employment. The model could be criticized for being rather rigid and limited in treating all four variables as exogenous. However, it provides a framework for posing questions about the growth process. Many subsequent theories have addressed the problem of whether equilibrium can be consistent with the natural rate of growth.

11.6.3 Neoclassical growth model

The **neoclassical growth model** responds to the problem of the uniqueness of the warranted and natural growth rates by showing that movements in factor prices may lead to adjustments in the warranted rate. In the **Harrod model** the capital–output ratio, v, was assumed to be fixed, whereas the **neoclassical model** has a production function where output is related to capital (K) and labour (L) inputs, i.e.

$$Y = f(K, L)$$

The factor intensity will vary according to relative factor prices. If we have a position where the warranted rate is less than the natural rate this will imply growing unemployment:

$$G_w < G_n \quad \text{i.e.} \ \frac{s}{v} < n + t$$

In these circumstances we might expect real wages to be depressed and labour to be substituted for capital, in which case the capital–output ratio will fall. If the value of v falls then this will raise the value of s/v, that is, the warranted rate will rise towards the natural rate. In this way the market responds to a difference between the natural and warranted rates and leads to appropriate adjustments in the latter. The **neoclassical model** does not address the other problem referred to by Harrod as it assumes that the actual and warranted rates will always be equal.

There may be many reasons why the adjustment process we described is not as smooth as our account suggests. Imperfections in competition may mean that the wrong price signals are given. The market economy may be very slow to respond to change in relative prices so that the process of adjustment may be prolonged.

11.7 Economic growth in the UK

11.7.1 Causes and effects of economic growth

There is considerable disagreement among economists over the causes of economic growth. One of the difficulties is the interpretation of the empirical evidence: it is generally not easy to distinguish cause from effect. For example, some countries with high growth rates spend a relatively high proportion of GDP on investment; but it is not clear whether this is a cause or a consequence of rapid growth. Similarly, countries with rapidly growing economies have tended to be highly competitive in international trade and enjoyed rapid export growth; but again cause and effect are in doubt.

It is fairly safe to assume that economic growth involves the interplay of several factors and growth can generate or be associated with changes that themselves promote growth. For example, rapid increases in productivity help to keep inflation low and, *ceteris paribus*, improve a country's competitive position, which in turn eases the constraints on the growth rate. The increases in demand associated with improved competitiveness will tend to stimulate investment which is likely to lead to further productivity gains. This is one example of the cumulative aspects of growth and illustrates the difficulty of isolating causal factors from the associated effects.

11.7.2 An overview of growth performance

For 25 years after the Second World War nearly all industrial countries, including the UK, enjoyed a period of unprecedented rapid growth. In the UK concern centred on the economy's poor performance in comparison with other countries. We consider these issues in our discussion below as well as the possible reasons for the slow down in growth rates in all countries since 1973.

Table 11.1 Comparative growth in various economies

UK growth rate 1870–1987
(annual percentage growth of total output)

1870–1913	2.2
1913–50	1.7
1953–73	3.0
1974–87	1.7

Growth of GDP in major economies 1953–87
(annual percentage change)

	1953–73	1974–87
USA	3.4	2.5
Japan	9.6	3.8
West Germany	5.5	1.9
France	5.3	2.3
UK	3.0	1.7
Italy	5.3	2.4
OECD	4.5	2.5

(OECD *Economic Outlook*, December 1987)

It is useful to put our discussion in context by considering the relative position of major economies and how they have changed over the years. The table below shows how these countries compare with the UK:

Table 11.2 GDP, per head, per worker and per hour worked, 1984

	GDP per capita (UK = 100)	GDP per worker (UK = 100)	GDP per hour worked (UK = 100)	Participation rate (%)	Hours worked per person per year
USA	143	133	124	45.5	1630
Sweden	139	115	120	51.0	1460
West Germany	120	124	112	41.0	1680
France	114	124	121	39.1	1550
Japan	111	98	69	48.0	2150
Belgium	110	125	116	37.2	1640
Netherlands	106	130	121	34.5	1640
UK	100	100	100	42.4	1520
Italy	91	104	101	36.9	1570

(Feinstein, *Economic growth since 1870*, 1988)

Comparisons of this type are difficult to make because of the problems of converting to a common currency; nevertheless, some comments can be made on these figures. In terms of the living standards indicated by GDP per head of population, nearly all the major economies have achieved a higher level than the UK, with the USA over 40 per cent above the UK. We get a rather different picture if we consider relative efficiencies by examining GDP per worker and GDP per hour worked. The latter measure shows, with the exception of Japan, that all countries lie in a narrower range than that suggested by the first column. The gap between the high GDP per head countries, USA and Sweden, and the UK and Italy is roughly halved when output per hour is considered. The difference is accounted for by the higher participation rate (i.e. a larger proportion of the population working) in the USA and Sweden and, in the case of the USA, by a greater number of hours worked. Indeed these two factors account for the fact that Japan's low GDP per hour is not reflected in its ranking of GDP per head.

The figures for GDP per hour are support for the **convergence hypothesis** which suggests that countries will converge on the highest productivity levels and practices. In the 19th century the UK had the highest levels. In 1870 **labour productivity** in the USA was about 10 per cent lower than in the UK and it was roughly 50 per cent less in France, Germany and Italy. Japan's productivity was only about a fifth of the UK's. By the turn of the century the USA had become the world leader in terms of productivity. The convergence on the USA has been particularly noticeable in the post-Second World War period, as Table 11.3 below indicates.

Table 11.3 Business sector labour productivity levels relative to USA (%)

	1968	1973	1979	1986
Japan	31.2	46.4	54.2	64.6
West Germany	46.4	58.5	69.2	77.3
France	44.1	59.9	70.3	82.0
UK	48.9	58.1	61.5	67.3
Italy	48.6	65.4	71.1	76.8

(OECD *Economic Outlook*, December 1987)

Convergence occurs because of the diffusion of technology, the adoption of best management practices and techniques and the development of capital markets and other institutional arrangements associated with exploitation of the best productivity levels. This view helps us understand why countries other than the USA and the UK were able to grow faster over most of the period: they were **catching up** on the productivity levels of the UK and USA. On this interpretation, the fastest growing country in the post-war period, Japan, achieved its remarkable performance because it started from such a low base. This allows us to argue that the UK's relatively poor performance this century, in terms of growth rate, has in part been the consequence of its past success.

While this view offers a context within which to examine differences in growth rates, it leaves many questions unanswered. What determines the speed of the catching-up process? Why do some countries converge on the best performer more rapidly than others? Why did the UK, which had broadly similar or better productivity levels than Italy, West Germany and France in 1968 (see Table 11.3), fail to make the progress of the others in catching up with the USA; and why was there a slow down in growth in the 1970s?

11.7.3 Supply-side explanations of growth

We have said that we can think of economic growth as an outward shift of the **production possibility curve**. The position of the curve depends upon the quantity of factors, labour (L) and capital (K) and their productivity (P_T). This last term, which is often referred to as **total factor productivity** or **multi-factor productivity**, is determined by technology, the way inputs are organized and other factors (as we shall see below). This is the framework for the **supply-side approach** which explains growth in terms of the growth of these inputs and their productivity.

We can express this in the following way:

$$\dot{Q} = a\dot{L} + b\dot{K} + \dot{P}_T$$

where the dots over the variables signify percentage rates of change. So $\dot{Q}$ is the growth of output (or GNP) and $\dot{L}$, $\dot{K}$ and $\dot{P}_T$ are the rates of growth of labour supply, capital and total factor productivity. The coefficients a and b indicate the responsiveness of growth to changes in factor inputs.

Growth accounting uses this framework to attempt to analyse the sources of growth. To do so it makes certain assumptions to allow available data to be used. It is normally assumed that there are constant returns to scale, so an *x* per cent increase in inputs leads to an *x* per cent increase in output; so the coefficients *a* and *b* sum to 1. It is then generally assumed that there is perfect competition, which means we can use the share of factor income in GNP as the way of providing the relative weight of capital and labour, i.e. the values of *a* and *b*. We can demonstrate this for labour by assuming that *K* and P_T are zero; then

$$a = \frac{\dot{Q}}{\dot{L}} = \frac{\Delta Q}{Q} \cdot \frac{L}{\Delta L} = \frac{\Delta Q}{\Delta L} \cdot \frac{L}{Q}$$

$\Delta Q/\Delta L$ is the marginal product of labour (it shows how output changes when an extra worker is employed other factors being constant). Under perfect competition the wage (*W*) will be equal to the marginal product so we can write:

$$a = W \cdot \frac{L}{Q}$$

which is the share of wages in national income. (See Chapter 17 for further discussion on marginal productivity.) A similar approach can be adopted to demonstrate that *b* equals capital's share in national income.

Using data on the quantity of capital and labour and weighting them by the shares of factor incomes in GNP, it is then possible to calculate the growth of total factor productivity in the following equation:

$$\dot{P}_T = \dot{Q} - a\dot{L} - b\dot{K}$$

This approach produces measures that imply that most growth is attributable to productivity changes rather than the growth of factor inputs. In an attempt to break down growth factors further an augmented version is often employed where a measure of **quality** as well as **quantity** of factor inputs is used. There are also attempts to add **supplementary effects** such as output benefits resulting from the transfer of resources from low productivity agriculture to higher productivity uses elsewhere in the economy.

We can summarize this type of approach undertaken recently by Angus Maddison:

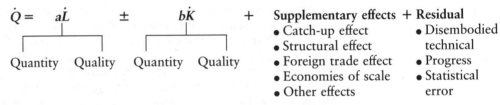

$\dot{Q} = \quad a\dot{L} \quad \pm \quad b\dot{K} \quad +$ **Supplementary effects + Residual**

Quantity Quality Quantity Quality

- Catch-up effect
- Structural effect
- Foreign trade effect
- Economies of scale
- Other effects

- Disembodied technical
- Progress
- Statistical error

He allowed for quality changes in the case of labour by taking account of the sex composition (women are weighted more lowly because it is assumed that their lower pay levels reflect lower productivity) and educational level of the workforce. Capital quality is assumed to improve because new technology may be embodied in new machinery. This is calculated by assuming that countries with a higher proportion of new capital have enjoyed a greater quality improvement. As well as estimating quality changes, Maddison identifies nine supplementary effects that should be taken into account when measuring the sources of growth. We have isolated four of these and grouped the others together:

1 The **catch-up effect** relates to the opportunities for productivity improvement that countries which lag behind the USA are offered when they adopt practices employed by the leader. This catch-up effect is assumed to be related to the size of the gap between the leader and follower and the rate at which it is being closed.

2 The **structural effect** is a measure of the output gains that result from the transfer of resources from low to high productivity areas of the economy. One of the main sources of these gains has been the movement of labour from agriculture to industry.

3 **Economies of scale** mean that output can rise proportionally more than the increase in inputs. In many of the growth accounting studies a supplementary allowance is made for this source and it is often quite important, amounting to nearly 10 per cent of growth in many cases. Maddison believes that the gains are more modest and assumes they are 3 per cent of growth.

4 Many commentators on growth believe that the **liberalization of trade** after the Second World War, with the removal or reduction in tariffs, and for European countries the formation of the **European Community**, helped generate the period of faster growth. Trade volume grew at an average annual rate of over 9 per cent between 1950 and 1973

compared with about 0.5 per cent between the two World Wars and 3.6 per cent more recently (1973 to 1984). Maddison has included estimates for the impact of this and called it the **foreign trade effect**.

5 Other effects include such factors as the **drag on growth** produced by the rise in energy prices and the benefit for some countries, including the UK, of the discovery and exploitation of oil and gas reserves.

Maddison's estimates are shown in Table 11.4. The **residual** represents **disembodied technical progress** (technological advances that are not embodied in new machinery) as well as **statistical and other errors**. If we compare the UK with other countries, the table indicates that the UK has grown more slowly because of a low increase in the quantity of capital, a smaller contribution from the catch-up effect (compared with countries other than the USA) and less benefit from structural effects. Most countries emerged from the Second World War with a much higher proportion of the labour force in agriculture and there is widespread agreement that this permitted faster growth than was possible for the UK. Indeed some accounts would give greater weight to this than Maddison's figures imply.

There are many critics of the growth accounting approach and even its advocates accept the limitations of unreliable data and the need to make assumptions about the contribution of various factors. Critics argue that assumptions about perfect competition (used to provide weights to evaluate the contribution of different factor inputs) are unjustified and undermine the whole process. They are also critical of treating capital as a homogeneous factor. The advocates of the approach argue that despite the limitations it does provide a framework within which to examine the growth process (critics generally have no alternative to offer). At best, though, it can be regarded only as a starting point because so many other questions need to be answered.

Table 11.4

	UK		USA		France		W. Germany		Japan	
	1950-73	1973-84	1950-73	1973-84	1950-73	1973-84	1950-73	1973-84	1950-73	1973-84
GDP	3.02	1.06	3.72	2.32	5.13	2.18	5.92	1.68	9.37	3.78
Labour quantity	−0.11	−0.93	0.85	0.95	0.01	−0.86	−0.03	−0.90	1.09	0.40
Labour quality	0.09	0.20	0.29	0.36	0.35	0.48	0.18	0.07	0.52	0.41
Capital quantity	0.99	0.77	1.02	0.85	1.10	1.20	1.63	1.03	2.49	2.17
Capital quality	0.52	0.38	0.51	0.43	0.56	0.43	0.53	0.35	0.58	0.38
Catch-up effect	0.14	0.29	0.00	0.00	0.52	0.49	0.68	0.40	1.02	0.44
Structural effect	0.10	−0.26	0.12	−0.07	0.46	−0.12	0.36	0.05	1.22	0.21
Foreign trade effect	0.16	0.06	0.05	0.02	0.19	0.06	0.21	0.06	0.26	0.05
Economies of scale	0.09	0.03	0.11	0.07	0.15	0.07	0.18	0.05	0.28	0.11
Other effects	−0.02	0.03	−0.04	−0.28	−0.02	−0.16	−0.12	0.55	0.64	−0.43
Total explained	1.96	0.57	2.91	2.33	3.32	1.59	4.29	0.99	8.73	3.74
Residual	1.06	0.49	0.81	−0.01	1.81	0.59	1.63	0.69	1.27	0.04
% explained	65.00	54.00	78.00	100.00	65.00	73.00	72.00	59.00	93.00	99.00

(Maddison, *Growth and Slowdown in Advanced Capitalist Economies*, 1987)

12 Inflation, unemployment and monetarism

12.1 Introduction

It should be clear from the last few chapters that monetarists and Keynesians disagree on many aspects of macroeconomic policy. In this chapter we will draw together some of these arguments by presenting an overall view of **monetarism** and considering the **Keynesian critique**. In the process, we shall review the differing views on inflation.

Many Western governments adopted monetarist-style policies in the 1980s. One of the first of these was the Thatcher government and we assess the operation of this policy at the end of the chapter.

This chapter will:

- define monetarism
- explain and illustrate the gradualist monetarist (adaptive expectations) view of the Phillips curve
- review the gradualist policy prescription
- explain the new classical view of the Phillips curve
- outline the operation of monetarist policy in an open economy
- explain the Keynesian criticism of monetarism
- outline and assess UK policy since 1979

12.1.1 Examination guide

Inflation and **unemployment** are key economic and political issues. It is not surprising that examiners seek to test students on these topics. You will be aware from our discussion so far that the causes and cures for both of these problems are highly controversial. Most questions on inflation and unemployment will require you to discuss and assess both **Keynesian** and **monetarist** positions. The emphasis of the question may be on the theoretical or empirical aspects of the topic. If the question is not explicit on this then you should consider both. For example, an answer to a question on an assessment of the monetarist view of inflation should discuss the theoretical difference between Keynesian and monetarists and indicate what support the two groups may draw from the empirical evidence.

12.2 What is monetarism?

There is no strict, universally agreed definition of **monetarism**. It is a phenomenon that has developed in the last 20 years and embraces a set of ideas originating with economists and stretching into the practical arena of politics. Within this range of ideas and policies there are some quite marked differences of opinion. We have already remarked that some eclectic (or pragmatic) monetarists adopt positions fairly close to some Keynesians. We will discuss two main types of monetarism: **gradualism**, an approach associated with **Milton Friedman**, and **new classical monetarism**. Despite the differences, there are three common views which all monetarists hold: the **quantity theory of money**, the **long-term Phillips curve** and the **rejection of policy activism**.

12.2.1 The quantity theory of money

Monetarists believe that **changes** in **nominal income** (that is, GDP in current price terms) are caused by **changes** in the **money supply**:

$$\Delta M \rightarrow \Delta Y$$

If the **money supply** increases more than **real income** then **monetary growth** will cause **inflation**. So

$$\Delta P = \Delta M - \Delta O$$

where ΔO is the increase in real income or output. This leads to the view that **zero**

inflation occurs when the money supply rises by an amount that is sufficient to meet the increase in real demand for money arising from growth in real incomes in the economy.

The underlying view of the **quantity theory** is that in the long run increases in the money supply lead to price rises. Output (or real income) will tend towards the full employment or the natural level because the labour market clears at the natural rate of unemployment.

12.2.2   Vertical long-run Phillips curve

Monetarists regard the **long-run Phillips curve** as **vertical** (see Figure 12.1). The **Phillips curve** shows the relationship between unemployment and inflation. The original Phillips curve, which we introduced in Chapter 2, suggested that lower unemployment was associated with higher inflation. If it is vertical, as the monetarists suggest, there is no trade off between the two variables: it is not possible to secure lower unemployment at the cost of higher inflation. The Phillips curve is vertical at the natural unemployment rate. (We discuss this more fully in section 12.3.)

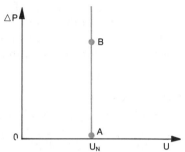

Fig. 12.1 Vertical long-run Phillips curve

12.2.3   Rejection of policy activism

Monetarists are opposed to the Keynesian approach to demand management: they reject the fine tuning of aggregate demand, or **policy activism,** to affect real variables like unemployment and output. They argue that a rise in aggregate demand cannot lower unemployment in the long run and merely increases inflation. Attempts to reduce unemployment and increase output depend upon micro-policies designed to reduce the natural rate of unemployment. This is why it is an easy step for many **monetarists** to advocate **supply-side policies** (see discussion in Chapter 11), though it should be remembered that this is not normally regarded as a necessary aspect of monetarism.

The **rejection** of **Keynesian policy activism** is in many ways the most important aspect of monetarism. It strikes at the heart of the Keynesian approach to macro-policy which dominated the period from 1945 up to the end of the 1970s. In some senses monetarism is part of a wider pro-market tide which is sweeping not only capitalist but socialist economies. However, this argument should not be overstated: it would not be inconsistent to agree with widespread intervention to change the distribution of income or affect the allocation of resources and at the same time accept the main features of monetarism. Indeed, there are some Marxists who would accept some aspects (e.g. the quantity theory of money) of the monetarist analysis.

12.3   Gradualist monetarism

We introduced the gradualist monetarist model in the last chapter in an aggregate demand and supply framework. Here we review the main features of that analysis and consider in particular the relationship between unemployment and inflation.

12.3.1   Monetarist view of unemployment

Monetarists believe that labour markets move towards an equilibrium position—that is they tend to clear. Movements in the real wage will eliminate excess demand and supply. The level of unemployment associated with equilibrium is known as the **natural rate of unemployment.** It will depend upon frictions in the labour market arising from occupational and geographical mismatches between vacancies and the unemployed as well as imperfect information. There will also be **voluntary unemployment** where the benefit level is regarded as sufficiently high to make the after-tax wages from work unattractive. (This is explained more fully in section 11.4.) **Unemployment** will diverge from the natural level when the real wage is not at the equilibrium level. This may simply reflect the fact that time is needed for the real wage to adjust to some change in the demand for or supply of labour. However, the main argument put forward by monetarists like **Milton Friedman** is that when unemployment differs from the natural rate it is a consequence of **incorrect expectations** about prices (see sections 11.3.4 and 12.3.2). But this **unemployment** is temporary because **expectations** will **adapt** and this will lead to wage adjustments which will return the market to the natural level of unemployment. This tendency towards the natural level is the basis of the vertical Phillips curve and the attack on Keynesian demand management policies.

12.3.2 Monetarist view of inflation

Inflation, according to monetarists, is caused by excessive expansion of the money supply. The foundation for this view is the **quantity theory of money**, discussed more fully in Chapter 10:

$$MV = PO_N$$

Increases in the money supply (M) lead to an increase in spending (or monetary demand) because the velocity of circulation is considered stable. In the long run output (O) or real income will be at the natural level (O_N) or full employment level, so the extra demand will raise prices. As the natural output level will grow over time, monetary expansion in excess of this will cause inflation; that is

$$\Delta P = \Delta M - \Delta O_N$$

This view of the inflationary process leads monetarists like Friedman to argue that the **control of the money supply** is both a necessary and sufficient condition for the reduction of inflation. However, Friedman's view of the short-run relationship between unemployment and inflation, the Phillips curve, leads him to urge a gradual approach to an anti-inflationary policy.

12.3.3 Gradualist monetarist view of the Phillips curve

The orthodox Phillips curve (which was referred to in Chapter 2) suggests that **wage inflation** (ΔW) is a function of **unemployment** (U):

$$\Delta W = f(U)$$

Monetarists argue that because workers and firms are interested in real wages, then the relationship should be written as

$$\Delta W = f(U) + \Delta P^e$$

where ΔP^e is the expected inflation rate. This means that money wage settlements (ΔW) will take account of expected inflation as well as the pressure of demand in the labour market ($f(U)$). This means we have a different Phillips curve for every expected inflation rate. In Figure 12.2 we show three Phillips curves. Notice that the Phillips curve shifts outwards when the expected inflation rate rises. This poses severe problems for governments which try to lower unemployment below the natural rate, as we will see later. However, even at this stage we can see the essence of the problem: a lower level of unemployment will involve a higher rate of inflation (a movement up a Phillips curve). But the higher rate of inflation leads to a higher expected inflation rate which shifts the Phillips

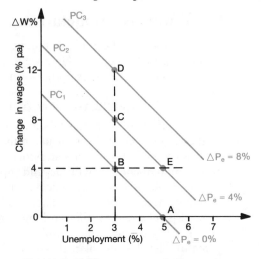

Fig. 12.2 Phillips curves and expectations

curve further upwards so that a given unemployment rate is associated with an even higher rate of inflation. This in turn leads to a further upward shift of the Phillips curve. Unemployment levels below the natural rate are associated with accelerating inflation because the Phillips curves shift as expectations respond to higher inflation. This is essentially the gradualist position: it suggests that **expectations** are formed **adaptively–** that is by people modifying their expectations in the light of experience.

An example will illustrate a number of the properties of this **monetarist model**. To make it easy to follow, we make three simplifying assumptions. First, that the Phillips curve is linear, i.e. a straight line, with the following values:

$$\Delta W = 10 - 2U + \Delta P^e$$

This means that if unemployment were 3 per cent and the expected inflation rate were zero, then the rate of wage increase would be 4 per cent. If unemployment remained the same but inflation was expected to be 6 per cent then wages would rise by 10 per cent.

Our second simplifying assumption is that wages and prices rise at the same rate, i.e.

$$\Delta P = \Delta W$$

Normally we would expect **productivity increases** to reduce the impact of wage rises on price inflation (see section 12.6.3 for a discussion of this point), but excluding this here keeps the example simple without damaging the conclusions. The overall equation is

$$\Delta P = 10 - 2U + \Delta P^e$$

The third assumption explains how expectations are formed.

$$\Delta P^e = \Delta P_{t-1}$$

It states that expected inflation in one period is equal to actual inflation rate in the previous period. It is a simple and crude example of **adaptive expectations**, with expectations responding fully and solely to what was experienced in the last period. **Gradualist monetarists** would suggest that **adaptive expectation formation** would be more complex than this (for example, extending the relevant period on which expectations are based), but again the general conclusions are not significantly affected by our simplification.

Table 12.1 Relationship of inflation and unemployment

Year	Unemployment	Inflation	Expected inflation
	U	ΔP	ΔP^e
1	5	0	0
2	5	0	0
3	3	4	0
4	3	8	4
5	3	12	8
6	4	14	12
7	4	16	14
8	5	16	16
9	5	16	16
10	6	14	16
11	6	12	14
12	7	8	12
13	7	4	8
14	7	0	4
15	5	0	0

Table 12.1 illustrates the path of **inflation** and **unemployment** over a period of years. We start off with zero inflation and none expected and an unemployment rate of 5 per cent. Suppose the government pursues an expansionary policy in year 3 by increasing the money supply. The unemployment rate falls and the inflation rate rises. We move from A to B, along the lowest Phillips curve in Figure 12.2. Notice from the Phillips curve and the table that the expected inflation rate is still zero because prices were not rising in year 2. In year 4 expectations will adapt to the 4 per cent inflation experienced in year 3 and the Phillips curve will shift up to PC_2. This makes it clear that if unemployment is to be maintained at 3 per cent this will now be associated with an 8 per cent inflation rate (see point C). Again we will have a situation where the actual inflation rate (8 per cent) exceeds the expected rate (4 per cent), so expectations will adjust further. PC_3 is the Phillips curve where the expected inflation is equal to 8 per cent. This shows that a further acceleration of inflation is required to 12 per cent, if unemployment is to stay at 3 per cent (see point D in Figure 12.2 and year 5 in Table 12.1).

Before proceeding further with the example, let us pause to underline a couple of points. This **monetarist view** of the Phillips curve means that the orthodox trade-off relationship between unemployment and inflation (whereby society can 'buy' lower unemployment at the cost of a higher rate of inflation) is temporary. The shifting Phillips curve in our illustration means that lower unemployment is associated with accelerating inflation (from 4 per cent to 8 per cent to 12 per cent).

Secondly, we can show the temporary nature of the trade off in another way. At point B unemployment has fallen to 3 per cent but the inflation rate has risen to 4 per cent and this causes the Phillips curve to shift upwards. If the government had chosen to keep the inflation rate at 4 per cent (rather than let it rise, as in our example) then unemployment would have returned to 5 per cent and in terms of the diagram we would have moved to E. Both of these points show the reason for monetarists' objection to a Keynesian reflation policy designed to reduce unemployment. Either it sustains lower unemployment at a mounting cost of accelerating inflation (points A to B to C to D) or it has only a temporary effect on jobs, with unemployment returning to the original level but at a higher rate of inflation (A to B to E).

Let us return to our example with inflation at 12 per cent and unemployment at 3 per cent. In years 6 and 7 the expansionary policy is not pursued as strongly and unemployment rises to 4 per cent. Notice that this increase in unemployment does not produce a fall in inflation–it merely slows the rate of increase to 2 percentage points per year instead of 4 percentage points, as the table and Figure 12.3 illustrate. We are still in a situation where inflation is greater than expected. In year 6, for example, inflation is 14 per cent yet the expected rate is 12 per cent, so when expectations adapt the Phillips curve shifts up again. It is only in years 8 and 9, when unemployment returns to 5 per cent, that we experience a **stable rate of inflation**–not price stability but a rate of inflation that is neither increasing nor declining. This again underlines the objection to demand management policies. We have returned to the original unemployment level but with a very much higher inflation rate: the few years of unemployment below 5 per cent have cost us dearly, with inflation rising to the peak of 16 per cent. As we shall now see, to reduce this inflation rate we shall have to allow unemployment rates to rise above 5 per cent.

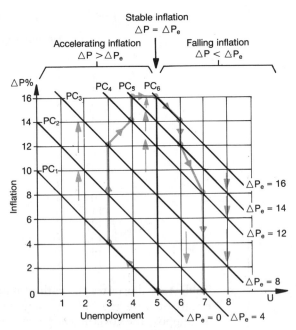

Fig. 12.3 Unemployment and inflation

In year 10 the government reduces the rate of growth in the money supply and inflation starts to fall (from 16 per cent to 14 per cent); but unemployment rises to 6 per cent. It is clear from the Phillips curve, PC_6, that inflation could have been reduced further, but the unemployment cost would have been greater. Indeed, zero inflation could be obtained; but the unemployment rate would have soared to 13 per cent. However, the same result can be achieved with a lower unemployment rate providing we are prepared to wait a number of years. So, for example, in year 11 the expected inflation rate falls to 14 per cent (as it adapts to the lower inflation in year 10) and shifts the Phillips curve downwards from PC_6 to PC_5. This means that an inflation rate of 12 per cent can be associated with unemployment of 6 per cent. In the remainder of the example a tighter monetary policy reduces inflation by 4 percentage points per year and this somewhat faster reduction of inflation compared with years 10 and 11 is associated with a slightly higher unemployment rate of 7 per cent. Throughout this process lower inflation causes expectations to be reduced and this shifts the Phillips curve inwards so that lower inflation is associated with any given unemployment level. This is the grounds for arguing for **gradualism** – spreading anti-inflation policy over a number of years keeps the unemployment costs to a minimum. The 'cold turkey' alternative of eliminating a high inflation rate immediately means massive unemployment. Typically, **Friedman** has advocated a four- to five-year programme to give time for expectations to adapt to the lower inflation produced by a tighter monetary policy.

By year 15 we have returned to our starting position: zero inflation and 5 per cent unemployment. We can now see even more clearly why this analysis leads to a rejection of Keynesian demand management policies. The demand expansion to reduce unemployment below 5 per cent led to accelerating inflation; to return to price stability it was necessary to raise unemployment above 5 per cent. As **Milton Friedman** has pointed out, you can have a binge but there is a hangover afterwards. If this analysis is correct, it is difficult to justify **reflationary policies**. If you examine Table 12.1 and Figure 12.3 you will see there is something rather special about the 5 per cent unemployment rate: it is the unemployment level where the inflation rate is stable (16 per cent in years 8 and 9, and zero in years 1, 2 and 15) and where the expected rate is equal to the actual inflation rate. This is the **natural rate of unemployment**, where the labour market is in equilibrium. The equilibrium may be associated with any rate of steady inflation – zero and 16 per cent are just two examples. As the labour market tends to clear in the long run then the long-run Phillips curve is a vertical line at the natural rate of unemployment. This shows what we have already discovered: that there is no trade off between unemployment and inflation in the long run.

According to monetarist analysis, the **labour market** would always be at the natural rate were it not for **mistaken expectations**. As we can see, every other unemployment rate is associated with a difference between expected and actual rates of inflation. Below the natural rate of 5 per cent the actual inflation rate is greater than the expected rate. It is mistaken perceptions that allow output to rise above the natural levels. Both firms and workers interpret expansionary policies as an increase in real demand for their goods and services. However, this is with **expectations** that are based on an earlier rate of inflation and previous demand policies. When **expectations adapt** to the current inflation rate, the labour market returns to equilibrium and the demand expansion is recognized as something that affects nominal variables only. This is what is happening in the example we referred to earlier, in Figure 12.2, when an expansionary policy causes a movement from A to B and then subsequently to point E when expectations adjust. The reverse occurs with unemployment above the natural level, where actual inflation is less than the expected rate. Here tighter policies cause a temporary loss of output and increase in unemployment, until expectations adjust downwards to lower inflation.

We can summarize this position as follows:

$$U = U_N + f(\Delta P^e \quad - \quad \Delta P)$$

$$\Delta M$$

If the actual rate of inflation is the expected one then the term in parenthesis is zero and unemployment is equal to the natural rate. However, if an **expansionary monetary policy** produces an inflation rate greater than the one expected, unemployment will be below the natural rate. This effect can only be temporary because expectations will adapt to the actual rate of inflation and unemployment will return to its natural level. If the authorities wish to maintain a lower than natural rate of unemployment then they need to increase the money supply at a faster rate so that inflation will be above the rate expected. The basis of unemployment reduction is fooling people about the inflation rate. As Friedman says, 'only surprises matter' in affecting real output and employment.

Our summary equation also shows why **gradualism** is advocated. Lower rates of monetary expansion reduce inflation; but if this is done sharply there is a large difference between actual and expected rates and unemployment rises significantly above the natural rate. A gradual approach keeps the actual rate closer to the expected and avoids the need for unemployment to rise to a high level.

12.4 New classical monetarism

When we discussed **new classical monetarism** in the last chapter we said that it was based on two main views: **rapid market clearing** and **rational expectations**. It is the way that expectations are formed that largely distinguishes this approach from the gradualism discussed in the last section. **Rational expectations** assumes that people will make the best use of available information (including economic models where appropriate). They will not necessarily forecast correctly, as there will be many reasons why mistakes could occur, but they will avoid systematic errors. In our previous example of adaptive expectations it was possible for people to be systematically wrong; but this implies irrational behaviour and will not occur under rational expectations.

Suppose the prevailing view of the cause of inflation is one based on the quantity theory of money; then under **rational expectations** people will use information on the **money supply** to form **expectations** about inflation. The equation used for adaptive expectations needs to be amended to

$$U = U_N + f(\Delta P^e - \Delta P)$$
$$\uparrow \qquad \uparrow$$
$$\Delta M^e \leftarrow \Delta M$$

So expected inflation depends upon what people expect the growth in money supply (ΔM^e) to be. This will in turn be affected by **actual growth, monetary targets** and **government policy announcements**. If there were perfect knowledge ΔM^e would equal ΔM, ΔP^e would be the same as ΔP and unemployment would be equal to the natural rate. Any expansionary policy would be fully anticipated and there would be no effect on real variables such as output and employment. In terms of the Phillips curve both the short-run and the long-run curves would be vertical (see Figure 12.1 where the effect of an expansionary policy is a move from A to B).

The **rational expectations hypothesis** does not assume perfect knowledge, so there will be errors, i.e.

$$U = U_N + e$$

where e stands for the **errors** in **expectations**. These arise because models are not perfect, nor is information on policy variables such as the rate of monetary growth. However, the errors cannot have a systematic pattern to them or this information itself could profitably be incorporated in the forecast. So there cannot be a systematic demand management policy designed to affect real variables. The error term, e, is random, so unemployment will be randomly distributed around the natural rate.

The analysis so far suggests that there is no need for gradualism in reducing inflation. A policy of **immediacy** (a sudden reduction in inflation, rather than the gradual approach discussed earlier) could be pursued. For example, the government may announce that it is about to stop expanding the money supply; providing the policy is believed, **expectations** will change and so too will **inflation**. It is worth noting that if markets respond very quickly then an alteration in inflation may precede the money supply changes, reversing the sequence normally associated with the quantity theory. As this response to policy suggests that there are no unemployment costs (in terms of Figure 12.1 we move from B to A), this implies a policy recommendation of **immediacy** rather than **gradualism**.

Many **criticisms** have been raised against the new classical position. One has centred on the assumption of **rational expectations**. We discussed this in Chapter 11 and we will not repeat those points here except to say that the hypothesis is fairly robust to criticisms. Much more contentious is the assumption of **very rapid market clearing**. In practice we know there are price contracts and annual wage settlements so there will be a certain steadiness to prices. **New classical models** can incorporate this type of inflexibility but price contracts and annual wage settlements tend only to produce a very short-lived effect on real variables.

12.5 Monetarism in an open economy

Economies like the UK's are very **open**—that is **international trade** is **significant**. It is important to consider the impact of this for monetarist analysis and policy. We will concentrate our attention on the **exchange rate** and the role it plays. This section contains material that is somewhat more difficult than the rest of the chapter and may be omitted if your course does not require you to consider how **monetarism** operates in an **open economy**.

12.5.1 A simple view of exchange rate determination

An exchange rate shows the rate at which one currency converts into another, for example $2 to £1. The exchange rate is determined in foreign exchange markets and for countries that operate under a **floating exchange rate system** (where there may be little or no government intervention) the rate may vary considerably. Many factors will influence the movement of exchange rates (considered more fully in Chapter 20); but here we concentrate on **relative inflation rates**. This is based on **purchasing power parity** theory, which has a long tradition in economics.

This theory suggests that subject to transport costs, tariffs, etc., prices in terms of a common currency (e.g. dollars) will tend to equalize–if they did not people would buy in the relatively cheap market and not purchase goods in the expensive area. So if prices were to double in the UK, and stay the same elsewhere, the exchange rate would halve (e.g. shift from $2:£1 to $1:£1) to maintain the same prices in a common currency ($). So a good whose sterling price was £1, and sold for $2, would now cost £2 but would still sell for $2. Of course if prices in all countries were to double, exchange rates would be unaffected–it is **relative** exchange rates that are important. We can summarize the position:

$$\Delta E = \Delta P_W - \Delta P_{UK}$$

where E is the exchange rate (the price of sterling in dollars), ΔP_{UK} is the UK inflation rate and ΔP_W is the world inflation rate.

We can extend this analysis to incorporate the **quantity theory of money**. If we adopt a simplified view of the quantity theory where the inflation rate is equal to the rate of monetary growth (ΔM), we can interpret exchange rate changes in terms of differences in monetary policy.

$$\Delta E = \Delta P_W - \Delta P_{UK}$$
$$\uparrow \qquad \uparrow$$
$$\Delta M_W - \Delta M_{UK}$$

So if monetary policy were more expansionary in the UK than in the rest of the world the inflation rate would be relatively higher and the exchange rate would depreciate.

Another way of looking at **purchasing power parity** is that it maintains a country's competitiveness. We can say that although the **nominal exchange rate** adjusts to changes in the price level, the **real exchange rate** remains constant. The **real exchange rate** is the nominal exchange rate (E) adjusted for the inflation rate, so where prices double and the nominal exchange rate halves, the real exchange rate and competitiveness remain unchanged.

In practice **purchasing power parity** does not hold with any exactness even over a number of years. Nevertheless, as we shall see in section 12.5.3, it proves helpful in understanding monetarist policy in the context of an open economy and we can explain some of the departures from purchasing power parity. Before doing so, it is important to distinguish between two types of market which display different degrees of price flexibility.

12.5.2 Fixed and flexible price markets

Price flexibility varies between markets. In some cases prices alter by the minute, (for example, the foreign exchange and stock markets). In other markets price changes are infrequent: in the labour market wages are typically fixed for a one-year period and for many products annual price lists are not uncommon. While there is a spectrum of price adjustments, we can classify markets into two types: **fixed** and **flexi-price**. Flexi-price markets have the feature of **continuous market clearing**. Prices are continually adjusting to ensure the market is in equilibrium. These are sometimes called **auction markets**.

In contrast, **fixed price markets** display price **rigidities**. Prices are not adjusted immediately when there is excess demand and supply. This may partly reflect the cost of price adjustments; but, more importantly, there are many markets where buyers prefer a degree of certainty over price to facing the day-to-day fluctuations which reflect changing market conditions. These are sometimes known as **customer markets**. In these markets there is an **implicit contract** or understanding that prices will be raised only when underlying costs rise; customers can feel relieved of the constant need to search around for lower prices.

The **labour market** in particular is characterized by rigidities. In many cases there are explicit **contracts** in the form of **wage agreements**: in others there may be implicit contracts whereby wage rates are changed periodically, usually on an annual basis. It is an interesting feature of **labour markets** that they tend to be characterized by relatively fixed prices and variable quantities. This doubtless expresses a desire to reduce uncertainty over wages; but it also reflects the fact that quantity adjustments (or employment changes) are normally made at the margin, so the majority of workers are not affected if jobs are lost because wages are above market-clearing rates.

12.5.3 Monetarist policy in an open economy

We are now in a position to consider how a **monetarist anti-inflation policy** operates in the setting of an **open economy**. There are a number of channels through which the policy may work.

The announcement of a policy to reduce the rate of monetary growth, assuming it is believed, will produce an immediate reaction in **financial markets**. These markets are of the auction-type with flexi-price properties so they are able to respond to the new policy immediately. The **nominal exchange rate** will appreciate, as suggested by the **purchasing power parity theory**. However, as many product markets and labour markets display price rigidity, the real exchange rate rises and the competitiveness of the economy declines. This causes a fall in output and a rise in unemployment, which in turn exerts a downward pressure on wage and price inflation. The appreciation of the exchange rate lowers import prices in sterling and helps lower the overall index of prices. Eventually, as wages and prices adjust, competitiveness is restored, and output and unemployment return to their natural levels. These effects are additional to the impact of slower monetary growth on domestic spending. However, many monetarists would recognize the importance of the influence of monetary policy via the exchange rate. The effects are summarized in Figure 12.4 and the following diagram:

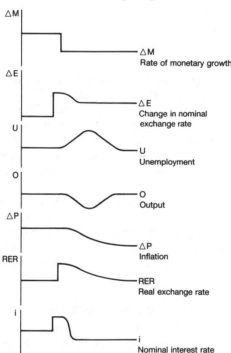
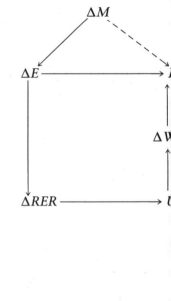

Fig. 12.4 Effects of monetary policy

One feature of a **monetarist anti-inflation policy** which we omitted from our simplified account is the tendency for the exchange rate to **overshoot**. This occurs when monetary policy is tightened and the interest rate rises. This causes the exchange rate to appreciate by a larger amount than we described earlier because higher interest rates attract an inflow of foreign currency. However, as inflation adjusts to the new monetary policy so does the demand for money and interest rates fall. (This is shown by the dotted line in Figure 12.4.)

Notice that interest rates fall below the original level after the initial rise. This is because nominal interest rates (i) will be affected by the rate of inflation. Whether or not an interest rate is attractive to a borrower or lender will depend on the rate of inflation. For example, a 10 per cent interest rate offers very cheap borrowing if the inflation rate is 30 per cent but it is relatively expensive if prices are rising by 2 per cent. It is helpful to distinguish between nominal (i) and real (r) interest rates. The real interest rate is the interest rate adjusted for the rate of inflation (ΔP):

$$r = i - \Delta P$$

For monetarists the real rate of interest (like other real variables) is unaffected in the long run by the money supply, but is determined by the motives of savers and borrowers. The nominal rate will tend to move with the rate of inflation:

$$i = r + \Delta P$$
$$\uparrow$$
$$\Delta M$$

and be affected by the rate of monetary growth. So although tighter monetary policy raises interest rates in the short run, it lowers them in the long run.

12.6 The Keynesian view

In earlier chapters we considered a number of aspects of the **Keynesian view** of employment and money. Here we summarize the main points relevant to our discussion of **monetarism**, **inflation** and **unemployment**.

12.6.1 Keynesian critique of monetarism

12.6.1.1 Quantity theory of money

Keynesians have expressed a number of reservations about the **quantity theory**. There are doubts about the **stability** of the demand for money and hence the **predictability** of the velocity of circulation. This means that controlling the money supply may not be a reliable way of affecting spending. Even if it were, most Keynesians believe that the impact of anti-inflationary monetary policy is on output rather than prices and inflation.

12.6.1.2 Phillips curve

The fear that **output** rather than **inflation** will be reduced as a result of tight monetary policy stems from the Keynesian view of the Phillips curve. Most Keynesians would reject the monetarist view of the vertical Phillips curve. Over the short and medium term, **labour markets** may fail to clear so changes in demand can affect output. An extreme Keynesian position would be that the **Phillips curve** is **horizontal**. (We discuss the Phillips curve further in section 12.6.4.)

12.6.1.3 Policy activism

Monetarists argue that there is no need for **policy activism** (i.e. demand management policies) because the market will return the economy to the natural level. They believe that attempts to lower unemployment through reflationary demand policies will be either ineffective (**new classical position**) or have only a temporary impact at the cost of higher inflation (**gradualist monetarists**). **Keynesians** flatly reject this view. They do not believe market economies are self-regulating. **Deficiencies** in aggregate demand may occur and the resulting unemployment will persist unless there is government intervention to stimulate demand. Many Keynesians also believe that intervention through an **incomes policy** is necessary if high employment and low inflation are to be simultaneously enjoyed.

12.6.2 Keynesian view of unemployment

The distinguishing characteristic of the **Keynesian view of unemployment** is that it can occur through a **deficiency** in **aggregate demand**. The reasons for this were fully discussed in Chapter 5. Keynesians would not deny that unemployment can occur for frictional and structural reasons, nor would they disagree that some unemployment is voluntary—though generally they do not emphasize this point as much as monetarists do. Keynesians will accept that supply-side and micro-policies directed at the labour market have a role; but so too do aggregate demand policies to raise spending to eliminate demand-deficient unemployment.

12.6.3 Keynesian view of inflation

The **Keynesian view** of **inflation** is often described as **cost push**. This is in contrast to the **demand pull** approach of the monetarist, where increases in the money supply cause excess demand which leads to rising prices.

The Keynesian approach tends to stress the imperfectly competitive nature of product markets and argue that prices are set by **adding a margin to costs**. It is the behaviour of **costs** which determines the path of prices. Demand plays an indirect role and affects inflation only to the extent that it influences costs.

An outline of this approach is shown in Figure 12.5 (overleaf). From the macro-economic viewpoint there are three influences on prices. The least important stems from **changes in** indirect taxes, though on occasions these can have a significant impact. We can expect changes in VAT, duties and subsidies to have an effect on the price level. In 1979 the large increase in VAT, which rose from 8 per cent to 15 per cent, is estimated to have contributed 4 percentage points to the inflation rate in 1980. This was an unusually large change–normal budget and other adjustments have a much smaller impact. We should also recognize that **fiscal changes** have a once-and-for-all effect, changing the price level (and therefore the inflation rate) in a particular year and subsequently affecting inflation only to the extent that they trigger a price–wage spiral.

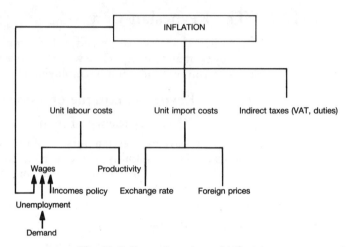

Fig. 12.5 Keynesian view of inflation

In an open economy like the UK's, **changes** in **sterling import prices** will affect the rate of inflation. Typically we might expect a 10 per cent rise in import prices to raise overall prices by 2.5 to 3.0 percentage points. We can identify two reasons for changes in the sterling price of imports. First, alterations in the **exchange rate** will affect the price of imported goods and services. A depreciation, or devaluation, of sterling will raise the price, in pounds, of imports and an appreciation will produce the reverse effect. The second factor which can operate even if exchange rates do not alter is foreign prices changing at a different rate from those in the UK. The most dramatic examples have been the rises in oil prices in 1973–74 and 1979–80 and the subsequent decline in 1986.

The most important influence on inflation is **wage costs**. The relevant concept is **unit labour costs** (ULC). This is the **labour cost per unit of output**. This will normally change by a smaller amount than the rise in money wages (ΔW) because productivity improvements (ΔQ) will offset some or all of the wage increases. We can represent the relationship as

$$\Delta ULC = \Delta W - \Delta Q$$

So if wages rise by 5 per cent and so does productivity, there is no increase in labour costs per unit of output; but if wages increase by 8 per cent this will imply a 3 per cent increase in prices. There is some cyclical variation in productivity around its long-term trend: it tends to increase in the upswing of a cycle and decline in a recession. Most of the changes in ULC are attributable to changes in wage inflation which leads us to ask what determines the **rate of wage increases**.

Keynesians have tended to emphasize the role played by **trade unions** in the labour market, arguing that workers' aspirations to raise living standards generally and to improve, or at least maintain, wage differentials are a powerful **potential inflationary force**. They assume that workers have a target increase in real wages. This implies that inflation (actual or expected) affects the rate of wage increases. As this, in turn, affects inflation we have a **wage–price spiral**. This may be heavily dampened or may produce accelerating inflation. (We discuss this further in the next section.)

Wage inflation may be affected by an **incomes policy**. A successful policy will reduce the rate of wage increase, *ceteris paribus*. Unemployment is likely to influence wage settlements too, though many Keynesians would argue that it is only when it rises to high levels that it exerts an important downward pressure. We discuss this more fully in the next section.

Let us summarize the **Keynesian position on inflation**. Most Keynesians do not explain it in terms of excess demand generally nor by the growth of the money supply in particular. There may certainly be occasions when the economy is working at full capacity and when demand pull inflation may be a problem. But this is not typical of the last 20 years and Keynesians prefer to explain inflation through the behaviour of costs. Demand may or may not have a strong influence on cost inflation. Keynesian explanations would tend to stress that external sources (commodity and oil price increases and sterling devaluation) provided an important explanation for the dramatic increase in inflation in the mid-1970s. The situation was made worse by the Heath government's incomes policy which provided for **indexation** (automatic increases in line with inflation) of wages when the **retail price index** increased above a threshold point. The subsequent slow down in inflation could be largely attributed to the Wilson–Callaghan governments' (1974–79) incomes policy under which the rate of wage inflation came down from 27 per cent to 10 per cent. However, this policy subsequently broke down and attempts to catch up on wage increases denied in the early stages of the policy led to an increase in wage inflation later. This was greatly exacerbated in 1979–80 by a further sharp increase in oil prices and the VAT increases which were mentioned earlier. Since then, when inflation rose to 18 per cent, the decline in inflation can be explained in terms of sterling appreciation (early 1980s), the decline in oil prices (mid-1980s) and the record unemployment levels.

12.6.4 Keynesian view of the Phillips curve

Many early Keynesians were aware of the **inflationary dangers** of pursuing **high employment policies** and a number argued that unemployment might have to be kept high enough to prevent an inflationary wage spiral from developing. In the event, unemployment fell to levels well below what most people could have hoped for (less then 2 per cent, 1950–70) and although inflation was regarded as a problem it was below−4 per cent for most of that period. Inflation did seem to respond cyclically and the publication of Phillips' article on the relationship between unemployment and wage inflation in 1958 provided, for some economists, a useful adjunct to the Keynesian model. It allowed the inflationary effect of demand management policy to be considered, as well as its impact on unemployment. It also seemed to offer a guide to policy makers. However, by the late 1960s and early 1970s the orthodox relationship was breaking down. onetarists augmented the Phillips curve with **inflationary expectations** (as we described earlier) whereas a number of **Keynesians** concluded that **wage inflation** had become uncoupled from market pressures in the labour market. The growing power of unions, combined with changing attitudes and aspirations shaped by 25 years of full employment, was thought to be a significant factor in determining inflation. It was stressed that the **labour market** of the 1970s was quite different from that of earlier periods and evidence cited by monetarists of previous decades or centuries was not relevant.

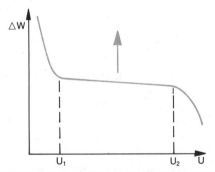

Fig. 12.6 Simplified Keynesian position

A simplified representation of the position of many Keynesians in the late 1970s is shown in Figure 12.6. At very **low unemployment** levels, below U_1, the Phillips curve is steep as the economy is operating at full capacity and **demand pull pressures** become important. However, this range was not regarded as relevant in the 1970s because the economy was experiencing relatively **high unemployment rates** compared with the earlier postwar period. It was suggested that the economy was operating between U_1 and U_2, and in that range the Phillips curve was very flat, showing that **wage inflation** was quite **unresponsive** to demand reductions and higher unemployment. Some **extreme Keynesians** even argued that it was horizontal. However, this view did not mean that the inflation problem could be disregarded, because the nature of the wage-bargaining process in attempting to raise real wages meant that the curve tended to shift upwards. However, this might be controlled by an incomes policy. In the late 1970s Keynesians suggested that there would be a rate of unemployment−U_2 in Fig. 12.6−above which wage inflation would decline significantly; but it was argued that this rate was unacceptably high. It would mean a large amount of excess capacity and this was felt to be outside the range of **politically acceptable unemployment rates**. This latter view turned out to be wrong.

Most **Keynesians** accept that unemployment in the UK rose to levels at which behaviour in the labour market was modified, though many would stress that it was the **change** in unemployment (ΔU), rather than its **level**, which played a significant role in the process. They are much more sceptical about the **monetarist** view that **high unemployment** is a **temporary** cost of bringing down inflation. Unless the structure and practices of product and labour markets are fundamentally changed then the unemployment cost of keeping inflation under control may be a high and rising one. There is growing evidence that the impact of long-term unemployment on the rate of wage inflation is minimal. This partly reflects employer attitudes on the suitability of people who have been out of work for a year or more for employment and it results from many of the long-term unemployed having become so demoralized that they have given up the search for work. So a pool of long-term unemployed created during a period when inflation-reducing policies were followed may not exert a long-term downward pressure on inflation; it may be very difficult to reabsorb the long-term unemployed into the workforce.

Keynesians also tend to point out that even the shorter-term **unemployed** have a **limited impact** on **wage settlements**. If institutional arrangements were different and all the jobs in a firm were periodically auctioned off, then the unemployed could put in bids alongside existing employees. In practice the labour market rarely operates like this. Although unions will be conscious that there is likely to be a trade off between wages and jobs, the majority of workers may feel that their jobs will not be jeopardized by relatively high wage settlements. Instead, given the turn over of labour, this will affect only the chances of new entrants and the unemployed obtaining a job. A deep recession, like 1980–81 in the UK when unemployment more than doubled in less than two years, extends the threat of job loss to a large section of the labour force; but that type of threat cannot be sustained over a long period of time.

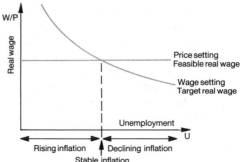

Fig. 12.7 Layard's view of stable inflation

A recent presentation of some of the views expressed in this section is to be found in the writings of **Richard Layard**. Firms **set prices** by adding a **mark up** to costs. Workers aim for wage increases that will achieve a target increase in real wages, given the expected inflation rate. We represent this diagrammatically in Figure 12.7 where the price-setting line shows a real wage increase that is compatible with the increase in productivity: the feasible real wage. The wage-setting schedule indicates that the real wage target is influenced by unemployment. Where the two schedules cross, the target real wage is compatible with the feasible real wage and **inflation** is **stable**. This is sometimes known as **NAIRU**: the non-accelerating inflation rate of unemployment. Lower unemployment levels raise the target wage and produce accelerating inflation.

Table 12.2 Wages, productivity and inflation

Year	Target real wage ΔW^* (1)	Expected inflation ΔP^e (2)	Money wages ΔW (3 = 1 + 2)	Productivity change ΔQ (4)	Inflation ΔP (5 = 3 − 4)
1	5	0	5	3	2
2	5	2	7	3	4
3	5	4	9	3	6
4	3	6	9	3	6
5	3	6	9	3	6
6	1	6	7	3	4

Table 12.2 gives a highly simplified illustration. We ignore the influence of the price of

imported goods and services and we assume that expected inflation (ΔP^e) is equal to last year's actual inflation rate (ΔP), that is, $\Delta P_t^e = \Delta P_t$. Further, we assume that target real wages (ΔW^*) are achieved. Money wages (ΔW) are set by

$$\Delta W = \Delta W^* + \Delta P^e$$

That is, given the **real wage target**, money wage increases are adjusted according to the **expected rate of inflation**. Prices are set on the basis of **unit labour costs**, in the manner discussed earlier:

$$\Delta P = \Delta W - \Delta Q$$

That is, productivity improvements can offset some or all of the money wage increases.

Years 1 to 3 in Table 12.2 illustrate a situation where the **target real wage** exceeds the **feasible real wage** (3 per cent). Here inflation increases from 2 per cent to 4 per cent to 6 per cent. Suppose in year 4 the government were to introduce a deflationary policy to dampen the target real wage to one that was feasible; the inflation rate would then stabilize at 6 per cent. Bringing inflation down means depressing the target real wage further by, say, further increases in unemployment. As the long-term unemployed have a weak impact on the target real wage, using recession as an anti-inflation policy could push the unemployment rate that gives stable inflation to the right on Figure 12.7. This arises because the **unemployed** affect the inflationary process only in the **short term**. If they become long-term unemployed they add to the unemployment totals without exerting a downward pressure on prices—more newly-created unemployed have to be produced if inflation is to be lowered further.

12.6.5 Keynesian policy on inflation

Keynesians generally believe that there is a **fundamental conflict** between **full employment** and low **stable inflation rates**. They tend to emphasize the high (and perhaps increasing) cost of using deflationary policies, or employment, as an anti-inflation policy.

Carefully targeted schemes may reduce unemployment without adding to inflation. This would particularly apply to schemes designed to bring jobs to the long-term unemployed, e.g. training schemes or public works programmes. However, most Keynesians recognize that a general reduction in unemployment requires a demand expansion that is likely to produce inflationary side effects. So some form of incomes policy is central to the policy recommendation of many Keynesians.

Various types of incomes policy have been tried in the post-war period. Some have been voluntary, others statutory. Their scope has varied from a concentration on wages to policies which include dividends and price controls. The experience of these policies is not entirely encouraging. In the short term a number of incomes policies have produced short-term benefits. The most dramatic was the one introduced by the Wilson and Callaghan governments, referred to earlier, which seems to have had a significant impact on inflation in the mid-1970s. However, the longer-term impact seems less beneficial. In many cases it appears that the policies postponed inflation rather than reducing it because after a couple of years of operation pressures and anomalies build up and this has tended to produce a **wage explosion** as workers seek to regain what they feel they lost during the early stages of a policy. Tightly controlled incomes policies produce many administrative and 'policing' problems, but more flexible policies tend to be far less effective in reducing inflation.

An approach which claims to overcome most of these difficulties but is as yet untried in the UK is a **tax-based incomes policy (TIP)**. Its chief advocate, Professor Layard, suggests that the policy will allow lower unemployment to be achieved without accelerating inflation. In terms of Figure 12.7 it will shift the wage-setting schedule to the left. The basis of the policy is straightforward. A **reference level** of wage increase would be agreed. This would take account of the **rate of productivity increase** and be set according to inflation targets. Firms who paid wage increases above the reference level would be taxed on the excess payments. The rate would have to be set high enough to discourage all but the most determined firms from paying more than the reference level. Not only would TIP stiffen employers' resistance to wage claims above the norm, it would tend to moderate union pressure for higher wage settlements because the loss of jobs would be much greater because firms would have to pay tax as well as the extra wages.

The scheme has certain advantages over a more conventional incomes policy. It is not rigid or unduly uniform in what it permits. Firms may pay more than reference level where they can afford to, for example, where there are severe skills shortages or where particularly beneficial productivity deals have been agreed. TIP means that normal collective bargaining is not suspended; it merely has to take account of the tax imposed on above-norm pay deals. There is no need for a large or elaborate administrative apparatus to police the scheme. It is suggested that the tax could be assessed and paid quarterly as part of the PAYE system.

The scheme is not without drawbacks. Generally, productivity deals whereby firms pay workers larger than normal wage increases to forgo certain working practices may be hit by TIP. Profit sharing could similarly be discouraged. Both of these could be accommodated by **gateways** or **exemptions** to the policy, though there would need to be safeguards to ensure that they did not turn into loopholes. Allowances would similarly have to be made for newly established firms and those resulting from mergers and buy outs. The tax would have been devised (and presumably amended with time) to ensure maximum compliance. Although the scheme could be applied to public corporations, some alternative way of dealing with the rest of the public sector would have to be devised, e.g. comparability or review boards.

Monetarists would argue that advocates of a conventional incomes policy fail to pinpoint the cause of inflation–excessive increases in money supply–and then apply an inappropriate remedy which tends to distort the allocation of resources. Some of the monetarist critics of TIP suggest that it is a weak substitute for properly tackling the power of trade unions through legislation to weaken their rights. **Keynesians** in turn point to the application of monetarist policies under Mrs Thatcher and argue they have proved a costly experiment in non-Keynesian control of inflation.

12.7 Monetarist policy in the UK

Mrs Thatcher's government came to power in 1979 with the declared intention of reducing inflation and replacing the existing consensus on managing the economy by an alternative approach. This has been described as a **monetarist experiment**. There may be some dispute over the extent to which the policies were monetarist (**Milton Friedman** was certainly critical of some aspects of the approach), but there is little doubt that the rhetoric of ministers has largely been monetarist and that government policy, particularly in the early 1980s, has strongly resembled that advocated by monetarist economists.

12.7.1 Monetary and fiscal policy

The centrepiece of the fight against inflation was the **medium-term financial strategy** (**MTFS**). This involved setting target growth sales for M3 (or sterling M3 as it was then known) for a four-year period. These targets are shown in Table 12.3. This approach is in keeping with the **gradualist policy recommendations** which suggest that it is necessary to allow sufficient time for expectations to adapt. Some statements by the Chancellor in 1980 and 1981 suggested that there was a hope, at least, that expectations might be formed rationally and that a sharp downward adjustment in wage settlements would avoid high unemployment costs. The MTFS was quoted to give credibility to the policy stance. However, the massive overshoot of monetary growth in 1980–81 did not help in this task. There were some special factors involving the abolition of controls such as the corset arrangements (see section 10.4) which account for some of the excessive growth. It was also the case that many firms who found themselves in financial difficulties were forced to increase their borrowing.

Table 12.3 Medium-term financial strategy: targets and out turns ($\Delta\pounds$M3 % pa)

	79–80	80–81	81–2	82–3	83–4	84–5	85–6	86–7
June 1979	7–11							
March 1980		7–11	6–10	5–9	4–8			
March 1981			6–10	5–9	4–8			
March 1982				8–12	7–11	6–10		
March 1983					7–11	6–10	5–9	
March 1984						6–10	5–9	
March 1985							5–9	4–8
March 1986								11–15
Out turn	11.2	19.4	12.8	15.3	10.6	10.0	13.8	20.0

It was **fiscal policy** which made the anti-inflation policy credible. As we explained in Chapter 10, **public sector borrowing requirement** (**PSBR**) targets were part of the MTFS designed to avoid very high interest rates as the rate of monetary growth was slowed down. The PSBR rose in 1980 (see Figure 12.8) as the effects of recession hit tax revenues and rapidly rising unemployment pushed up public expenditure on benefits. By 1981 the UK was in the middle of the deepest recession since the 1930s: unemployment had risen from 1.1 to 2.2 million. It was at this point that the Chancellor introduced a highly deflationary budget. This underlined the macro-policy change in approach and the determination to reduce inflation. There was a growing emphasis on fiscal policy and a move away from money supply targets. Monetary aggregates both broader and narrower than M3 were included for consideration. By 1987 M3 was abandoned and no targets were published for it. The PSBR as a proportion of GDP fell from a peak in 1979–80 and reducing it still further emerged as an important policy objective. However the target shifted somewhat from one year to another. Although it was still clear that government policy was committed to low inflation, a greater emphasis on short-term changes on fiscal stance, combined with a reduced attention to monetary targets, led many commentators to argue that monetarism had been abandoned.

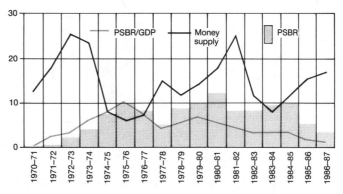

Fig. 12.8 PSBR as a percentage of GNP and M3 growth (1970–87)

12.7.2 Exchange, inflation and unemployment

Although the money supply targets were overshot, the policy stance in 1979 was generally a tight one. Interest rates were relatively high and fiscal policy was restrictive. The nominal exchange rate (illustrated by the sterling index in Figure 12.9) appreciated by about 20 per cent from early 1979 to the beginning of 1981. This was at a time when the UK was experiencing a faster rate of inflation than other major countries. The real exchange rate rose even more (by around 50 per cent). The measure of this in Figure 12.9 is **relative unit labour costs (RULC)** measured in a common currency. The figure indicates that UK costs rose nearly 50 per cent more than our competitors': a massive deterioration in competitiveness. (Exchange rates and the different ways of measuring them are explained more fully in Chapter 20.) Anti-inflation policy was not the only reason for sterling's appreciation—the emergence of the UK as a major oil producer and the hike in oil prices were also important.

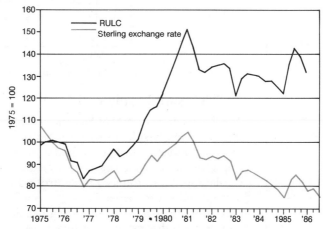

Fig. 12.9 Sterling exchange rate and relative unit labour costs (*RULC*), (1975–86)
(RULC: normalized IMF index, 1975 = 100)

The loss of competitiveness, combined with tight domestic policies, led to a 5.5 per cent fall in real GDP between the second quarter of 1979 and beginning of 1981. During this time unemployment nearly doubled and continued rising until 1986. The appreciation of sterling and the dampening effect of high unemployment on wage inflation brought inflation down. By 1986, helped by the decline in oil prices, it had reached levels not enjoyed since the late 1960s. Figure 12.10 shows the Phillips curve relationship from 1970. If we recall our illustration of the monetarist view then the period 1970–78 would seem to be a good illustration of what we might expect. However, if that is the case then the period from 1978–83 would seem to be another loop around a rising natural rate.

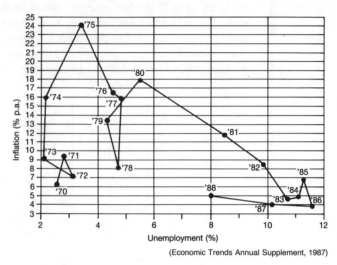

(Economic Trends Annual Supplement, 1987)

Fig. 12.10 Inflation and unemployment (1970–86)

The point is illustrated in Figure 12.11(a). There are many ways of interpreting the evidence. For example the whole period may represent one very large loop with a short-lived indentation between 1975 and 1978 produced by the incomes policy. We considered the Keynesian explanation of both the rise and fall of inflation in section 12.6. This would emphasize the high unemployment cost of bringing down inflation. It is probably fair to say that the unemployment costs of the policy have been higher than most monetarists suggested in the 1970s; but it should also be pointed out that the policy has achieved lower inflation rates than were thought likely.

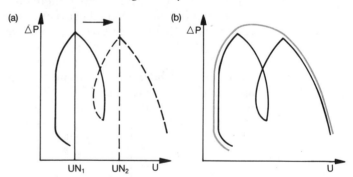

Fig. 12.11 Loop round a rising natural rate of employment

12.7.3 Supply-side policies

The Thatcher government has rejected **Keynesian demand-side policies** but has laid great stress on **supply-side initiatives**. Cutting marginal tax rates was an important objective and the standard rate was lowered from 33p to 25p in the pound between 1979 and 1988. Top rates of tax were cut more dramatically. A policy of **privatization** was followed and legislation was introduced to **control trades union powers**. Some steps were taken in the housing market to increase labour mobility, though council house sales were prompted by other objectives as well. **Lowering benefits** is politically sensitive, but tying them to the **retail price index** means that they tend to rise less than wages.

Supporters of the government's policy would claim that these measures, combined with the shaking out of inefficient firms and practices by the recession, have produced a new **enterprise culture** with some significant productivity gains. Productivity growth in manufacturing has certainly been high by the standards of most of the 1970s; but as Figure 12.12 shows it is not widely different from that of the 1960s. If a significant change in attitudes has occurred we will need a few more years before we have clear evidence of its impact.

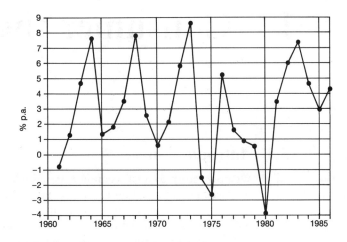

Fig. 12.12 Productivity growth (1960–86, output per person in manufacturing)

12.7.4 Was the policy a success?

Both supporters and critics can find evidence and arguments to back up their point of view. Critics point to the worst post-war recession and a decade of very high unemployment. Supporters emphasize the success in controlling inflation and point to the respectable growth since 1982 as evidence of new attitudes and practices.

The **rhetoric** of policy has remained largely **monetarist**. The practice of policy has contained some shifts in emphasis, as we indicated earlier. This has given rise to debate on how far monetarism has been discarded. What is indisputable is that the commitment to full employment through demand management policies was abandoned and replaced by the priority of reducing inflation.

13 Consumer theory

13.1 Introduction

We now return to microeconomic issues which we considered in Chapters 4 and 5. One of the basic tools of economics, as we have seen, is demand and supply. In this and the next few chapters we look more closely at what lies behind the demand and supply curves. We begin by considering **consumer theory** and **demand**. Our attention here is on the **demand** of the **individual** rather than the aggregate demand that has been our concern in the last few chapters. The two main approaches to explaining consumer behaviour which we will consider are **utility theory** and **indifference curve analysis**. Apart from explaining the analysis we will illustrate its application and conclude by briefly considering approaches to **forecasting demand**. This last section can be understood without following the discussion on consumer theory which precedes it.

The chapter will:

- explain the distinction between total and marginal utility
- explain the conditions for consumer equilibrium
- show how the demand schedule is derived from the marginal utility curve
- explain 'consumer surplus'
- illustrate and explain consumer equilibrium using indifference curve analysis
- show the effect of income and price changes using indifference curves
- explain income and substitution effects
- distinguish between normal, inferior and Giffen goods
- outline different approaches to forecasting consumer demand

13.1.1 Examination guide

Some questions will concentrate entirely on the theoretical aspects of this topic, while others will require analysis. The former type of question is usually more straightforward, although there are a number of points which need close attention. You should make sure you can use diagrams for this topic and to answer questions on **utility theory** you must be able to explain the conditions for **consumer equilibrium** and the relationship between **marginal utility** and **demand**. **Indifference curve analysis** requires you to master the basic diagram showing consumer equilibrium; but the most important single aspect is understanding **income** and **substitution effects**.

The analysis may be applied to a wide range of areas but as a rule the same approach is required for each. However problem-orientated the question, the examiner will expect to see evidence that you understand the basic theory (whether it is explicably mentioned in the question or not) and that you can relate the topic of the question to that analysis. In many cases, examiners are testing whether you can explain and identify the **income** and **substitution effects**. For example, questions asking about the relative merits of subsidies and income support, minimum wage legislation compared with income supplements and the incentive effect of tax cuts, are all concerned with income and substitution effects.

13.2 Utility theory

There are two basic approaches to **consumer theory**: **ordinal** and **cardinal**. The former is based on consumers' ranking or ordering different bundles of goods and services, so that, for example, consumption pattern A is preferred to consumption pattern B. However, this tells us nothing about the intensity of feeling or satisfaction consumers have for A and B. **Indifference curve analysis** uses the ordinal approach, which is considered in section 13.3. The cardinal approach, **utility theory**, suggests that **utility** can be measured in some way. To illustrate this, we will use an imaginary unit, which we can call utils. This allows us, in principle at least, to show the intensity of preference as well as the relative ranking of different consumption patterns. So, for example, consumption pattern A may give 120 utils of utility whereas B produces only 80 utils.

13.2.1 Total and marginal utility

The **utility** approach to consumer theory suggests that as the **quantity** of a good or service increases the **total utility** or satisfaction will rise. There will be some level, the saturation point, after which total utility will decline. **Marginal utility** is the additional utility derived from the consumption of an extra unit of the good. It is assumed to decline as the total utility increases. So although additional consumption will raise total utility (up to the saturation point), each extra unit consumed will successively add less. This is illustrated in Figure 13.1(a). Notice that marginal utility is zero at saturation point, A, and negative beyond that as total utility declines.

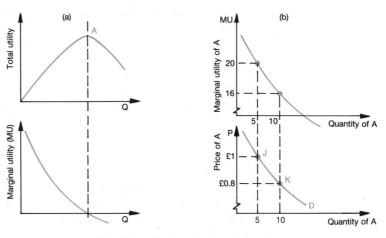

Fig. 13.1 Total and marginal utility

13.2.2 Consumer equilibrium

We assume that consumers are **utility maximizers**. To achieve this they must make sure that their expenditure is spent in such a way that it could not be reallocated to increase utility. The condition that achieves this is where the last penny spent on each of the goods and services bought yields the same utility—the ratio of the marginal utility to the price of each commodity bought is equal.

$$\frac{MU_A}{P_A} = \frac{MU_B}{P_B} = \frac{MU_n}{P_n}$$

$$\frac{20}{£1} = \frac{40}{£2} = \frac{300}{£15}$$

If more of A were consumed this would lower its marginal utility (remember that marginal utility diminishes as the amount consumed increases) meaning that additional utility per pound for A would fall below the 20 achieved on other commodities.

13.2.3 Marginal utility and the demand curve

13.2.3.1 Derivation of the demand curve

We can consider the relationship of the marginal utility and demand curve with the aid of the Figure 13.1(b), where the price of A is equal to £1. The consumer is in equilibrium when five units of the commodity are purchased and marginal utility is 20. This price–quantity combination is shown in the bottom diagram as point J. If the price of A were to fall to £0.80 the existing consumption of A would not be in equilibrium. We will assume that expenditure on A forms such a small part of the total budget that the impact on other commodities is so negligible that it can be ignored. With the fall in price, $MU/£$ has risen to 25:

$$\frac{MU_A}{P_A} = \frac{20}{£0.8} = 25$$

This is the signal to increase expenditure on A. As more is bought MU declines. In our example it falls to 16 when an extra unit is bought. This will restore equilibrium as the ratio MU:price has returned to 20. This allows a further point, K, to be identified on the price–quantity diagram. Exploring other prices for A would identify further points; these could then be joined to form the dotted line shown. This, of course, is the demand curve: it shows what quantities consumers will purchase at different prices and as such it shows points of **consumer equilibrium**.

In effect, the **marginal utility** and the **demand schedule**, given our assumption that the MU:price ratio of all other commodities is unaffected, are the same thing, with utils being converted into sterling at the rate of 20 utils to £1. This assumption of the **constant marginal utility** of money is one which we will retain.

13.2.3.2 Marginal utility and elasticity

It should be clear, therefore, that the shape of the demand curve is determined by **marginal utility**. In the diagram, if the MU schedule had been steeper, this would have produced a steeper demand curve, with the quantity demanded less responsive to price change. This discovery allows us to explain why **price elasticity** is not related to whether goods are necessities or luxuries. **Price elasticity**–responsiveness to price changes–clearly depends upon **marginal utility**, whereas statements which suggest that commodities are necessities are based on the concept of **total utility**. Water is necessary for life and its total utility is presumably high; but consumption may well occur at a point where demand is highly elastic. If water is not metered and there is only a flat-rate charge, then additional gallons are obtained at zero price, so consumers will use water up to the point where $MU = 0$. It is likely that the MU schedule is fairly flat in this range, so demand is highly elastic and a small charge per gallon will produce a relatively large reduction in consumption.

13.2.4 Consumer surplus

We can now use the analysis we have developed to illustrate and define the important concept of **consumer surplus**. In our earlier example, when the price of a good was £1, the consumer was in equilibrium when 5 units were consumed. In this position the consumer is likely to enjoy a surplus of utility gained over the utility lost through payment for the commodity.

This arises because the same price is normally paid for each unit of good purchased (in this case £1); but the MU of earlier units exceeds that of the last one consumed. Our consumer would, if necessary, be prepared to pay £3 for the first unit–this would match the utility enjoyed. But notice that this represents a surplus of £2 because he or she only has to pay £1. With declining MU the consumer enjoys less additional utility with the second unit and is therefore prepared to pay a lower price, £2; but this still represents a surplus over the price that is actually paid. The same analysis can be applied to other units until the final one where the surplus is zero (see Table 13.1).

Table 13.1 Marginal utility

Unit consumed	Price consumer would be prepared to pay (£)	Price paid (£)	Surplus (£)
First	3.00	1.00	2.00
Second	2.00	1.00	1.00
Third	1.60	1.00	0.60
Fourth	1.20	1.00	0.20
Fifth	1.00	1.00	0

This is the shaded area ABC in Figure 13.2. The monetary equivalent of the total utility enjoyed by the consumer is $OBCD$, the expenditure (or utility sacrificed) is $OACD$, i.e price (£1) times quantity (5), and the difference between the two, ABC, is the **consumer surplus**.

The concept of **consumer surplus** is much used in economics and we shall refer to i again in Chapters 18 and 20. However, one limitation needs to be made on the use o **marginal utility analysis**. Even if we were to accept that we can in principle devise a measure of an individual's utility, there is no scientific basis for adding such measures together to produce an **aggregate utility schedule**. We cannot know the utility per pound received by different individuals. Even apparently similar people may be prepared to pay a different price for the marginal utility of a good. To make these concepts operational we have to make some untestable assumptions.

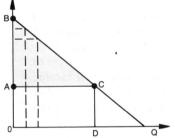

Fig 13.2 Consumer surplus

13.2.5 Applications of the analysis

Despite the practical difficulties and the rather abstract nature of the analysis, the utility approach is helpful in analysing a number of economics problems. Consider public expenditure projects which produce both benefits and costs to society. The notion o **consumer surplus** provides a way of measuring these benefits.

We consider examples of this type of analysis in Chapter 18. Here we consider only a

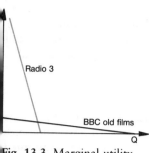

Fig. 13.3 Marginal utility schedules

brief illustration. How should a broadcasting corporation like the BBC decide how to allocate its resources? Audience figures or ratings are a useful starting point but not a complete answer. Consider the case of Radio 3, which attracts a relatively small number of listeners, even compared with the late-night audience for old movies on TV. The benefits derived from each service cannot be obtained simply by counting heads–ideally we wish to know the **marginal utility schedule** for each. In both cases consumption will take place until $MU = 0$, but the total utility obtained is likely to be different. Figure 13.3 shows a hypothetical position, with most of the comparatively few hours enjoyed by Radio 3 listeners generating high additional utility compared with the many viewers watching often-repeated films. This type of result, if it were obtained, would justify more attention being given to minorities than ratings alone would suggest.

The analysis reminds us that **marginal utility** underlies the demand curve and that it can help to explain the paradox of value raised by **Adam Smith** two centuries ago. Smith asked why diamonds, which were a luxury, commanded a high price while water, which was essential for life, did not. We now know that the reference to the essential/luxury nature of products is based on **total utility** concepts whereas price depends upon demand (**marginal utility**) and supply. Plentiful water means that consumers are operating at the bottom of their marginal utility schedules, whereas the scarcity of diamonds means the reverse.

13.3 Indifference curve analysis

Our second main approach to **consumer theory** avoids the difficulty of measuring the intensity of utility or satisfaction and adopts an **ordinal** approach which simply ranks consumer preferences by showing one preferred position compared with another. The main way of illustrating this approach is through the use of **indifference curves**.

13.3.1 Constructing indifference curves

An **indifference curve** joins points of equal satisfaction or utility. So in Figure 13.4(a), the combination A, 36 units of Y and 1 unit of X gives the same satisfaction as B which involves the consumption of $16 Y$ and $2X$. Any other combination shown by the curve (e.g. C and D) also yields the same utility. Different **indifference curves** show a different level of utility, so the curve IC_2 which shows larger bundles of goods (e.g. A combines more X with a given amount of Y) represent a higher level of satisfaction than IC_1. Similarly IC_3 is preferred to IC_2. Notice that we are merely ranking preferences–we make no attempt to quantify how much IC_2 is preferred to IC_1.

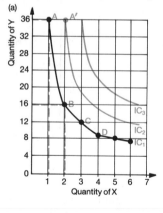
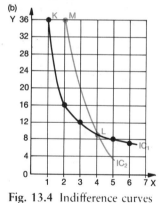
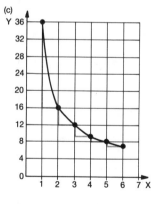

Fig. 13.4 Indifference curves

We assume that consumers are consistent in their behaviour; it therefore follows that **indifference curves** cannot cross. In Figure 13.4(b) we conclude from the indifference curve IC_1 that K and L yield the same utility: yet the other indifference curve, IC_2, the coloured curve, suggests that M and L give the same satisfaction. That cannot be correct because comparison of K and M clearly shows that M is preferred to K, because the former combines more X with the same amount of Y. The diagram displays a logical inconsistency and as we reject the possibility of such behaviour by consumers we conclude that **indifference curves cannot cross.**

Why are indifference curves normally drawn with a **convex** shape? It is because we assume that consumers will be willing to give up relatively large quantities of Y when they have little X; but as the amount of X consumed increases the utility from extra units of X declines and a constant utility indifference shows that consumers give up less Y. This is illustrated in Figure 13.4(c). As we move along the indifference curve we see that the consumer gives up 20 units of Y to acquire the second unit of X but is willing to give up only 4 units to obtain the third unit of X. The fourth and subsequent units show that the constant utility of the indifference curve involves further declines in the amount of Y sacrificed. The amount of Y a consumer is prepared to give up to acquire an extra amount of X is known as the **marginal rate of substitution** of Y for X (MRS_{YX}). More formally,

$$MRS_{YX} = \frac{\Delta Y}{\Delta X}$$

It is the slope of the **indifference curve** and, as we generally expect the MRS_{YX} to decline as more of X is acquired, the **indifference curve** is convex. The slope of an indifference curve at a particular point is the slope of a tangent to that curve. The measure we adopted for the sake of simplicity in our illustration is not exactly the same, because we were in effect measuring the slope between two points (e.g. A and B).

13.3.2 Consumer equilibrium

13.3.2.1 The budget constraint

Indifference curves show us consumers' preferences—they cannot tell us what quantities will be bought. To discover this we need to know what the consumer is capable of purchasing and this is shown by the **budget line**.

Consider a consumer with an income (I) of £48 and a situation where the price of X (P_X) is £16 and the price of Y (P_Y) is £1. Table 13.2 shows four possible ways (A to D) of spending this money.

Table 13.2 Budget constraint (income (I) = £48)

	Quantity of X (P_X = £16)	Quantity of Y (P_Y = £1)
A	0	48
B	1	32
C	2	16
D	3	0

This is also shown in Figure 13.5. The line is the **budget line**. It shows the consumer's purchasing possibility given:

1 a certain level of income;
2 the prices of Y and X.

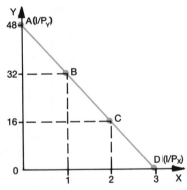

Fig. 13.5 The budget line

The intersection with the Y axis (point A in the diagram) is the quantity of Y that can be bought if none of X is purchased and is equal to I/P_Y. The line intercepts the X axis (point D) at I/P_X. The slope of the schedule reflects relative prices and is equal to P_X/P_Y. So changes in income with the same relative prices will shift the budget line in or out. However, changes in relative prices will alter the **slope** of the line. We will see examples of both of these in sections 13.3.3 and 13.3.4.

13.3.2.2 Consumer equilibrium

We can now illustrate and explain a position of **consumer equilibrium**. We assume that the consumer wishes to maximize utility: this means that he or she will wish to be on as high an **indifference curve** as possible but will, of course, be constrained by the size of his or her budget. Point B in Figure 13.6 represents a position of **consumer equilibrium**. Point D offers a higher level of satisfaction but lies outside the **budget line** and is therefore beyond the means of the consumer. Points A and C are possible positions but are suboptimal because they place the consumer on lower indifference curves. It is possible to raise utility by moving towards point B.

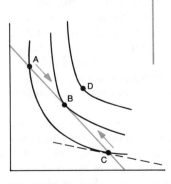

Fig. 13.6 Consumer equilibrium

Geometrically, **consumer equilibrium** is where the **budget line** is a tangent to the **indifference curve**. This, if you recall our earlier discussion, is where

MRS_{YX} $=$ P_X/P_Y
(slope of (slope of
indifference budget line)
curve)

This is a position where the rate at which the consumer is prepared to substitute one good for another (MRS) is equal to the rate at which the market trades one good for another: P_X/P_Y. At any other point the MRS is not equal to the ratio of prices and it is possible to improve the consumer's position. At point C, for example, the consumer requires relatively little additional Y to compensate him or her for giving up a unit of X: but the market possibilities mean that much more Y can be obtained for one unit of X (compare the slopes of the indifference curve at C with the slope of the budget line). Therefore, it will pay the consumer to reduce expenditure on X and raise it on Y, i.e. move towards B. This argument applies to all such points where $MRS_{YX} < P_X/P_Y$. A similar type of reasoning can be used to show that points like A where $MRS_{YX} > P_X/P_Y$ are also suboptimal.

13.3.3 Income change

We now explore the effect on consumer equilibrium of a change in income. We assume that prices are unchanged. A rise in income will shift the budget line out to the right (see Figure 13.7) because the consumer is now able to buy more of goods X and Y. This will produce a new equilibrium as the consumer is able to move on to a higher indifference curve–see the move from A to B in Figure 13.7(a). In 13.7(b) we illustrate a number of income changes. The line through the equilibrium points is known as the **income consumption curve** (*ICC*). It allows us easily to see how consumption responds to income changes. The illustration shows X as a normal good, that is, consumption rises as income increases. If X is an inferior good, the *ICC* will be backward sloping (see Figure 13.7(c)).

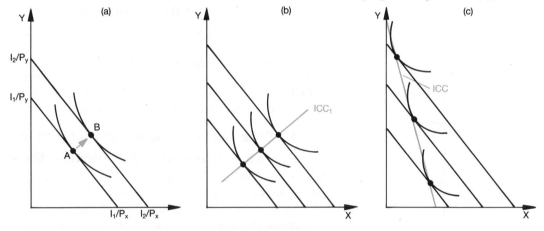

Fig. 13.7 Income consumption curves

13.3.4 Price changes

13.3.4.1 Illustrating a price change

If the price of one good changes and income remains the same then the budget line will swivel in the way shown in Figure 13.8(a).

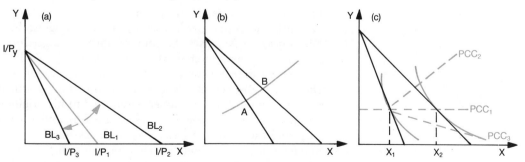

Fig. 13.8 Effect of price change on the budget line

A lower price for X will increase the maximum amount of X that can be bought, but will not affect the maximum quantity of Y (because income and the price of Y do not change). The budget line therefore moves from BL_1 to BL_2. A rise in the price of X will cause the budget line to move in the opposite direction (BL_1 to BL_3).

A fall in price will allow the consumer to move on to a higher indifference curve and will produce a new equilibrium position as shown in Fig. 13.8(b) where the consumer moves from A to B.

13.3.4.2 Price consumption curve (PCC)

A line that joins points of **consumer equilibrium** which result from price changes is known as the **price consumption curve (PCC)**, see for example the coloured curve on Figure 13.8(b). It is analogous to the **income consumption curve** except it refers to **price** rather than **income** changes. The *PCC* may be upward, downward, or even backward sloping, as we shall see below.

13.3.4.3 Elasticity

The shape of the *PCC* can tell us something about the elasticity of X, providing we know how expenditure on X changes. We can know this if we assume that Y represents expenditure on goods and services other than X. In Figure 13.8(c) the fall in price of X leads to an increase in the quantity of X consumed from X_1 to X_2; but there is no change in the quantity of Y consumed. As the price of Y is unchanged the total expenditure on Y remains the same. With income constant the expenditure on X, therefore, cannot have changed, so the demand for X must have unitary elasticity. We can conclude that providing Y represents all goods other than X, a horizontal *PCC* means that **price elasticity of demand** for X is one.

If the *PCC* slopes upwards (e.g. PPC_2 in Fig. 13.8(c)) then the new equilibrium position following a fall in the price of X are associated with increased consumption of Y. This means total expenditure on Y is increasing and people must therefore be spending less on X. If expenditure on X is reduced following a price cut then demand is inelastic. It follows that if the *PCC* is downward sloping (PCC_3) then the demand for X is elastic.

13.3.4.4 Derivation of the demand curve

Figure 13.9 shows how we can derive a **demand curve** using **indifference curves**. In the top diagram, at the equilibrium point A consumers are willing to purchase X_1 of X when the price is P_1. We show that information in the bottom diagram where the price of X can be plotted against quantity of X. So point M represents this equilibrium position. If the price of X falls, say to P_2, we get a new equilibrium position, B, and this is shown in the bottom diagram by point N. Joining up points M and N gives us a **demand curve**.

13.3.5 Price changes: income and substitution effects

13.3.5.1 What are income and substitution effects?

There are two effects operating when there is a change in price. First, there is a **change in relative prices**. So, when the price of X falls, X is cheaper in relation to Y. We would expect consumers to substitute some of the cheaper X for Y. This is known as the **substitution effect** and shows the response of consumers to a change in relative prices. Second, the change in price affects consumers' real income. When the price of X falls there is an increase in **real income**. That is, although money income is constant it is capable of buying more goods and services because the price of one commodity has fallen. This is the **income effect** which shows the impact of a change in price through its effect on consumers' real income.

13.3.5.2 Illustrating the income and substitution effects

Both of these effects are present in the price changes we discussed and illustrated earlier. Our task now is to show how analysis can distinguish between the two. In Figure 13.10 a fall in price of X causes the equilibrium to change from A to B with the quantity of X consumers wish to purchase rising from X_1 to X_2. We illustrate the two effects if we isolate the increase in real income resulting from the price fall, so leaving us with the **substitution effect**. The most common way of doing this is to hypothetically take away the increase in real income until the consumer is returned to his **original indifference curve**. In terms of our diagram, we take the new budget line, BL_2, and move it inwards, retaining the slope of BL_2 (and therefore the new relative prices) until it becomes a tangent to the original indifference curve at point C. Here the consumer is enjoying the original level of utility which is how this approach interprets a constant real income, but the budget line BL reflects the new relative prices. We therefore represent the substitution effect as the move along the original indifference curve (A to C) which shows how the consumer would

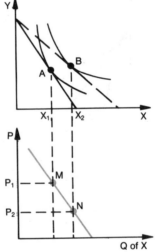

Fig. 13.9 Demand curve derived from indifference curves

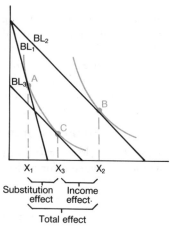

Fig. 13.10 Income and substitution effect

respond to the price change if utility were constant. In our illustration this would involve an increase in the consumption of X, from X_1 to X_3. Given the shape of the indifference curve, the **substitution effect** will always be negative: that is a fall in price will always lead to an increase in consumption and vice versa.

The income effect, which is the amount we hypothetically deducted to leave the substitution effect, is represented by CB, that is an increase in consumption of X_3 to X_2. Unlike the substitution effect, we cannot be certain whether the income effect will be positive (as it is here) or negative. This gives rise to three possible outcomes of a price change: **normal**, **inferior** and **Giffen** goods.

13.3.5.3 Normal goods

A normal good is the case we have already illustrated where the income effect is positive. This reinforces the substitution effect.

13.3.5.4 Inferior goods

Inferior goods are where there is a negative income effect which offsets some of the substitution effect. Figure 13.11(a) shows a fall in the price of X as previously described; but here the income effect (CB) is negative X_3 to X_2. This means that the total effect on consumption (X_1X_2) is equal to the substitution effect (X_1X_3) less the income effect, (X_3X_2).

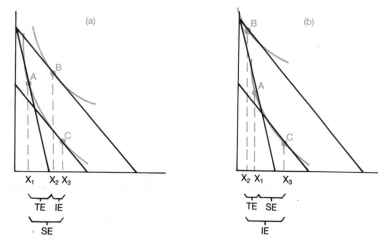

Fig. 13.11 Inferior and Giffen goods

13.3.5.5 Giffen goods

It is possible that the negative income effect is so large that it outweighs the substitution effect, in which case a fall in price actually leads to a fall in consumption. This possibility is illustrated in Fig. 13.11(b) where the negative income effect (CB) or in terms of quantity of X, (X_3 to X_2) is greater than the substitution effect (AC, X_1 to X_3); the total effect is that consumption of X falls from X_1 to X_2 as the consumer moves from an equilibrium at A to a new equilibrium at B.

This is a rather special case because it would produce an upward sloping demand curve. It is generally known as a Giffen good, after a 19th century statistician who suggested that the demand for bread among the poor might have this exceptional slope. For this group, bread formed a major part of their expenditure, so the income effect of price changes was likely to be large. It might so improve the real income of the poor that they might reduce bread consumption and buy some meat instead.

Nobody would suggest that the Giffen good is of practical importance; but it is a useful way of exploring income and substitution effects and courses that include it are likely to test your knowledge of it.

13.3.5.6 Summary of different cases

Table 13.3 below classifies the effects of a fall in the price on quantity consumed; the signs would be reversed for a rise in price.

Table 13.3 Effect of a fall in price of X on the quantity of X

Type of good	Substitution effect	Income effect	Total effect
Normal	+	+	+
Inferior	+	−	+
Giffen	+	−	−

13.3.5.7 How to show the income and substitution effects correctly on a diagram

Drawing **indifference curve diagrams** correctly, especially to show particular income and substitution effects, is often a source of difficulty. But this need not be the case if you combine a sound understanding of the concepts with a technique like the one described here to systematically build up the diagram. Do not try to learn the diagram by memorizing the shapes and patterns—this will almost certainly let you down. Figure 13.12 shows you how to construct the diagram in stages—we illustrate a fall in price for the cases of normal, inferior and Giffen goods. You will see that the technique involves drawing the indifference curves at the last stage.

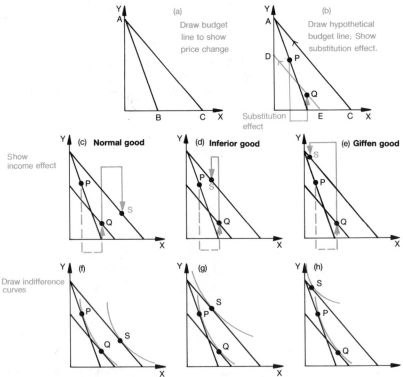

Fig. 13.12 How to draw indifference curve diagrams

1 Draw the budget lines:

- Draw the **original budget line** (AB).

- Draw the **new budget line**. If the price of X falls the new budget line will swivel on point A and look like AC.

2 Show substitution effect:

- Draw the **hypothetical budget line** (which helps to identify income and substitution effects) DE, parallel to AC, the new budget line (reflecting the new price ratio).

- Show the **substitution effect**: mark a point P on the original budget line and point Q on the hypothetical budget line (DE) as shown in Fig. 13.2(b). Point P will be the original consumer equilibrium position. PQ represents the substitution effect. In the final stage we will draw an indifference curve that passes through both P and Q, but it is wiser not to do so at this stage.

3 Drawing the income effect—we can now locate a point S which allows us to show the **income effect**. Where point S is constructed depends upon which of the following cases we wish to illustrate.

- Normal good—here the **income effect** will reinforce the **substitution effect** (see summary table in previous section) so point S will be to the right of point Q.
- Inferior good—here the impact of higher income (as represented by the difference between DE and AC) will have a **negative effect** on consumer spending and will work in the opposite direction to the substitution effect. Point S will be to the left of Q—but will lie between Q and P.
- Giffen good—the negative income effect is so strong the point S will be to the left of P. Point S will be the new equilibrium position. As it represents a lower consumption of X than the original point (P) it demonstrates the distinguishing characteristic of a Giffen good: cuts in price are associated with lower demand.

4 Draw **indifference curves**. One should touch both P and Q (this is the original indifference curve); the other is tangential to the new budget line (AC) at point S. Remember when drawing them that indifference curves do not cross. Particular care will have to be taken with the Giffen good case. You can then mark off on the X axis the substitution effects (X_1X_3), the income effect (X_3X_2) and the total or overall effect (X_1X_2).

13.3.6 Subsidies versus income support: an application of indifference curve analysis

A common application for **indifference curve analysis** is the policy problem of whether to provide **extra income support** for those on low incomes or use **subsidies** for goods and services. This may be applied to a variety of areas: housing, food, transport, etc. We can briefly show the main points of how to tackle this type of problem with the aid of Figure 13.13.

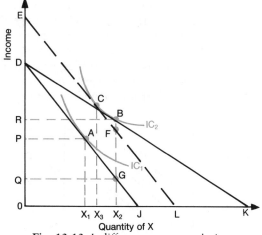

Fig. 13.13 Indifference curve analysis

The original equilibrium position is A, where X_1 quantity of X—say, housing—is consumed. We plot the income of the consumer on the Y axis. If the government wish to help the poor with housing they may subsidize it—for example through rent subsidies. A subsidy will effectively lower the price of X which will cause the budget line to swivel from DJ to DK. (If the government subsidy is introduced to halve rentals then OJ will equal JK.) The consumer moves on to a higher indifference curve and equilibrium point B where X_2 is consumed.

How would this policy compare with an alternative which raised income by some income support scheme? We can show this by drawing a budget line (EL) parallel to the original one (hence reflecting the unsubsidized rents) to produce a point of tangency (C) with IC_2. The income support programme, therefore, gives the same utility to the consumer as the subsidized rents (C and B are on the same indifference curve) but the substitution effect (C to B) X_3X_2 means more housing would be consumed with the rent subsidy scheme than with income support.

How do the costs of the schemes compare? The income support scheme will cost the amount necessary to shift the budget line upwards and this is clearly shown as extra income, DE, on the Y axis. The cost of the rent subsidy scheme can be obtained by less direct means. After the subsidy's introduction the consumer spends DR on housing (calculated by subtracting the expenditure on other goods OR from income OD). But to have enjoyed X_2 amount of housing before the subsidy the consumer would have been at point G on the old budget line and spent DQ (OD less OQ spent on other goods) on housing. The cost of the subsidy is, therefore, RQ (DQ less DR). We can make a direct comparison between the two schemes by considering the perpendicular line drawn at X_2. BG is the cost of the subsidy scheme (= RQ) and FG the cost of the income support scheme (= DE). So the latter is cheaper—in fact it will always be cheaper, given the shape of indifference curves—so why should we ever consider subsidies?

There may be several powerful reasons for preferring a subsidy. There may be externalities involved—that is, there may be some extra benefits in good housing (e.g. less illness, vandalism, and so on) which are not included in the consumer preference curve. Second, a paternalist/maternalist view of the state may suggest that society needs to take some responsibility for children to ensure they are brought up in decent surroundings.

This leads to a third argument, that housing is a **merit good**. This may be related to strongly held views on equality of opportunity. Poor housing (though it is correlated with many other factors) seems to be a contributor to poorer performance in education, perhaps because it causes more illness and restricts the opportunity for study. Lastly society may be more willing to pay taxes to subsidize housing than it would to pay money for income supplements.

13.4   Forecasting consumer demand

It is important for firms and public sector institutions to be able to **forecast consumer demand** for goods and services. There are several approaches. In most cases use is made of past data on sales; but we need to issue a warning on how this should be interpreted. In Figure 13.14 we illustrate some possible interpretations to be placed on two sets of observations, one showing higher quantities combined with lower prices (Figure 13.14(a) and (b)) and the other where higher quantities are associated with higher prices (13.14(c) and (d)). In Figure 13.14(a) the data will identify the demand with shifts in the supply curve. In the other illustrations the data do not correctly reveal the shape of the demand curve. In Figure 13.14(b), although the data appear to be points on a demand curve this is not the case because the points are a consequence of both demand and supply curve shifts. Figure 13.14(c) illustrates a situation where there is a stable supply curve and demand curve shifts. The resulting points reveal the shape of the supply curve but tell us nothing directly about demand. In Figure 13.14(d) the pattern of observations is seen to be the outcome of both demand and supply curve shifts.

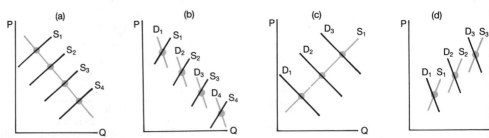

Fig. 13.14 Consumer demand

The difficulty that this poses for estimating demand is known as the **identification problem**. There are approaches in econometrics for dealing with this problem to try to ensure that what is obtained is an estimate of the demand for a product. We need to be wary of how we interpret data on product sales.

We can now briefly outline three broad approaches to forecasting demand.

13.4.1   Time-series forecasting

One approach to forecasting is to use past data on sales directly to make a forecast. This is essentially a matter of detecting the pattern in these **time-series data** and using it to make projections. The simplest of all approaches is to extrapolate a trend (see Figure 13.15(a)). Trends may be linear, as in the illustration, or non-linear. Often this method will not give reliable results because the time-series pattern is more complicated than the one shown.

Moving averages provide the basis for some simple and crude forecasts. So, for example, we may take the average of the last 12 observations to forecast the next period. We could use **weighted averages** if we wanted to give more importance to recent data. We could incorporate techniques to adjust forecasts for past errors in forecasts.

Many time series will have various identifiable components to them: trends, cyclical and seasonal factors. There will also be an unsystematic or irregular element (see Figure 13.15(b)). We can use techniques to decompose a time series into these various parts and then use them for forecasting. Some sophisticated computer software packages are now available designed to detect patterns and incorporate them into forecasts.

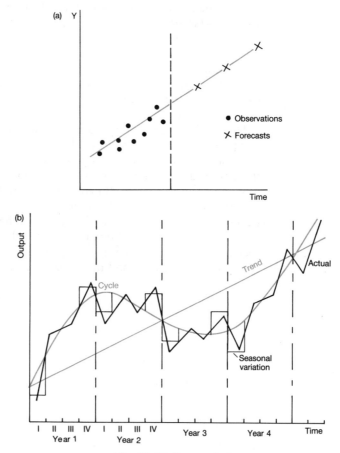

Fig. 13.15 Extrapolation

13.4.2   Causal models

We have concentrated on trying to identify factors that will influence demand—we have tried to develop a causal model. The economists' approach to forecasting demand will normally use these factors to estimate an equation that can be used for forecasting purposes. So we can approach the task using our basic framework for a demand for a product X (Qd_x):

$$Qd_x = f(P_x, P_o, Y, Z)$$

where P_x = price of X; P_o = other prices; Y = income and Z = tastes and other factors.

Using past data on the relevant variables, we can use a technique known as multiple regression to provide estimates of the coefficients in the equation. As an example, see the following hypothetical equation for beer, brand X:

$$Qd_x = 4 - 0.01P_x + 0.006P_o + 0.03Y + 0.002TEMP + 0.02POP + 0.0003ADVERT$$

This gives estimates of how the demand for brand X is affected by the price of the product and other variables (e.g. income, tastes). The latter will account for shifts in demand. The three taste variables are mean temperature ($TEMP$) to reflect the increase in demand that occurs during hot summers; the number of 18- to 35-year-olds (POP) to capture the demographic influence on demand because beer drinking is more favoured by the young; and finally an advertising variable ($ADVERT$) as measured by the firm's expenditure on this item.

We could use an equation of this type for forecasting if we have estimates of, or are able to make assumptions about, these variables. This approach allows us to try to explain the influences on a product and it is more capable of forecasting in changed circumstances (e.g. if there is a significant change in the tax on beer) than the time-series approach.

13.4.3 Indicators and surveys

A further approach to forecasting demand is to attempt to find a leading indicator for sales. For example, housing starts (i.e. the number of new houses that builders have started to construct) may be a good indicator for certain products—for example sanitary ware.

Surveys of intentions of buyers may be a useful guide to future sales. The CBI regularly publish the result of surveys they conduct among retailers and producers of goods and services. Market research, involving the questioning of customers or potential customers, may be important in a number of ways. It will help to identify the profile of customers and perhaps, the factors influencing their purchases. This could be directly useful in forecasting demand or it could assist in the development of causal models. Market research is particularly useful for making forecasts for new products when appropriate past data are unavailable. It also has an important role to play in testing consumer reaction to different types of products and packaging before deciding which one to launch.

This final section on forecasting is a reminder of the practical use of economics. Firms and public sector institutions (including local and central government) all have a need to forecast the demand for goods and services. Similarly they frequently need to understand the main factors affecting consumer spending so that they can attempt to influence it. The economist can make a useful contribution in this area.

In this chapter we have developed the microeconomic analysis of demand to shed more light on consumer behaviour. This approach has concentrated on the individual's demand for a product or service. You are reminded that the macroeconomic theories of consumer spending were discussed in Chapter 8. Together they provide insights into both consumption generally and the demand for particular products.

14 Production and costs

14.1 Introduction

In this and the next three chapters we explore the background to **supply**. A key element determining the quantity that a firm supplies is its costs of production. In this chapter we consider the approach of cost-minimizing firms to the **production choices** they face and we will explain the main **measures of costs** used in economics. The determination of **factor prices** is considered as part of the topic of distribution of income in Chapter 17. The decision on what level of output to produce will depend upon revenue as well as costs and this is examined in the next two chapters on competition and monopoly.

The chapter will:

- explain what is meant by a production function
- explain the distinction between short run and long run
- define and illustrate isoquants and isocosts and use these to explain the equilibrium position of the firm
- define and illustrate total, average and marginal product
- explain the law of diminishing returns
- define and explain economies of scale
- discuss and illustrate the economist's view of costs
- illustrate and explain the following cost concepts: total (fixed and variable), average (total, fixed and variable) and marginal costs
- distinguish between short- and long-run costs
- derive and explain the long-run average costs curve

14.1.1 Examination guide

This area of economics will require you to have a sound knowledge of different **costs** and be able to distinguish between **short-** and **long-term costs**. Courses will vary in how far you will be expected to explain the underpinning of costs. Most will require you to understand the notion of marginal productivity and diminishing returns, though many courses will not expect an understanding of **isoquants** and **isocosts**.

You should be able to draw the costs diagrams correctly, and here there is no substitute for practice. Make sure that costs bear the correct relationship to each other, for example, that the marginal cost curve cuts average total and variable cost at their lowest point. Test yourself by drawing them without the assistance of the book then check them and, if incorrect, understand why you went wrong–do not just learn the shapes. Keep practising until you get them correct.

Make sure you can correctly distinguish between short- and long-run costs. The former relates to a situation where one or more factors is fixed, whereas all factors are variable in the long run. It follows, therefore, that diminishing returns to a factor is a short-run phenomenon and helps explain short-run costs curves. This should not be confused with **economies** and **diseconomies** of scale which refer to situations where **all** factors are variable.

14.2 Theory of production

14.2.1 Production function

Firms and **public sector institutions** are producers of goods and services which transform inputs into output. A **production function** summarizes the process: generally

$$Q = f(F_1, F_2, \ldots \ldots F_n)$$

where Q is output and $F_1 \ldots F_n$ refers to factor inputs. More specifically, we will normally simplify the discussion by using a two-factor function:

$$Q = f(K, L)$$

where K is capital and L labour. Firms will usually face **production choices** between different ways of producing a given level of output, so production may be relatively capital- or labour-intensive. We explore these choices in the next two sections; but clearly changes in production technique do not normally take place immediately in response to some stimulus, so we distinguish between the **short-** and **long-run** changes.

14.2.1.1 Short run

The **short run** is defined as a period during which some factors can be varied and some are fixed. So, for example, capital may be fixed but output may be raised by increasing labour input:

$$\overset{\uparrow}{Q} = f(\overset{-}{K}, \overset{\uparrow}{L})$$

14.2.1.2 Long run

In the long run all factors may be varied, so in our illustration the scale of operations may be increased by using more labour and capital:

$$\overset{\uparrow}{Q} = f(\overset{\uparrow}{K}, \overset{\uparrow}{L})$$

The factor intensity too, may vary in the long run, as capital might be substituted for labour or vice versa.

The distinction between the short and the long run is important and is one we shall use frequently in this and the next chapter. Sometimes reference is made to the very long run—this is when technological change can alter the production function so that increased output could be produced with the same quantity of inputs, e.g.

$$\overset{\uparrow}{Q} = \overset{\uparrow}{f}(K, L)$$

Clearly in the **very long run** all elements in the production process may change. In contrast, in the **very short run** neither output nor factor inputs can change so, in effect, supply is perfectly inelastic.

14.2.2 Isoquants

There will normally be many possible ways of **producing** a good or a service. Table 14.1 shows one possible way of producing product X, which we can call activity 1.

Table 14.1 Production of X: activity 1

Output of X	Inputs Labour	Capital
1	5	20
2	10	40
3	15	60
4	20	80

In Figure 14.1 the line marked Activity 1 plots these points. Other methods of producing X will generate similar activity lines—a further three are shown in the same figure. If we concentrate on the production of 2 units of X, these activity lines reveal several ways of producing the same output. However, we can reject activity 3 as technically inefficient because it uses the same amount of capital as activity 2 yet requires more labour.

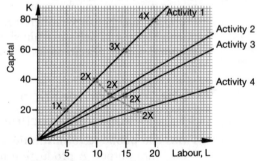

Fig. 14.1 Constructing an isoquant

If we join **technically efficient points** that produce the same output we obtain an **isoquant** or **equal product curve**. We normally assume that there are many ways of producing a good (that is, there are many activity lines), so the **isoquants** are drawn as curves (see Figure 14.2). The non-linear shape suggests that labour and capital are not perfect substitutes. As the amount of capital used diminishes then increasing amounts of labour are needed for every unit reduction in capital. (See the move between *A* and *B* compared with *C* and *D*, both of which involve a reduction in capital of 10 units.) The ratio of ΔK to ΔL is known as the **marginal rate of transformation** (**MRT**) or **marginal rate of technical substitution**. It declines as we move down the isoquant because it becomes less easy to substitute labour for capital as the quantity of capital is reduced.

We can consider more closely how output responds to changes in factor inputs, first under conditions where some factors are fixed (section 14.2.3) and then under conditions when all factors can vary (section 14.2.4). The former is known as **returns to a factor** and the latter **returns to scale**.

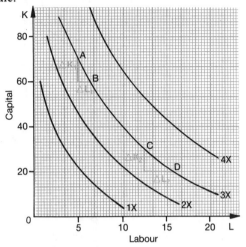

Fig. 14.2 Isoquant curves

14.2.3 Diminishing returns to a factor

In Figure 14.3, let us assume that the stock of capital is fixed at K_1. The points *A* to *D* show that ever-larger increases in labour are required for equal rises in output. This is known as **diminishing returns to a factor**.

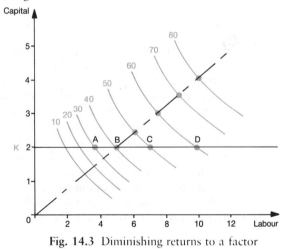

Fig. 14.3 Diminishing returns to a factor

The same situation is presented in Figure 14.4 (overleaf) where the quantity of *X*, or total product, is plotted against the variable factor, labour. In the range 5 to 11 units of labour, although output rises as more labour is applied, the increments in output are diminishing. We can see this more clearly if we look at Figure 14.5 where the **marginal product** (**MP**) is plotted. The **marginal product** of a factor is the change in total product resulting from a change in the factor used. In our example:

$$MP = \frac{\Delta TP}{\Delta L}$$

The marginal product declines when more than 4 units of labour are used, as each additional unit of labour adds less in extra output than its predecessor. This outcome is to be expected when more labour is added to a fixed amount of capital. This is sometimes known as the **law of diminishing returns**, which states that at some point diminishing marginal returns will occur if more of a variable factor is combined with a fixed amount of other factor(s). In our illustration the marginal product becomes negative when 12 units of

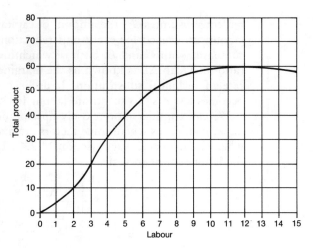

Fig. 14.4 Diminishing returns to labour

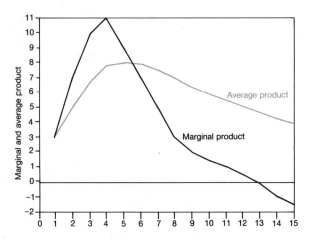

Fig. 14.5 Average and marginal product

labour are employed. At this point adding extra labour not only fails to raise output any further but causes total production to fall. This position would be reached when, for example, extra workers impeded production by taking up useful space. There may be a range where we experience increasing returns to a factor. There will be many instances when a relatively low quantity of the variable factor means that the fixed factor is significantly underutilized. In our illustration the marginal product rises between 1 and 4 units of labour, as extra workers allow a fuller use of machinery and a more extensive division of labour to develop. This does not contradict the law of diminishing returns, which argues that increasing returns cannot be sustained when extra variable factors are added; at some point **diminishing returns** set in.

We can consider the **average product** of a factor as well as its marginal product. The **average product** (*AP*) is defined as

$$AP = \frac{TP}{L}$$

In our illustration this is shown as the coloured line in Figure 14.5. *AP* will decline at some point. As the diagram shows, it will be cut from above by the marginal product curve and will fall after that as the marginal product is less than the average.

14.2.4 Returns to scale

We can now examine the relationship between **factor inputs** and **output** when all factors can change, as they can do in the long run. In Figure 14.6(a) the line from the origin allows us to consider equal proportional changes in factor inputs. There is an equal distance on the diagram between successive isoquants, which means that a doubling of factor inputs will lead to a doubling of output. This is an example of **constant returns to scale**.

Returns to scale are not necessarily constant. **Increasing returns** occur when a doubling of inputs leads to more than a doubling of output (see Fig. 14.6(b)). Raising the scale of operations permits a more extensive division of labour; it may also allow fuller advantage to be taken of capital indivisibilities which on a lower scale of operations means that machinery is underutilized. Managerial economies may also occur. (We consider the issue of **economies of scale** more fully in section 14.3.3.)

There may be **decreasing returns to scale** (or diseconomies of scale) when a doubling of inputs leads to less than twice the output (see Figure 14.6(c)).

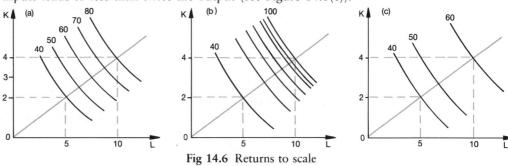

Fig 14.6 Returns to scale

14.2.5 Isocosts and equilibrium

The **isoquants** look like indifference curves and are a clearly similar concept except they refer to points of equal output rather than equal utility. The similarity of approach does not end here. Households seek to maximize utility given their budgets and firms wish to obtain the highest output for a given outlay or expenditure on factors. Just as we could not determine consumer equilibrium without the budget line, so we cannot know the firm's equilibrium position without an equivalent measure: the **isocost line**. The **isocost line** shows what quantities of factors could be bought for a given sum of money. For example, if a firm had £100 to spend and capital cost £20 per unit and labour £12.50, it could at one extreme buy 5 units of capital and no labour or at the other extreme 8 units of labour and no capital. It will more probably buy some combination of the two factors and the **isocost line** shows these possibilities (see Figure 14.7).

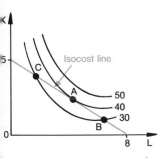

Fig. 14.7 Isocost line

The firm will be in equilibrium at A where the **isocost** line is a tangent to the **isoquant** (for an output of 40). Here it is achieving the maximum output for a given expenditure on factors. Points B and C would be suboptimal because the firm would be spending the same amount of money to achieve a lower output; it could clearly improve its position by reallocating its expenditure and moving towards A. Point A represents a cost minimization position for the firm. We can see this if we consider a firm wishing to produce an output of 40 at the minimum cost. It will want its **isocost** line to be as near the origin as possible; but as the illustration shows: it could not lower costs any more and still produce 40 units of output. At the equilibrium position the **marginal rate of transformation** of capital for labour (**MRT**) is equal to the ratio of the prices of labour (P_L) to capital (P_K):

$$MRT = \frac{\Delta K}{\Delta L} = \frac{P_L}{P_K}$$

which means that the rate at which the market trades factors (as shown by relative prices) is the same as the rate at which firms wish to substitute one factor for another to maintain a given output.

Changes in **factor prices** will alter the slope of the **isocost line** and produce a new equilibrium position. Consider the case illustrated in Figure 14.8 of the firm wishing to produce an output of 40 and initially in equilibrium at A with isocost line ICL_1. A lower wage will alter the relative price of factors and hence the slope of the isocost line. The new cost-minimizing position for a firm producing an output of 40 will be at B where ICL_2 (reflecting the new relative prices) is tangential to the isoquant. The lower wages not only reduce total costs but lead to the substitution of more labour (L_1 to L_2) for less capital (K_1 to K_2). This analysis leads us to expect that more labour-intensive methods will be associated with lower wages, *ceteris paribus*.

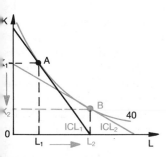

Fig. 14.8 Effect of price changes on isocost line

14.3 Costs

14.3.1 The economist's view of costs

The economist's view of costs is sometimes at odds with other approaches. There are doubtless many benefits and conveniences from the accountant's way of measuring costs, but the economist can claim some insights which are of particular value in decision making.

The economist's approach is to use **opportunity cost**. The cost of inputs to a firm is measured by the benefit that is sacrificed by not using them in the best alternative way. For many explicit costs this is a straightforward principle to apply and is no different from other approaches to costing. For example, if a firm pays £200 000 for raw materials, labour and energy, this sum of money is a reasonable measure of the opportunity cost to a firm: it has given up £200 000 that could have been spent on some alternative use. However, there are other areas where recognition of the **opportunity** (or **alternative**) **cost** principle raises differences from other approaches.

14.3.1.1 Implicit costs

Some **opportunity costs** incurred by a firm are not always correctly recognized. Take as an example a small firm which is managed by its owner and makes a profit of £35 000. The **opportunity cost** of the owner's management skill should be treated as a cost. It would be measured by the salary the owner could obtain by working for someone else. Let us suppose this is £30 000 but that the owner is drawing only a salary of £20 000 from his own firm. The explicit cost (of £20 000) underestimates the implicit opportunity cost by £10 000; a further £10 000 should therefore be added to the firm's costs.

A similar argument can be applied to finance provided by the owner or from retained profits. There is an opportunity cost to this, which is the rate of interest that could be obtained by loaning it out. So if, for example, £100 000 were provided internally and the market rate of interest were 10 per cent then the opportunity cost of this finance would be £10 000. Finally, building and other property rights (e.g. franchises) have an **opportunity cost** because they could be rented out. The **market value** of the best alternative use should be counted as a cost. For our illustration let us suppose this is £20 000. These costs are illustrated in Table 14.2.

Table 14.2 Opportunity costs (£)

Using explicit costs	
Revenue	235 000
Less explicit costs	(200 000)
Profit	35 000
Using opportunity costs	
Revenue	235 000
Less explicit costs	(200 000)
Implicit managerial costs	(10 000)
Opportunity costs of finance	(10 000)
Opportunity costs of buildings	(20 000)
Profit	− 5000

Using this approach a profit of £35 000 becomes a loss of £5000. On the basis of these figures the owner would be better off closing the firm and working for someone else, lending out his money and renting out his buildings.

14.3.1.2 Depreciation and bygones are bygones

What we have said so far would suggest that conventional costing practices underestimate **opportunity costs**; but there may be occasions when the reverse is true. Take, for example, the treatment of **depreciation**. Suppose our firm bought a machine last year for £50 000 and it was expected to last for five years and was therefore depreciated at £10 000 a year. This may not correspond to the **opportunity cost** of using the machine. If the machine was highly specific and had a negligible market value, then the opportunity cost would be approximately zero and the expenditure of £50 000 (or for that matter £1 million) would be irrelevant to assessing cost today. The inclusion of a £10 000 depreciation charge would inflate costs and, as far as the economist is concerned, would not give a true picture of profitability. Thus historic costs are not necessarily a good measure of current opportunity costs.

Opportunity cost may not always be an easy concept to grasp and there are certainly occasions when it is difficult to measure; but it is an important aid to decision making. Maurice Chevalier captured the approach when he was asked how he felt about old age and he replied, 'Fine, relative to the alternative'.

14.3.1.3 Social and private costs

From the point of view of society, an **optimum allocation** of resources requires decisions to be based on **social** rather than **private** costs. A divergence may occur because of **externalities**. In the case of pollution a firm may not pay the full cost of production that has to be borne by the community. This was discussed in Chapter 3 and is considered more closely in Chapter 18. We will concentrate until then on how decisions are made by firms on the basis of **private costs**.

14.3.2 Short-run costs

In the short run some factors are fixed while others are variable. This means that there will be some costs that have to be paid whatever the level of output–these are known as **fixed costs**. In contrast, the use of variable factors will depend on the level of output and this gives rise to **variable costs**. Examples of **fixed costs** are most of the management and administration of the organization, security staffing and much of the plant and machinery. Raw materials, energy and probably the hours worked by the operative staff are often regarded as **variable costs**.

14.3.2.1 Definitions of costs

1 Total fixed and variable costs–Table 14.3 shows the hypothetical costs of a firm. The **total fixed cost** (*TFC*) is unaffected by output (*Q*) and the **total variable cost** (*TVC*) must by definition be zero when no output is produced and then rise as output increases. The **total cost** (*TC*) facing the firm is obtained by adding together *TVC* and *TFC*.

Table 14.3

Quantity	Total cost TC (TFC + TVC)	Total fixed cost TFC	Total variable cost TVC	Marginal cost MC ($\Delta TC/\Delta Q$)	Average total cost ATC (TC/Q)	Average variable cost AVC (TVC/Q)	Average fixed cost AFC (TFC/Q)
0	12	12	0				
1	22	12	10.0	10.0	22	10.0	12.0
2	29	12	17.0	7.0	14.5	8.5	6.0
3	34	12	22.0	5.0	11.3	7.3	4.0
4	37	12	25.0	3.0	9.3	6.3	3.0
5	39.5	12	27.5	2.5	7.9	5.5	2.4
6	42.5	12	30.5	3.0	7.1	5.1	2.0
7	46	12	34.0	3.5	6.6	4.9	1.7
8	50	12	38.0	4.0	6.3	4.8	1.5
9	55	12	43.0	5.0	6.1	4.8	1.3
10	61	12	49.0	6.0	6.1	4.9	1.2
11	69	12	57.0	8.0	6.3	5.2	1.1
12	79	12	67.0	10.0	6.6	5.6	1.0
13	92	12	80.0	13.0	7.1	6.2	0.9

2 Average costs are obtained by dividing the various total costs by output (see the final three columns of Table 14.3). So **average fixed cost** (*AFC*) is *TFC/Q* and, as Figure 14.9 shows, *AFC* steadily declines as fixed costs become spread over a larger output. Both the **average variable cost curve** (*AVC*), obtained by dividing *TVC* by *Q* and average total cost (*ATC* = *TC/Q*) have a similar shape, with the *AVC* getting closer to the *ATC* as *AFC* declines with higher output.

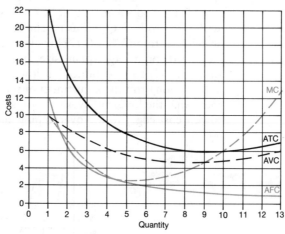

Fig. 14.9 Average costs

3 Marginal cost is our final short-run cost concept. This is the additional cost of producing an extra unit of output:

$$MC = \frac{\Delta TC}{\Delta Q}$$

Like the average variable and average total cost curves it is U-shaped.

14.3.2.2 Explaining the shape of cost curves

Why should the **marginal cost** fall then increase in this way? The explanation is to be found in our earlier discussion of marginal product. We suggested then that as more of a variable factor (e.g. labour) is added to a quantity of a fixed factor then the marginal product (that is, the additional output produced by an extra worker) may rise to begin with but that eventually diminishing returns will mean that it declines. We illustrated this in Figure 14.4. There is a simple relationship between marginal cost and product:

$$MC = \frac{P_v}{MP}$$

where P_v is the price of the variable factor and MP is its marginal product. This would be the wage in the case of labour. If factor prices are taken as given, then MC and MP move inversely. So, in effect, the MC curve is the mirror image of the MP curve: the rise in MP causes MC to decline and the fall in MP leads to a rise in the MC.

A brief account of this interrelationship will help explain why the two move in opposite directions. When MP is rising, extra workers add more to output than their predecessors. Assuming they all receive the same wage, this means that the labour cost per unit of output is declining. If, for the sake of simplicity we assume that labour is the only variable factor, the marginal cost (which is the additional cost of producing extra output) is falling. When the MP falls, additional workers add less and less extra output; the labour cost of each unit therefore rises, pushing the marginal cost upwards.

So it is **diminishing returns** that cause the short-run marginal cost curve to rise and increasing returns that are responsible for its fall. The behaviour of the average product (AP) curve accounts for the shape of the AVC and (in conjunction with AFC) ATC:

$$AVC = \frac{P_v}{AP}$$

$$ATC = \frac{P_v}{AP} + AFC$$

The **marginal cost curve** will cut the average variable and average total cost curves at their lowest points. When the marginal cost becomes greater than the average it causes average cost to rise, in the same way that a cricketer's average rises when his last score is above his average. Care should be taken when drawing these cost curves to make sure that the marginal cost does cut the average curves at their minimum.

14.3.3 Long-run costs

In the **long run** all factors are **variable** and the scale of operations may be adjusted in response to changes in actual or anticipated output. We can understand the nature of long-run costs and their interrelationship with short-run costs through a simple illustration. In Figure 14.10, three possible plant sizes, A to C, are shown. If the firm intends to produce an output of Q_1 it will choose plant A. If it subsequently finds that it wishes to produce Q_2 it has no choice in the short run but to incur higher average costs—which rise from OX to OY. However, in the long run when all factors are variable the firm can decide on a larger plant size. In this case it will choose plant B which will allow an output of Q_2 to be produced at lower average cost, OZ, than is possible with plant A.

In the long run the adjustment of the scale of operations to secure the lowest costs will mean that the long-run average cost is given by the heavy line that forms the envelope (or **lowest cost edge**) to the overlapping short-run curves. Care should be taken in drawing

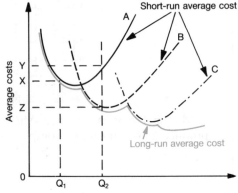

Fig. 14.10 Long- and short-run cost curves

this diagram so that the long-run curve follows the outer edge of the family of short-run curves. It will not be above these short-run curves because this implies that lower cost options have not been exploited, even though the long run allows the scale of operations to be adjusted; and it cannot be below these curves because it must operate, at any particular time, on a short-run curve. If there are a large number of short-run cost curves, reflecting a wide choice in plant size, then the bumpiness in Figure 14.10 will disappear and the long-run average cost curve will appear smooth.

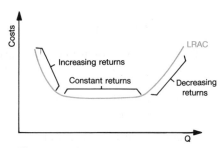

Fig. 14.11 Long-run average cost curve

The **long-run average cost curve** (*LRAC*) in Figure 14.11 illustrates **increasing, constant** and **decreasing returns to scale**. **Increasing returns** mean that there are **economies of scale** which produce a fall in long-run average costs as output rises. This may arise for a variety of reasons. Technical economies may occur because a doubling of volume does not require a twofold increase in surface area. This is clearly important for warehouses and oil tankers. Larger-scale operations may allow greater benefits of specialization to be secured. Division of labour may be extended and this may allow productivity to be raised, as assembly line production in many industries has shown. There will be certain indivisibilities in many production processes which mean that small-scale operations cannot afford certain equipment or cannot fully utilize it if it is purchased. Managerial economies are really an example of indivisibilities—a halving of output will not generally allow the number of managers to be reduced in the same proportion. Financial or marketing economies are also likely to occur. For example, the cost of a market research exercise is not likely to cost twice as much if the output of the firm doubles. All these factors may be regarded as **internal economies of scale**.

In addition there may be **external economies of scale**. These arise when the growth of an industry as a whole produces opportunities that lead to a lowering of costs of individual firms. For example, after a certain size it may be profitable for specialist firms to be established to meet certain of the industry's needs, for example, waste disposal, testing of materials, training. Similarly, where industries are concentrated in a particular location (e.g. pottery around Stoke-on-Trent) there will be a pool of labour that has the skills and tradition of working in the industry. All these developments are likely to lower the costs of firms in the industry. These **external economies** result from the expansion of the industry whereas **internal economies** arise from the growth of the firm.

Figure 14.11 also shows a range of constant returns where long-run costs remain the same when plant size is altered. This is likely to occur when the economies of scale we have discussed are exhausted. This may also be a point beyond which **decreasing returns** or **diseconomies of scale** arise. In this situation rising long-run average costs may occur because of managerial diseconomies arising from a large bureaucratic organization.

A long-run total cost curve may be derived and if the average cost curve is broadly U-shaped the total cost curve will have a shape similar to the total variable cost curve shown in Figure 14.9. Remember, as there are no fixed costs there is only one long-run total cost curve. From this curve a long-run marginal cost curve can be derived. It shows the additional cost of producing extra output when the scale of operations can adjust to the cost-minimizing position.

Clearly, costs are only half the information needed to understand why firms choose their output levels; the other half concerns revenue. How revenue varies as output changes depends on the structure of the industry and whether it is competitive or monopolistic. We consider these two situations in the next two chapters.

15 Perfect competition model

15.1 Introduction

Perfect competition is one of the basic models of economics which plays an important role in helping us to understand the **behaviour of firms**. It explains how competitive firms determine their output and it can be used to derive a supply curve and to show how competitive industries respond to changes in demand.

The chapter will:

- define perfect competition
- explain the profit maximization condition $MC = MR$
- explain the equilibrium position of the perfectly competitive firm
- show you how to draw perfect competition diagrams correctly (with losses and profits illustrated)
- explain how an industry supply curve is derived
- explain the short- and long-run response of the firm and the industry to a change in demand

15.1.1 Examination guide

All courses which include the **perfectly competitive model** will require students to show a clear understanding of the **profit maximization principle** and the **equilibrium position** of **the firm**. You will also need to explain how the firm and the industry responds in the short and long run to changes such as shifts in demand. Generally, diagrams will be expected or even demanded. They are often a source of error in examination; but as we explain in this chapter an understanding of a few basic principles combined with a correct approach to drawing them will overcome these difficulties.

Many questions concentrate on testing knowledge of the theory, though others will be more applied. Questions that ask about agriculture may well be asking for (or can benefit from) the use of the perfectly competitive model. Some questions might ask for a comparison with a monopoly situation or ask about government policy towards competition. We deal with these in the next chapter, though we make use of the analysis covered here.

15.2 Revenue and profit maximization

The **total revenue** (**TR**) of a firm is clearly equal to the quantity it sells times the price for the product:

$TR = P.Q$

where P is price, and Q is quantity. The **average revenue** is TR/Q, which is equal to the price of the product. There is one further revenue concept which we will use more than the others and that is **marginal revenue** (**MR**). **Marginal revenue** is the change in total revenue resulting from sale of an extra unit:

$$MR = \frac{\Delta TR}{\Delta Q}$$

We are assuming that all output is sold at the same price. This will be an assumption we make throughout this chapter and we explain it in section 15.3.1. A different approach to the relationship between revenue and quantity is considered in the chapter on monopoly. However, it does not affect the key points we make in this section.

Profit is the difference between total revenue and total cost:

$PROFIT = TR - TC$

So when $TR > TC$, as it is between Q_1 and Q_3 in Figure 15.1, then the firm is making profits. Elsewhere $TC > TR$, so there are losses. The lower half of the figure plots losses and profits explicitly. Maximum profits are at Q_2 where the gap between TR and TC is at its greatest. Expanding output above Q_2 or contracting it below Q_2 will reduce profits.

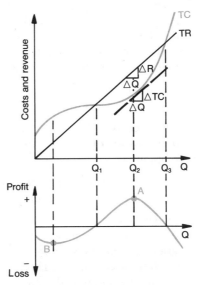

Fig. 15.1 Costs and revenue

We can take a different approach to defining the same position, using **marginal** concepts. **Marginal revenue** (**MR**) is the slope of the total revenue schedule ($\Delta TR/\Delta Q$). The point of **profit maximization** will be where the slope of the TR schedule is equal to the slope of the TC curve (measured by the slope of a tangent to it) as in Figure 15.1. The slope of the TC curve is $\Delta TC/\Delta Q$, which is how we defined **marginal cost** (**MC**) in the last chapter. So we can say that **profit maximization** occurs where $MR = MC$.

A more straightforward explanation is provided in Figure 15.2. The **marginal revenue** is constant because of our assumption that all output is sold at the same price. The **marginal cost curve** has the shape we discussed in the last chapter. Q_2 is the **profit-maximizing output** where $MC = MR$. We can explain this easily by considering output levels above and below Q_2. At Q_1, $MR > MC$, that is, the firm is adding more to revenue than it is to costs and it pays the firm to expand output as long as this is the case. At Q_2 it adds the same to revenue as it does to cost and further expansion is no longer indicated. However, consider the position above Q_2, say at Q_3. Here $MC > MR$, so the extra output adds more to cost than it does to revenue. This indicates that output should be cut back.

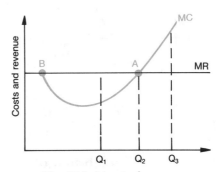

Fig. 15.2 Marginal revenue

We can consider the condition $MC = MR$ as the rule for **profit maximization**. However, it is necessary to add a qualificaton to this because, as Figure 15.2 shows, there are two points A and B where $MC = MR$. In contrast to A, B is a point of **profit minimization** (the two points are also marked on the lower part of Figure 15.1). Strictly, we require an additional condition to make it clear which of the $MC = MR$ points refers to profit maximization. This can be achieved by requiring it to be the point where MC is rising. (Having made this qualification we will not keep repeating it.)

15.3 Perfect competition model

15.3.1 Assumption of the perfect competition model

Economists distinguish between different types of market structure ranging from **perfect competition** to **monopoly**. In this chapter we concentrate exclusively on the **competitive** extreme. **Perfect competition** is normally defined through a number of assumptions or conditions:

1 The most important of these assumptions is that firms are so numerous and insignificant in relation to the market as a whole that no single firm has an impact on prices. Firms are **price takers**–they have to accept market determined prices and can sell as much as they wish at the prevailing price. The other assumptions/conditions are in many senses necessary to ensure that firms remain price takers.

2 Under perfect competition it is assumed that firms (and therefore resources) are **free to enter** and **exit** from the industry.

3 It is necessary for all relevant transactors (consumers, entrepreneurs, owners of factors) to be **aware** of **market conditions**. If they are not then markets will become less competitive.

4 The products of firms under perfect competition should **not** be **differentiated** from one another–if they are it reduces the competitive nature of markets.

Given these assumptions (or conditions) it seems highly likely that few examples of perfect competition will be found in practice. **Foreign exchange, commodity** and **agricultural markets** are very close to the textbook definition; but most of industry fails to match these conditions. This does not mean that the model we are exploring is of no use. Our discussion on methodology in Chapter 2 made it clear that models do not have to be realistic to be useful. The **predictions** of the **perfect competition model** may give satisfactory results concerning the behaviour of firms even though the industry may fail to meet the conditions outlined above. Where there is a marked absence of **competition** then the **monopoly model** discussed in the next chapter, (or another **non-competitive model**), may be more appropriate.

15.3.2 The firm's demand curve under perfect competition

Under **perfect competition** each firm is faced by a horizontal or perfectly elastic demand curve at the market price. In effect it can sell all that it wants at the prevailing price. **Marginal revenue** is equal to **price** because with a constant price each extra unit sold will raise revenue by the sale price. So as Figure 15.3(a) shows, the firm's demand (or average revenue) is equal to marginal revenue at the market price P_1.

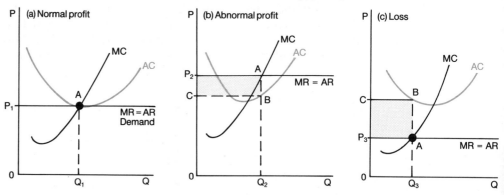

Fig. 15.3 Normal profit, abnormal profit, and loss

15.3.3 Equilibrium of the firm under perfect competition

We assume that firms are **profit maximizers**, so they will seek to produce at a point where $MC = MR$ as this is the condition for **profit maximization** (see section 15.2). In Figure 15.3(a) this will be at point A at an output of Q_1. We can determine if this position is profitable by comparing average revenue and average cost for this level of output. The **average cost** of producing an output OQ_1 is Q_1A ($= OP$), which is the same as average revenue at Q_1. As $AC = AR$ it appears that the firm is not making a profit (though it is not making a loss either). However, the firm will be earning **normal profits**. This is a profit which gives the firm a return that is sufficient to keep it operating in the industry. **Normal profits** are included in average total costs because without this payment for undertaking risks being covered, at least in the long run, the firm would leave the industry.

We can understand this point more fully if we consider cases where **abnormal profits** and losses are made. In Figure 15.3(b) the price is P_2 and firms maximize profits (where $MC = MR$) at an output of Q_2. Average cost is Q_2B ($= OC$), but price and average revenue is higher at Q_2A ($= OP_2$), so a profit of AB per unit is being made. Total profit is the shaded area ($ABCP_2$) i.e. AB (average profit) multiplied by OQ_2 (output). As normal profits are included in average costs, the profits marked on the diagrams are over and above what is necessary to keep the firm in the industry and they are known as **abnormal**. In Figure 15.3(c) a case where a relatively low price leads to losses is illustrated. Again, the profit-maximizing rule $MC = MR$ will determine the most profitable output, Q_3. In this case it turns out to be the point that minimizes losses because the average cost of this output is Q_3B (= OC), which is greater than average revenue Q_3A (= OP_3), so a loss of AB per unit is being made. Total losses are the shaded area $ABCP_3$ ($AB \times P_3A$). Although loss-making firms do not make a normal profit they may still stay open and operate in the short run providing they cover variable costs (see section 15.3.5). In the long run if the situation is unchanged they will leave the industry. Each of these positions represent firms in short-run equilibrium—maximizing profits.

As we shall see below only the first of these positions, where **normal profits** are being made, is a sustainable, long-run equilibrium position.

15.3.4 How to draw perfect competition diagrams correctly

The basic diagrams used in discussing perfect competition are those in Figure 15.3. They are fairly straightforward, but they do seem to pose problems under examination conditions. The point where MC cuts the AC curve seems to be compellingly attractive and many examinees cannot resist incorporating it into the illustration of profit/losses or output determination; but as you can see from Figure 15.3 it has nothing to do with these aspects of short-term equilibrium.

Avoid the device of a thick pencil and small diagram to conceal ignorance because it tends to have the reverse effect and draw attention to the problem. Do not try to memorize diagrams—it is a thoroughly unreliable method. The following two-stage approach is straightforward and foolproof (see Figure 15.4).

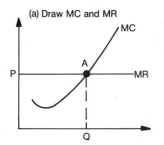 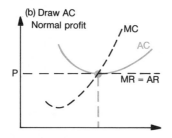 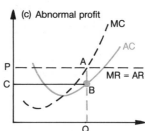 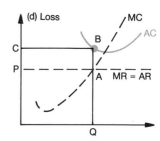

Fig. 15.4 How to draw perfect competition diagrams

1 Determine output—use MC and MCR:

- Draw MC and MR.
- Determine the profit-maximizing output where $MC = MR$ and draw a vertical line to indicate it—see AQ in Figure 15.4.

2 Determine profit/losses—use AC and AR. Having determined what output the firms will produce you can now show positions of profits or losses. This involves comparing average revenue with average cost at Q, the profit-maximizing output. Recall that $AR = MR$, so you have already drawn the AR schedule and it only needs to be labelled. Stage 2 involves drawing an appropriate AC curve. Remember that the MC cuts AC at its lowest point. Where the AC curve is drawn depends whether there are profits or losses being earned. We consider three possible cases.

- If the firm is earning **normal profits** then $AC = AR$, so in this case the AR schedule will be a tangent to the AC curve as shown in Figure 15.4(b).
- In the case of **abnormal profits**, AC will be less than AR at the profit-maximizing output, Q, so the AC curve will pass through the line AQ at a point below A, for example B. Mark B on your diagram then draw on the AC curve passing through it, but remember, that AC will be cut at its lowest point by the MC schedule so it should look like Figure 15.4(c). The distance AB represents the profit per unit so total profits is shown by the area $ABCP$ (i.e. profits per unit (AB) times quantity ($OQ = CB$)).
- **Losses** arise when $AC > AR$, so as average revenue is equal to the distance AQ, we need AC to be higher than this, say at point B on Figure 15.4(d). Having marked a point B, draw on AC crossing MC at its lowest point. AB is the loss per unit, so the $ABCP$ represents the total loss.

15.3.5 Derivation of the supply curve

We can derive a **supply curve** for the firm and industry under **perfect competition** very easily. The quantity a firm will supply (Q) will be where $MC = MR$. As MR equals price (P) this produces a price–quantity combination which will represent a point on the supply curve. In Figure 15.5(a), point A is such a position: the firm will produce a quantity of OQ_1 when price ($= MC$) is P_1. If prices were to rise to P_2 ($= MR_2$) then the profit-maximizing firm will make sure it still equates MC and MR (now at point B) and will therefore produce OQ_2 output. We can trace out similar points to A and B for higher prices (e.g. P_3 and P_4) which gives us other quantities (Q_3 and Q_4) that will be supplied. In effect, the firm's supply curve is its **marginal cost curve**.

However, there is an important qualification to be made. The lower the price becomes the more likely it is that a firm will operate at a loss. Will a firm still supply goods and services if it is making losses? In the long run it will not, but in the short run it will, providing it can cover variable costs and make a contribution to fixed or overhead costs. In Figure 15.5(b), at a price of P_1 the firm is just covering its variable costs. Above that price, until P equals P_2, it will experience losses but as $P > AVC$, some of the fixed costs will be paid. Below P_1 this will not be achieved, so it is cheaper to shut down and produce nothing and thus not pay the variable costs. The supply curve is therefore horizontal at P_1. Above that the **marginal cost curve** is the firm's short-run supply curve. The industry's **supply curve** is the sum of the **firms' supply curves**. We consider the long-run supply at the end of the next section.

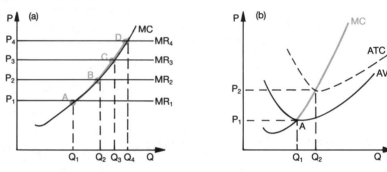

Fig. 15.5 Supply curve under perfect competition

15.4 The perfectly competitive industry and firm in the short and long run

We can now look at the **interrelationship** between firm and industry and see the response at both levels to a change such as a shift in demand for the product. This will help us appreciate more fully what is involved in the supply and demand model developed earlier in the book.

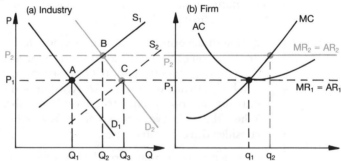

Fig. 15.6 Firm and industry demand

In Figure 15.6 the position of the industry is depicted in the lefthand panel and that of the firm on the right. The initial **industry equilibrium** is at P_1 with output Q_1. The **industry demand curve** will be downward sloping because it reflects consumer preferences for the product, though demand facing individual firms will be perfectly elastic because they are in a perfectly competitive situation. The firm is in equilibrium producing q_1 and earning normal profits ($AR = AC$). If there were a change in preference for the product so that the demand curve shifted out from D_1 to D_2 this would cause the price to rise. As price takers, firms will now be faced by a demand curve (which is equal to MR) at a higher price. Being profit maximizers they will wish to equate MC and MR, so they will expand output.

A **short-run equilibrium position** is established at B where price has risen to P_2 and output increased to Q_2. The higher output results from firms raising production, as Figure 15.6(b) shows. At P_2 the firm equates MC and MR at Oq_2. But as we can see, at an output of Oq_2 abnormal profits will be earned. This acts as a signal for new firms to enter the industry. As they do so the industry's output is raised, the short-run supply curve shifts outwards and prices will start to fall. A long-run equilibrium position is established at C where prices have returned to P_1 but industry output is OQ_3. The supply curve has shifted to S_2. For the individual firm output will return to Oq_1 at the origin price, P_1, and only normal profits are earned. The extra output in the industry (Q_1Q_3) has been supplied by **new entrants**. In the situation we have described the long-run supply curve is horizontal, suggesting **constant returns to scale**. Note that in our illustration costs do not rise, which implies that we have assumed that factors of production are in perfectly elastic supply to the industry.

Our example shows what lies behind the adjustment of supply to changes in demand and it provides a fuller explanation than we gave in Chapter 4. You should be able to work out the consequences of a fall in demand which will produce losses, causing firms to exit the industry until a situation is restored where normal profits are being earned. A change in costs is slightly less straightforward, though the principles for analysing it are the same. Higher fuel costs or increased factor prices will cause the firm's average total cost curve to rise leading to losses. These losses will be established at higher prices but with a lower output.

The **perfectly competitive model** not only provides a demonstration of how the market generates and responds to signals resulting from changes in preferences and costs; it can also be used to explore the issues of **efficiency** and **optimality**. This discussion is undertaken in Chapter 18.

16 Monopoly and imperfect competition

16.1 Introduction

At the other extreme from the perfectly competitive model is **monopoly**. In this chapter we examine the **monopolistic market structure** and show how output prices and profits are determined. We compare the two extremes of perfect competition and monopoly and outline government policy in this area. **Nationalized industries** have been some of the most prominent monopolies in the UK. We briefly review the arguments about their operation and the case for privatization. We conclude by explaining other market structures: **oligopoly** and **monopolistic competition**.

The chapter will:

- define monopoly
- explain the derivation of marginal revenue under monopoly
- explain and illustrate the determination of equilibrium under monopoly
- show you how to draw a correct diagram depicting monopoly equilibrium
- explain how price discrimination works
- compare perfect competition and monopoly and assess the strengths and weaknesses of each
- outline government policy towards monopoly, competition and mergers
- explain the background to nationalization and outline the debate over privatization
- explain the meaning of monopolistic competition and oligopoly

16.1.1 Examination guide

Most courses will expect students to have a sound knowledge of the analysis of **output determination under monopoly and competition** and be able to discuss the strengths and weaknesses of each (including diagrams). Section 16.3 presents the main points which can provide a framework of an answer. The topic of **nationalized industries** often produces comments so extreme that they would be out of place in a party political broadcast. If you have strong feelings on this issue, keep them under control and stick to analysis and arguments that have some empirical support.

16.2 Monopoly

16.2.1 What is a monopoly?

A **monopoly** literally means a sole seller. The analysis of **monopoly** is based on this definition, which means that the firm and the industry are in effect the same. This simplifies analysis; but do such extreme market structures actually exist? There are a number of cases that come very close to fitting this definition, such as electricity and gas supply, British Coal and a number of services provided by local authorities. However, **monopoly analysis** is generally considered applicable to situations where a firm is not a sole supplier but nevertheless dominates the market, e.g. British Telecom. Section 16.3 discusses how to measure the degree of monopoly and absence of competition.

16.2.2 Marginal revenue under monopoly

Given our definition of **monopoly**, the firm's and the industry's demand curve will be the same. As the firm is the **sole producer** it can decide at which point of the demand curve it wishes to operate. It is a **price maker**, in contrast to the perfectly competitive firm, which is a **price taker**. However, it cannot choose both output and price, so higher output can be sold only with lower prices. This means that **marginal revenue** is no longer equal to price because cutting prices to sell more will normally involve reducing prices on **all** units sold, not just the last one. We can illustrate the point simply with Figure 16.1. One unit (X_1) is sold at a price of £10 (P_1) and total revenue, P_1AX_1O, is £10. To sell two units involves cutting the price to £9. **Total revenue** (*TR*) is now £18 and is shown by the area P_2BX_2O. Marginal revenue,

$\Delta TR/\Delta Q$, is £8, which is less than price, In fact we can think of MR as being the price gained for the last unit sold (CBX_1X_2) less the revenue lost by cutting price on previous units (in this case P_1ACP_2). The MR schedule will look like Figure 16.1. For a straight-line demand schedule it will bisect the distance between the Y axis and the demand curve and at some point become negative. Given our earlier explanation this is not too surprising because at some point as the price gets lower the additional revenue from the sale of an extra good is not likely to cover the revenue lost from cutting the price on a large number of previously sold units. The relationship is the one we discussed in section 4.6 on elasticity, except that we then concentrated on the consumer's expenditure rather than the firm's revenue. MR will be positive when demand is elastic, zero with unit elasticity and become negative when demand is inelastic.

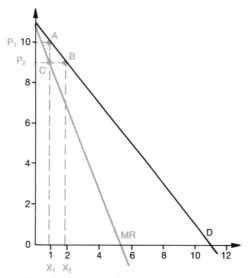

Fig. 16.1 Marginal revenue under monopoly

We have assumed that the monopolist has to charge the same price for all his output. This is very often the case; but there may be occasions when **price discrimination** can occur. If we had a **perfectly discriminating** monopolistic firm then it would be able to charge a separate price for each unit and in this special circumstance marginal revenue would equal demand. (See section 16.2.5 for a discussion of **price discrimination**.)

16.2.3 Equilibrium for a monopolist

The monopolist, like any other firm, will maximize profits where $MC = MR$. In Figure 16.2 this will be at an output of OQ_1 which is sold at P_1. This does not necessarily mean that the firm is earning profits; this is merely a profit-maximizing/loss-minimizing point. However, in this case it will enjoy **abnormal** or **supernormal profits**. The average cost of an output of OQ_1 is Q_1B but average revenue is AQ_1, so it is making profit AB per unit. The total profit ($AB \times OQ_1$) is the shaded area $ABCP_1$. If average cost had been above price (or AQ_1), then the monopolist would be making losses.

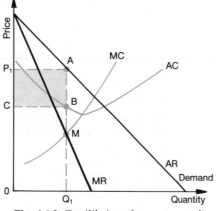

Fig. 16.2 Equilibrium for a monopolist

The equilibrium position shown here can be both short- and long-run. There is no freedom or ease of entry into a monopolistic market, so abnormal profits (i.e. above those necessary to keep the firm in the industry) may be earned even in the long run.

16.2.4 How to draw the monopoly equilibrium diagram

This diagram is often drawn incorrectly. There are even more tempting intersections of schedules here than with perfect competition—most of them should be ignored. If you take care and are prepared to build up the diagram logically stage by stage you will have no problems.

1 Determine the profit-maximizing output $MC = MR$. The profit-maximizing/loss-minimizing output will be where $MC = MR$; if these schedules are drawn as in Figure 16.3(a) then this output, Q_1, can be determined.

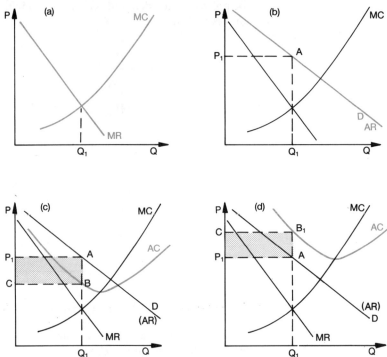

Fig. 16.3 How to draw the monopoly equilibrium diagram

2 Determine price of product: add AR schedule. We can find out what price the monopolist will charge by drawing in the demand or average revenue schedule (see Figure 16.3(b)). In doing so, remember the relationship between the AR and MR we described earlier: the marginal revenue schedule bisects the horizontal distance between the demand curve and the vertical axis. The price (P_1) can be marked on the diagram and the appropriate point on the demand curve is A.

3 Show profits/losses and compare AR and AC. For this final stage ignore the marginal curves. We are now concerned with AC and AR in order to establish the profit and loss being made. We can illustrate both cases.

(i) If abnormal profits are being earned, this means that $AR > AC$, so we need to draw AC below AQ_1 at the output of Q_1. Mark a point like B in Figure 16.3(c). Draw the AC curve through B, remembering that MC will cut AC at its lowest point. The area representing profits P_1ABC can be shaded in if required. (Notice that the following intersection points are **not** involved in showing profits: $MR = MC$; $AR = AC$; $MC = AC$; $MC = AR$.)

Point B has to be on the perpendicular line at Q_1, but this could obviously include the point where $MC = MR$. There is no economic reason why it should be that point, so it is best to avoid it. Examiners often find it very difficult to resist the conclusion that its selection was prompted by uncertainty or ignorance. (It would not be clear which of the cost/revenue schedules were responsible for determining output and the level of profits.) You should by now have the knowledge and confidence to mark the points described earlier unambiguously.

(ii) The procedure for the monopolist making losses is the same as the one described for profits except that AC will be greater than AR. Extend the perpendicular from Q_1 above A and mark a point B_1. The loss per unit will be AB_1, so total losses are AP_1CB_1. Whether the monopolist will produce at this point in the short run will depend upon whether $P > AVC$. If it is then the firm will minimize losses at Q_1 and be making a contribution to fixed costs.

16.2.5 Price discrimination

As a sole seller a monopolistic firm may be able to charge different prices for its output. For example, firms set prices differently for home and foreign markets or for industrial and domestic consumers. Customers could be charged higher rates for the first few units of electricity and gas than for subsequent units. An essential requirement for **price discrimination** is the ability to **separate markets**; if this cannot be done purchasers will always have the option of buying in the cheaper market and this will clearly undermine the attempt to charge different prices.

Monopolists can increase their revenue through **price discrimination**. An extreme case would be the perfectly discriminating monopolist referred to earlier. In this case a different price would be charged for each unit sold. We consider a less extreme situation where there are two markets, A and B, each with its own distinct demand curve–see Figure 16.4(a) and (b). The total demand and MR curves are shown in Figure 16.4(c). These curves are obtained by adding together those in markets A and B. Above a price of £2 nothing is bought in market A, so the total demand and marginal revenue is the same as market B. The total curves are the horizontal sum of the curves in the two markets. So at a price of £1, 20 units will be demanded in market A and 40 in market B; total demand is therefore 60. The MR schedules are similarly added together horizontally. Marginal revenue of £1 is obtained when 10 units are sold in market A and 20 sold in market B; therefore a marginal revenue of £1 is associated with total sales of 30. The firm's output is determined by equating marginal cost and the combined marginal revenue (see Figure 16.4(c)) and will be equal to QT, a quantity of 30.

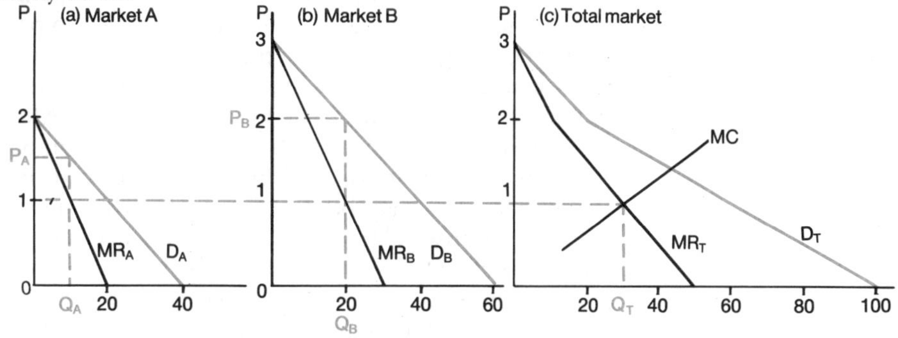

Fig. 16.4 Price discrimination

How should this be distributed between the markets? The monopolist will wish to equate the marginal revenues in the two markets. If this was not done and MR_A was greater than MR_B, it would pay the firm to reallocates output from B to A. Such a situation occurs if a price of P_1 which is the price indicated by the total demand curve at the profit-maximizing output, were charged in both markets. Figure 16.4 shows that equating marginal revenues will involve 10 (OQ_A) being sold in market A and 20 (OQ_B) in market B. The prices that will be charged can be seen from the demand curves, with the higher price £2 (P_B) being charged in market B and £1.50 (P_A) in market A. Where price discrimination occurs, prices will be higher in markets where the demand is less elastic. If the elasticities are the same in both markets it will not pay the monopolists to discriminate in prices.

16.3 Competition and monopoly

16.3.1 Perfect competition and monopoly compared

We can now make a comparison between perfect competition and monopoly and use this to consider the strengths and weaknesses of the two market structures.

Let us assume that we have a perfectly competitive industry that becomes monopolized. What difference would this make? We can make a direct comparison using Figure 16.5(a). This shows the demand curve for the firm's product and the marginal cost curve which, for the perfectly competitive industry, is, in effect, its supply curve (see section 15.3.5). Equilibrium under perfect competition will be at Q_c with a price of P_c. In comparison, a monopoly industry will operate where $MC = MR$ so its output will be at Q_m with a price of P_m. The monopolist restricts output and raises prices compared with a competitive position.

A major objection to monopoly is that it prevents the efficient allocation of resources. We can understand this if we recall that demand indicates the marginal utility of consumers: it shows the marginal benefits consumers receive. The marginal cost indicates the additional resources used in producing a particular output level. Perfect competition means that output takes place at the point where marginal benefits equal marginal cost. This is a point of **allocative efficiency** because it is maximizing the net benefits to society. Any other level of

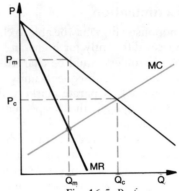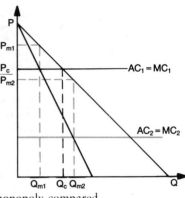

Fig. 16.5 Perfect competition and monopoly compared

output would be less efficient in terms of the use of resources. For example, at an output above Q_c the additional cost would exceed the extra benefit so production would use too many resources. The monopolist position, where output is less than Q_c, is also suboptimal. At Q_m the extra benefits exceed the additional costs and raising output would involve adding more to benefits than to costs. This expansion can be justified in terms of a more efficient allocation of resources until output reaches Q_c, when extra costs are the same as extra benefits. (The argument we are applying here to net benefits in analogous to the one used to consider the profit-maximizing output for the firm.)

We can now summarize the position: under competition $P = MC$ so the extra benefits, as represented by the price (P) people are prepared to pay, is equal to the additional cost of resources, marginal cost, whereas under monopoly $P > MC$, so extra benefits exceed additional cost and insufficient resources are allocated to the production of the produce. We explore this point further, together with cases where there are **externalities**, in Chapter 18.

Our discussion so far has assumed that costs will be the same under monopoly as they would under competition. This may not be the case and arguments can be put forward to suggest that they may be lower or higher. If a monopolized industry can secure extra efficiency because of larger-scale operation, then cost curves will be lowered and consumers may obtain the product at a lower price than under competition. This is illustrated in Figure 16.5(b), where for convenience we have drawn constant average costs (which will be equal to marginal costs). AC_1 represents the costs under competition. Equilibrium for the perfectly competitive industry is at Q_c with price equal to P_c. If monopolized industry had the same costs then it would operate at Q_{m_1} and charge a price P_{m_1}. If lower costs are obtained under monopoly the costs curve may be something like AC_2, in which case consumers enjoy a lower price, P_{m_2} than under competition and a larger quantity. However price will still exceed marginal cost under monopoly. Certainly if we were to create perfectly competitive conditions in some industries that are presently highly concentrated, this would mean sacrificing some economies of scale.

However, monopolies may operate with higher costs because the lack of competition means they are under less pressure to reduce costs. Managers and workers may take advantage of their monopoly position to enjoy an easy life and operate less efficiently than under competition. This is known as **X-inefficiency**. If this occurs in the absence of scale economies the cost curve under monopoly would be higher than AC_1, so consumers would pay even higher prices. If **X-inefficiency** is combined with scale economies then the cost curve may be higher or lower than the competitive equivalent, depending on the relative size of the two effects.

In Chapter 3 we distinguished between the notions of **static** and **dynamic efficiency**; this distinction is relevant here. We are concerned with maximizing benefits and output over time and it is possible that although monopoly does not involve an optimum allocation of resources at one particular point in time (i.e. it does not display **static efficiency**), it may be capable of generating faster growth. This means that there will be a time when this faster growth will compensate for allocative inefficiency.

Schumpeter was an economist who believed that monopoly was superior to perfect competition because it was dynamically more efficient. He argued that monopolies would be more likely to innovate than competitive firms, for two interrelated reasons. First and foremost there was the **incentive**, because monopolists know that profit generated by innovation will not be competed away: development costs can be fully recovered. Second these high profits provide the finance for the research necessary for innovation. There is little incentive for the competitive firm to incur the costs of product or production improvement if they can be readily copied by others. So in the end the consumer is better off with an innovating monopoly, despite its charging a price greater than marginal cost, than with rather stagnant competitive industry even though it can produce the conditions for static allocative efficiency.

This view of monopoly and innovation is not universally accepted. It can be argued that because a monopoly dominates a market and is not threatened by competition it feels no pressure to innovate and may simply enjoy the higher profits that its monopolist position permits. This could be contrasted with a picture of a competitive industry which has to innovate to survive. According to this view there will be constant pressure on firms to lower costs through new methods and processes and firms who fail to keep up will become unprofitable and eventually have to exit from the industry.

16.3.2 Monopoly and potential competition

There may be circumstances when a monopoly may be forced to operate like a competitive firm even though it is the only firm in the industry. This would occur if the industry were a **contestable market**. A contestable market is one where new firms can enter the industry without incurring irrecoverable costs. There would be no sunk or irrecoverable costs if a firm could recover the investment costs necessary to operate in the market without loss. In such cases a firm may enter an industry, even though fixed costs may be very high, with the knowledge that if the venture is not successful it can recover all the capital costs. Such a situation means that there may be a hit-and-run entry into the industry to take advantage of any monopoly profits. If these conditions exist then the incumbent firm in the industry is under constant threat from potential entrants and it will not operate as a monopoly. The market is said to be **contestable**.

The theory of contestable markets is a useful reminder that the number of firms in an industry may be an unreliable guide to the conduct of the industry; so a single firm may conceivably operate like a firm under perfect competition if there are a number of potential entrants ready to pounce and snatch any monopoly profits. However, sunk or irrecoverable costs may be significant, in which case the incumbent will generally have an advantage which it can exploit; it may also devise strategies to discourage entrants. We consider this further at the end of the chapter.

16.3.3 Competition and monopoly policy in the UK

Economic theory offers no evidence for the superiority of competition over monopoly or vice versa. Some uncompetitive industries have impressive innovative records while others do not. In these circumstances it is perhaps not surprising that government policy towards monopoly is pragmatic. It recognizes that the operation of monopolies and their formation is sometimes in the public interest, while in others it is not. We can now identify five aspects of monopoly and competition policy:

16.3.3.1 Monopoly policy

The pragmatic approach to monopolies was established in 1948 with the setting up of a Monopolies Commission. This had the power to investigate firms (or a group of firms acting together) who controlled more than a third of the market for a product to see if they were operating in the public interest. Subsequent legislation extended the policy to investigation of restrictive practices (1956) and mergers (1965). The Office of Fair Trading (OFT) was set up in 1973 with the overall responsibility of coordinating competition policy. The critical market share was reduced to 25 per cent. The 1980 Competition Act gave the power to conduct a preliminary investigation of 'anti-competitive practices'. If any changes it seeks to make are not forthcoming it may then refer cases to the Monopolies and Mergers Commission (MMC) for a more detailed inquiry. The operation of monopoly policy has often been criticized for being slow in the investigation stage and weak in carrying out the MMC recommendations: there is heavy reliance on voluntary cooperation.

16.3.3.2 Restrictive practices

An area where policy has been fairly influential in changing behaviour is **restrictive practices** legislation. **Restrictive practices** are arrangements by firms to limit competition, for example by requiring purchasers to sell at manufacturer's stipulated prices (known as **retail price maintenance**) or colluding over price setting. The 1956 Act required firms to register practices which affected the supply of goods and these had to be justified before a restrictive practices court as serving the public interest. Many practices were dropped in preference to registration and of those which were registered many were later withdrawn. Resale price maintenance, a particularly restrictive practice, was the subject of separate legislation in 1964 and although a few exemptions were permitted (e.g. books), the practice was effectively ended. The legislation was extended to services in 1976.

There is general agreement that the most blatant restrictive practices have been ended and that legislation has modified behaviour. However, this does not mean that all agreements and practices, although they are acceptable in terms of legislation, are completely free from restrictions. As with most legislation, these are ways of observing the letter of the law but avoiding the spirit.

16.3.3.3 Mergers

Since 1965 the MMC has had the powers to investigate and prohibit mergers if they are expected to operate against the public interest. Any mergers which would create a monopoly (defined as a percentage of the market or involving assets of more than £30 million) can be referred under the legislation. The vast majority of mergers (over 95 per cent) have not been referred, though some that have been investigated have led to a merger being stopped. The policy almost certainly has a deterrent value, with firms avoiding mergers which would be likely to be investigated.

16.3.3.4 EC legislation

Since entry into the European Community, the UK has been subject to EC legislation. This refers to restrictive agreements (Article 85 of the Rome Treaty) and abuses of a dominant position such as monopoly (Article 86). The legislation is mainly concerned with restrictions which affect trade between member states. The Commission of the European Community may initiate inquiries into behaviour and practices but individual firms may complain to the commission or take cases to the European Court. After 1992 the single market is likely to have an important effect on competition. The opening up of markets is likely to expose many firms to more intensive European Community competition; but it will also offer the opportunity to take advantage of greater scale economies which may reduce competition.

16.3.3.5 Deregulation

The final strand of competition policy is **deregulation**, which involves lifting restrictions on entry into various markets and effectively qualifies monopoly powers in certain areas. For example, in the energy field private gas producers were able, after 1982, to rent what were then publicly owned pipelines and similarly, private electricity producers could use the nationalized distribution system. Mercury has been permitted to compete with British Telecom. Deregulation of bus transport removed restrictions of entry to any route providing the carrier meets certain safety requirements.

16.3.4 Mergers and concentration in the UK

16.3.4.1 Mergers

We can identify three types of merger. **Horizontal mergers** are between firms engaged in the production of similar products (e.g. two drink manufacturers), whereas **vertical mergers** involve the acquisition of firms engaged in different stages of the production process (e.g. purchase of pubs or hop growers by a brewery). Finally, there are **conglomerate mergers** which lead to a diversification of interests. Most mergers are horizontal, but conglomerate mergers have increased in importance in the 1980s to around one third of all mergers. Vertical mergers are not very common.

The number and value of mergers is shown in Table 16.1. The latter half of the 1970s and the early 1980s were a quiet period for mergers compared with the intense merger activity of the 1960s and early 1970s and the mergers boom since 1984.

In 1978 a Green Paper considered the evidence on the post-merger performance of companies and concluded that in roughly half the cases examined, merger had had an unfavourable or neutral effect on profitability. Of course, this may still be an improvement on what may have occurred had merger not taken place. The criterion of performance success—profitability—may not have been the best indicator of economic benefits. However, a DTI paper on mergers policy in 1988, which surveyed the evidence of studies conducted since the Green Paper, concluded that the earlier findings of 'disappointing or inclusive performance' were supported.

16.3.4.2 Industrial concentration

Mergers can obviously lead to an increase in industrial concentration and about half of the rise in **concentration** since the late 1950s has occurred by this means. Concentration is normally measured by the share of a market output accounted for by the largest concerns. Concentration shows how much market power is concentrated in a few hands; it therefore provides an indication of how competitive markets are. Of course, the picture is not conclusive: two industries with the same level of concentration may display a different degree of competitiveness depending on the size and behaviour of the dominant firms. Collusion and informal linkages may limit competition even if concentrations are low. One

Table 16.1 Acquisitions and mergers by industrial and commercial companies within the UK 1964–87

| | | Expenditure | |
Year	Number of companies acquired	Current prices £m	Constant (1986) prices £bn
1964	940	505	3.5
1965	1000	517	3.4
1966	807	500	3.2
1967	763	822	5.1
1968	946	1946	11.5
1969†	907	935	5.3
1969†	846	1069	6.1
1970	793	1122	5.9
1971	884	911	4.4
1972	1210	2532	11.4
1973	1205	1304	5.4
1974	504	508	1.7
1975	315	291	0.8
1976	353	448	1.1
1977	481	824	1.7
1978	567	1140	2.2
1979	534	1656	2.8
1980	469	1475	2.1
1981	452	1144	1.5
1982	463	2206	2.6
1983	447	2343	2.7
1984	568	5474	5.9
1985	474	7090	7.2
1986	696	14 935	14.9
1987	1125	15 363	14.8

(*Business Monitor MQ7*)

†Based on company accounts up to 1969, and on the financial press and other sources since 1969.

simple and highly aggregated measure of concentration is to take the share of the largest 100 enterprises in manufacturing net output. This ratio rose from 25 per cent before the Second World War to around 40 per cent in the late 1960s; since then it has remained fairly stable. It seems likely that in the rest of the economy concentration rose in the early 1970s, but declined in the latter half.

We can measure industry concentration by taking the ratio of output of the five largest firms to total output. This is known as the **C5 measure**. However, given the growing importance of foreign trade, as indicated by the growth in import penetration, we ought to adjust the ratio to take account of this. For example, a firm may produce most of the UK output of a product which would imply a monopolistic position; but if most of the output was exported and imports accounted for a high share of UK purchases of the product the firm may be in a highly competitive position.

Table 16.2 allow us to see the changes in concentration ratio since 1970. The adjusted ratio takes account of foreign trade whereas the unadjusted measure is based solely on UK output. The changes in the classification of industries means measures for the mid-1980s are not strictly comparable with those for the early 1970s, but this does not invalidate the general trend which the figures indicate.

Table 16.2 Average C5 concentration ratios for manufacturing, 1970–84

	Unadjusted U	Adjusted for foreign trade	
		A	U − A
1970	49	41.3	7.7
1973	50.9	40.9	10.0
1977	48.9	38.1	10.8
1979	48.5	36.5	12.0
1979	51.4	39.3	12.1
1981	50.9	37.6	13.3
1984	49.1	33.8	15.3

(DTI, *Mergers Policy*, 1988)

The unadjusted ratio is broadly stable, with a slight rise in the early 1970s followed by a decline thereafter. When adjusted for the effects of foreign trade the concentration ratio declines significantly. The downward adjustment necessary for foreign trade $(U-A)$ has consistently increased over the period, reflecting the growing importance of foreign trade.

16.4 Nationalized industries and privatization

16.4.1 Nationalized industries

Industries may be nationalized for a variety of reasons: strategic (to secure a domestic supply); social (e.g. to ensure essential services to remote areas); large externalities (where there are large external benefits–e.g. transport links to regions) and because industries are natural monopolies (e.g. gas, electricity, water).

We need to take a closer look at natural monopolies. We referred to them in Chapter 3 where we observed that it is not always practicable to expect competition to exist for certain goods and services. Consumers cannot be presented with a choice of electricity, gas, water, telephone, roads, etc. These are **natural monopolies** because they offer such economies of scale that a dominant supplier would be bound to emerge from any attempt to introduce competing suppliers. They pose particular problems and are likely to require some regulation whether they are in private or public hands. In Figure 16.6 the declining average cost reflects the point we have just made about natural monopolies. If this industry were in unregulated private hands the firm would equate marginal cost and marginal revenue and produce OQ_1 and charge P_1 (and P_1AFD abnormal profits). However, this would not be a point of allocative efficiency because the marginal benefits, as shown by the demand curve and the price that is paid, are in excess of the marginal cost of producing the good.

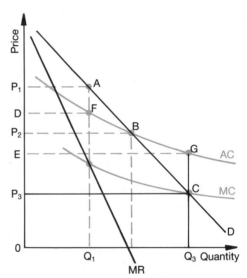

Fig. 16.6 Costs under monopoly

We learned in section 16.3.1 that $P = MC$ is the condition for achieving a social optimum. If this price were charged then the concern would operate at C, with output equal to Q_3 and a price of P_3. Although this would be socially efficient it would involve losses $(= CGEP_3)$. There are two possible ways of responding to this problem. One is to use a two-part tariff through a standing charge which will increase revenue but still ensure that prices are set equal to marginal costs. The other approach is through a tax subsidy programme with the government paying and financing the loss incurred by producing at C.

It is important to appreciate that loss making by a nationalized natural monopoly is not necessarily a sign of inefficiency. Indeed, it may be just the reverse. Point A (with Q_1) would yield profits but would be socially less efficient than C.

As we observed at the beginning of this section there are a variety of reasons for nationalization; but the post-war Labour government, which was responsible for bringing many of these concerns into public ownership, hoped that they could all be run in the public interest rather than along narrower profit-maximizing lines. However, the guidelines on objectives proved too vague and White Papers in 1961, 1967 and 1978 sought to clarify them. Financial targets were set in 1961. The 1967 policy introduced marginal cost pricing, required a discount rate (that was thought to be comparable with the private sector) to be applied to new investment and explicit subsidies to take account of external benefits were paid to British Rail. The 1978 White Paper laid down a somewhat similar but looser criteria that reflected a concern to control the financial demands on central government. The 1980 Competition Act allowed nationalized industries to be referred to the MMC as a means of checking on and improving their efficiency.

These reports have been critical of aspects of nationalized industry, but they have also commented favourably. Over the years there have been many investigations into nationalized industries. One of the common comments is that too much government interference, some of which is not in keeping with the government's own guidelines, mitigates against reasonable medium-term planning. Nationalized industries have been criticized for not being very successful in applying efficient (i.e. marginal cost) pricing policies. It is also suggested that there is too much cross-subsidization, with profit-making activities subsidizing those produced at a loss.

The heyday of nationalization may have passed. During the 1980s the Conservative government has been privatizing these publicly owned concerns. We turn now to consider the policy of privatization.

16.4.2 Privatization

16.4.2.1 What is privatization?

Privatization involves:

1 selling nationalized industries, such as British Telecom, British Gas, etc;

2 contracting out services, such as cleaning and catering in the health service, and local authority services such as refuse collection;

3 deregulation, which exposes state industries to competition.

The last two aspects of privatization tend to increase competition, whereas the first does not necessarily do so, particularly where privatization involves transfer of natural monopolies from the public to the private sector.

16.4.2.2 Objectives of privatization

Apart from the ideological preference for private rather than public provision, there seems to be a variety of motives for the sales.

1 A primary motive seems to be the **improvement in efficiency** of the industries being privatized. It is suggested that greater freedom for management and a financial independence from the government will assist in this process. To many advocates of privatization, the private sector produces goods and services more efficiently than the public sector. The increased competition resulting from contracting out and deregulation, it is suggested, will tend to raise productivity and lower costs.

2 The proceeds from the sales (which count as negative government spending) help to achieve **PSBR targets** and assist **monetary control**. This became less pressing as a reason for the policy in the mid 80s when the budget deficits were reduced and later surpluses were produced.

3 The way the privatization of nationalized industries has been conducted has been designed to **extend share ownership** among the general public. It has also been recognized that encouraging share purchase by workers may lead to more involvement in the firm concerned.

16.4.2.3 Are private concerns more efficient?

There is no simple answer to this question, either from a theoretical or empirical point of view. Economic theory helps clarify some of the issues. We can recognize two types of inefficiency: **allocative inefficiency**, where an enterprise operates with prices higher than marginal cost, and **production inefficiency** where the costs of production are higher under one type of operation compared with another. (We considered these issues in section 16.3.1.) **Allocative inefficiency** is associated with **monopoly**, so it may occur in public or private sector concerns. Privatization will not necessarily reduce allocative inefficiency unless it involves introducing competition. If competition is not or cannot be introduced (because the industry is a natural monopoly), then dealing with this inefficiency will depend on the effectiveness of regulatory controls.

Production inefficiency may also occur in both the private and public sector. However, this type of inefficiency may be greater and more persistent in the public sector because in the private sector high cost producers should be bought out by those who could run the firm at a lower cost. This should occur because purchasers will be willing to pay a price high enough (because of their ability to run the firm at a lower cost) to induce the inefficient producer to sell. This option is not available with nationalized industries, so production inefficiencies could emerge and persist. Indeed they may be sufficiently large for losses to be made and the consequences of this is not the same in the private and public sectors. In the former the firm would eventually be forced out of business, taken over or have to rectify the high costs; but with the nationalized industry these market pressures do not exist and losses may continue as long as governments are prepared to pay for them. We should not necessarily conclude that public enterprises will operate in this way. Whether or not they do so will depend on the competitive pressures on them and the objectives that are set, as well as the means of monitoring these concerns.

Where privatization involves taking a nationalized monopoly and creating a private competitive industry then the analysis covered earlier in section 16.3.1 is relevant. Regulatory controls on nationalized or privatized industries may have important effects on efficiency. For example, in the USA attempts to control private electricity supply in order to reduce allocative costs have involved profit regulation. This has the effect of reducing the incentive to keep production costs down, so the attempt to resolve one problem has made another worse.

It would be helpful if empirical studies could clarify whether private concerns are more efficient than those in the public sector. Unfortunately, the results are not conclusive. Surveying the evidence of many countries, Kay and Thompson (1986) concluded that **competition** is a key element which tends to improve the performance of all firms – public or private. Public enterprises perform better than private enterprises in industries where competition is absent and private concerns are subject to regulation. Such regulation, as we said earlier, may induce inefficient practices.

The firmest conclusion we can draw is that the introduction of competition is most likely to improve efficiency. Where this cannot be achieved because the industry is a natural monopoly then care needs to be taken that regulatory control does not have undesirable side effects. A number of approaches may ameliorate these. One is franchising the right to a monopoly, as is done with ITV companies. Where the monopoly can be allocated on a regional basis (e.g. water boards) then comparison of costs helps to reveal information about the operation of an enterprise. Finally, there may be ways of limiting the monopoly. In the case of gas pipelines there clearly cannot be effective competition, but there can be competition among the gas producers and gas sellers who use the pipeline.

16.4.2.4 Privatization in the UK

The UK **privatization programme** started with sales of £377 million in 1979–88 but had risen to £5 billion by 1987–88, with plans for sales to run at this level into the 1990s. Sales have included some large concerns such a British Telecom, British Gas, British Airways and British Steel. Many of these concerns will not necessarily become more competitive because of privatization, and those like British Gas and British Telecom, which are natural monopolies, will need to be regulated. The performance of these concerns may depend upon whether the regulatory bodies turn out to be more successful than the government policy and ministerial control in operation when they were nationalized.

Deregulation has been more limited. Bus transport deregulation has been introduced, giving companies greater freedom. In 1983 electricity supply was deregulated so that private suppliers could operate and make use of the publicly owned distribution network. Contracting out has not resulted in widespread introduction of privately provided services in either the NHS or local authorities. The tendering out of services will have focused the attention on the need to control costs. Instances of cost cutting resulting from contracting out have certainly occurred; but so too have complaints about the quality of some privately provided services.

Overall it is too soon to assess the impact of privatization policies. It will always be difficult to do so because we can never be certain what performance would have been like if privatization had not occurred. But there will be many opportunities over the next few years for researchers to try and assess its effects.

16.5 Monopolistic competition and oligopoly

We have concentrated our discussion on the perfect competition and monopoly. These analyses have widespread application, but nevertheless represent extreme positions. We conclude the chapter by briefly outlining two market structures that occupy positions between these extremes.

16.5.1 Monopolistic competition

As the term **monopolistic competition** implies, it includes elements from both of the models we have previously discussed. Like a monopolist, a firm in monopolistic competition has a downward sloping demand curve – it can expect to sell less if it raises prices and more if it lowers them. But in almost every other respect this market structure resembles perfect competition. There are many relatively small firms with freedom of entry and exit.

The clearest examples of monopolistic competition are retailers. The local shop or garage generally has a **local monopoly** – it is the sole seller in the immediate area but it is also in competition with similar outlets nearby. So it may be able to take advantage of its local monopoly position to a limited degree before customers consider it worthwhile travelling the extra distance to a competitor. Firms which produce a differentiated product but nevertheless operate in a market where there are many producers of similar products are in a similar position. Each firm has a monopoly of its product because it is differentiated; but the existence of many similar products means that this monopoly is limited and firms also have to face competition.

We represented the short-run equilibrium position of a firm under monopolistic competition in Figure 16.2. In this sense it is like a monopolist and can earn abnormal profits. But this can only occur in the short run because these abnormal profits will attract new entrants. So the long-run position is shown in Figure 16.7, where the firm operates at the point where $MC = MR$ but earns only normal profits, so $AR = AC$: i.e. the demand schedule will be tangential to the average cost curve at this point. You will notice that it is not possible for firms to be at the bottom of their average cost curves in the long run, so they must operate with some spare capacity. This is known as the **excess capacity theorem**. Rather than necessarily implying that firms produce inefficiently, it can be interpreted as an effect of consumers' wish for differentiated products. If consumers did not want differentiated products then the equilibrium point would lie close to the least cost position and the market would take on more of the characteristics of perfect competition. The greater the desire for differentiated products, the steeper the demand curve and the further to the left of the least cost position the equilibrium position will be.

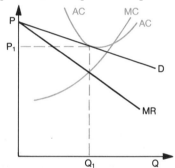

Fig. 16.7 Long-run equilibrium of the firm under monopolistic competition

16.5.2 Oligopoly

Oligopoly is a situation where the market is dominated by only a few producers. This means that the actions of one firm are likely to have a noticeable impact on others, so their reactions have to be anticipated when considering the consequence of actions such as price cutting. This makes the analysis of oligopoly behaviour both fascinating and complex. We will illustrate just one frequently quoted feature of oligopolistic markets – the 'kinked' demand curve.

16.5.2.1 Kinked demand curve

In Figure 16.8 (overleaf) there is a 'kink' in the firm's demand at P^*. This arises because the firm believes that if it cut its price its competitors would follow suit; so demand is not very responsive to the price cut. In contrast, if the firm raised its prices it believes others would not do the same, so it would lose a relatively large volume of sales. The marginal revenue curve is discontinuous at the kink in the demand curve. The profit-maximizing point will be at Q_1 (where P^* is charged). This explains why prices may be fairly 'sticky' for an oligopolist: quite large shifts in MC can occur without there being any change in price. If this price is believed to be one that competitors are likely to maintain, then the profit-maximizing output resulting from many demand shifts will be associated with this price.

A more common explanation of sticky prices, which is consistent with the discussion of Chapters 11 and 12, is that oligopolies face constant marginal costs over a range of output in the region of full capacity and they base prices on these costs through a mark-up procedure. If we assume that price changes are fairly costly and that the customer–market relationships we discussed in earlier chapters operate, then firms will adjust output, rather than prices, to demand changes. However, cost changes will lead to an alteration in prices charged. Notice that this is different from the prediction of the kinked demand curve, which

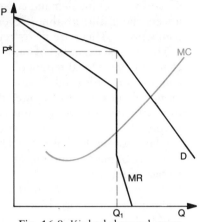

Fig. 16.8 Kinked demand curve

suggested that price would not be affected by cost changes which occurred in the range where *MR* was discontinuous. The mark-up-on-costs approach seems to accord more with our experience of oligopolies than that of the kinked demand curve.

16.5.2.2 Game theory and the behaviour of oligopolies

An important feature of oligopoly is the interdependence of the few firms in the industry on each other. **Game theory** allows us to explore the strategies and likely outcomes for the players in this field, who in our application are the participating firms. We can illustrate the approach in Table 16.3.

Table 16.3		Firm B	
		High	Low
Firm A	High	100 / 100	0 / 400
	Low	400 / 0	300 / 300

This shows the possible strategies of two firms in an industry and the expected profit associated with these actions according to the expected response of the other firm in the industry. Each firm has the option of producing a high or low output; the effect of this on profits will depend upon what the rival does. The expected profit of *B* is shown in the top righthand corner of each box and that of firm *A* in the bottom lefthand corner. We assume that higher output in the industry will depress prices and profits. If firm *A* were to produce a high output its success would depend on what firm *B* did. If firm *B* is expected to produce a high output then prices will be more depressed and profits correspondingly lower than if firm *B*'s output is expected to be low. The latter is the most profitable position for *A*, with profits equal to £400 because prices are not depressed by *B* as it is only selling a low output. In contrast, when *B* produces a high output profits for *A* are only £100. The least profitable position for *A* is shown in the bottom lefthand corner. Here *A* produces a low output while *B*'s production is high. If both firms were to produce a low output then prices would be relatively high and profits for each would be £300.

Which strategy will each firm follow? Both firms will go for a high output. It is the best strategy for *A* to produce a high output whatever *B* produces. (If *B*'s output is low, *A*'s profits would be £400 with a high output and £300 with a low output; if *B*'s output is high, *A*'s profits will be £100 with a high output and zero if production were low.) Similarly it pays *B* to produce a high output. The outcome is that both firms enjoy profits of £100. However, this game shows that there are benefits from collusion because the most profitable outcome for both parties is to produce a low output and earn £300 profits each. This helps explain why collusion may occur under oligopoly.

This is a fairly simple game with predictable outcomes depending on whether we assume cooperation or not. Other situations may be much more complex with larger number of players and options and the strategy to be employed may be far less obvious.

17 Distribution

17.1 Introduction

The topic of the **distribution of income** has arisen at various stages in earlier chapters, though so far we have said very little about what determines payments to factors of production. In this chapter we concentrate on the **marginal productivity theory** explanation of factor payment. This is the approach taken by orthodox economic theory and the one that most introductory courses consider. Most of the discussion is applied to wages and payments to labour but rewards to other factors are considered briefly. The division of income between factors of production is known as the **functional distribution of income**. We conclude the chapter by considering another aspect of distribution, **personal income distribution**, which shows the division of income between different households.

The chapter will:

- explain marginal revenue product
- show how the demand for labour is derived under competitive conditions
- discuss the shape of the supply of labour curve
- explain and illustrate equilibrium factor payments
- explain economic rent and transfer earnings
- consider factor payments under monopoly and monopsony
- discuss the role of trade unions in wage determination
- outline the personal distribution of income and wealth in the UK

17.1.1 Examination guide

Most courses will consider the topic of **distribution of income**. The basic theory for analysing distribution in introductory courses is the **marginal productivity theory**. This theory can be applied to all factors, though the discussion is often conducted in terms of wages. You should be able to explain the derivation of the demand for a factor and why changes in factor prices lead to firms wishing to employ a different quantity of factors. You also should be aware of the meanings of **economic rent** and **transfer earnings**. Courses will vary concerning the examination of factor price determination under imperfect competition. If your course covers this area, make sure you can distinguish between the effects of a monopoly seller and sole buyer (monopsonist) and that you are able to bring the two together as bilateral monopoly. The other main aspect of this topic is the distribution of income in the UK. This is considered in section 17.6 but is developed further in Chapter 19 (see sections 19.3 and 19.4).

17.2 Marginal productivity theory

17.2.1 Marginal product and the demand for a factor

17.2.1.1 The profit-maximizing principle

The **marginal productivity theory** applies the maximizing principles we encountered in Chapters 14 to 16 for the factor market. The theory states that profit-maximizing firms will employ extra units of a variable factor up to the point where the additional cost of the factor equals the extra revenue it produces.

17.2.1.2 The firm's demand for labour

In this section we will concentrate on perfectly competitive markets (other situations are discussed in section 17.3). Using labour as an illustration, the additional or marginal cost of the factor to a firm will be the wage rate – each firm will be able to employ as much labour as it wishes at the prevailing rate. The additional revenue a firm receives from employing an extra unit of a factor is known as the **marginal revenue product** (MRP). This will depend on the extra output produced and the amount for which it is sold. The extra output will be the **marginal physical product** (MPP), which we discussed in Chapter 14. Under perfect competition each unit of output will be sold for the same price because the firm is a price taker and therefore faces a perfectly elastic demand curve. Table 17.1 below provides a numerical example to clarify the position.

Table 17.1

Units of labour	Marginal physical product (MPP)	Price of product (P)	Marginal revenue product (MRP = MPP × P)	Wage (W)	Additional profit MRP − W
1	3	10	30	70	−40
2	7	10	70	70	0
3	10	10	100	70	+30
4	11	10	110	70	+40
5	9	10	90	70	+20
6	7	10	70	70	0
7	5	10	50	70	−20
8	3	10	30	70	−40
9	2	10	20	70	−50

The second column shows the effect on the *MPP* of employing different quantities of labour. The marginal revenue product (which is often known as the **marginal value product (MVP)** under perfect competition) in column 4 is obtained by multiplying the *MPP* by the price of the product (*P*). The marginal cost of labour will be the same as the wage, which in this example is £70. We can calculate the addition to profit by subtracting the wage from the *MRP*. The profit-maximizing position will be where six people are employed. Up to that point it is possible to raise profits by employing more; beyond it profits are reduced because extra employment adds more to costs than revenues. Figure 17.1 shows the *MRP* and the profit-maximizing position.

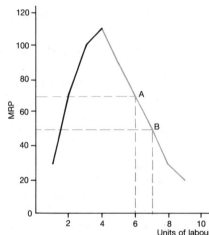

Fig. 17.1 *MRP* and a profit-maximizing position

Although the wage equals the *MRP* when two people are employed, it should be clear that this is not a point of profit maximization because profits can be increased when more workers are taken on. It is the downward sloping section of the *MRP* that is relevant to determining the numbers employed. This part of the schedule is, in effect, the firm's demand curve for labour. We can see this if we consider what would happen if the wage were to fall to £50. The firm would no longer be maximizing profits at *A* but would move to *B* and take on an extra unit of labour. Points like *A* and *B* (and any other point on the downward sloping *MRP* schedule) show the possible wage–employment combinations for this firm.

17.2.1.3 The industry and the firm's demand for a factor

We have to recognize that if each firm takes on more workers when the wage falls and produces extra output, this will depress the price for the product and the *MRP* will fall. We can see this in Figure 17.2 where the *MRP* schedule shifts inwards (from MRP_1 to MRP_2), so that instead of moving from *A* to *B* the firm maximizes its profit at point *C* on MRP_2. The firm's demand curve for labour is shown by the coloured line (*D*) passing through *A* and *C*. How much steeper this is than the *MRP* schedules depends on how much prices are depressed by the extra output the industry produces. This will depend on the elasticity of demand for the product – the more elastic it is, the more elastic will be the demand for labour.

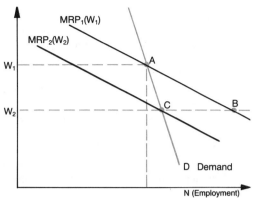

Fig. 17.2 The firm's demand curve for labour

We can obtain an industry's demand curve for the factor by aggregating firms' demand curves. This demand curve depends upon the marginal physical product of the factor and the elasticity of demand for the product.

We have largely conducted this analysis in terms of labour, although it should be clear that it could apply to any variable factor: there will be a marginal physical and revenue product of capital and land as well as labour.

The discussion has been based on one variable factor while others have been fixed. If all factors were variable we would need a different approach. A relevant approach is the one using isoquants which was discussed in Chapter 14. The main point to note here is that when all factors are variable, a change in relative factor prices will cause the cheaper factor to be substituted for the more expensive one. There will be a **substitution effect**.

17.2.2 Supply of factors

17.2.2.1 Supply curve

We have derived a demand curve for a factor; we now need a supply curve so that we can determine the **equilibrium factor price**. In many cases we can expect the supply curve of a factor to be upward sloping in the conventional way. In the short run supply is likely to be more inelastic, and in some cases may be perfectly inelastic, but in the longer run quantity is likely to respond to higher factor prices.

However, the case of labour supply needs to be considered more carefully. When wages rise this raises the rewards for working and we would expect people to substitute more work for leisure. There will be an **income** as well as a **substitution effect**. Higher wages raise income, and assuming leisure is a normal good (as opposed to an inferior good), people will wish to consume more of it and work fewer hours. If the income effect outweighs the substitution effect higher wages can lead people to work less. In this case the supply curve will be backward bending or negatively sloped. In Figure 17.3 the range *AB* displays this effect.

Fig. 17.3 Income and substitution effect

17.2.2.2 Non-monetary influences – equal net advantage

Non-wage factors are likely to be important in influencing the supply of labour. Working conditions, status and job security will be taken into account, as well as the wage, when deciding between job opportunities. These non-monetary matters are likely to be less influential with other factors of production but may not be totally absent: owners of capital may be affected by political considerations (e.g. objections to certain regimes), or wish to be well regarded by the community. We assume in supplying factors, owners will be interested in the **net advantage**, that is the sum of monetary and non-monetary (which may be positive or negative) benefits. In a perfect market with homogeneous factors we would expect the net advantage to be equalized.

17.2.2.3 Human capital and education

Labour possesses skills and experience. We can think of this as **human capital**. It is analogous to physical capital: it can be increased by investment (more spending on education and training) and it tends to depreciate over time. Education generally offers higher earnings later in life but low income while studying. In determining the supply of labour, the human capital approach suggests that individuals will assess the costs of education in relation to its benefits. In doing so account will be taken of non-monetary benefits and costs, so full-time students will include the advantages of student life which will offset some of disadvantages of a low income from the grant.

17.2.3 Determination of factor prices

Factor prices will be determined by the demand for and supply of the factors. So in Figure 17.4 if demand is D_1 then the equilibrium price, in this case wage, will be W_1. An increase in demand for the product, an increase in the productivity of the factor or the rise in price of a substitute factor will cause the demand curve to shift outwards, say from D_1 to D_2. We can expect this to raise wages and employment. The elasticity of supply, which will determine how much wages rise, will depend upon the mobility of factors: this is likely to be greater in the long run than the short run.

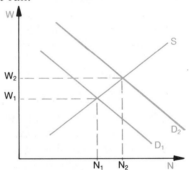

Fig. 17.4 Determination of factor prices

Factor prices, according to this approach, depend upon their marginal productivity (demand) of factors and their scarcity (supply). So relatively high factor payments are the result of high productivity and/or the consequence of the use of the factor being unattractive compared with alternative uses.

17.2.4 Economic rent and transfer earnings

When factor earnings rise in response to an increase in demand, as in our previous example, existing factors will receive additional payments that are known as **economic rent**. As the term **rent** is used in everyday language to refer to a payment for land or property, it is important to be clear about the way it is generally used by economists. **Economic rent** refers to a payment over the amount necessary to retain a factor in its present use. The payment that is just sufficient to keep it in its present employment is known as **transfer earnings**. These concepts are illustrated in Figure 17.5. The wage is *OB* and *ON* are employed. The shaded area *ABC* shows the economic rent paid because it represents payments over and above the wage required to supply the factors to the industry. Transfer earnings are shown by the area under the supply curve *OACN*. The last unit of labour employed is at the margin of leaving the industry and receives only transfer earnings, while earlier units receive some economic rent. The importance of the rent element will depend upon the elasticity of supply. In the extreme case of a perfectly inelastic supply curve, all of the payment is rent, whereas with a perfectly elastic supply curve factor there is no rent element in the payment – it is all transfer earnings. The analysis is equally applicable to other factors. For example, a highly specific piece of capital equipment will have zero or very low transfer earnings and nearly all the payment will be rent. In the short run, when factors are fixed in supply and all the payment is rent, this is known as **quasi-rent**. This is only a short-run phenomenon because in the longer run factors can move and transfer earnings will be positive.

Where factors are in limited supply (e.g. city centre land, test cricket players) there is likely to be a large rent element to their earnings. In the case of test cricketers, they are limited in supply and they enjoy a high income. Their transfer earnings are generally fairly low

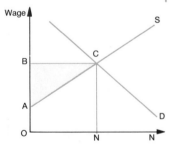

Fig. 17.5 Economic rent and transfer earnings

because they could not command similar pay elsewhere and they derive a great non-pecuniary reward from playing the game. In the past the regulated nature of payments in cricket kept the rent element in earnings fairly low. However, Kerry Packer, the Australian entrepreneur, realized that payments were below the market rate and was able to organize a breakaway group of top players. This led to revision in payment levels so that there is now a much larger element of economic rent in the income of test players.

17.3 Labour and wages

17.3.1 Demand for factors in non-competitive product markets

In the last section we concentrated on the determination of factor payments in competitive markets. We can now briefly consider the differences when markets are non-competitive.

If product markets are not competitive, firms face a downward-sloping demand curve. So selling extra output involves cutting prices. This means that the marginal revenue is less than price. So to calculate the marginal revenue product (*MRP*), we need to multiply *MPP* by *MR*, not price, as in the competitive model:

$$MRP = MPP \times MR$$

Table 17.2 provides a numerical illustration using the marginal product data from Table 17.1 and incorporating a demand curve for the product, which allows us to show the price at which the product can be sold and the marginal revenue associated with that level of sales. The final two columns show the marginal revenue product under competitive (*MPP* × *Price*) and monopolistic conditions (*MPP* × *MR*) respectively. In comparison with perfect competition, the demand for labour will be less at any given wage rate.

Table 17.2 Marginal revenue product under competition and monopoly

Employment	Total product	MPP	Price[1]	Total revenue	Marginal revenue[2]	MRP (Competition)	MRP (Monopoly)
1	3	3	38.5	115.5	37	115.5	111.0
2	10	7	35.0	350.0	30	245.0	210.0
3	20	10	30.0	600.0	20	300.0	200.0
4	31	11	24.5	759.5	9	269.5	99.0
5	40	9	20.0	800.0	0	180.0	0.0
6	47	7	16.5	775.5	−7	115.5	−49.0
7	52	5	14.0	728.0	−12	70.0	−60.0

[1] The equation of demand is $Q = 80 - 2P$ (where Q is quantity and P is price);
[2] Marginal revenue $(MR) = 40 - Q$.

17.3.2 Monopsony

A firm may be a sole buyer of labour (known as a monopsonist). In this case the firm faces an upward-sloping supply curve of labour. The marginal cost will be greater than the wage paid because to attract an extra worker the firm will have to pay higher wages to all employees as well as the additional worker. This is illustrated in Figure 17.6.

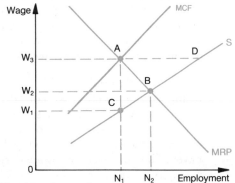

Fig. 17.6 Wage determination under monopsony

The monopsonist will maximize profits where the marginal cost of the factor (*MCF*) equals the marginal revenue product (*MRP*):

$$MCF = MRP$$

This will be at point A. The wages paid will be W_1 and employment N_1. This can be compared with a non-monopsony position when employment would be N_2 and the wage W_2 (point B).

17.3.3 Trade unions and wages

17.3.3.1 Unions operating in competitive markets

We can use the analysis developed to comment briefly on the role of trade unions in determining wages. We will assume that the union has control over the supply of labour and that it can use this power to affect wages. There are many possibilities according to the objectives of the union (e.g. wage or employment maximization), attitude towards technical and organizational change which affect productivity and the market situation in which they operate (competitive or non-competitive).

In Figure 17.7 we start in a position where the wage rate is W_1 and employment is N_1. If the union successfully pushes for a wage increase to W_2, it will achieve this at the cost of jobs, as employment will fall from N_1 to N_2, and some of the workers will be unemployed. However, if it limited the supply of workers to N_2 so that the supply curve passed through point B, then there would be no unemployment among trained workers; but some who wished to enter the trade or profession would have been prevented from doing so.

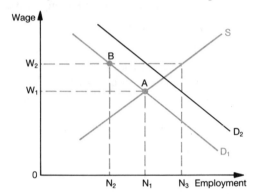

Fig. 17.7 Wages and employment

The union might encourage or participate in a productivity deal so that the demand curve shifted out to the right (D_1 to D_2), in which case employment would remain at N_1 but with the higher wage of W_2. There would still be some unemployment but not as much as in the first illustration.

17.3.3.2 Unions and monopsony buyers of labour

In a case where there is a monopsonist buyer of labour, there is a possibility of a union organizing workers and raising wages without losing jobs – indeed there is the option of combining higher wages with more jobs. If the original position is the one illustrated in Figure 17.6, with a wage of W_1 being paid, and a union organizes labour in the industry, it has a number of options. One possibility is that it offers the industry ON_2 workers at a wage of W_2. The supply curve (and the marginal cost curve) becomes horizontal up to point B on the supply curve. In this case firms employ ON_2 workers at a wage W_2 and the union has raised employment and wages. It may forgo the opportunity to raise employment and press for a wage of W_3. Here the supply curve would be perfectly elastic up to point D; but firms maximize profits at A and AD workers who would like jobs will not be offered them; but the existing workforce of ON_1 would secure a rise in wages from W_1 to W_3.

17.3.3.3 Bilateral monopoly

In the previous section we considered a union's concern with wages and employment objectives. Another approach suggests that if the union is a sole supplier of labour it may act like a monopoly seller of products. The implications of this are shown in the bilateral monopoly model where the monopoly seller of labour (the union) is confronted by the single buyer of labour (the monopsonist firm). In Figure 17.8 we can see that the firm would wish to employ N_1 workers at a wage of W_3. However the union, if it acts like a monopolist in the product market, will seek to sell a quantity at a point where the marginal revenue equalled the supply of labour. (To make the diagram easier to follow we have shown this at the employment level N_1 too.) The wage at which the monopolist union would seek to sell labour would be at W_1. This would mean that employers would want to pay W_3 and the union would want to receive W_1. The outcome would depend on bargaining between the two parties.

This model presents the union as a **rent maximizer**. It is unclear how far this model is applicable to a labour market where the union does not own labour but acts as an agent on its behalf. There is a further objective that could be considered, though it too is of doubtful

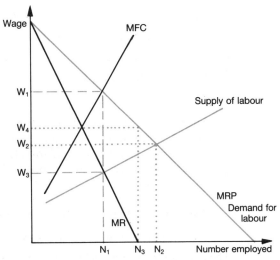

Fig. 17.8 Bilateral monopoly

relevance to modelling union behaviour: wage bill maximization. This would require the union to press for a wage of W_4 where N_3 would be employed, because here the marginal revenue would be zero and at this point total wages revenue would be maximized.

17.3.3.4 Collective bargaining and strikes

Although trade union membership fell in the early 1980s, around 40 per cent of workers are in unions and **collective bargaining** is clearly an important feature of wage determination. The union cannot ignore market forces, except perhaps in the short run, where it has an effective control over the supply (a **closed shop**); however, in many cases there is an area of indeterminacy over wages and bargaining has an important role to play. The union can use its power to withhold labour – to strike – and management can use its power as wage payer to try to keep wages lower than unions wish. If there is a strike then both parties will face costs which they would be prepared to avoid by making concessions on their original bargaining positions. If the negotiators are aware of each other's position then a compromise settlement can be reached. However, if one party makes a mistake about the resolve of the other then a strike may result. In the process the bargaining positions of both parties will become clearer, though sometimes this is only after a protracted conflict. It should be recognized that some disputes are concerned with issues beyond the apparent subject of the strike and are directed at asserting the power of the union or the management.

17.4 Limitations of marginal productivity theory

The **marginal productivity theory** of factor prices is widely used in economics. It has its critics and its limitations. It is only a theory of demand and therefore requires a theory of supply to explain factor prices. The theory is built on the assumption that the objectives of organizations is profit maximization. Other objectives would give different predictions concerning the demand for labour. The theory becomes more difficult to apply and test where factors are heterogeneous; in the labour market there is a great variety of skills and experience even within given occupational categories. Finally, the theory is much less successful at explaining the macroeconomic distribution of income than it is in accounting for factor payments at the micro level.

17.5 Alternative theories of distribution

Dissatisfaction with marginal productivity theory has led to the development of a number of different approaches. Some of these developments have roots in earlier thinking of political economists like Ricardo and Marx. Here we can do no more than provide a simple introduction to the type of thinking involved.

Let us start from a position where national income (Y) can be divided into two classes of income, wages (W) and profits (P):

$Y = W + P$

and expenditure comprises capitalist consumption (C_c), workers' consumption (C_w) and investment (I). If we assume that the economy is in equilibrium with income equal to expenditure, then

$Y = C_w + C_c + I$

A simple manipulation of these equations gives us the following expression for profits:

$$P = (C_w - W) + I + C_c$$

If we assume that workers' savings are zero (i.e. $C_w = W$) because they spend all of their income on consumption, we get an amended expression for profits:

$$P = I + C_c$$

The interpretation of this that is normally given is that capitalists' expenditure (investment plus their consumption) determines capitalists' income, profits. This view of distribution is captured in the remark attributed to Kalecki, a Polish economist: 'Workers spend what they get but capitalists get what they spend'. That is, capitalist income, P, is equal to capitalist expenditure, $I + C_c$.

17.6   Personal distribution of income in the UK

17.6.1   Distribution in the UK

The main sources of household income are shown in Table 17.3. Wages and salaries are by far the largest single category. Income from self-employment is a much more important source of income for the rich than it is for the poor: the top 1 per cent of income earners get 26 per cent of their income from this source whereas the comparable figure for the bottom 25 per cent is 1 per cent. Similarly, investment income (rent, dividends and interest) accounted for 14 per cent of income for the top 1 per cent but for only 6 to 8 per cent for the remainder. Conversely, benefits account for 64 per cent of income for the bottom quarter of income recipients and 45 per cent of the income of the next-to-bottom 25 per cent, whereas only 5 per cent of income for the top 25 per cent is from this source.

Table 17.3 Household income: national totals, 1986

Income (%)	
Wages and salaries	60
Income from self-employment	9
Rent dividends and interest	7
Private pensions, annuities, etc.	8
Social security benefits	13
Other current transfers	3
Direct taxes (% of household income)	
Taxes on income	15
National insurance contributions	4
Contributions to pension schemes	2

(*Social Trends*, 1988)

Table 17.4 shows how income is distributed before and after tax. We can see that the distribution is unequal, with the top 10 per cent receiving about 30 per cent of income before tax and the bottom 50 per cent getting less than a quarter of total incomes. Taxation makes the distribution more even. The impact of the state on distribution is discussed further in Chapter 19.

Table 17.4 Percentage shares of income before and after tax 1984–85

Quintile group	Before tax	After tax
Top 1%	6.4	4.9
2–5%	12.1	11.1
6–10%	10.9	10.5
Top 10%	29.5	26.5
11–20%	16.8	16.6
21–30%	13.0	13.0
31–40%	10.3	10.4
41–50%	8.2	8.6
51–60%	6.6	7.1
61–70%	5.4	6.0
71–80%	4.4	4.9
81–90%	3.5	4.2
91–100%	2.3	2.7
Median income	£5480	£4990
Mean income	£7520	£6340
Gini coefficient	41	36

(*Economic Trends*, November 1987)

17.6.2 Measuring inequality

A common way of depicting the distribution of income is through the Lorenz curve. This shows on a graph the cumulative income share against the population share of income. The diagonal line in Figure 17.9 would depict complete equality. The distribution is more likely to look like the coloured line. This shows, for example, that 50 per cent of the population receives only 25 per cent of the income. The larger the shaded area the more inequality exists.

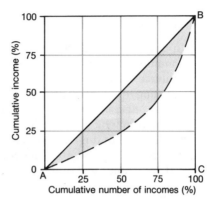

Fig. 17.9 Measuring inequality – a Lorenz curve

A common measure of inequality is the **Gini coefficient**. This expresses the shaded area as a percentage of the triangle *ABC*. The latter shows the area that marks the extremes between complete equality (the diagonal line) and complete inequality (point *C*). The Gini coefficient may lie between perfectly equal incomes when it will be zero and complete inequality when it will be 100.

Table 17.4 shows that the size of the Gini coefficient is reduced by the impact of taxation, thus confirming that income tax produces a more equal distribution of income.

18 Welfare economics

18.1 Introduction

In our overview of the market economy in Chapter 3 we suggested that under certain conditions an **unregulated market economy** could achieve an **optimal allocation of resources**. This seems a remarkable result in a situation where millions of people are pursuing their own selfish interests. However, we recognized that we could expect circumstances to prevent optimal allocation and called this **market failure**. In this chapter we want to look again at these issues in the light of our discussions in Chapters 13 to 16. Section 18.3 of this chapter may treat the subject in more detail than your course, but it can be omitted without affecting your understanding of subsequent sections.

This chapter will:

- explain the concepts of social costs and benefits
- outline the conditions for an efficient allocation of resources
- explain the conditions under which a market economy can achieve an optimum allocation of resources
- explain Pareto optimality and its limitations
- discuss the problems for efficient resource allocation of imperfections in competition
- consider externalities and discuss the necessity for government intervention
- explain the nature of public goods and the need for intervention
- illustrate, through a study of the problem of pollution, the approaches that may be taken to achieve an optimum allocation of resources where there are external benefits and costs

18.1.1 Examination guide

Many questions in economics are concerned with the way resources are allocated and the extent to which particular practices or policies assist in achieving an optimum allocation of resources. Although some of the material in this chapter may be more advanced than your course requires, the more elementary treatment in the first part of section 18.2 should be suitable for most courses. The condition that any optimum allocation of resources requires social marginal utility to be equal to social marginal cost is a useful starting point when answering a wide variety of questions concerned with public versus market provision (e.g. health, education and housing). Market failure (externalities, imperfections, etc.) can be considered from this standpoint as indicated in section 18.3.

18.2 Competition and the efficient allocation of resources

18.2.1 Social costs and benefits

The overall problem we are considering in this chapter is the **optimum**, or best, **allocation** of society's resources. We can apply the rules for maximization used in earlier chapters and illustrate this problem in Figure 18.1. Here the *SMC* represents the **social marginal costs** of producing the output of this good or service, that is, the extra costs society has to bear to produce additional output. The downward sloping schedule, *SMU*, shows the additional utility society derives from consuming an extra unit of the good or service. The conditions for **maximizing net benefits** (i.e. utility less costs) are obtained where social marginal utility equals social marginal cost:

$SMU = SMC$

This point is at an output level of Q_1. Other levels of output represent inferior positions. At Q_3, $SMC > SMU$, so society is adding more to costs than to benefits; it would consequently gain by reducing output. Whereas too many resources are devoted to the production of this good at Q_3, the reverse is true at Q_2. Here additional benefits are greater than the extra cost ($SMU > SMC$), so society can gain by applying more resources to its production. This will be the case until Q_1 is reached. Can an **unregulated market economy** achieve a point where $SMU = SMC$?

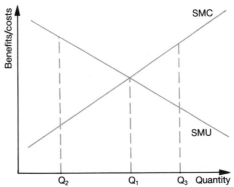

Fig. 18.1 Optimum allocation of resources

18.2.2 Conditions necessary for an efficient allocation of resources

A **perfectly competitive economy**, if it satisfies certain conditions, can achieve a point where $SMU = SMC$. Before we spell them out it will be helpful to recall some of the conclusions we reached in earlier chapters. In Chapter 13 we showed how the **demand curve** could be derived from the **marginal utility schedule** (Figure 13.1). In our earlier discussion we said that, in effect, the demand curve represented the **marginal utility** of the consumer. We assume that the price the consumer pays for the product is a measure of additional benefit or marginal utility derived from consuming the last unit.

We established in Chapter 15 that the supply curve is the sum of the firms' marginal cost curves. Figure 18.2(a) and (b) are a reminder of this derivation. Firms under **perfect competition** will produce where $P = MC$. So, with the demand curve indicating MU and the supply curve representing marginal cost, the equilibrium price under perfectly competitive conditions is also a point where $MU = MC$. If, for the moment, we assume that the marginal utility represented by the demand curve is the same as the extra utility to society (SMU), and similarly that the supply curve shows the marginal cost to society as well as firms, we have demonstrated a remarkable result. It shows that consumers seeking to maximize their own utility and firms pursuing profit maximization achieve the best allocation of resources in the way we defined them in the previous section: $SMU = SMC$. We can summarize this as:

$$SMU = SMC$$

$$SMU = MU = P = MC = SMC$$

Our discussion of supply and demand and perfect competition leads us to expect that changes in preferences and costs will lead to output changes. These changes can now be seen as an adjustment which will reallocate to a new optimum. For example, a shift in demand will raise price and in the short run there will be abnormal profits; but this will act as a signal for new entrants to the industry. A new equilibrium will be established where price equals long-run marginal cost and this again will be where $SMU = SMC$.

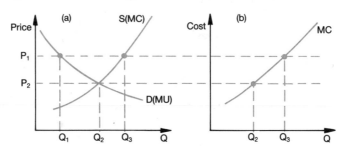

Fig. 18.2 Perfect competition and optimum resource allocation

A perfectly competitive economy will only produce at a point where $SMU = SMC$ if certain conditions are satisfied. As there are good grounds for supposing these conditions will be violated, it is important to be clear what they are.

18.2.2.1 Externalities

First, **private benefits** (MU) and **costs** (MC) must be equal to **social benefits** (SMU) and **costs** (SMC). Resources are allocated on the basis of private costs and benefits, so if there is a divergence from benefits enjoyed by the community and the costs it pays, then an optimum allocation will not be achieved. A divergence arises in the case of **externalities**. We consider this more fully in section 18.3.1.

18.2.2.2 Public goods

A second condition is that there must be no public goods if an unregulated market economy is to achieve the best allocation of resources. A public good exists where a good or service is provided and it is not possible to exclude non-payers from the benefits. Defence, law and order, street lighting and lighthouses are often cited as examples. The problems of properly allocating resources to public goods are discussed below, but we can state the difficulty fairly simply at this stage. It is not likely that the benefits consumers receive from public goods will be translated into a demand curve (in the manner we described earlier) because the non-excludability of these goods means the benefits can be enjoyed without payment. So the opportunity for everyone to be a **free rider** will mean that no demand curve emerges and inadequate resources will be allocated to the production of public goods.

18.2.2.3 $P = MC$

A third condition is that **price equals marginal cost**. While this condition is met under perfect competition it will not be achieved in a market economy that has imperfections. We learned in Chapter 16 that under monopoly conditions price will be greater than marginal costs. We explore the welfare loss associated with this a little more closely in section 18.3.1. Other imperfections such as **consumer ignorance** and distortions in the factor market will prevent an optimum from being achieved.

We can present a different picture of the optimum allocation of resources using an approach first adopted in Chapter 3. Figure 18.3(a) shows a **production possibility curve** and a set of **indifference curves**. Recall that the production possibility curve shows the maximum amounts of Y and X that a society can produce with given resources. Showing society's preference for Y and X is not so straightforward. There is no scientific basis for adding up the preference of individuals as we cannot know how much enjoyment one

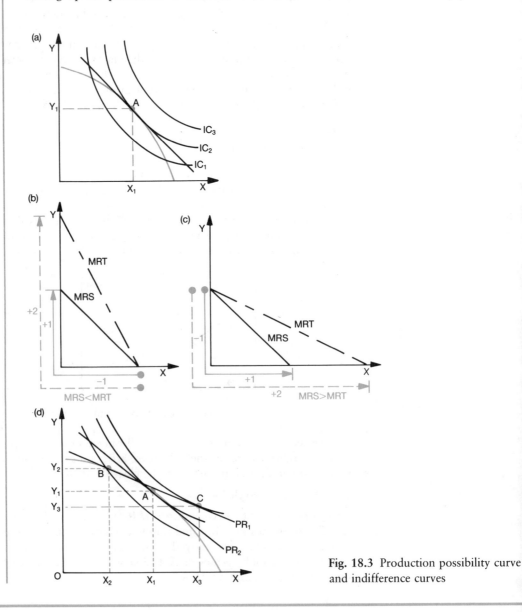

Fig. 18.3 Production possibility curve and indifference curves

person derives from consumption compared with someone else. The expression of preferences through demand in the marketplace reflects the distribution of income so redistribution will give a different weight to these preferences. The difficulties in trying to derive a set of community indifference curves is discussed a little further in the next section. Here, we shall get round the problems by assuming that there is only one consumer.

Point A is clearly a position of **maximum utility** (given these preferences) and **allocative efficiency**. We can explore what this position involves and relate it to the operation of a market economy. The slope of the production possibility curve at A shows the **marginal rate of transformation** (*MRT*):

$$MRT = \frac{\Delta Y}{\Delta X}$$

That is, it shows how much Y has to be given up, when resources are fully employed, to obtain a small amount extra of X. We can relate this to costs and prices. The **marginal cost** (*MC*) is the change in total costs resulting from an incremental change in output, so

$$MC_X = \frac{\Delta TC_X}{\Delta X}$$
and
$$MC_Y = \frac{\Delta TC_Y}{\Delta Y}$$

where MC_X is the marginal cost of X and MC_Y the marginal cost of Y. If we are considering a small move along the production frontier, the increase in total cost of producing more X is the same as the reduction in costs of producing less Y, i.e.

$$\Delta TC_X = \Delta TC_Y$$

(ignoring signs). This is because we are moving a given amount of factors from Y to X and in competitive markets factor prices will be the same for both.

We can use the equality of ΔTC to show that the ratio of marginal costs of X to Y is equal to the *MRT*:

$$\frac{MC_X}{MC_Y} = \frac{\Delta TC/\Delta X}{\Delta TC_Y/\Delta Y} = \frac{\Delta TC_X}{\Delta X} \cdot \frac{\Delta Y}{\Delta TC_Y} = \frac{\Delta Y}{\Delta X} = MRT$$

Under perfect competition firms will produce where $MC = P$, so from the production side we have

$$MRT = \frac{\Delta Y}{\Delta X} = \frac{MC_X}{MC_Y} = \frac{P_X}{P_Y}$$

The position of the consumer can be stated much more briefly. The slope of the indifference curve shows the **marginal rate of substitution** (*MRS*) and we know from Chapter 13 that the consumer is in equilibrium where

$$MRS = \frac{\Delta Y}{\Delta X} = \frac{P_X}{P_Y}$$

We can put these results together:

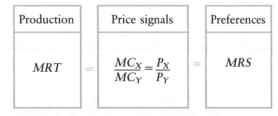

Production		Price signals		Preferences
MRT	$=$	$\frac{MC_X}{MC_Y} = \frac{P_X}{P_Y}$	$=$	MRS

From Figure 18.3(a) we can see that a point of tangency of the production possibility curve and indifference curve will give the maximum utility. We have now established that this is where $MRS = MRT$ and the result we have just derived shows that a perfectly competitive economy which responds to price signals has maximization conditions that are consistent with a position of allocative efficiency. That is, firms maximize profits where $P = MC$ and consumers maximize utility where $MRS = P_X/P_Y$, so the relationships shown in the price signals box, above, is what we would expect to find in a perfectly competitive economy. However, we must repeat the qualifications made earlier that the existence of externalities and public goods will mean that market price signals (based on private costs and benefits) are not an accurate reflection of the *MRT* and *MRS* for society as whole.

We delve a little deeper into the meaning of an **optimum allocation of resources** if we consider more closely the condition $MRS = MRT$. At this point the ratio of gains to losses in society's output following a shift in resources is exactly the amount necessary to keep society's utility constant. If MRS does not equal MRT these are potential gains. In Figure 18.3(b), which is a situation where $MRS < MRT$, MRT shows that reducing the output of X by 1 will lead to an increase of 2 in Y. The MRS shows that an increase of 1 unit of Y is sufficient to compensate the consumer for the loss of 1 unit of X. The move of resources produces a net gain: we can keep the utility constant and still have 1 unit of Y left over.

There are net gains to be obtained when the $MRS > MRT$, as Figure 18.3(c) shows. If we start at point B and reduce the consumption and output of Y by one unit then the MRS shows that one extra unit of X will be sufficient to maintain consumer satisfaction; but the MRT shows that society can gain 2 units of X by reallocating resources. As both of these positions allow net gains to be made they can be regarded as suboptimal.

We can view them in terms of a much used criterion of optimality in economics put forward at the turn of the century by **Vilfredo Pareto**. A position is **Pareto optimal** (or **Pareto efficient**) when no one can be made better off without making someone else worse off. The cases we illustrated are not Pareto optimal because we gain more output than is necessary to maintain utility. Thus we are in a position to make someone better off without making anyone worse off. Where such an improvement can be made to achieve a Pareto optimum, it would generally be acceptable to society to make the change because there would be no losers. However, most changes we can contemplate involve loss as well as gain. Most people would not necessarily rule out such changes because they cannot be justified under the Pareto criterion. However, as there is no scientific basis for evaluating one person's utility loss compared with another's gain, the foundation for such redistribution must be ethical. Different distributions of income will generate different community indifference curves and we cannot demonstrate, scientifically, that one set is superior to another. Of course research into various aspects of the distribution of income (e.g. child mortality and illness amongst the poor or the incentive effects of income) may influence our opinions; but ultimately it is a matter of belief which distribution is preferable. There will be a different position of **Pareto optimality** associated with each set of community indifference curves, so the analysis of economists is largely concerned with examining the conditions necessary to achieve an optimum position produced by a set of preferences resulting from a given distribution of income.

Is a **Pareto-inefficient** position likely to generate price signals that will move resources towards an optimum position? In Figure 18.3(d) the Pareto-optimum position is at A; but suppose output is at B with firms producing OY_2 of Y and OX_2 of X with prices equal to marginal cost. The price ratio is represented by the slope of the production possibility curve at B, shown by the line PR_1. Consumers will try to purchase X_3 of X and Y_3 of Y because point C represents an equilibrium for them; but this involves excess demand for X (X_2 is produced but X_3 is demanded) and excess supply for Y (Y_2 is produced but only Y_3 is demanded). We would expect the price of X to rise and that of Y to fall. These price signals lead to losses in the Y industry but abnormal profits in X which should lead resources to move towards X and away from Y. This adjustment will be complete when the price ratio is PR_2 and production is at A.

While the **price system** is capable of producing appropriate price signals and responding to them, this may not happen, or at least not in a satisfactory way. We are here concerned with the dynamics of adjustment and as we saw in Chapter 5 the introduction of time lags may produce a cyclical response which could be unstable. The reallocation of resources from B to A may involve a very protracted adjustment.

18.2.3 A closer look at Pareto optimality

A useful device that allows us to consider the conditions of **Pareto optimality** more fully is an **Edgeworth box**. This is a diagrammatic approach which shows the various ways in which two products may be divided between two consumers. We illustrate this in Figure 18.4 where we have an output of $O_A X$ food and $O_A Y$ beer to be divided between two consumers, Annette and George. If Annette consumes $O_A F_A$ of food and $O_A B_A$ of beer this leaves the remainder, $F_A X$ food and $B_A Y$ beer for George. We can show George's consumption by recognizing that the top righthand corner of the box can represent the origin of axes showing the quantities he consumes. So he consumes $O_G F_G$ (= $F_A X$) food and $O_G B_G$ (= $B_A Y$) beer. As he moves away from O_G his consumption increases, so the further left along $O_G Y$ and the further down $O_G X$, the more food and beer he will consume, respectively.

We can draw a set of indifference curves for Annette (A_1 to A_4) and for George (G_1 to G_4) (remember his origin is O_G, so they are drawn convex from that point and utility increases the nearer the curves are to the bottom lefthand corner).

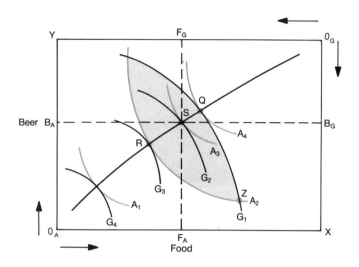

Fig. 18.4 An Edgeworth box diagram

We can draw a line through the points of tangency of the two sets of indifference curves. This line, which is known as the **contract curve**, shows **Pareto-optimum points**. We can understand this better by taking a point off the curve such as Z. This lies on George's indifference curve G_1 and Annette's curve A_2. It is not Pareto efficient because we can improve Annette's position without making George worse off by moving along G_1 towards Q. Alternatively we can make George better off without worsening Annette's position by moving along A_2 towards R. We could of course, improve both persons' position by moving from Z to any point in the shaded area. However, when we reach a point where their indifference curves are tangential to each other it is not possible to improve one person's position without making the other worse off. So, for example, at point S, Annette's position can be improved by moving to the right; but that will force George on to a lower indifference curve. Similarly a leftward move would improve George's position but to the cost of Annette's. The contract curve joining points of tangency shows the **Pareto-optimum conditions** and any point off it is not Pareto-efficient because improvements can be made that will raise the utility of one or both parties.

Off the contract curve the marginal rate of substitution of the two people differs, so mutually beneficial trade can take place. This is no longer possible when each MRS is equal to the other. The Pareto criterion does not allow us to choose between points along the contract curve (e.g. R, S and Q) because any of these will make one party worse off.

We can use an Edgworth box diagram to consider how a limited supply of factors of production can be divided between two firms, B and F. In Figure 18.5(a) (overleaf) the total quantity is indicated by the horizontal sides of the box which show the quantity of labour, and the vertical sides which show the quantity of capital. Firm B has an origin in the bottom lefthand corner and firm F in the diagonally opposite corner. Four of firm B's isoquants are shown by B_1 to B_4 and firm F's isoquants are shown as F_1 to F_4. Using exactly the same reasoning as we did with consumers, we can draw a contract curve joining points of tangency which will represent **Pareto-optimum positions**. In this case it is where the **marginal rates of technical substitution** ($MRTS$) are equal to each other. Along this curve raising one firm's output can be achieved only by reducing that of the other. Points off the curve are Pareto inefficient (e.g. M) so the output of one firm can be raised without the other suffering (e.g. M to J, or M to K) or both parties may benefit (e.g. M to L).

The contract curve gives us different output combinations, varying from O_B where output of B is zero and all the factors are used by firm F to produce its output, food. The opposite extreme is shown at O_F, where all the factors are used to produce beer, the output of firm B. These points along the curve, which show Pareto-efficient production conditions can be used to draw the **production possibility frontier** (see Figure 18.5(b)).

Let us suppose that society's preferences mean that its utility is maximized at T where $O_A X$ units of food are produced and $O_A Y$ units of beer. We can draw an Edgeworth box within the production frontier to show how this output could be divided between our two consumers. The optimum position will be:

1 where **marginal rates of technical substitution** are equal to each other;

2 where **marginal rates of substitution** are equal to each other;

3 where the **marginal rate of transformation** equals the **marginal rate of substitution**.

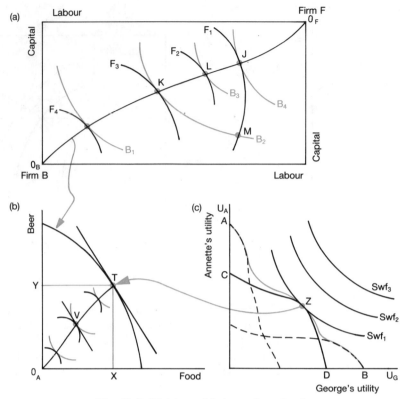

Fig. 18.5 Division of factors of production

The first condition is satisfied because any point on the production possibility curve is one where the *MRTS* are equal, as we saw when we explained the derivation of the production frontier. The second condition is the one which places consumers on their contract curve, as we discussed earlier.

The final condition connects consumption and production conditions. It requires the **marginal rate of transformation** (which shows what output has to be sacrificed to obtain an extra unit of another good) to be equal to the **marginal rate of substitution** (which is the rate at which consumers will exchange the goods to maintain the same level of utility). If the two are not equal then we are not at a point where maximum gains are being made, as we saw in the previous section. We also noted that the *MRT*, at a point like *T*, would be equal to the ratio of the marginal costs and in turn this would equal the ratio of prices. Graphically this is shown by the slope of the tangent line at *T*. The optimum position for consumers will be where the *MRS* is equal to the ratio of the prices, which in our diagram will be at *V*. We see here, as we did in the single consumer case, that a perfectly competitive market is capable of generating the prices that are required for a Pareto optimum.

Finally we turn to how point *T* is determined. We can draw a **utility possibility curve** on a diagram like Figure 18.5(c) for every consumer contract curve. So the line CD is the one that corresponds to the contract curve O_AT in the box in Figure 18.5(b). The **utility possibility curve** shows that as we move along the curve one person's utility improves at the expense of the other. The Pareto criterion does not allow us to say one position on the line is superior to any other; however, points within the curve are inferior because it is possible to make one party better off without the other being worse off. There will be a different contract curve for every point like *T* on the production possibility curve and hence a different utility possibility curve in Figure 18.5(c). Only four of these are shown in the diagram. We can construct a **utility frontier** from the outer edges of these and this is the line *AB* in the diagram. Every point on this frontier is a Pareto optimum and we cannot say, using that criterion, that one is preferable to another.

We still have not shown how point *T* is obtained: this requires one final step – the construction of a **social welfare function**. This shows society's views on the relative worth of the utility of one person compared with the other. With this social welfare function we can determine point *Z* as the preferred position and as this is a point on the utility possibility frontier constructed from the contract curve in Figure 18.5(b) it means that *T* is the preferred position on the production possibiliity curve. The **social welfare function** essentially represents an ethical position on who is deserving. Its construction is not straightforward. It may be imposed by a dictator or be the outcome of the democratic process or express the preference of officials.

18.2.4 Pareto and other criteria

The **Pareto criterion** attracts widespread support – up to a point. That is, it would be generally accepted that changes which better some people without making others worse off should be pursued. However many policy changes will involve making some groups worse off while benefiting others. Society is not prepared to rule out all such changes, so is there an alternative criterion that helps in these circumstances? One suggestion is that if those who gain can sufficiently compensate the losers to make the change worthwhile to both parties it should go ahead. However the initial distribution of income may give certain groups much greater opportunity to exercise their preferences than others; had the initial distribution been different so might the outcome of the compensation exercise. Another approach is to argue that there needs to be an **explicit social welfare function** that can be used to decide changes where there will be loss as well as gain.

18.2.5 Market economies, socialism and optimality

It may be helpful to briefly summarize some of the points made and clarify some of the limitations. We have shown that under certain conditions a market economy can achieve an **optimum allocation of resources**. This is a remarkable outcome for a decentralized system in which the participants are all pursuing their own selfish interests. However, the conditions necessary for an optimum are unlikely to be realized, so our view of the market economy must be qualified. (We consider the issue of **market failure** in the next section.) We should remember, too, that there is not one optimum position but many, each associated with different distributions of income.

The discussion so far has been in terms of **market economies**; but the rules for maximization apply to any economy seeking allocative efficiency. So they may be used to guide planners or prices may be used in a **socialist economy** to act as signals to individual enterprises.

18.3 Market failure

18.3.1 Market failure and efficiency

We have stressed at various points in the chapter that a market economy may achieve an optimum allocation only under certain conditions: when **imperfections**, **public goods** and **externalities** are absent. In practice we cannot expect to find such a market economy, so it is useful to briefly analyse the consequences of what is usually described as market failure.

18.3.1.1 Imperfect competition

Under **imperfect competition** price will not equal marginal cost so the correct price signals will not be given and resources will not be optimally allocated. In Figure 18.6 the marginal cost is assumed to be constant and competitive equilibrium will be at Q_c, with price, P_c, equal to marginal cost, MC_1. Under monopoly, MC will be equated with MR and the profit-maximizing output will be Q_m, where the price, P_m, is greater than MC. This means that insufficient resources are applied to the production of this product because the marginal benefits (as indicated by the demand curve) exceed the additional costs.

We can go a little further in showing the objection to monopoly. If we compare the monopoly position with that of perfect competition in Figure 18.6 we can see that monopoly involves a loss of consumer surplus equal to P_mACP_c. There will, however, be a producer's surplus, P_mABP_c, where the price received is greater than the costs of purchasing factors. In our illustration this involves the transfer of benefits from the consumer to the producer. However there are some consumer benefits that are lost altogether and this is shown by the shaded area ABC. This is known as the **deadweight loss** (i.e. a loss without any compensating gains) and is a measure of the cost to society of monopoly.

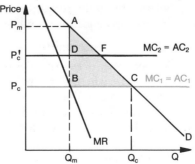

Fig. 18.6 Imperfect competition

In Chapter 16 we argued that a monopoly may result in lower costs, compared with perfect competition, because of economies of scale. We can illustrate this on the diagram i we assume in this case that the competitive costs are represented by the line MC_2 and the competitive price will be P'_c. The monopoly position is the same as before so the monopoly price is still greater than the competitive one and there is a loss of consumer surplus equal to $P_mAFP'_c$. The deadweight loss is ADF, but there are now some extra benefits to conside arising from the lower costs. These are shown by the area $P_cDBP'_c$.

Extra costs may result from monopoly. These may arise because managers and worker use the opportunity of a monopolistic situation to go for the 'quiet life' which leads to highe costs. This phenomenon is known as **X-inefficiency**. These various costs and benefit underlay the pragmatic approach to monopoly policy in the UK that we discussed i Chapter 16.

18.3.1.2 Public goods

An unregulated market economy will not achieve an optimum allocation of resources whe there are **public goods**. **Public goods** are goods which, when they are provided, are availabl to all. The classic example is defence. If a country is provided with a defence system a citizens are defended with public goods: one person's consumption does not detract from another's. This affects the way market demand curves are derived. With private good demand curves are added horizontally (as in Figure 18.7(a)). In the case of **public goods** when a quantity is provided, for example OQ in 18.7(b), then the whole of that quantity ca be enjoyed by everybody so we can add the demand curves vertically. The equilibrium for private good is where price is equal to each individual's marginal rate of substitution whereas for a public good it is equal to the sum of the MRS.

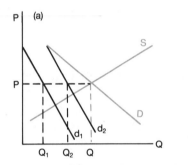 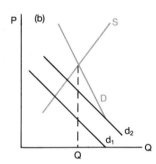

Fig. 18.7 Public goods

There are severe difficulties in providing the optimum level in a market economy. A majo difficulty arises in getting people to reveal their **demand**. With goods like defence th exclusion principle breaks down so people can enjoy the benefit without paying. In this cas everyone is tempted to be a **free rider**. There is widespread acceptance that certain publi goods, such as defence, law and order and street lighting, should be provided by governmer (central or local). However, this does not solve the problem of revealing **true preferences fo public goods**; if stating preferences is connected with payment then there is an incentive t understate demand (**free-rider problem**) and if it is divorced from payment there will be tendency to overstate preferences. Even if these difficulties were resolved a further probler exists concerning the **pricing of public goods**. Optimum resource allocation requires that zero price is charged where the marginal cost is zero. Extra people can be defendec additional viewers can watch a TV transmission and more motorists can use uncongeste roads and bridges without incurring extra costs, so the marginal cost is zero. Not chargin these consumers prevents the private market from operating and also means that an attempt by public authorities to use charges as a way of revealing preferences, as a means c improving allocation, conflicts with **optimal pricing policies**.

18.3.1.3 Externalities

The existence of **externalities** poses a problem for a market economy achieving an optimun These arise where there are benefits or costs that are **external** to the consumer or produce For example, pollution creates costs for a neighbourhood that are not paid for by th producer. We can see this illustrated in Figure 18.8(a), where S_1 shows the private margin: cost. The total cost to society is shown by S_2: the difference between the two curves is measure of the **externality**. As the market operates on the basis of private costs and benefi it will produce an output of Q_P. However the social optimum, where $SMC = SMU$, is at Q The market allocates too many resources to the production of this good because the margin:

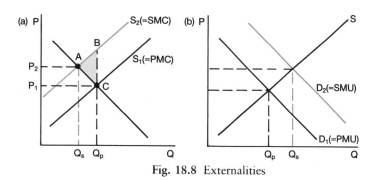

Fig. 18.8 Externalities

costs to society (as shown by the *SMC*) are greater than the additional benefits as shown by the demand curve. The triangle *ABC* is a measure of these excess costs.

There can be **external benefits** as well as costs. For example, vaccination confers benefits on society as whole, as well as the persons vaccinated, because it reduces the incidence of the disease. We show this in Figure 18.8(b), where D_2 shows the benefits to society (= *SMU*) and D_1 presents the benefits of those people who are vaccinated. Again private demand and supply will determine the level of output which will be Q_P. But this is sub-optimal because the benefits to society exceed the cost and output should rise to Q_S.

18.3.1.4 Imperfect information

If firms and households do not have full and correct information about the market then resources will not be optimally allocated. **Imperfect information** may occur in a number of ways. Transactors may not have full knowledge of prices so they may buy in relatively expensive markets and sellers may supply at lower prices than prevail elsewhere. Here **price signals** are not correctly perceived and resources are correspondingly **inappropriately allocated**. There may well be **imperfect information** about the quantity and even existence of goods and services. While lack of information is often the problem, there are occasions when **too much information** – the result of persuasive advertising – may distort demand by making exaggerated and incorrect claims about products.

The market itself is likely to respond to the problem of imperfect information. Consultants, market advisers and consumers' associations may provide advice, test reports and recommendations to help purchasers make better informed decisions. The **optimum position** for the individual consumer is to acquire additional information as long as the marginal benefits of the information exceed the marginal cost. Achieving this optimum is not without its difficulties. For consumers to assess the value of the extra information they need to acquire it. Nevertheless, it is likely that experience will establish the appropriate amount of information, for example, the extent to which it pays to shop around and the value of reading *Which* reports.

Most modern industrial economies are not content to leave the market to deal with all of the deficiencies of information. Where there are economies of scale and/or the exclusion principle breaks down and information takes on the nature of a public good, then **public provision** may be the socially efficient approach. A common form of **government intervention** is the establishment of minimum standards for products. So, for example, cars and drugs have to demonstrate they meet safety standards before they can be marketed.

18.3.1.5 Static and dynamic efficiency

The various aspects of **market failure** that we have discussed so far would prevent an optimum allocation of resources occurring at any particular point of time. If these obstacles were not present or were successfully remedied, there would still be doubts about the ability of market economies to allocate resources **optimally over time**. This problem was discussed in Chapter 3 (see sections 3.3.3 and 3.5.1.6); here we summarize the main points. The absence of a comprehensive set of future markets means that price signals about the future are not generated and therefore resources may not be allocated in a way that will maximize welfare or utility in the future. An optimum position over time may not be achieved because of the public good nature of economic growth. If we assume that there is a general preference for faster growth but that this involves sacrificing present consumption and accepting a more rapid application of technology (producing less job security as new skills and products are required), then there are doubts whether a socially optimal point will be achieved. Most people cannot be excluded from the benefits of growth as general living standards rise, so there is a free-rider problem as individuals may consume the benefits of growth without paying the costs or making the sacrifices. This is likely to distort the allocation in favour of maximizing present consumption at the expense of the future.

18.3.1.6 Merit goods

Many areas of public provision arise because some goods and services (e.g. health and education) are regarded as **merit goods**. These are goods which policy makers regard as being under-provided by an unregulated market economy. While these goods are often associated with **externalities** and their provision also meets **redistributional goals**, the underlying basis for regarding them as **merit goods** is ethical. So, for example, state education may be supported because it assists equality of opportunity or promotes social cohesion. Similarly, the view may be taken that in a civilized society everyone should have equal access to health care. **Merit goods** are an expression of the view that some goods should be provided collectively rather than by the demands of the market place.

18.3.2 Market and government failure

Market failure seems to provide a prima facie case for **government intervention**; but it needs to be stressed that such intervention may make matters worse. The point has already been made that the problem with public goods, the failure of the exclusion principle, that prevents the market from responding to preferences makes it difficult for the government to identify demand correctly. Some of the leading examples of monopolistic provision are (or in some cases, were, before privatization) to be found in the **public sector**. There can be no presumption that they are immune from the objections raised against private sector monopolies (for example, lack of responsiveness to consumers' wishes and weak incentive to be efficient). There have been attempts to require nationalized industries to charge prices that reflected long-run marginal costs; but many other aspects of efficiency were not fully addressed and ministerial interference, it is frequently suggested, made matters worse. Indeed, the basis of the argument in favour of privatization is that efficiency will be increased where competition is introduced and where it is not, regulated private monopolies will perform in a superior way to their state-owned predecessors.

State intervention to counter deficiencies in information may not be socially optimal. For example, the benefits from establishing safety standards have to be weighed against the cost of discouraging new products from coming on to the market. So the patients who are saved from dying by imposing rigorous requirements for the sale of new drugs have to be compared with those who might have been saved by laxer standards which would almost certainly have meant the introduction of more drugs. Regulatory bodies are likely to be more sensitive to criticism that they have passed as safe a product that has subsequently killed people, than to arguments that their standards are too rigorous; hence some economists have argued that government intervention is too restrictive and sub-optimal.

Markets may be more capable of dealing with other aspects of market failure than our account earlier suggested. Some **externalities** may be settled between the affected parties. Suppose firm A produces an external cost which falls on firm B. This means that firm A will produce a greater output than the social optimal level as explained in section 18.3.1.3 and illustrated in Figure 18.8(a), if it has to take account only of its internal costs. But it is likely that litigation or negotiation will force firm A to take account of the externality. If a system of property rights is established so that firm B can require compensation from firm A then the latter will have to pay for the nuisance it causes, so internalizing the costs. But if these property rights do not exist it will pay firm B to offer money to A up to the amount of the external cost as payment for reducing output and the externality.

While a response to the problem of **externalities** may be found in the case cited, in many other cases a solution without government intervention is unlikely. This will be the case where the externalities are spread over a community and where it would be impossible to exclude households from the benefits of reducing nuisance. In this case the externality can be regarded as a **public bad** and negotiating with the offending firm will encounter the **free-rider problem**. But it is also the case that establishing the extent of the externality will pose a problem for a government achieving a satisfactory solution.

Market failure undoubtedly exists; but you will find that its extent and significance is a matter of dispute. Those who favour market solutions are inclined to suggest that it is not a major problem, while the opposite is the case with those who are more critical of the workings of the market. Even where market failure occurs there is disagreement over whether intervention improves the position.

18.3.3 Theory of the second best

Where **market failure** occurs then it seems obvious that this should be remedied by achieving the socially optimum position: for example, ensuring that price equals marginal cost where there are imperfections in competition and that marginal social benefits and costs are equated rather than private costs and benefits in cases where are are externalities. The involves trying to achieve **first-best solutions**, i.e. conditions that correspond to those we discussed earlier in the chapter that are required for an optimum allocation of resources.

But if it is not possible to achieve first-best solutions throughout the economy, what should the response of policy markets be? Two economists, **Lipsey** and **Lancaster**, demonstrated in the mid-1950s that the **second-best solution** may involve departing from **first-best solutions** if these conditions are violated elsewhere. A simple illustration may provide an intuitive grasp of the argument. Suppose an unavoidable externality in one part of the economy means that industry A is producing at an output level above the social optimum; the theory of the second best suggests that if the government can control an industy B, which is a substitute for A, then departure from the first-best position (i.e. where $SMU = SMC$) would be justified. This departure would be directed at transferring resources away from A towards B, say through a subsidy to B.

18.3.4 Pollution: a case for control

Pollution is an **externality** which means that the optimum output is not being produced. There are various ways of dealing with the problem. It may be tempting to argue for total prohibition and for some pollutants that are particularly hazardous this may be appropriate. But there is a more general argument that weighs the costs of pollution against the costs of controlling it and so seeks an optimum control of the problem. The point is illustrated in Figure 18.9, where the costs of pollution increase as the amount of pollution rises. Also illustrated are the control costs, which are very high if there is little or no pollution but decline as more pollution is allowed. The total (or combination of the two costs) is shown by the coloured line. The low-cost position, Q_1, is regarded as the optimum. Government may then limit pollution to that amount. This may be done in a variety of ways.

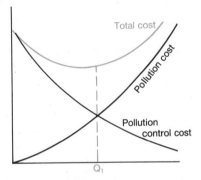

Fig. 18.9 Costs of pollution and pollution control

Controls could involve statutory powers which would prohibit the pollution to the level associated with an output of Q_1. Alternatively the government may issue permits allowing pollution of the amounts associated with Q_1. These permits may be traded in a market. Those firms who found it relatively cheap to limit pollution would do so rather than purchasing permits. A major problem with trying to produce an optimum control of pollution is obtaining the information on the relevant costs, i.e. both the cost curves shown in Figure 18.9 which make up the total cost curve.

An approach that involves slightly fewer demands on information is to impose a tax equal to the externality so that optimum output is produced. So, referring back to Figure 18.8(a), a tax equal to BC would mean that output would decline to Q_S. Of course this requires an understanding of the divergence between private and public costs, and this may not be easily ascertained where the costs are borne by the community. There seems little doubt that environmental issues are likely to be more seriously debated in the years ahead; yet even our cursory treatment shows that there are costs as well as benefits from policies designed to improve the environment (or to prevent its further deterioration, depending on your view point). Often neither the costs or benefits are well understood. The discussion is further complicated where future generations are likely to bear the costs (for example, destruction of the ozone layer or hazards of radioactive waste) and scientific evidence is not clear cut.

19 Public finance

19.1 Introduction

A recurring theme throughout this book has been the role of government in the economy. The branch of economics which makes a particular study of the role and impact of government is known as **public finance,** and we consider it in this chapter. This largely centres upon the analysis of **public expenditure** and **taxation.**

The chapter will:

- provide an outline of public expenditure in the UK
- consider the causes of public expenditure growth
- outline the basic principles of taxation
- distinguish between the benefit and ability to pay principles
- outline the structure of taxation in the UK and consider how it compares internationally
- consider the economic arguments for local government
- outline the role of local government in the UK

19.1.1 Examination guide

Public finance is often neglected or receives little emphasis in many introductory courses. However, most courses will consider the analysis of the **incidence of taxation** and many of these will extend this to examine the basic principles of taxation (see section 19.3). An awareness of the size and composition of government expenditure and taxation in the UK is useful in many questions. Similarly, many applied questions on a variety of topics involve an awareness of the distribution of income and the way governments can affect it. There are many mistaken ideas in this area. For example, the importance of benefits in kind in redistribution is often not appreciated.

Local government, despite its relative importance in the economy, may not be covered in many courses, except those concerned with public administration. Our brief coverage is intended to provide the framework for answers on the economic rationale of local government.

19.2 Public expenditure

19.2.1 Public expenditure in the UK

The importance of government in the UK economy can be gauged when it is realized that central and local government expenditure is around 45 per cent of GNP. In some ways this underestimates government influence because its power over the legal framework, which is not reflected in spending levels, can have an important impact on the behaviour of the private sector. In other respects the figure gives an inflated impression of the government's command over resources because it includes **transfer payments** (pensions, unemployment pay, social security payments, etc.) which are merely a redistribution of income from one group to another. The recipients determine which goods and services are purchased. Nearly half of all government expenditure is on transfer payments.

Table 19.1 shows that exhaustive expenditure or spending which involves the government directly purchasing resources is around 23 per cent of GDP. This table and Figure 19.1 show the increase in government spending since 1890. It has risen much faster than GDP generally, from less than 10 per cent of GDP in 1890 to more than 40 per cent in 1986. Within this overall increase, transfer payments have grown in relative importance: they were only about 25 per cent of government spending in the early 1890s, whereas more recently they represent half of expenditure.

Table 19.2 shows how the main categories of government spending have changed in the last 200 years. The most striking changes are the growth of social and economic services (final two columns), and the decline in importance of the first three categories: administration

Table 19.1 Government spending as percentage of GDP

	General government expenditure	Exhaustive spending	Transfer payments
1890	9.0	6.7	2.3
1900	14.4	12.6	1.8
1910	12.2	9.7	2.5
1920	26.6	16.6	10.0
1930	24.4	12.3	12.1
1940	51.9	43.3	8.6
1950	33.8	20.1	13.7
1960	34.1	19.4	14.7
1970	40.1	22.0	18.1
1980	45.1	23.7	21.4
1986	42.8	22.9	19.9

(*Economic Trends*, October 1987)

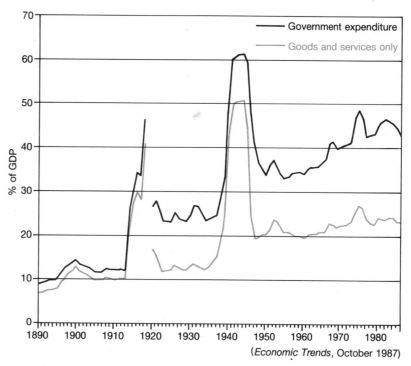

(*Economic Trends*, October 1987)

Fig. 19.1 Government expenditure as percentage of GDP in the UK

Table 19.2 Government expenditure by category
(as percentage of total expenditure)

	Administration	Debt interest	Defence	Social services	Economic and environmental service
1790	17	39	26	9	9
1840	16	42	23	9	9
1890	22	15	28	20	15
1910	14	7	27	32	20
1932	7	25	10	45	14
1951	6	11	25	43	15
1961	7	10	20	47	16
1977	6	10	11	50	22
1985	7	11	12	52	18

(Veverka, 1963)

debt interest and defence. These changes reflect a significant shift in ideas about the role of government and the working of the market economy. ***Laisser-faire*** views, which dominated the first half of the 19th century, presented a limited role for the state, with activities largely confined to defence, law and order and diplomatic relations. The provision of other services, including what we now call social services, was left to the private sector. The old, the poor and the sick were looked after by their families, charity or, as a last resort, the state. But the latter's help was made so unpalatable and unattractive that only the desperate made use of it. Around 80 per cent of government expenditure was devoted to defence, interest on the national debt (itself partly the result of war-time borrowing) and the cost of administration of parliament, external relations and tax collection. Social services (health, income support, education, etc.) and economic services (transport, water and sanitation, street lighting, etc.) accounted for less than a fifth of spending.

Today the proportions are almost reversed. Social and economic services are 70 per cent of spending and the remainder is devoted to defence, debt interest and administration. This change started in the last quarter of the 19th century when it was realized that industrialization and urbanization posed problems (e.g. public health hazards, need for basic education) that the market economy could not successfully resolve. This arose because of the **public good nature** of some of these services (e.g. street lighting and public health), the presence of **externalities** (e.g. education) and the **natural monopoly** properties of public utilities (gas, electricity). In the 1890s there was a change in attitude towards poverty. There was a growing realization that there was a vicious circle of unemployment, poverty and ill health which arose not from personal weakness or idleness but from the workings of the economic system. In the 20th century there has been a large growth in social services. Two notable landmarks in this development were the liberal reforms before 1914 and the founding of the modern welfare state after the Second World War. An analysis of general government expenditure in the mid-1980s is presented in Table 19.3.

Table 19.3 Analysis of total expenditure, 1988
(£million, percentage of total expenditure)

	£million	%
General public services (Parliament, finance and tax collection, external)	7879	5
Defence	18 306	12
Public order and safety (police, fire, law courts prison)	6166	4
Education	17 505	11
Health	17 837	11
Social security	45 894	29
Housing and community amenities	6798	4
Recreational and cultural affairs	2280	1
Fuel and energy	1642	1
Agriculture, forestry and fishing	2821	2
Mining mineral resources, manufacturing and construction	2441	2
Transport and communication	4098	3
Other economic affairs and services	3831	2
Other expenditure	20 034	13
Total	157 532	

(*Financial Statement and Budget Review, HM Treasury*)

Our discussion so far has been in terms of general government expenditure. Table 19.4 provides a breakdown which shows the relative importance of central and local government.

Table 19.4 Central and local government expenditure

	Central government 1975	1985	Local authorities 1975	1985	General government 1975	1985
Total final consumption (£million)	13 534	45 975	9597	28 037	23 131	74 012
(percentage of GDP)	12.8	13	9.1	7.9	21.9	20.9
Capital expenditure (£million)	1252	3699	3734	3457	4986	7156
(percentage of GDP)	1.2	1	3.5	1	4.7	2
Total (£million)	14 786	49 674	13 331	31 494	28 117	81 168
Percentage of GDP	14	14	12.6	8.9	26.6	22.9

(*Economic Trends Annual Supplement*, 1988)

The position for central government, as a proportion of GDP, is broadly the same in 1985 as it was a decade earlier, while expenditure by local authorities has relatively declined. In part this reflects council house sales, which are regarded as negative investment, and the slight reduction in spending on education in real terms.

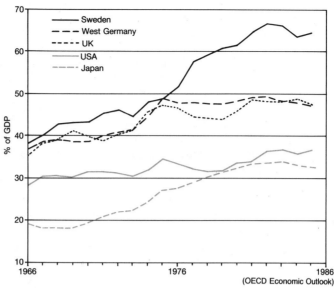

Fig. 19.2 Government expenditure as percentage of GDP in other countries

The growth in government expenditure has been a feature of all countries, as Figure 19.2 shows. Although there is a variation in the importance of the public sector between countries, it is significant in all of them. Even in Japan, where public spending has been low in comparison with other countries, in the mid-1980s it was nearly a third of GDP. Sweden has an unusually high public spending to GDP ratio. The UK is slightly below the European average.

19.2.2　The growth of public expenditure

The growth in public expenditure as a share of GDP has been such a distinctive feature of 20th-century economies that a number of explanations have been put forward to account for its occurrence. One of the oldest and most well known is **Wagner's law**.

In the late 19th century, Adolph Wagner, a German political economist, suggested that there was a tendency in industrial economies for public expenditure to rise faster than GDP. He thought industrialization would give rise to the need for increased welfare expenditure, more government regulation and state investment in public utilities. Wagner recognized that financial stringencies might restrict the growth of public expenditure but he thought that this restraint would be temporary.

An explanation of public expenditure growth which suggests a much more central role for the financing of public expenditure is one put forward in the early 1960s by **Peacock** and **Wiseman**. They argue that at any particular time there is a **tolerable tax burden**, that is, a level of taxation that the public is prepared to pay. This acts as a financial constraint on the growth of public spending, with politicians reluctant to raise tax rates above the level acceptable to the electorate. Periods of social upheaval, such as wars, can raise the tolerable tax burden as people are prepared to pay higher taxes in certain crises. This is known as a **displacement effect**, because Peacock and Wiseman argue that once higher taxes have been accepted as an emergency measure they do not fall back to the original level. This allows a higher level of spending. Raising the financial constraint may be reinforced by an **inspection effect** which can occur during a war (or other crisis) when there is a review of the nature of society and its services and opportunities. This review may lead to a resolve to produce a better society which at least in part requires increased public spending. The feelings behind the slogan 'a land fit for heroes' in the First World War and the Beveridge plans for a welfare state during the Second World War are examples.

Marxists have tended to explain the growth of state expenditure in terms of underlying **crises of capitalism**. There is considerable diversity in their explanations, with some emphasizing the threat of slump and mass unemployment while others have stressed the profitability crisis of capitalism. In the former case, state expenditure is regarded as an important addition to aggregate demand, which would otherwise have proved deficient. Those who argue that the major crisis facing capitalism is low profitability are divided on the cause. Some who adopt an orthodox Marxist approach argue that the accumulation of capital through investment lowers the rate of profit. Others stress that full employment following the Second World War until the mid-1970s, led to a rise in the power of workers which caused an upward pressure on wages and a squeeze on profits.

In the 1970s a number of Marxists referred to the **fiscal crisis of capitalism** which some (for example, James O'Connor in USA) considered had arisen because pressures to increase state spending (for oppressive purposes – police and military – and to avoid discontent – welfare expenditure) had tended to outstrip tax revenue. The resulting budget deficit tended to lead to inflationary finance. To these Marxists the attacks on government spending in the 1980s are an attempt to come to terms with the fiscal crisis. To many others the spending cuts are seen as a deflationary move designed to raise unemployment, to weaken workers' power and an attempt to reduce the **social wage** (social services provided by the state and consumed whether people work or not) in order to strengthen the incentive to work.

We conclude this section by briefly considering empirical investigations on the growth of public expenditure. There have been two broad approaches to these studies: **cross-sectional** and **time-series**.

Cross-sectional studies involve examining the relationship between GNP and government spending (or revenue) for different countries at a point in time. There are great difficulties in trying to establish reliable and comparable measures of the variables because of differences in definitions and methods of measurement. There are further problems in expressing values in a common currency. Most studies suggest there is a broad positive correlation between GDP levels and the share of government expenditure in national income. However, the correlation is far less impressive if the group of high income countries is considered by itself; similarly it breaks down within the group of low income countries. There are clearly factors other than the level of GDP operating which affect the extent of government spending.

A similar conclusion can be drawn from the time-series approach which considers the ratio of government spending to GDP over time. As Figure 19.1 showed, there has been an upward trend over the century and as income has increased over the period the data is consistent with Wagner's law. Peacock and Wiseman have argued that there is evidence of a displacement effect too. Some other interpreters have suggested that the evidence, if transfer payments are excluded, is consistent with attempts by government to raise its expenditure in line with the growth of GNP.

It is important to recognize that as GNP has increased over time, the correlation of GNP with the government expenditure – income ratio is likely to reflect the political, cultural and intellectual changes that have occurred over the period, as well as rising living standards. Some of these changes were referred to earlier in the chapter. In the 1980s, UK government policy has been directed at limiting the role of the state and controlling public expenditure. This marks a change in attitude and philosophy from earlier post-war governments. This new approach is not confined to the UK. It remains to be seen whether or not this marks the beginning of a longer lasting change which reverses a century of growth of public expenditure and state power.

19.3 Taxation

19.3.1 Principles of taxation

The major means of financing public expenditure is the revenue from taxation. In this section we consider a number of aspects of taxation.

19.3.1.1 Direct and indirect taxes

Taxes are often categorized as **direct** or **indirect**. **Direct taxes** are normally imposed on individuals (or groups) who bear the main burden of the tax, for example, income and corporation taxes. **Indirect taxes** are largely imposed on goods and services and the main burden will not necessarily fall on those who are formally responsible for paying the tax – instead there will be an attempt to shift payment on to the consumer. Customs and excise duties (on tobacco, alcohol and petrol) and value added tax (VAT) are examples of indirect taxes. They illustrate the idea of shifting the burden of taxation because the **formal incidence** of the tax (that is, the legal tax point: for example, the brewer or distiller in the case of alcohol duties) will not necessarily be the same as the **effective incidence** which shows who bears the burden of the taxation.

19.3.1.2 Incidence of taxation

In Chapter 5 we used demand or supply analysis to consider the incidence of taxation. Figure 19.3 illustrates the main points by using the example of a specific sales tax which imposes a tax of a given amount for each unit sold. The pre-tax equilibrium is at B with a price of P_1 and Q_1. A sales tax shifts the supply curve upwards by the amount of the tax and the new equilibrium is at A with a price of P_2 and quantity Q_2 (see section 5.4.1 for a fuller explanation). The total tax paid is shown by the rectangle P_3P_2AC with consumers paying P_2P_1DA. The effective incidence depends upon the relative elasticities of demand and supply. If demand were perfectly inelastic then all of the tax would be passed on and the

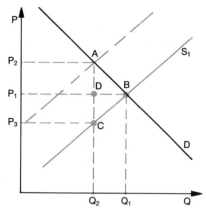

Fig. 19.3 Incidence of a sales tax

price would rise by the amount of the tax. On the other hand, if supply were perfectly elastic, producers would pay all of the tax and price would be unaffected. In both of these extreme cases the quantity traded would be unaffected by the imposition of the tax. Normally equilibrium quantities, and hence the allocation of resources, will be affected. We turn now to consider the welfare costs of this.

19.3.1.3 Efficiency and taxation

Following the approach we adopted in the previous chapter, let us assume the pre-tax position at B (on Figure 19.3) represents an efficient allocation of resources with social marginal cost (shown by the supply curve, S_1) equal to social marginal utility (represented by the demand curve). The imposition of the tax ($= AC$) drives a wedge between society's benefits and costs, so SMU is greater than SMC and with output at Q_2 (compared with the pre-tax Q_1) production is below the optimum. We can consider this in terms of the net loss of benefits. P_2ABP_1 represents the loss of consumer surplus and P_1BCP_3 the loss of producer surplus. However, there will be benefits arising from the tax revenue, P_2ACP_3. This leaves the triangle ABC which is the deadweight loss of the tax, that is, losses that are not offset by benefits. This distortion of the efficient allocation of resources is relatively small if demand or supply is highly elastic.

Although taxation is a cause of allocative inefficiency where the market would have achieved an optimum, there are circumstances when taxation may improve efficiency. This will occur where externalities produce a divergence between social and private costs or benefits. Here the unregulated market does not produce the most efficient output and taxation (in the case of external costs) or subsidies (where there are external benefits) can be used to improve the allocation of resources by shifting the supply curve and the equilibrium output to a socially optimum point. (See Chapter 18 for a fuller discussion of this point.)

A particular concern over the impact of taxation on the allocation of resources has come from those advocating supply-side policies. They stress the **disincentive effect** taxation may have on the supply of factors of production. It is suggested that tax cuts, especially on high marginal rates of income tax, will raise output and growth. There is little disagreement that there will be some high rates at which taxation will have a harmful effect on effort, but the debate in recent years has been about whether the UK has been operating at that point. (See Chapter 11 for a discussion of supply-side arguments.)

19.3.1.4 Equity and taxation

An important issue in taxation is **equity**. At one level there is the view that public expenditure should be financed in a fair and equitable way. There is also the more positive position that taxation can be used to redistribute income and create a more equal society. Notions of fairness and equity are open to different interpretations. Within public finance, two principles which represent different approaches to fairness are normally considered. The **benefit principle** suggests that the taxes people pay should be related to the benefits they receive from public expenditure. The second principle is the **ability to pay**. These, in turn, raise two ideas of equity: **horizontal** and **vertical equity**. Horizontal equity suggests that people in the same position should pay the same taxes, whereas vertical equity implies that people on different incomes should pay different amounts of tax, according to their ability to pay. We consider these ideas briefly in the next two sections.

19.3.1.5 The benefit principle

The idea that people should pay taxes according to the benefits they receive from public expenditure corresponds to a certain notion of fairness. It is the basis on which goods and services are bought in the private sector and for those who wish the public sector to mimic the private this approach has a strong appeal. It provides a close tie between spending and revenue, so the problem of financing expenditure is simultaneously solved. However, with many publicly provided goods it is not easy to identify and quantify the benefits received by different tax payers, so the use of specific benefit taxes would be limited. Furthermore it does not satisfy the redistribution objective of government.

19.3.1.6 Ability to pay principle

There is no doubt that the ability to pay principle has a strong appeal because it corresponds to most people's idea of fairness that the rich should pay more taxes. However there is considerable disagreement over how much more the better off should pay. Economic theory can give us guidelines on how to approach the problem, but is not able to give us definite tax rules for the amounts different income groups should be taxed.

Under the ability to pay principle, taxes are levied so that people sacrifice an equal amount of utility or welfare. There are two related ideas of equity associated with the principle. **Horizontal equity** suggests that people on equal incomes should pay equal amounts of tax and assumes that all people on equal incomes enjoy the same level of utility, so that there is an equality of sacrifice. If we assume that different incomes produce different levels of utility, the principle of equal sacrifice requires tax payments to vary with income – this is known as **vertical equity**. While this requires the rich to pay higher taxes than the poor, it does not give us a clear guide as to whether taxation should be **progressive** (where tax as a proportion of income rises as income increases), **regressive** (where the proportion declines) or **proportional**. This will depend on what view we take on the relationship between utility and income; while it is generally assumed that the marginal utility of income declines as income rises, its rate of decline becomes important when deriving tax rules. The progressiveness of the tax system will depend on how we interpret the concept of equal sacrifice; it could mean that everybody gives up the same amount of utility in absolute terms or that the sacrifice is proportionally the same. The interpretation that gives the most progression has everybody attaining the same marginal utility of income after the tax has been paid which, assuming utility schedules are the same, is where post-tax incomes are equalized.

Applying the ability to pay principle is not entirely straightforward. A major difficulty is finding an appropriate and workable definition of income. It should be wide enough to ensure that people do not obtain income in a non-taxable form (e.g. payment in kind) and exemptions, included in most income tax systems to respond to different family responsibilities, need to be tight enough not to be 'loopholes'.

19.3.1.7 Features of a 'good' tax system

It is generally recognized that a tax system should have the following characteristics:

1 The tax system should be **well understood** by taxpayers and be free from arbitrary judgments by tax collectors.

2 The **administrative costs** of collecting taxes and in ensuring that taxes are complied with should be **low**.

3 A tax system will be more acceptable and enforceable if it is generally regarded as **fair** and **equitable**. (There are different interpretations of fairness, as we discussed earlier.)

4 In most instances a good tax system should **not distort the allocation of resources**. However, there are circumstances where an unregulated market system fails to achieve an optimum allocation and the **reallocative effect** of taxation may improve the situation (see section 19.3.1.3).

5 For Keynesians, the tax system should be one which aids the conduct of a **fine-tuning aggregate demand policy**. This involves a preference for those taxes that have rapid impact on demand and are capable of being changed easily.

19.3.2 The UK tax system

19.3.2.1 Structure of Tax in the UK

Table 19.5 shows the main sources of government revenue. Income tax is the largest single revenue raiser and accounts for about nearly a quarter of government receipts. The proportion has steadily fallen since 1975 when it was approaching 40 per cent. Over the same period taxes paid by corporations have nearly doubled. The share of total revenue arising from indirect taxes rose significantly in 1979 when the rate of VAT was raised from 8 per cent to 15 per cent.

Table 19.5 Sources of government revenue, 1988–89
(percentage of total revenue)

Income tax	23
National insurance contributions	17
Value added tax	14
Local authority rates	10
Road, fuel, alcohol and tobacco duties	10
Corporation tax	9
Capital taxes	3
Interest and dividends	3
North Sea taxation	2
Other	9

(HM Treasury, *Financial Statement and Budget Report*, March 1988)

19.3.2.2 International comparisons

How does the tax burden in the UK compare with other countries? Table 19.6 shows total taxes (including social security contributions) as a percentage of Gross National Product (at factor cost).

Table 19.6 Taxes and social security contributions as percentage of GNP, 1985

Sweden	59
France	53
West Germany	46
UK	44
Japan	31
USA	31

(*Economic Trends*, December 1988)

By this measure the UK is neither a highly- nor lowly-taxed country. In 1985, out of 17 OECD (Organization for Economic Cooperation and Development) countries, the UK was ranked tenth in terms of the share of GDP paid in tax and social security contributions. The UK occupies a similar position when the relative importance of direct taxes is considered. The UK used to have very high marginal income tax rates on high incomes. Reductions in 1979 and 1988 (when all rates above 40 per cent were abolished) mean this is no longer the case.

There is considerable variation in the way different countries raise their tax revenue, as Table 19.7 shows. Compared with many other countries, the UK places a relatively heavy reliance on indirect taxes and company taxation and raises a comparatively small proportion from social security contributions.

Table 19.7 International comparison of tax revenue sources, 1985

	Taxes on household income	Taxes on profits and capital	Indirect taxes	Social security contributions
France	15.3	6.1	35.1	43.7
West Germany	25.0	5.5	30.3	39.2
Japan	23.8	19.9	27.5	28.8
Sweden	38.9	3.4	32.8	25
UK	27.7	13.3	41.1	18
USA	37	8.9	29.2	24.9

(*Economic Trends*, December 1988)

19.3.2.3 Progression in the UK tax system

We can consider the progressiveness of the UK tax system by examining the proportion of income paid in direct and indirect taxes. Table 19.8 shows non-retired households ranked into five groups by original income. Income tax turns out to be progressive, as we would

Table 19.8 Income tax and employees' NIC as percentage of gross income of non-retired households ranked by gross income

	Quintile group					
	Bottom	2nd	3rd	4th	Top	Total
Income tax	1.2	9.4	12.1	14.0	18.2	13.8
Employees' NIC	1.5	5.6	6.2	6.3	5.2	5.4
Total	2.7	15.0	18.3	20.3	23.4	19.2

(*Economic Trends*, July 1987)

expect, with the bottom fifth of households paying 1.2 per cent of their income in tax, whereas the top quintile pays 18.2 per cent. There is a ceiling on national insurance contributions so they become regressive after a point and the top quintile pay a lower proportion than all other groups except the bottom fifth of households.

Indirect taxes, on the other hand, tend to be regressive, the most regressive being the duty on tobacco (Table 19.9). In nearly every category the top 40 per cent (and particularly the top fifth) pay a lower proportion in taxation. For top income earners this is partly the result of them spending less because they devote a higher proportion of income to saving. So if tax were expressed as a proportion of expenditure the system would appear more progressive.

Table 19.9 Indirect taxes as a percentage of disposable income for non-retired households, 1985

| | Quintile group | | | | | |
	Bottom	2nd	3rd	4th	Top	Total
Rates	3.9	4.8	4.1	3.7	2.8	3.6
VAT	7.7	8.0	7.8	7.7	7.3	7.6
Duty on:						
Beer	1.2	1.3	1.1	1.1	0.9	1.1
Wines/spirits	0.8	0.9	0.9	1.0	1.1	1.0
Tobacco	5.3	3.3	2.5	1.8	1.2	2.2
Oil	1.2	1.6	1.7	1.7	1.5	1.6
Car tax, VED	0.8	1.1	1.1	1.1	1.0	1.0
Other	2.1	1.9	1.6	1.4	1.1	1.5
Intermediate	5.7	5.5	5.1	4.9	4.5	4.9
Total	28.6	28.3	25.9	24.4	21.4	24.5

(*Economic Trends*, July 1987)

19.4 The impact of expenditure and taxation on the distribution of income

We should recognize that the impact of the state on the distribution of income is not confined to the tax system. Public sector expenditure, through the provision of cash benefits and benefits in kind (education, health, travel and housing subsidies, welfare foods), has a significant effect too.

Figure 19.4 shows the various stages at which governments may affect the distribution of income. **Original income** is the income received by households before government

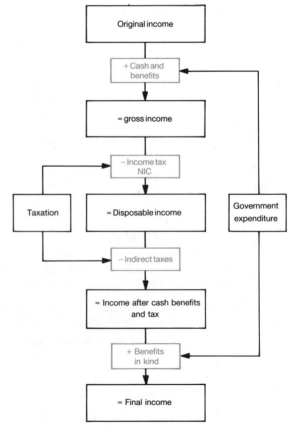

Fig. 19.4 Government intervention to affect income distribution

intervention and arises from wages and salaries, occupational pensions and investment income. This may be supplemented by cash benefits (state pensions, social security benefits, family allowances, etc.) and we call the result **gross income**. When income tax and national insurance contributions (NIC) are deducted we obtain **disposable income**. Some of the spending out of disposable income will be received by the government as indirect taxes (VAT, duties, rates, etc.). When this is subtracted we get **income after cash benefits and taxes**. Finally we recognize that households receive benefits in kind such as education and health. When we add these in we arrive at **final income**, the income enjoyed by households when account is taken of the effects of all state taxes and benefits.

To examine the impact of the distribution of income, we divide households into five groups (quintiles) according to their original income. The bottom fifth in 1985 had barely any original income (the average annual income for this group was only £120). The group has few economically active people (only 1 in 18 households had someone in work) and nearly two thirds were retired. In contrast, the top fifth group had an average annual income of £22 300. Cash benefits are significantly progressive, (see Table 19.10) accounting for nearly all of the income of the bottom quintile group but only 3 per cent of the top group.

Table 19.10 Benefits as percentage of income, 1985

Quintile group	Cash benefits % of gross income	Benefits in kind % of final income
Bottom	96	35
2nd	49	28
3rd	13	21
4th	6	16
Top	3	10
Average of all households	16	18

(*Economic Trends*, July 1987)

Benefits in kind are also highly progressive. The receipt of health and education services forms a much higher proportion of the income of the poor than it does the better off. Expressed as a percentage of final income they account for over a third of the income of the bottom group but only 10 per cent of the top quintile.

We can see the overall impact of taxes and benefits in Figure 19.5. The spread of original incomes is considerably reduced by these policies. We use Gini coefficients, in Table 19.11, to provide a more detailed account. The Gini coefficient is a measure of the distribution of income; the lower the coefficient the more equally income is spread (refer back to section 17.6.2).

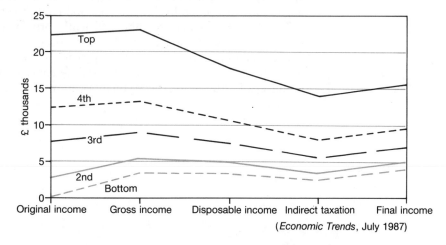

(*Economic Trends*, July 1987)

Fig. 19.5 Effects of taxes and benefits in 1985 (on quintile groups of households)

Table 19.11 Gini coefficients for each stage in the tax−benefit system

	1975	1985
Original income	43	51
Gross income	35	38
Disposable income	32	35
Income after cash benefits and taxes	33	38
Final income	31	34

(*Economic Trends*, July 1987)

We can see in Table 19.11 that the largest single impact on the distribution of income is achieved by cash grants, which reduces the Gini coefficient by 13 points in 1985. Income tax and NIC reduce the coefficient by a further 3 points but this is reversed when account is taken of the impact of indirect taxes. Benefits in kind provide a further more equal spread of income. The overall impact of taxation in 1985 was broadly neutral in its effect on distribution of income, with the main redistributional thrust coming from benefits. Comparison with 1975 reveals a less equal distribution of income. There is a large increase in the dispersion of original income mainly as a result of higher unemployment and the increased number of retired people. The operation of the tax—benefit system has ensured that the increase in the spread of final income is less marked than that of original income.

19.5 Local government

Most countries do not rely solely upon central government for public expenditure: some spending is the responsibility of lower tiers of government. In this section we consider the economic rationale for local government.

Market failure provides a prima facie case for government intervention; but why should local rather than central provision be preferred?

Firstly, there may be a better coincidence of benefits and costs at a local level. Leisure centres, street lighting, refuse collection, etc. confer benefits that are largely confined to a particular area. It seems more appropriate that decisions about resource allocation are taken at that level rather than by a national government with responsibility for a country, most of which is unaffected by a particular service (for example, a proposed leisure centre in a small town).

Secondly, preferences for publicly provided services may be more clearly revealed at a local level; local authorities are likely to be better informed than central government about the wishes of people in their areas. Local government may reveal preferences in another way: where there are differences in the range of services offered by different authorities, people may move to those areas which best meet their needs. Some will choose high spending/high tax areas, others the opposite. For some people social service provision will be all important, while for others, the standard of schools will be a priority. In this way resources may be allocated according to preferences of individuals. Compared with this, a standardized provision of services throughout the country would be sub-optimal and people would not be able to reveal their preferences by voting with their feet. This approach to local government and an explanation of its significance was first put forward by an economist, Tiebout. The **Tiebout model** achieves an optimum allocation of resources only under very restrictive conditions, for example, perfect information about what each authority provides, no costs of moving from one area to another and no externalities (which might allow people to live in one area and enjoy the benefits of another).

Thirdly, services may be more efficiently provided because local provision means a greater degree of accountability than may occur with a large and perhaps bureaucratic national administration. Diversity of provision among many local authorities also means that services are likely to be provided at different costs and this may help expose inefficient producers. Furthermore, successful innovations by one authority are likely to be copied by others.

20 The open economy

20.1 Introduction

The UK is a highly **open economy** with over a quarter of GDP exported and a similar proportion imported. The reasons why countries trade are considered in the first part of the chapter and the effects of **tariffs** are examined. The **balance of payments** has frequently been mentioned elsewhere in this book and here we provide a more detailed look at what it means. Since **exchange rates** were allowed to float in the early 1970s, their movements have attracted much interest. We explain various measures of the exchange rate and consider different explanations of their movements. We discuss the arguments for a **fixed exchange rate system** and compare this with a regime of **floating exchange rates**.

This chapter will:

- outline the importance of international trade to the UK economy
- explain the theory of comparative advantage
- show the main effects of tariffs
- explain what is meant by the balance of payments
- define real, nominal, bilateral and effective exchange rates
- outline the main theories of exchange rate determination
- consider the case for fixed versus floating exchange rates

20.1.1 Examination guide

Questions about the open economy for introductory courses most commonly look at the benefits derived from trade; tariffs and protection; and exchange rate systems. The first of these areas requires an understanding of the theory of comparative advantages; you should be prepared to explain it. A graphical approach, as used in this chapter, will avoid the pitfalls sometimes associated with numerical examples. You need to be clear about the main effects of tariffs and the arguments for and against protection. Many questions on exchange rates require you to discuss the advantages of fixed and floating rates; your arguments must be considered within a clear framework — a set of criteria is suggested in section 20.5.7.1.

20.2 International trade

20.2.1 International trade and the UK economy

International trade is very important to the UK: the value of exports and imports as a percentage of GNP is around 27 per cent. This is comparable to the position in West Germany but is nearly twice as large as the percentage in Japan. The USA has a large impact on the world economy because of its size, but it is a relatively **closed economy**, with exports accounting for around 10 per cent of GNP. The post-war period has seen a very rapid growth in world trade with most countries becoming very much more open. This has meant that **import penetration** has increased. In the UK imports of manufactures in relation to home demand rose from 16.6 per cent to 25.7 per cent during the 1970s. Although manufacturers exported a larger proportion of their output, the UK's share of world trade in manufactures declined from around 9 per cent in 1970 to 6 per cent in the mid-1980s.

Manufactures dominate UK trade in commodities, accounting for about 70 per cent of both exports and imports. **Raw materials** and **food** account for around 20 per cent of imports. The trend in the destination of UK visible exports reflects the UK's membership of the European Community (EC), with the share going to the EC rising from 36 per cent to 48 per cent between 1976 and 1986. By 1986 the EC accounted for more than half the UK's imports, as compared with 37 per cent a decade earlier and 28 per cent in the early 1970s. A notable feature of the UK's trading position is the importance of **invisibles**: transport, travel, investment income and financial services. The receipts the UK earns from invisibles are second only to the USA and the UK surpluses from these services are the largest of all countries except the USA.

20.2.2 The reasons for trade

Why do countries trade with each other? There are several explanations, but we will concentrate on one given more than 150 years ago by **David Ricardo**: the **theory of comparative cost** or **advantage**. This is an important principle which demonstrates the gains from trade in circumstances where they are not intuitively obvious. We begin by considering a position that is more straightforward: **absolute advantage**.

20.2.2.1 Absolute advantage

There will be circumstances when trade between countries seems obvious because one country has a clear advantage in producing a particular product. For example, we buy bananas from the West Indies because the resources we would require to grow them are much greater than those needed in the Caribbean. This type of advantage is reflected in the hypothetical data in Table 20.1.

Table 20.1

	Output per worker (units)	
	Bananas	Pottery
UK	10	20
WI	40	10

The output per worker with bananas is four times greater in the West Indies than in the UK; but UK productivity in pottery is twice that in the West Indies. In this case both countries can gain from concentrating on the product in which they have an advantage and trading with each other. World production of both commodities can be raised by reallocating resources in this way. Table 20.2 below shows the effect of shifting a worker from the production of bananas towards pottery in the UK and reallocating a worker in the opposite direction in the West Indies.

Table 20.2

	Bananas	Pottery	Movement of one worker
UK	−10	+20	From bananas to pottery
WI	+40	−10	From pottery to bananas
Net effect	+30	+10	

In this type of situation we say the West Indies has an absolute advantage in the production of bananas and the UK has an absolute advantage in the production of pottery. It is not surprising that specialization and trade occur in these circumstances. However, what is far less obvious is that there are similar benefits from such a situation when a country has an absolute advantage in both products.

In the example in Table 20.3, USA productivity is higher in both products *A* and *B* – that is, it has an absolute advantage in both.

Table 20.3

	Output per worker	
	A	*B*
USA	10	10
UK	2	8

As the USA is better at producing both products it would appear that it has nothing to gain from trading with the UK. However, its advantage in both products is not the same and, as we shall see, this is the basis for a gain to be made from trade. The superiority of the USA over the UK is much greater with product *A* than with *B*. We say that the UK has a **comparative advantage** in producing *B*. We can see this clearly if we examine the opportunity costs of producing the two products (Table 20.4).

Table 20.4

Opportunity cost of producing *A*
(cost of 1 unit of *A* in terms of units of *B*)

USA	1
UK	4

Opportunity cost of producing *B*
(cost of 1 unit of *B* in terms of units of *A*)

USA	1
UK	0.25

The opportunity cost of producing A is higher in the UK, where 4 units of B have to be sacrificed to secure 1 unit of A. In contrast, the UK can produce a unit of B at a lower opportunity cost – it only has to give up 0.25 units of A to obtain a unit of B whereas the USA loses 1 unit of A for every unit of B produced. It is the difference in these opportunity costs that provide the basis for gains from trade.

In Table 20.5 below we consider the effects of reallocating resources in the two countries.

Table 20.5 Reallocation of resources

	A	B	
USA	+10	−10	Movement of 1 worker from B to A
UK	−4	+16	Movement of 2 workers from A to B
	+6	+6	

A move towards specialization in A in the USA and in B in the UK shows overall gains. This increase in net output means there is an opportunity for **mutual gains from trade**. For example, if the countries established a trading ratio of 2 units of B for 1 unit of A, this would represent a better position for the UK because, as we have seen, its opportunity cost position involved giving up four units of B to obtain one unit of A. But the USA also gains, because it can now obtain 2 units of B for 1 unit of A, which is twice as good as its domestic opportunity cost position.

The principle we have illustrated is known as **comparative advantage**. It shows that countries can gain from international trade by specializing and trading in those commodities which they can produce at a lower opportunity cost, i.e. in which they have a **comparative advantage**. It is important to emphasize that this does not rely upon the existence of an absolute advantage. Indeed, a country could be a world leader in every product, but it would still be worthwhile for it to trade providing there were opportunity cost differences between itself and other countries. The principle is an important one which underlines the benefits from specialization and exchange and has a more widespread application than international trade. For example, the person who is both a leading surgeon and an expert gardener would be better off concentrating on surgery and employing a gardener because the surgeon is likely to possess a comparative advantage in medicine.

20.2.2.2 Market prices, exchange rates and comparative advantage

The **trading ratio** we used in our example to demonstrate the gains from trade is expressed as a **barter ratio** of 2 units of B for 1 unit of A. If barter were the basis of trade we might expect a mutually beneficial ratio such as this to be established because both countries can gain. But would the market system produce a set of prices which allows these gains to be realized? Generally, we can expect that, in the absence of obstructions, there will be a tendency for this to occur. We can extend our illustration to show how this might work (Table 20.6).

Table 20.6

	Output per worker		Unit labour costs Wage (US = $200) Wage (UK = £80)		Price in $		Exchange ratio
	A	B	A	B	A	B	
USA	10	10	$20	$20	$20	$20	
UK	2	8	£40	£10	$40	$10	£1 : $1
					$80	$20	£1 : $2
					$20	$5	£1 : $0.50

With wages $200 in the USA and £80 in the UK, the unit labour costs (i.e. the labour cost per unit of output) can be calculated by dividing the wage (i.e. cost per worker) by the output per worker. These ULCs are shown in columns 3 and 4. To keep the example simple we will ignore other costs and assume that prices are equal to ULC. Whether the USA will buy from the UK or vice versa will depend upon the exchange rate. Suppose the exchange rate is £1 : $1; then we can use this to convert sterling prices into dollars so we can compare prices. In this case product B would be exported from the UK to USA and product A would be imported by the UK. There are many other exchange rates which would produce the same result, but would market forces be likely to produce such a rate? We can answer this by considering the limits of mutually profitable trade. For example, if the exchange rate were $2 : £1 then there would be no price advantage to the Americans in buying from the UK; if the ratio went any higher both products would be cheaper in the USA so the UK would import both.

But with no products exported and both imported there would be enormous downward pressure on the exchange rate, pushing the rate below $2 : £1 (see section 20.5 for a more detailed discussion of exchange rates). At the other extreme of £1 = $0.50, both goods are on the verge of becoming cheaper in the UK compared with the USA and the pressure on the exchange rate would be in the opposite direction. From this simple illustration we can conclude that **market forces** will tend to push **exchange rates** to levels where the benefits of comparative advantage can be enjoyed.

20.2.2.3 Graphical illustration of comparative advantage

We can use a simple but dramatic diagrammatic approach to show the gains from comparative advantage. Table 20.7 shows the production possibilities of two countries, UK and USA, for two commodities, pottery and wheat.

Table 20.7 Production possibilities

	Pottery	Wheat
UK	60	30
USA	60	90

These are also shown in Figure 20.1(a) and (b). The straight lines mean that opportunity costs are constant and the slopes indicate that the opportunity cost of pottery in the UK (0.5 units of wheat) is less than the USA (1.5 units of wheat). The pre-trade positions are marked on Figure 20.1(a) and (b) as *A* for the USA and *B* for the UK.

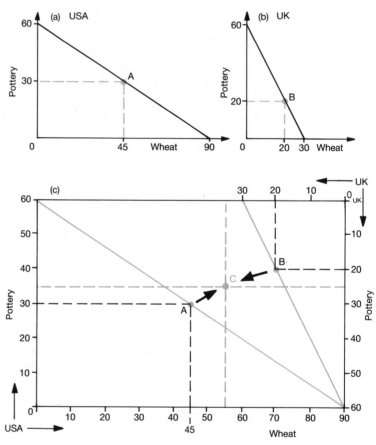

Fig. 20.1 Production possibilities – gains from trade

We can show the gains from trade if we turn the diagram of the UK position (Figure 20.1(b)) upside down so that its origin, 0_{U_K}, is at the top righthand side of what becomes a box in Figure 20.1(c). The USA has a comparative advantage in wheat and the UK in pottery. As we have simplified the illustration by assuming constant opportunity costs, specialization will be complete in both countries. So the USA puts all its resources into wheat production and the UK concentrates completely on pottery. The position after trade is established will depend upon preferences in the USA and UK and the exchange rate, but Table 20.8 shows a typical position.

The USA produces 90 units of wheat, 55 of which it retains for home consumption and 35 of which it exports to the UK. With the UK producing 60 units of pottery and keeping 25 for

Table 20.8

	USA		UK	
	Wheat	**Pottery**	**Wheat**	**Pottery**
Production	90			60
Export	35			35
Imports		35	35	
Home consumption	55	35	35	25
Pre-trade home consumption	45	30	20	20
Gain	+10	+5	+15	+5

the home market, the USA is able to import 35 units of pottery from the UK. The after-trade position is represented in Figure 20.1(c) by point C. This reveals that the USA has moved off its **production possibility curve** (which is impossible without trade) from A to C, increasing its consumption of both wheat and pottery. But this has not been achieved at the expense of the UK suffering reductions in consumption. Indeed, if anything the UK's position has improved even more dramatically. It has moved beyond its production possibility curve from B to C and it too has increased its consumption of both products. In this case the UK ends up consuming more wheat than it could possibly have produced before trade even if it had consumed no pottery and pushed all its resources into wheat production.

We have demonstrated an apparently impossible outcome: we have shown that although two countries are producing efficiently and the maximum amount that is possible with given resources (i.e. they are on their **production possibility frontiers**) that **specialization** and **trade** can improve the living standards of both. This graphical approach provides a simple way of illustrating the gains from trade arising from **comparative** advantage. You do not need to include numbers to illustrate the point in a figure:

1 Draw a box with the two production possibility curves (see Figure 20.2(a)). Select a point C between the two production possibility curves. This will be the post-trade position and the quantities can be marked off as in Figure 20.2(a).

2 Mark points A and B on the production frontiers but within the dotted lines drawn through point C, to show the pre-trade positions for the two countries (Figure 20.2(b)).

3 Indicate the before-trade (BT) and after-trade (AT) positions and the gains from trade (shaded rectangles) (see Figure 20.2(c)).

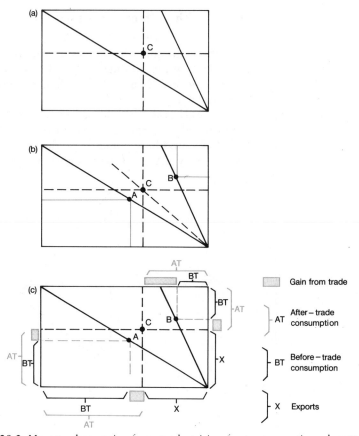

Fig. 20.2 How to show gains from trade arising from comparative advantage

20.2.2.4 Other reasons for trade

The **theory of comparative advantage** provides a major insight into the reasons why countries trade with each other. However, we need to make a few qualifications to the simplified illustrations we have given. First, we have ignored transport costs, which will affect the picture, particularly for high-bulk/low-value goods. Furthermore, in practice specialization will not be complete because opportunity costs will not be constant but will rise; so comparative advantage will cease at some point. We ignored **trade restrictions** (e.g. **tariffs, prohibitions, currency controls**) which will clearly shape the pattern of world trade.

Other factors should be taken into account when explaining world trade. Some countries **export goods** because firms there invented and patented them. Even in these cases if the opportunity cost of production is much higher than abroad it will pay the innovating firm to **locate production elsewhere**. Finally we have to recognize that there are a number of commodities which a country both exports and imports in significant quantities. This may not be inconsistent with the theory of comparative advantage because within a commodity classification, such as cars, there will be what amounts to different goods – for example, family saloons and luxury sports cars. However, there are cases where the products are very similar. Such trade arises from the desire of consumers for **choice**; because of the need for economies of scale in many industries, it is not always possible to provide a range of goods from within a country's boundary, hence the need for trade.

20.3 Tariffs

20.3.1 Tariffs and protection

There are a number of ways in which free trade between nations may be impeded. The most obvious, which we will concentrate on, is **tariffs**; but there are others. **Quotas** which set quantitative limits on the amount that can be imported have a similar effect to tariffs. **Currency controls**, which restrict the acquisition of foreign currency effectively limit imports and exports, thus providing protection to domestic producers. Protection may also arise through less obvious means. For example, **safety** or other **standards** may favour home producers. The arguments arising from the move towards standardization within the European Community are a clear sign that adopting a particular standard is not necessarily neutral in its effect on the manufacturers of different countries. Given the possible benefits from trade that we discussed in the previous section it is important to assess the effects of **protectionism**.

20.3.2 The effects of a tariff

The effects of a **tariff** are best considered with the aid of a diagram. In Figure 20.3 the supply curve shows the quantities domestic producers are willing to supply at different prices. If the world price of the product is P_1 and if the foreigners' supply is perfectly elastic then the domestic price will be P_1, OQ_4 will be demanded and OQ_1 will be produced by domestic firms with Q_1Q_4 imported. If a tariff of P_1P_2 were imposed then the new overseas supply curve would be perfectly elastic at a price of P_2. Here imports would have fallen from Q_1Q_4 to Q_2Q_3 and domestic production risen from Q_1 to Q_2. This is the **protective effect of the tariff** and shows how domestic producers gain from its imposition. Consumers will suffer because they have to pay higher prices and therefore consume less. A measure

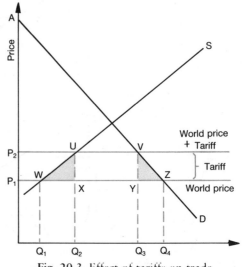

Fig. 20.3 Effect of tariffs on trade

of their reduced satisfaction is their loss of consumer surplus. This was equal to AZP_1 before the tariff; after it consumer surplus was AVP_2. The loss is, therefore, equal to P_1P_2VZ.

Some of the loss is offset by gains elsewhere. There is an increase in producer surplus P_2UWP_1 and there is the tariff revenue $UVYX$ which will provide benefits through tax cuts or increased government expenditure. But these benefits do not fully compensate for the loss. We are left with the shaded triangles, YVZ and WUX – these are known as the dead-weight loss. The represent a **net loss** to society from the **imposition of a tariff**.

20.3.3 Are tariffs justifiable?

As we have demonstrated, there are winners and losers from tariffs. To the person whose job has been preserved and for the firm which has been saved from bankruptcy, tariffs would seem to be justified. On the other hand the consumer would always like the opportunity to buy in the cheapest market. In assessing **tariffs** (and many of the arguments apply to other forms of protection) we shall take more of an overview.

The **overriding objection to tariffs** is that they prevent the full gains from trade being enjoyed and they involve some uncompensated losses, as we saw in the previous section. Society may decide that it prefers to accept a lower standard of living in order to gain some benefits from protection. It may, for example, wish to preserve certain key industries for defence purposes. **Adam Smith**, who favoured free trade, argued that governments should place 'defence before opulence'. Society may also wish to preserve some traditional ways of life and skills that are associated with certain threatened industries and might regard the cost of the tariff as an acceptable price to pay.

Infant industries are often put forward as an acceptable case for tariffs. The argument is that an industry in its infancy may not be able to withstand the pressures of international competition, so it requires some short-term protection; but when it becomes established it will demonstrate its **comparative advantage** and be able to stand on its own feet without the need for tariff support. In principle this is a reasonable argument. We are interested in maximizing gains over time, so there will be occasions when benefits in the long run will justify short-run costs. However, two doubts need to be raised. If there are clear benefits in the future from an industry, despite short-term losses, we would expect the market to recognize this and invest accordingly. Second, experience has shown that infant industries have a tendency never to grow up and resist any attempts to remove protection.

The **strategic/defence**, **social** and **infant-industry** arguments for protection are not necessarily best served by tariffs. A **subsidy** could achieve the same result. This would have certain benefits over a tariff: consumers would still pay world prices and would not lose consumer surplus in the way shown in Figure 20.3. However, taxation would have to be raised to pay for the subsidy (although there would still be a deadweight loss, it would be confined to WUX, thus avoiding the other net loss, associated with the tariff, YVZ). The tax–subsidy approach tends to make the cost of protection more visible than a tariff.

Tariffs may be imposed for **revenue-raising** purposes by some countries. This may be justified for some developing countries whose tax system is not well established and where tariffs are a more effective and least-cost method of raising revenue.

We have concentrated here on the **microeconomic resource allocation** aspects of tariffs. There may be a **macroeconomic argument** for tariffs as a means of overcoming a balance-of-payments constraint on the achievement of full employment – we consider this briefly in Chapter 20 (**Questions and answers**, Chapter 20, Essay question 1, answer 2(f)).

20.4 The balance of payments

20.4.1 What is the balance of payments?

The balance of payments is a set of accounts that records the transactions between one country and the rest of the world. As such it will always balance. We therefore need to explain what is meant by a balance-of-payments deficit/surplus. The current official presentation of the UK balance of payments is discussed in the next section. Here we use a hypothetical set of accounts, presented in a slightly different way, to illustrate certain key aspects (Table 20.9, overleaf).

The **visible balance** (sometimes referred to as the balance of trade) shows the difference between payments for imports of goods and receipts from exports. In this case there is a deficit of £400. The **invisible balance** refers to services (such as insurance, shipping, tourism, etc.), interest, profits and dividends. The two balances give us the current account. This is the balance which economists refer to most, though the press tends to give more prominence to the trade or visible balance. If economists speak of a deficit on the balance of payments without saying which balance they are referring to, it is usually the current account.

Table 20.9

	£
Visible balance	−400
Invisible balance	+200
Current account	**−200**
Investment and other capital flows	+50
Balancing item	+50
Balance for official financing	**−100**
Official financing	
Reserves (− additions to; + drawing on)	+50
Other official financing (+ borrowing; − repayments)	+50

Goods and services are only part of the total receipts and payments. In the UK over a third of the total money flows arise from investment and capital flows. These arise from purchases of foreign assets, physical and financial and lending. Similarly, there is a currency inflow as overseas people and institutions purchase our assets and we borrow from abroad. The **balancing item** arises because we cannot account for all the currency flows we record. So in our example, there is an unattributable net inflow, perhaps because of under-recording of exports.

We can now strike an overall balance – or what used to be called the **balance for official financing**. In this case it shows a deficit of £100. The remainder of the account, **official financing**, shows how this deficit is financed or, in the case of a surplus, how it is disposed of. In our example £50 of the deficit is met by running down reserves. These are the **official reserves** of **gold** and **foreign currency**. The remainder is financed by **official borrowing** – this could be from the **International Monetary Fund** or foreign governments.

The signs on these items need explanation. Notice that **drawing on reserves and borrowing** are indicated by a positive sign (adding to reserves and repayment of loans would be shown by a negative sign). This may seem odd, particularly in the case of reserves, but remember we are showing where we obtain money to finance a deficit, or in the case of a surplus, to what uses we put the money. Thus, **official financing** ensures that the balance of payments balances overall because the balancing item ensures that the balance for official financing equals official financing.

20.4.2　The UK balance of payments

Table 20.10 UK balance of payments 1986 (£million)

Visibles	
Exports	72 843
Imports	81 306
Visible balance	−8 463
Invisibles (balance)	
Services	+4 990
Interest, profit and dividends	+4 686
Transfers	−2 193
Current balance	**−980**
Transactions in external assets	
Overseas investment in UK	
Direct	−11 386
Portfolio	−22 870
Lending to overseas residents by UK banks	−53 898
Deposits and lending	
overseas by UK residents	−649
Official reserves	−2 891
Other external assets of central government	−535
Total transactions in assets	−92 229
Transactions in external liabilities	
UK Investment overseas	
Direct	5 420
Portfolio	8 202
Borrowing from overseas residents by UK banks	64 049
Borrowing from overseas by UK residents	
(other than banks and government)	3 644
Other external liabilities of central government	167
Total transactions in liabilities	81 482

(*Economic Trends Annual Supplement*, 1988)

Table 20.10 shows the UK balance of payments for 1986. At that time the visible balance deficit was the largest for the post-war period. Deficits on this balance are normal: it has been in surplus only six times in the 40 years from 1946 to 1986. Three of those occasions were in the early 1980s when large surpluses occurred, partly as a result of North Sea oil but also because of the severe recession which dampened the demand for imports. The invisible balance (discussed more fully below) has been in surplus every year since 1948.

The state of the current account shows greater variation, having been in deficit 15 times in the period 1950–87. Figure 20.4 shows the current balance as a percentage of GDP. In around half the years shown it has exceeded 1 per cent of GDP, but on only three occasions since the early 1950s has it been greater than 2 per cent. The first of these was in 1971, when the effect of the 1967 devaluation combined with a depressed economy in the early 1970s to give a large surplus. In 1974, before Britain became an oil producer, a quadrupling of oil prices and the after effects of faster growth produced a record deficit. Seven years later a deep recession and the revenue from North Sea oil gave the largest post-war surplus.

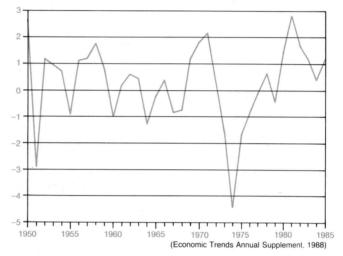

(Economic Trends Annual Supplement, 1988)

Fig. 20.4 Current account as percentage of GDP

The **transactions in external assets** and **liabilities** correspond to the investment and capital flows and official financing referred to earlier. **Transactions in external assets** means the purchase of these items and therefore involves a currency outflow. Direct investment is largely made up of net investment by UK companies in their overseas branches and subsidiaries, including the reinvestment of retained profits. **Real-estate transactions** are also included in this category. **Portfolio investment** refers to the purchase of stocks and shares.

Lending to overseas residents by banks includes **export credit**. **Official reserves** have been explained but note that the negative sign, as on the other items, means foreign assets are being acquired, so the reserves are increasing. Other **external assets of central government** includes intergovernment loans. The bottom part of the table shows the corresponding transactions in liabilities. Table 20.11 presents the invisible items in more detail.

Table 20.11 Invisible account, 1986 (£million)

	Credit	Debits
Services		
General government	508	1 907
Private sector public corporations		
Sea transport	3 339	4 276
Civil aviation	2 922	3 371
Travel	5 419	6 065
Financial and other services	12 804	4 383
Interest profits and dividends		
General government	760	1 668
Private sector	46 610	41 016
Transfer		
General government	2 135	4 370
Private sector	1 705	1 663
Total invisibles	76 202	68 719

(*Economic Trends Annual Supplement*, 1988)

You will notice the UK has a large surplus on **financial and other services**. This item includes insurance, banking and earnings from commodity trading and brokerage. Interest, profits and dividends have grown rapidly in the last few years, doubling between 1980 and 1986, twice the rate at which visible trade has grown. In part this reflects higher interest rates and increased capital mobility. The UK abolished exchange controls in 1979 and this removed obstacles to the purchase and sale of overseas assets by UK residents. **Private transfers** refers to gifts to and from the UK and **government transfers** include grants and subscriptions to and from international organizations, including the European Community.

20.5 Exchange rates

20.5.1 Real nominal and effective exchange rates

Anyone who has had a foreign holiday is well aware of what is meant by an exchange rate: it shows the value of one currency compared to another e.g. £1 to $2. The most quoted exchange rates, such as our dollar example, are **bilateral rates**. This is clearly the appropriate rate if we are interested in a holiday in the USA or we export to that country.

We are also concerned with knowing what is happening to exchange rates generally. We can obtain a measure of the **effective exchange rate** (*EER*) by taking the main exchange rates (R_1 to R_n) relevant to a country and weighting them according to their importance to a country's trade:

$$EER = w_1 R_1 + w_2 R_2 \ldots + w_n R_n$$

This means that if R_2 is relatively unimportant, as, for example, the Finnish mark is to the UK trade-weighted index, then the weight w_2 will be small; fluctuations in this exchange rate will have little impact on the **effective exchange rate**. In the UK this measure is known as the **sterling exchange rate index**. It has a 1975 base equal to 100. Movements in this index tell us if, overall, the pound is depreciating or devaluing. If the index rises, it means that the pound is appreciating against a **basket** of foreign currencies.

The **bilateral** and **effective exchange rates** we have described are known as **nominal exchange rates**, that is, they are not adjusted to take account of inflation rates. **Nominal rates** cannot really tell us about the competitive position of a country. For example, suppose the dollar:sterling rate halves from $2 : £1 over a period of time; it would be tempting to conclude that the UK has become much more competitive, as a product produced for £1 which formerly sold for $2, in the US, can now be sold for $1. However, we need to know what has happened to inflation in the two countries before we can say that the UK is in a more competitive position. If prices have doubled in the UK but are unchanged in the USA, then the UK competitive position has remained the same – the devaluation of sterling has simply offset the differences in inflation rates.

To measure competitiveness we need to calculate the **real exchange rate**. This adjusts the nominal exchange rates for alterations in prices. For example, the real dollar:sterling exchange rate (*RER$*) could be calculated in the following way:

$$RER\$ = R \cdot \frac{P_{UK}}{P_{US}}$$

A rise in the real exchange rate, which would signify a deterioration in UK competitiveness, could occur if UK prices, P_{UK}, rose faster than those in the US, even if the nominal exchange rate remained constant. Constant competitiveness would require, as our earlier illustration showed, a sufficient depreciation in the nominal rate to offset the faster rise in P_{UK}. The dramatic fall in UK competitiveness in 1979–80 occurred because a rise in nominal rates occurred at a time when UK inflation was above that of most of our competitors.

One difficulty that arises when measuring **real exchange rates** is knowing which price index to use. The **Retail Price Index** is not particularly suitable because it is chosen to be representative of the purchases of UK households and will include items which are not traded internationally. We could take an index of prices of goods which are traded on the world market. However, a worsening in competitiveness may not show up in prices if firms cut profit margins rather than raise prices in order to retain markets. One approach which is often employed is to take **relative unit labour costs** (*RULC*). So, for example, we could calculate a real dollar:pound exchange rate by adjusting the nominal rate by a ratio of UK to US unit labour costs:

$$RULC = R \cdot \frac{ULC_{UK}}{ULC_{US}}$$

We can construct a **real effective exchange rate** by adjusting the nominal effect rate for alterations in relative costs. Figure 20.5 shows these two measures. The rise in *RULC* in 1979 and 1980 shows the significant deterioration in competitiveness in those two years.

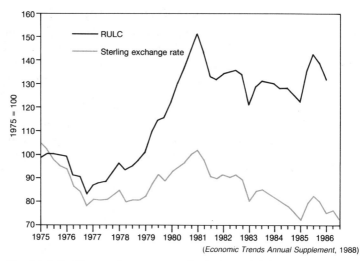

(Economic Trends Annual Supplement, 1988)

Fig. 20.5 Sterling exchange rate and relative unit labour cost, 1975–86
(RULC : normalized IMF index, 1975 = 100)

20.5.2 Determining the exchange rate

The exchange rates are determined in the foreign exchange markets by the demand for and supply of currencies. Figure 20.6 presents a highly simplified picture of this by looking at transactions between the USA and the UK. UK importers supply pounds on the foreign exchange market in order to acquire dollars to pay for imports. On the other hand, in the case of UK exports, US purchasers supply dollars and demand pounds. The direct and portfolio investment in the UK by Americans similarly gives rise to a demand for pounds. The demand for and supply of pounds are shown in the demand and supply diagram in Figure 20.7, where the vertical axis shows the price of a pound in dollars – that is, it represents the exchange rate. The slope of the demand schedule is not surprising because a lower exchange rate will make UK exports more competitive – e.g. a devaluation from $4:£1 to $2:£1 will permit the dollar price of exports to be halved, so we can expect to sell more goods and the quantity of pounds demanded will increase.

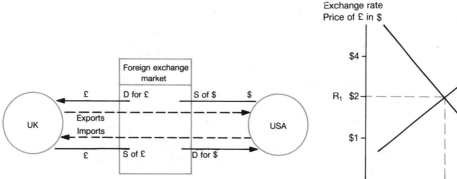

Fig. 20.6 Exchange rate determination   **Fig. 20.7** Demand and supply of sterling

The slope of the supply curve is not as straightforward. A devaluation will raise the sterling price of goods and reduce the demand for imports. Using our example, a $4 product which sold in the UK for £1 before devaluation will now sell for £2. Although we will import a lower quantity we will give a higher sterling price for each, so whether the quantity of pounds increases or decreases depends upon the elasticity of demand. In the case illustrated the demand is elastic because devaluation leads to a lower expenditure in sterling. The supply curve would have a negative slope if demand for imports were inelastic. That would not significantly affect the discussion below unless the supply curve were flatter than the demand curve. The evidence does not suggest this is the case and we shall ignore the possibility.

The **equilibrium exchange rate** is at R_1 where the demand for pounds is equal to supply. The equilibrium rate will clearly change if there is a shift in the demand or supply for sterling. However, what happens to the exchange rate depends on the **adjustment mechanism** or **exchange rate regime**. Several have been put into practice (we provide a brief historical outline later). It is helpful to be aware of two extremes: **fixed** and **floating**. We assess the merits and weaknesses of each in section 20.5.7.

20.5.3 Fixed exchange rates

Under a **fixed exchange rate system** the government agrees to maintain a given rate. We can see how this works in Figure 20.8. If the fixed exchange rate is R_1 and there is a decline in demand for sterling, from D_1 to D_2 (say because UK exports are less popular), there will have to be intervention in the foreign exchange markets if the exchange rate is to be maintained. In an unregulated market the rate would fall to R_2. However, if the central bank, on behalf of the government, buys up the excess supply of sterling (AB) with dollars then the exchange rate will stay at R_1. This excess supply of pounds is the counterpart of a deficit on the combined current and capital account (what we called the balance for official financing in section 20.4.1).

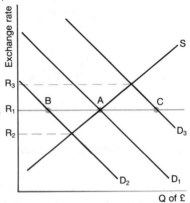

Fig. 20.8 Fixed exchange rate system

If it is a short-term phenomenon then there should be little problem in holding the exchange rate at R_1. But if it is a sign of a more fundamental problem then clearly there are limits to the ability of the authorities to buy up sterling because reserves are finite and the government has only limited powers to borrow foreign currency. At some stage the government will be forced to introduce policies to shift the demand and or supply curves to eliminate the deficit. For example, it could reduce domestic expenditure which would lower the demand for imports and shift the supply curve inwards. If it is unable or unwilling to adopt these policies it will have to give up its commitment to that exchange rate. This was the situation the Labour government found itself in in 1967 when it decided to devalue the pound from $2.80 to $2.40.

The government will need to intervene when there is excess demand (e.g. AC, when demand is at D_3 in Figure 20.8), as well as selling sterling. However, it is not quite symmetrical to the excess supply case, because there is not the same effective limit to acquiring reserves as there is on spending them.

20.5.4 Floating exchange rates

In the extreme case of freely floating exchange rates, there is no government intervention and no commitment to any given exchange rate parity. So in our illustration in Figure 20.8, a fall in demand would cause the market rate to decline to R_2 and a rise in demand lead it to increase to R_3.

Notice that when a new exchange rate like R_2 is established, the resulting devaluation eliminates the balance-of-payments deficit that existed at R_1. Clearly trade flows cannot respond as quickly as exchange rates can change, but they do not need to. Speculation should prevent the rate from going too low, because if it falls below a point that can maintain long-term equilibrium then speculators should buy up the currency because they can expect to make capital gains. In this way, excessive fluctuations should be prevented. However, experience suggests that markets do not always work well and there is often some intervention to smooth day-to-day fluctuations.

20.5.5 Other exchange rate regimes

There are many types of regime between these extremes of **fixed** and **floating**. Even a fixed exchange rate system permits small variations either side of the **stated exchange rate parity**. One approach which combines more flexibility with a fixed parity is to have **wide bands of fluctuations**. An alternative approach is the **adjustable peg system** which allows the central exchange rate parity to be periodically altered through devaluation and revaluations; the more adjustable, the more flexible the system is. A **crawling peg** regime might allow quarterly changes to the parity to occur. Even floating exchange-rate systems normally involve some intervention. This is known as **dirty floating** and the intervention may be based on a fixed but unannounced exchange rate target. Sometimes governments allow (or do not prevent) certain expectations to be formed. So it was widely understood, during 1987, that the Chancellor of the Exchequer wished to see the sterling:deutschmark rate stay close to, but below, DM3.

20.5.6 Historical outline of exchange-rate systems

20.5.6.1 Gold standard

The UK, like most major economies in the 19th century and early 20th century, belonged to the **gold standard**. This was a **fixed exchange rate system** in which each country fixed the price of its currency in terms of gold. The quantity of currency was generally tied or related to the countries' quantities of gold. The system was supposed to operate as follows: balance-of-payments deficits led to an outflow of gold and a contraction in the money supply which, according to the quantity theory of money approach, would lower prices and make the deficit country more competitive. The reverse occurred in a surplus country. The gold standard was disrupted by the First World War, and its operation in the 1920s was not so successful. Most countries abandoned it during the Great Depression.

20.5.6.2 Floating rates

Many countries operated under floating exchange rates after 1931. The regime gained a bad reputation from this period as countries desperate to lower unemployment became involved in competitive devaluations.

20.5.6.3 Bretton Woods adjustable peg

After the war there was an attempt to combine the stability benefits of **fixed exchange rates** with the **flexibility of floating rates**. The **adjustable peg system** was essentially the one we described earlier: fixed parities but with the provision to devalue/revalue. Countries were assisted in adjusting to balance-of-payments deficits by being able to borrow foreign currency to finance the deficit in the short term, thus preventing the need for sharp, deflationary action. The borrowing was from the **International Monetary Fund (IMF)**, with which all countries deposited a certain amount of gold and foreign currency. The **Bretton Woods system** coincided with a period of rapid growth in international trade. It may well have contributed to this expansion along with other factors such as trade liberalization and full employment policies.

The system had its critics. It turned out to be a system that was more fixed than floating – the UK, for example, stayed on the same exchange rate from 1949 to 1967. It tended to encourage **speculation** because the nature of the system meant that if an exchange rate was going to change it could be in only one direction. As a result, **speculation** became a **one-way bet**. The system relied heavily on the dollar as a **reserve currency** (that is, a currency which countries held, along with gold, as a reserve to be used for intervention in the exchange markets). By the end of the 1960s and early 1970s the world was awash with dollars (as a consequence of US budget and balance-of-payments deficits resulting from welfare and Vietnam War expenditure) and confidence in this key currency began to waver. By this time, too, fairly large differences in inflation rates were emerging and the **Bretton Woods system** could not cope with the strain.

20.5.6.4 Floating rates again

By 1972 the adjustable peg system had collapsed and most countries had adopted **floating exchange rates**. Some countries tied themselves to major currencies such as the dollar. In the EC, European currencies adopted various arrangements which led to the **European Monetary System (EMS)**. Various hopes have been expressed about a return to a more stable exchange rate system, but as yet no widespread alternative to floating rates has been adopted.

20.5.7 Fixed versus floating exchange rate systems

The superiority of fixed and floating exchange rate systems has been debated for decades. The experience of floating since 1972 has certainly led to many criticisms of the system. There is no doubt that it has coincided with a period of slower growth, increased unemployment and higher inflation as compared with the Bretton Woods era. It is highly debatable how far floating rates are to blame. The **floating exchange system** inherited serious problems of inflation and imbalance from its predecessor – indeed, that is why the former system broke down. The oil price shocks of 1973–74 and 1979 caused slower growth and higher inflation, and would have posed a strain on any system. The freer and more voluminous capital movements in the 1970s made life more difficult for exchange rate regimes. Nevertheless, the period of floating rates has produced a high degree of exchange volatility which some critics suggest has damaged the growth of world trade.

There are many facets to exchange rate systems which make it difficult to come to a clear-cut conclusion on the superiority of one over another.

20.5.7.1 Criteria for assessing exchange-rate changes

The following list of headings is helpful in assessing the strengths and weaknesses of different regimes.

1 Effect on trade
   Does the system encourage trade?
   Does it allow the gains from trade to be secured?
2 Stabilization policy
   How much freedom does the government have to pursue internal objectives?
3 Inflationary/deflationary bias
   Does the system tend to encourage inflation or does it tend to be deflationary (generate unemployment)?
4 Speculation
   Is speculation destabilizing?
5 Reserves
   Does the system make heavy demands on reserves?

20.5.7.2 Fixed exchange rates

1 A powerful argument in favour of **fixed exchanges** is the **certainty** it gives to **traders**. If there is no doubt about the exchange rate, fixing a price in dollars for the US market is not really any different from setting sterling prices. This should encourage **international trade**. However, if adjustments in the rate are permitted (as they were under the Bretton Woods system) then there will be occasions when there is uncertainty. For example, in the UK in the period 1964–67 there was a good deal of doubt about whether the rate would be maintained or devalued.

There may be a cost to keeping rates constant. If a country becomes uncompetitive because its rate of inflation is higher than its competitors, then this will tend to be damaging to trade. So there is a trade off between **flexibility** in the rate to **maintain competitiveness** and **fixity** to **reduce uncertainty** in selling prices.

2 An objection to **fixed exchange rates** is that they may constrain the use of **demand policies** to achieve internal objectives. So deficit countries will have to deflate demand to deal with balance-of-payments problems, unless they can devise an alternative to exchange-rate adjustment to improve competitiveness.

3 It is often suggested that fixed exchange rates display a **deflationary bias**. This is because there is an asymmetry to rectifying balance-of-payments imbalances. A deficit country, because of limited reserves (and borrowing powers), will be under more pressure to deflate than a surplus country which can, if it wishes, simply accumulate reserves. So although in the world as a whole deficits must equal surpluses, demand-reducing policies are not likely to be offset by an equivalent expansion in demand elsewhere.

Fixed exchange rates can only be maintained if inflation rates are similar so that countries which have a tendency to inflate relatively rapidly will be forced to try to contain the rate of price increases. On the other hand, low inflaters will tend to import higher inflation from other countries. It is generally argued that the net effect will be to keep the average rate of inflation below the rate that would occur under a more flexible regime.

4 If exchange rates were completely **fixed** then **speculation** would be **stabilizing**. But if there is provision for adjustment of the exchange rate, speculation is likely to be harmful. In these circumstances it will be a one-way bet, as we suggested earlier when considering the Bretton Woods system. For example, when a country displays the symptoms of being uncompetitive it will either devalue or leave the rate unchanged. Moving out of the currency will avoid capital losses if devaluation occurs, but if it does not the speculator can buy the currency again at around the same price.

5 There is a considerable need for **reserves** to maintain a fixed exchange rate system. This is necessary because policies to rectify a deficit will take time to impact. It is clear that there may be occasions when a currency comes under intense speculative pressure, for which very large reserves of foreign currency may be required.

The need for reserves would not be a problem if they were plentiful. Gold, the long established reserve and means of international payment, is physically incapable of growing at the same rate as world trade. As a result, key or major currencies such as the dollar have been used; but the acceptability of these very much depends upon the internal policies being pursued by the country in question. Attempts to find a **man-made substitute** for both gold and key domestic currencies have not been entirely successful. So a system that makes heavy use of **reserves** has some difficulties and generally needs arrangements or institutions like the IMF to help economize on reserves.

20.5.7.3 Floating exchange rates

Many of the arguments for and against floating rates are the opposite of those considered for fixed rates so we can be fairly brief in summarizing the main points.

1 A major objection to floating rates is the **uncertainty** that exchange rate volatility generates for **traders**. Empirical work has not been conclusive in establishing that it has damaged the volume of trade. Certainly there are ways of reducing the effects of volatility. Firms may cover themselves by buying in the forward exchange market or purchasing options on foreign currency and so eliminate the uncertainty for short-term contracts. They may hedge so that expected receipts are matched by payments in the same currency or spread their risk by trading and/or invoicing over a range of currencies. Firms may even engage in barter deals. Advocates of floating rates have argued that it is a system that allows the full benefits of trade to be secured because prices are free to move to reflect changes in cost conditions, whereas fixed exchange rates can mean that currencies become misaligned and this prevents efficient resource allocation.

2 Some critics of the **Bretton Woods system** who advocated floating rates argued that governments would be freer to pursue internal objectives, such as full employment, because movements in the exchange rate could deal with any **balance-of-payments difficulties**. Unfortunately the experience of the 1970s, at least for the UK, was not so agreeable. Depreciation of a currency makes exports more profitable and imports more expensive. The latter increases wage pressures and the former makes it more likely that wage demands will be conceded. The effect is that reflation/devaluation policies are likely to be inflationary.

3 It is generally felt that floating rates have an **inflationary bias**. The constraint imposed by fixed exchange rates on countries with an inflationary tendency is removed and although low inflation may be secured by other countries the net effect is likely to involve higher price rises.

4 The case on **speculation** has been argued both ways. As exchange rates can go up or down speculators have to be more circumspect than they were under the Bretton Woods system. It is suggested that they will form a view on the equilibrium exchange rate by taking account of available information on factors such as competitiveness, government policy, etc. If market rates tend to deviate from this they will intervene and in this way stabilize exchange rates around the equilibrium. Furthermore, as they are speculating with their own money there is a greater incentive to be correct in their expectations than there is for officials in a central bank or for the government. In contrast to this, there is the view that **currency speculation** has been **destabilizing** – causing large fluctuations. This approach suggests that speculators often take a very short view of what is likely to happen to exchange rates (in some cases hours, rather than weeks and months) and that **market sentiment** is subject to much volatility which is not well anchored to underlying economic indicators. It is probably the case that the critics of floating exchanger rates have tended to increase rather than diminish with our experience of this regime.

5 A **fully floating exchange rate system** does not require official **reserves** as there is no intervention by the authorities. The more **dirty** the float, the more **reserves** will be required.

20.5.8 European Monetary System

The **European Monetary System (EMS)** was formed in 1979 by members of the European Community. Although strictly the UK is a member of the EMS, it is not a participant in the exchange rate mechanism (**ERM**); the discussion in the 1980s about whether or not to enter the EMS was about joining ERM. We shall concentrate our brief discussion on the exchange rate mechanism and use this synonymously with the term EMS.

The ERM is similar to the adjustable peg system. Member countries agree to limit their exchange rate fluctuations to ±2¼ per cent (in the case of Italy, 6 per cent). A central rate for each currency is established against the **European Currency Unit (ECU)**. The ECU is a weighted basket of currencies whose weights are determined by a country's share in the Community's GNP. It helps establish the so-called **divergence indicators**, which are exchange-rate points which indicate that action has to be taken by affected countries. It is intended that both surplus and deficit countries should react once these warning points are reached. The action involves intervention in exchange markets and, where appropriate, adjustments in monetary policy or other economic measures. Credit facilities were set up to assist deficit countries. If these measures are insufficient then a currency can be realigned (i.e. devalued or revalued). There were 10 realignments between 1979 and 1987, though not all of these involved major currencies.

The **EMS** was intended to provide exchange rate stability for member countries. Although these European currencies are tied together they do float against other currencies such as the dollar, yen and sterling. How successful has the EMS been? This type of question is always difficult to answer because we do not know what would have happened if the EMS had not been established. However, it is fairly clear that fluctuations in nominal rates (bilateral and effective) within the EMS have been less since it was formed and show less volatility than major non-EMS currencies. A study by the London Business School (LBS) suggested this was not obtained at the cost of greater fluctuations in real exchange rates within the EMS. The LBS concluded that 'the EMS has been an island of relative stability'.

20.5.9 Exchange rate determination

Finally we consider why exchange rates change. There are a number of theories which try to explain the factors which determine exchange rates. We outline four main theories.

20.5.9.1 Purchasing power parity

We considered the purchasing power parity (PPP) theory in chapter 12 (section 12.5.1). It suggests that exchange rates movements (ΔR) will reflect differences in inflation rates, i.e.

$$\Delta R = \Delta P_W - \Delta P_{UK}$$

So if prices in the UK doubled compared with the rest of the world the exchange rate would halve. This approach suggests that the real exchange rate or competitiveness remains constant. Whilst significant differences in inflation rates are likely to be reflected in exchange rate changes, eventually experience shows that the PPP theory does not hold with any high degree of accuracy even over a number of years. PPP exchange rates can be calculated if it is assumed that PPP holds exactly and the exchange rate changes to reflect differences in inflation rates. This requires us to use a base-year exchange rate for the calculation. However choosing an appropriate base year is not an easy matter. If we can overcome this difficulty then a PPP exchange rate may give some broad indication of the direction in which the exchange rate may move in the future, though we cannot be sure about the timing of the change.

20.5.9.2 Monetarist theory of exchange rates

We can develop the PPP theory into a simple monetarist theory of exchange rates if we adopt a quantity theory view and regard inflation as being determined by the growth in the money supply:

$$\Delta R = \underset{\underset{\Delta M_W}{\uparrow}}{\Delta P_W} - \underset{\underset{\Delta M_{UK}}{\uparrow}}{\Delta P_{UK}}$$

According to this theory, changes in exchange rates are seen to occur because of difference in monetary policies, i.e.

$$\Delta R = \Delta M_W - \Delta M_{UK}$$

20.5.9.3 Traditional trade flow model

A more common explanation of exchange rate changes in the post-war period has been the traditional trade flow model. At its simplest the model suggests that exchange rate changes are a reflection of a country's current account position, balance-of-payments deficits leading to downward pressure on the exchange rate and surpluses causing currencies to appreciate. The balance-of-payments position may then be explained in terms of domestic policies (e.g. expansionary policies causing a rise in import levels leading to a deficit) and changes in world prices (e.g. a rise in commodity prices which produces a deterioration in the current account).

This approach had some appeal when capital movements were limited by currency regulations and restrictions, but it is far less convincing today when trade flows are extremely small compared with very large capital movements. This has led to more support being given to the fourth and last theory to be considered here.

20.5.9.4 Portfolio balance theory

In many ways this is a much more complicated theory than the previous three, but its basis is very straightforward. We should recognize that in the modern world individuals and institutions may hold portfolios of financial assets which can be represented in a simplified form as mixtures of money, bonds and foreign assets. Each portfolio will have an equilibrium position which will depend upon interest rates at home and abroad, and upon expectations concerning inflation, monetary and fiscal policy in the different countries. This is summarized in Figure 20.9.

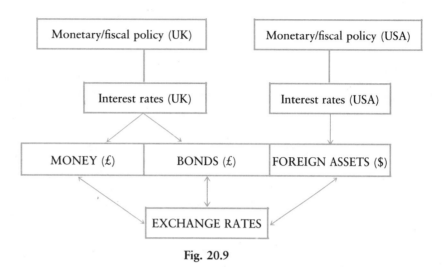

Fig. 20.9

Changes which disturb the equilibrium will lead to a readjustment of asset holdings which is likely to involve changes in the amount of foreign assets held. These will cause flows across the foreign exchanges and alterations in exchange rates. For example, an increase in the UK money supply will mean that individuals and institutions are holding more money than they want, so they will purchase more bonds and foreign assets. The latter, *ceteris paribus*, will lead to a decline in the exchange rate.

This approach allows a wide range of influences to be recognized as factors affecting exchange rates because of their impact on portfolios. For example, the current account position will affect the quantity of foreign assets held: an increase in a balance-of-payments surplus following new North Sea oil discoveries or higher oil prices will increase the number of dollars held and lead to portfolio adjustment causing the exchange rate to appreciate.

This chapter has covered a number of important topics relating to an open economy. International trade is becoming increasingly important to countries so it is important to understand the reasons for trade. Equally, for every trade flow there is a financial flow as money is paid to purchase these items. This side of activities lead us to consider a country's balance-of-payments and, in a world of changing exchange rates, to examine exchange systems. We have concluded that there are difficulties in finding an exchange rate system that allows a country to achieve both the full benefits of trade and an optimum allocation of international resources.

Questions and answers

Chapter 2

Self-test questions

1 The following information represents the production possibilities of an economy:

Production possibility	Good Y	Good X
A	50	0
B	49	1
C	45	2
D	40	3
E	32	4
F	20	5
G	0	6

(a) Plot the production possibility curve.
(b) Show on your diagram: a point of unemployed resources, R; an unobtainable point, S; economic growth, T.
(c) What are the opportunity costs of producing successive units of X (from 1 to 6)?
(d) Why do you think the opportunity costs are not constant?

2 Distinguish between positive and normative economics. Are the following statements positive or normative?
(a) An increase in tobacco duty will reduce consumption of cigarettes.
(b) The government ought to redistribute income in favour of the poor.
(c) The government ought to cut income taxes so that incentives may be improved and the growth rate increased.
(d) Market economies can be relied upon to produce full employment without the need for government intervention.
(e) The government ought to increase public spending if it wishes to reduce unemployment.

Answers

1 (a)

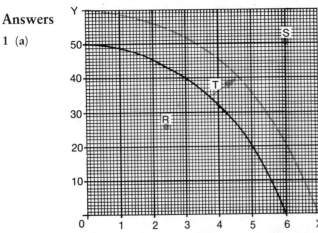

(b) See figure.   (c) 1, 4, 5, 8, 12 and 20
(d) Resources are not equally suited to the production of the goods. So moving resources from Y to X will reduce the production of Y by relatively small amounts in the first instance; but as resources are moved increasingly into X then the opportunity cost (in terms of Y) rises as those factors which are better suited to the production of Y (and are not very productive at X) are shifted to producing X.

2(a) Positive   (b) Normative

(c) Both: the relationship between tax cuts and incentives and growth is positive (because it is capable of being tested) but a tax cut recommendation is normative because it expresses a value judgement that higher growth is desirable.
(d) Positive, in principle, although statements like this correspond so closely to ideological positions (e.g. faith in markets and preference for individual rather than government solutions) that the division between normative and positive is not very clear.
(e) Positive, despite the use of the word 'ought', because the relationship between a public expenditure increase and a fall in unemployment is testable. But there is a qualification: the statement selects one policy solution (spending increases) from, presumably, a number of alternatives. This type of statement differs from (c) because here the statement itself does not express a value judgement but considers the means of achieving a particular objective.

Essay question

'Economics is the science which studies human behaviour as a relationship between ends and scarce means which have alternative uses.' (L. Robbins) Discuss.

This is a typical question on the scope and method of economics. We devoted some space to considering this particular quote in the chapter so here we concentrate on the essay plan.
1 Introduction
2 Scope of economics
(a) Explain the concepts of scarcity and opportunity cost.
(b) Illustrate the economic problem (e.g. using a production possibility curve).
(c) Explain and discuss Galbraith's criticism of the notion of scarcity.
(d) Consider the limitations of Robins's definition: well suited to orthodox microeconomics; it is not an accurate description of macroeconomics.

3 Method
(a) Explain what is meant by science and scientific method (refer to Popper, see section 2.4.1.2).
(b) Discuss differences between social and natural sciences.
(c) Outline the methods used by economists: theory and testing.
(d) Discuss the extent to which economics can be described as scientific and the problem of value judgements and ideology.

4 Conclusion

Chapter 3

Self-test questions

1 Explain the following terms:
(a) technical efficiency; (b) X-inefficiency;
(c) allocative efficiency.

2(a) Explain the functions performed by prices in a market economy.
(b) Illustrate how these functions would be performed in the case of a disease which damaged a significant amount of the Brazilian coffee plantations.

3 Are the following public goods, private goods or merit goods?
(a) beer; (b) lighthouses; (c) health services; (d) defence; (e) museums; (f) coal.

Answers

1(a) Technical efficiency is where resources are fully used in the technically most efficient way so that an economy is operating on its production frontier: maximum output is being obtained from given inputs.

(b) X-inefficiency is where practices and traditions prevent resources from being used to achieve maximum output.

(c) Allocative efficiency takes account of a community's preferences as well as technical possibilities and is the point on the production possibility curve where the satisfaction (or utility) of the community is maximized.

2(a) Rationing, information and incentives (see section 3.4.2).

(b) The disease would reduce the supply of coffee and prices would rise: this would ration the lower quantities and through higher prices transmit information about the state of the market to consumers who would, to some extent, substitute other beverages. There would be an incentive to areas unaffected by the disease to increase the number of coffee plants and firms would be encouraged to develop treatment for the disease or develop disease-resistant strains. Producers of substitute beverages would be encouraged to supply more of their product.

3(a) Private good; **(b)** Public good; **(c)** Merit good; **(d)** Public good. **(e)** Many are regarded as merit goods though some are private goods. **(f)** Private goods, despite the post-war period of nationalization – if you got this wrong, check on the definitions of public and private goods.

Essay questions

Many courses will test you at some stage (in coursework if not in the examination) on your understanding of how the market system operates. The question may be direct, as in our first illustration, or it may be applied to a particular area, as in the second question. We provide an outline of the answer for each but in both cases the analysis is essentially the same. The framework for the second answer would have been essentially the same if the examiners had chosen to set the question on some other area of the economy, for example, education or housing.

1 What are the advantages and disadvantages of the free market system as a means of allocating scarce resources? *ACCA*

1 Introduction

2 The market system
Briefly explain the economic problem of scarcity and how this involves choices about how resources are allocated. Explain what is meant by the market system:
(a) decentralized decision making by households and firms;
(b) price mechanism: how it rations scarce resources, transmits information and provides a system of incentives.

3 Advantages of the market system
(a) The price mechanism provides an efficient means of allocating resources. Give a brief illustration and compare with the problems of using planning to allocate resources.
(b) Consumer sovereignty: resources are allocated according to consumers' preferences.
(c) Competition: pressures for cost cutting and incentive to innovate.

4 Disadvantages
Explanation of market failure and why it means that an optimum allocation of resources will not be achieved:
imperfect information; monopoly; public goods; externalities; merit goods; dynamic efficiency; stabilization problems; distribution of income.

5 Conclusions
These should include an overall assessment of the arguments in 3 and 4 above and an indication of those areas where the market is relatively successful and those where state provision or intervention is more appropriate.

2 Compare and contrast the economic benefits of private and public provision of health services in the UK. *ICA*

1 Introduction

2 Health care in UK
(a) Brief background on the present provision for health in the UK: dominance of NHS.
(b) Financial problems of NHS: underfunding and excess demand (waiting lists).
(c) Current debate over role of private health care.

3 Arguments for state provision
(a) Merit good: a widely held view is that in a civilized society health care should be available to all. Illness is not evenly distributed and a caring society looks after those who are unfortunate enough to require treatment.
(b) Distribution of income: this relates closely to (a) and refers to the need to ensure the poor have access to health care.
(c) Monopsony (sole buyer) powers: the dominant position of the NHS (or state provision) means that inputs, materials and labour, can be obtained at lower prices.
(d) Economies of scale: the NHS can achieve economies of a large-scale organization, e.g. management, training, research.
(f) Imperfect information: consumer ignorance means market provision is inappropriate. State provision allows doctors the opportunity to decide treatment on medical grounds.
(g) Public good: most of the health service is *not* an example of a public good because non-payers can be excluded from the benefits but some aspects (e.g. public health and vaccinations) do fall into this category.
(h) Externalities: the benefits of good health are not confined to those receiving treatment but affect their families, firms and society generally.

4 Arguments against state provision
(a) Inherent underfunding problem: public will resist tax increases to pay for health yet demand greater provision. This is linked with
(b) Zero pricing (or free health service): this tends to overstimulate demand to a point where costs exceed benefits. This may produce or exacerbate excess demand but, more importantly, may lead to inefficient resource allocation as consumers are not aware of the costs. However, as consumers may not be aware of the benefits either, efficient resource allocation requires those who make the decisions to know what the costs are.
(c) Monopoly position: may lead to inefficiency and lack of orientation towards the consumer.

5 Arguments for private provision
(a) Links benefits to payment: this will help overcome problems 4(a) and 4(b) above.
(b) Competition will produce efficiency benefits of lower costs, more innovation and greater attention to what consumers want.
(c) Strengthens market incentives: if people get better health care if they pay more for it then this will increase the incentive to work harder because the rewards are greater, just as they are with other goods and services, e.g. housing, food, transport, etc.

6 Disadvantages of private provision
(a) Distribution: problem of those on low incomes.
(b) Problem of those with long-term illnesses.
(c) Consumer ignorance: unnecessary operations may be performed in order to maintain hospital/doctors' income.
(d) Competitive waste: more resources are likely to be devoted to promotion and marketing and there may be spare capacity in hospitals.
(e) Public good/externalities: where these conditions exist then private provision will not properly address them (see 3(g) and 3(h) above). However, some externalities may be dealt with, e.g. potential losses to firms because of illness may lead them to help finance health provision.

(f) Problems of private insurance: private health provision would involve the extensive use of private insurance. However, there are difficulties here because consumer ignorance may lead to under-insurance. Insurance companies would not cover high-risk groups or long-term illness. Insurance may lead to those who are insured not taking proper care of themselves and may involve expensive and unnecessary treatment because it will be covered and paid for by the insurance company.

7 Conclusions

Assess and summarize the arguments which centre on issues of equity and efficiency. Compromise positions are possible, where state provision has certain responsibilities and the private sector has a significant role. The NHS could remain as the major provider of health care but parts of the health service might be privatized (e.g. laundry and catering services). It is possible to introduce changes to the present state provision which would address some of the disadvantage of the NHS and mimic some competitive aspects of the market economy.

Chapter 4

Self-test questions

1(a) What are the main factors which affect the demand for a product?
(b) What are the main factors which affect the supply of a product?
(c) 'As firms will not produce goods if there is no demand, one of the determinants of supply must be demand.' Why is this incorrect?

2 Using the following data, answer the questions below:

Price £	Quantity demanded	Quantity supplied
6	20	65
5	24	60
4	30	50
3	40	40
2	60	30
1	120	0

(a) What is the equilibrium price?
(b) Describe the market position when the price is £2; £4.
(c) With reference to the demand schedule, how much would total expenditure vary as prices changed? What does this tell us about the price elasticity of demand?
(d) If a rise in income caused consumers to demand 20 more of the commodity at every price, what would the new equilibrium price and quantity be?
(e) If the government were to act as a sole buyer from producers and sole seller to consumers and if it guaranteed to producers to buy output for £5:
  (i) What quantity would it purchase and how much would it cost?
  (ii) What price would it have to charge consumers to sell all of this output?
  (iii) What would its net gain or loss on the intervention be?
  (iv) Assuming that any costs of the scheme were paid for through taxation, could we decide whether consumers were better or worse off because of government intervention?

3 The imposition of an expenditure tax leads to less being demanded and the lower demand causes prices to fall, so the effect of taxes is to lower prices.' Why is this statement wrong?

Answers

1(a) Price of the product, other prices, income, expected prices, tastes.
(b) Price of the product, other prices, factor prices, technology and other factors (e.g. weather, legislation).
(c) The statement is incorrect because the influence of demand is through its effect on price and that is already included as a determinant of supply. The point can be more clearly understood

if it is appreciated that we can draw a supply curve (showing the quantities that firms are willing to supply) without reference to demand.

2 (a) £3 **(b)** (i) excess demand; (ii) excess supply.
(c) No change; this means the demand curve has unit elasticity.
(d) £4, 50 units
(e) (i) 60 units at a cost of £300; (ii) £2; (iii) loss of £180; (iv) The total cost of the scheme to the consumer is £300: £120 that is paid for the product plus £180 in taxation. In other words, the consumer is paying, in effect, £5 each for the quantity of 60 units. In general terms we can conclude that consumers are worse off because this is a point off their demand curve, i.e. a position that they would not have voluntarily chosen; if they had to pay £5 they would wish to purchase only 24 units. However, we need to consider the distribution of the costs of taxation and who benefits from subsidized prices. The utility loss to tax payers may not be the same as the utility gain to consumers of the product. However, we have no scientific way of measuring this. The administrative costs of the scheme need to be set against any benefits.

3 This statement reveals a confusion between movements along the schedule and shifts of the demand curve. Higher taxes are likely to raise the equilibrium price and consumers will move up their demand curve and reduce the quantity they demand. It will not cause the demand curve to shift, so the suggestion in the quote that 'the lower demand will cause prices to fall' is wrong in this context.

Essay questions

1(a) Define each of the following terms: price-, income- and cross-elasticities of demand. Describe briefly the factors which affect each of them.
(b) Below is given the demand schedule for a product.

Price (£ per unit)	Demand (units per week)
10	400
9	500
8	600
7	700
6	800
5	900
4	1000
3	1100

Calculate the price elasticity of demand and comment on your results when
  (i) the price is reduced from £9 to £8 per unit;
  (ii) the price is reduced from £5 to £4 per unit.   ACCA

The structure of the answer to a question like this is not really a problem because the question itself defines it; but make sure you answer all parts. So in part **(a)** you need to describe the factors which affect the three elasticity concepts as well as defining them, and in part **(b)** do not overlook the need to comment on the results.

Part (a)

Introduction: Elasticity is concerned with responsiveness to changes.

$$\text{Price elasticity} = \frac{\% \text{ change in quantity demanded}}{\% \text{ change in price}}$$

Explain elastic, inelastic and unit elasticity.
Elasticity will depend on:
  (i) the availability of substitutes (the fewer the substitutes the more inelastic demand);
  (ii) the proportion of total income spent on the good (the smaller the proportion the lower the price elasticity).

$$\text{Income elasticity} = \frac{\% \text{ change in quantity demanded}}{\% \text{ change in income}}$$

Distinguish between normal goods where income elasticity is positive and inferior goods where an increase in income leads to a lower demand. Income elasticity will depend on standard of living and preferences. For example, it is only when incomes achieve a certain level that eating out, foreign holidays and second homes become highly responsive to income.

$$\text{Cross-elasticity} = \frac{\%\ change\ in\ quantity\ demanded\ of\ X}{\%\ change\ in\ price\ of\ Y}$$

Explain substitutes and complementary goods. Cross-elasticity: depends on how close goods are as substitutes and complements.

Part (b)
(i) 1.8; demand is elastic.
(ii) 0.6; demand is inelastic.

2(a) Explain briefly the difference between
(i) increases in supply and extensions in supply;
(ii) decreases in supply and contractions in supply.
(b) Explain the effects of the following changes on the demand for chocolate:
(i) a fall in the price of chocolate;
(ii) a health campaign that claims that chocolate makes you fat;
(iii) a rise in the price of chocolate substitutes;
(iv) a fall in consumers' income;
(v) an increase in the wages of chocolate workers.   *ACCA*

Part (a)

This refers to the distinction between a movement along the supply curve (extensions and contractions) and shifts of the schedule (increases and decreases in supply). The former occurs when the price of the product changes and its effect on the quantity supplied is shown by the supply curve. Shifts in the supply curve occur when other influences on supply alter (changes in other prices, factor prices, technology, etc.). Diagrams to illustrate the distinction would be helpful.

Part (b)

This requires a brief explanation of each point, preferably accompanied by a diagram.
(i) This will involve a movement down the demand curve.
(ii) This will cause an inward shift in the demand curve.
(iii) Consumers will substitute chocolate for the higher priced competitive products, so the demand for chocolate will shift outwards.
(iv) The response to lower income will depend on whether chocolate is a normal or inferior good. Assuming it is the former, the demand curve will shift inwards.
(v) The change in chocolate workers' wages will affect the supply of chocolate not the demand. The supply curve will shift inwards and through its interaction with demand will in all likelihood raise equilibrium price; but the demand curve will not be directly affected.

Chapter 5

Self-test questions

1 Trace the effects, on the markets listed below, of a disease which severely affects the supply of potatoes:
(a) potatoes; (b) fish and chips; (c) Chinese take-aways; (d) fish; (e) cod liver oil; (f) rice.

2 Using the data in the table:

Price (£)	Quantity demanded	Quantity supplied
5	20	65
5	24	60
4	30	50
3	40	40
2	60	30
1	120	0

(a) Show the effect of an imposition of a sales tax of £2 per unit. How does the equilibrium price and quantity change?

(b) What is the tax revenue received by the government?
(c) What is the incidence of the tax, i.e. how is the tax burden shared between the consumer and producer?

3 When a sales tax is imposed, under what circumstances:
(a) would the price rise by the amount of the tax?
(b) would both equilibrium price and quantity be unaffected?

4 Why has the Organization of Petroleum Exporting Countries (OPEC) failed to maintain high prices for its oil?

Answers

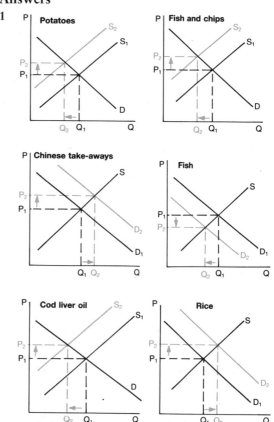

1

2(a) From £3, 40 units to £4, 30 units (b) £60
(c) Price to the consumer is raised by £1 and the after-tax price to the producer is reduced by £1.

3(a) If demand were perfectly inelastic or supply were perfectly elastic. (b) If supply were perfectly inelastic.

4 In the 1970s OPEC controlled a significant proportion of the supply of oil. In the short run demand and supply were highly inelastic. But in the longer run demand became more elastic as users substituted other energy sources and installed energy-saving methods and technology. In the longer run, too, the supply was more responsive and the high price encouraged the exploration and exploitation of other oil fields. In time this has meant that OPEC's share of output has diminished. This, combined with attempts by some members of the cartel to increase output beyond their quotas, led to the oil price collapse of the mid-1980s.

Essay questions

1 It is well established that if left to the free market, the prices of agricultural products and hence farm incomes will fluctuate widely. Describe the methods which may be used to stabilize farm prices and incomes, indicating the advantages and disadvantages of each.   *ACCA*

This topic is fairly well covered in the chapter so we confine the answer to a plan of the main points.

1 Introduction

2 Price and income fluctuations
(a) Price fluctuations occur because of:

(i) variation in supply (weather, disease);
(ii) the cobweb effect: many uncoordinated producers;
(iii) inelasticity of demand and supply in some cases (see 5.6.2.2.). For perishable products the difficulty of storage means that the supply curve will be inelastic in the short run.

(b) The extent to which incomes will fluctuate as a result of price variations will depend on the price elasticity of demand. For example, if it had unit elasticity then incomes would not change because expenditure would be constant.

3 Price stabilization schemes
(a) If supply can be controlled then prices can be stabilized, providing demand can be forecast.

Advantages:
(i) this provides coordination in a market where there are many producers and can be used to overcome the cobweb effect;
(ii) this can be used to regulate income.

Disadvantages:
(i) the problem of forecasting demand;
(ii) fluctuations due to weather cannot be prevented;
(iii) it is difficult to coordinate producers and ensure compliance.

(b) Intervention buying and selling can maintain a price by buying excess supply when harvests are plentiful and selling from stocks when poor harvests cause excess demand. Income stabilization will require some price fluctuation unless demand elasticity equals one (see section 5.6.3.1 and Figure 5.8).

Advantages:
(i) can respond to variations in supply due to weather;
(ii) in the short term does not require forecasts as intervention is simply adjusted to stabilize prices according to market conditions (but see disadvantage (i) below).

Disadvantages:
(i) If the price is stabilized around a level above the average equilibrium then stocks will accumulate (food mountains). To prevent this the intervention board needs to be able to estimate average equilibrium price.
(ii) Cost of storage of buffer stocks: sufficiently large stocks are needed to cope with a series of poor harvests.

4 Deficiency payments
This is a system of subsidies to farmers to give them a guaranteed price, while prices paid by the consumer can be equal to world prices (see section 5.6.3.2).

Advantages:
(i) no accumulated stocks storage costs;
(ii) consumer pays low (market) prices;
(iii) cost of scheme is fairly explicit.

Disadvantages:
(i) cost can be high, depending on the level of the guaranteed prices;
(ii) taxes must be raised to pay for the scheme;
(iii) does not stabilize prices to the consumer.

5 Import levies and export subsidies
Import levies and export subsidies are means of supporting a country's agricultural sector which will affect prices and incomes.

Advantages:
(i) lower tax costs than deficiency payments.

Disadvantages:
(i) prices to the consumer will rise above world prices;
(ii) intervention buying is required if prices are set above equilibrium.

6 Conclusion

2 Many governments impose controls on rents of private property with the objective of assisting low-paid workers. What are the likely consequences of such policies?   *ACCA*

1 Introduction
Rent controls were introduced in the First World War when around 90 per cent of all housing was privately rented. This sector has now shrunk to around 13 per cent, with owner occupation accounting for more than a half and council housing for nearly a third of the housing stock. Rent controls are common in most countries as a means of helping and protecting the poor.

2 Rent controls
(a) Explain rent controls. Use a supply and demand diagram (see Figure 5.3).
(b) Explain excess demand; this means waiting lists.
(c) Rent controls are usually accompanied by legislation to give security of tenure.

3 Effect on supply
(a) Short run: supply will be highly inelastic so the availability of rented property will be little affected but –
(b) Long run:
(i) Supply will be more elastic and the quantity of rented property will be reduced as it is less profitable and attractive to landlords. *Ceteris paribus*, this will increase excess demand and mean that it is more difficult for prospective tenants to find property.
(ii) In addition to lower rents, security of tenure legislation may make renting property even less attractive to landlords and the supply curve may shift inwards.

4 Overall effect on the housing market
The long waiting list for private rented property will increase the demand for council house accommodation and owner occupation. Security of tenure combined with waiting lists will tend to reduce the mobility of labour.

5 Distributional effects
To the extent that tenants are poorer than landlords, those who remain in controlled property will gain. However, those who are unsuccessful will be homeless, forced into higher rented uncontrolled property or having to seek owner occupation.

6 Conclusion
Rent controls reduce the size of the private rented sector and this poses problems for those seeking housing but offer benefits to successful tenants. There could be a brief reference to alternative ways of assisting the poor.

Chapter 6
Self-test questions

1 Which of the following would be included in the UK national income accounts?
(a) coal miners' wages
(b) concessionary coal received by coal miners
(c) tips paid to waiters
(d) wages of domestic servants
(e) housework
(f) food produced and consumed on farms
(g) purchase of company shares
(h) income of stockbrokers
(i) unemployment pay

2 Using the hypothetical data in the table, calculate the following:
(a) Total Final Expenditure   (d) GNP at factor cost
(b) GDP at market prices   (e) National Income
(c) GDP at factor cost

	£
Consumer expenditure	100
General government final consumption	50
Gross fixed capital formation	40
Value of physical increase in stocks	10
Exports	60
Imports	50
Taxes on expenditure	20
Subsidies	10
Net property income from abroad	25
Capital consumption	20

3 Distinguish between the Retail Price Index and the Consumer Expenditure Deflator.

4 The figures in the table are the nominal value of the student grant and the Retail Price Index (RPI) for the years shown. Calculate the real value of the grant and express it as an index number with 1962 = 100. What would the grant have been in 1986 had grant payments kept pace with inflation since 1962? Why is the RPI not an ideal index in this context. How could it be improved?

Year	Student grant (£)	RPI
1962	320	39.3
1965	340	43.4
1970	380	54.2
1975	740	100.0
1980	1430	195.6
1985	1830	276.8
1986	1901	286.3

Answers

1 All except (e), (g) and (i). (e) is not traded and it would be difficult to provide a value for it. The value of dealings in financial assets (g) is not counted as output as they are not goods and services. However, stockbrokers provide a service by buying and selling on our behalf so their incomes are counted. (i) is a transfer payment and is not included because it would involve double counting.

2 TFE = £260; GDP at market prices = £210; GDP at factor cost = £200; GNP at factor cost = £225; National Income = NNP at factor cost) = £205.

3 Technically the RPI is a Laspeyre index (using base quantities and current prices) whereas the CED is a Paasche index (using current quantities but base-period prices). The latter is an implicit deflator and is calculated by dividing consumer expenditure in current prices by consumer expenditure at constant prices. The CED therefore covers all consumer expenditure; the RPI does not include the expenditure of the top 4 per cent of incomes and it excludes those households who rely for more than 75 per cent of their income on state benefits and pensions (about 14 per cent of households). One particular item is treated differently by the two indices: owner-occupied housing. The cost of housing in the RPI is based on mortgage interest payments whereas in the CED imputed rents are used.

4

Year	Student grant	RPI (1975 = 100)	Real value of grant 1975 prices (1962 = 100)		Value of grant to maintain 1962 value (£)
1962	320	39.3	814.2	100.0	320
1965	340	43.4	783.4	96.2	353
1970	380	54.2	701.1	86.1	441
1975	740	100.0	740.0	90.9	814
1980	1430	195.6	731.1	89.8	1593
1985	1830	276.8	661.1	81.2	2254
1986	1901	286.3	664.0	81.6	2331

The RPI is not very suitable because it is not representative of a typical student's expenditure. Constructing such an index would involve surveying a sample of students to discover the relative weights of goods and services they purchase (presumably books, beer and chips would be more significant than in the RPI), then collecting regular information on the prices of these items.

Essay question

What problems are there in measuring a country's national income? To what extent is GNP a good measure of economic welfare?

Problems of national income accounting
a) A major problem is deciding what constitutes output and what should therefore be counted as expenditure, output and income. The response to this is partly one of principle but it is also pragmatic because some items are difficult or impossible to measure.

(b) There are problems in compiling the national income data:
(i) need to avoid double counting;
(ii) missing data: data are not available on every single item of output or every income, so surveys are used and estimates are made;
(iii) inaccurate and unreliable data;
(iv) mistakes in processing and transforming data: data are not always available in the form required by the national income accountant so they have to be processed and distortions may enter at this stage;
(v) transforming data from nominal to real terms poses difficulties and can give a misleading picture, e.g. using 1980 prices to present constant price GNP when relative prices have changed significantly;
(vi) depreciation or capital consumption data is not available in a satisfactory form so there are serious difficulties in obtaining accurate measures of net product and national income.

2 GNP as an indicator of economic welfare
GNP tends to underestimate the welfare benefits of economic activity (see (a) to (c) below) and to overestimate them (see (d) to (f) below). Making comparisons over long periods of time poses particular difficulties.

(a) Non-marketed goods and services are generally excluded, yet they generate benefits, e.g. housework, do-it-yourself.

(b) Leisure confers benefits yet is not explicitly counted in GNP; so an increase in productivity that allowed a society to enjoy the same quantity of goods and services but work fewer hours would, as far as the national income accounts were concerned, imply no change in economic welfare because GNP was unaltered.

(c) Quality of life benefits: in addition to leisure there will be other benefits that are associated with the growth of GNP but are not included in it, e.g. reduction in infant mortality.

(d) Amenity loss and the production of 'bads': account should be taken of these because they affect economic welfare, e.g. pollution. Appropriate deductions, in principle, ought to be made from GNP.

(e) In some cases resources will be devoted to remedying amenity loss but this activity will raise GNP without an equivalent rise in welfare because it is simply directed at keeping the stock of amenities intact. This expenditure ought therefore to be treated like capital consumption and be deducted from GNP when trying to obtain a measure of welfare.

(f) Capital consumption should be deducted from GNP when trying to obtain a measure of economic welfare. There are problems in obtaining an accurate measure. Some economists have suggested that the notion of capital consumption should be applied to human capital (i.e. the labour force), in which case much of the expenditure on education should be regarded as payment necessary to keep the stock of human capital intact.

(g) There are particular difficulties in using GNP to indicate welfare changes over time. There are likely to be important 'quality of life' changes, both benefits and costs, associated with significant changes such as urbanization, the decline of the extended family, and the transport revolution that has made people much more mobile. These effects are almost impossible to quantify but we should be aware of them. Some changes in GNP will certainly be misleading, for example the breakdown of the extended family, in which ageing grandparents would have been looked after by younger members of the family. Increasingly, older people are now being looked after in nursing homes, hospitals and by local authorities. As these are counted as part of national income but family care is not, some of the increase in GNP is overstated. There is also a problem arising from new products which make comparisons over time difficult.

Chapter 7
Self-test questions

1 Indicate which statements most correctly complete the sentences.

(a) If the consumption function is represented by the equation $C = bY$, then:

(i) the APC falls as income increases;

(ii) the MPC falls as income increases;

(iii) the APC equals the MPC;

(iv) the APC is greater than the MPC.

(b) The marginal propensities to consume and save:

(i) always sum to one;

(ii) are equal to each other;

(iii) sum to one in a two-sector model;

(iv) are equal to the respective average propensities.

(c) If the MPS = 1 then a fall in investment spending leads to:

(i) a decline of equal value in the equilibrium level of income;

(ii) no change in equilibrium income;

(iii) an indeterminate change in income;

(iv) an unending downward spiral of income.

2(a) Explain what is meant by equilibrium when referring to the general level of output and employment.

(b) What will be the effects on output and employment of each of the following:

(i) an increase in investment;

(ii) an increase in imports.   ACCA

3(a) Why does a change in the marginal propensity to import occur?

(b) What is the effect of a fall in the marginal propensity to consume which is matched by an equal rise in the marginal propensity to import?   ICA

Answers

1 (a) (iii); (b) (iii); (c) (i).

2(a) Equilibrium means that there is no tendency for output and income to change; planned expenditure is equal to the planned output of firms. It is normally expressed by:

$$\text{Income } (Y) = \text{Expenditure } (E)$$
$$\text{or} \qquad Y = C + I + G + X - M$$
$$\text{Withdrawals } (W) = \text{Injections } (J)$$
$$S + T + M = I + G + X$$

(b) (i) Assuming the economy is operating with spare capacity an increase in investment will raise output. It raises output by a larger amount than the increase in investment spending because of the multiplier effect. The size of the multiplier effect will depend on the marginal propensity to withdraw.

(ii) An increase in imports involves a higher level of withdrawals from the circular flow and will lead to a fall in aggregate demand, output and employment. The multiplier effect will mean that the effect on income is greater than the original change in imports.

3(a) The marginal propensity to import (MPM) is the ratio of the change in imports to the change in income. It can change for any of the following reasons:

(i) a change in competitiveness because of exchange rate changes or alterations in relative costs due to differences in inflation rates or productivity changes);

(ii) alteration in trade barriers;

(iii) increased specialization and desire for choice (e.g. motor cars) which means most countries have tended to experience increases in MPM;

(iv) degree of spare capacity: in the short term the MPM may increase if an increase in demand occurs when there is little or no spare capacity. Similarly, an increase may result from a sudden and sharp rise in demand to which domestic producers are unable to respond quickly.

The size of the multiplier will be affected by a change in the

MPM. There will also be balance-of-payments consequences of the change: a higher MPM will mean that a given growth of income will produce a larger volume of imports requiring a faster growth in exports if balance-of-payments deficits are to be avoided.

(b) Both changes involve an increase in the marginal propensity to withdraw, because a fall in the marginal propensity to consume implies that there has been an increase in the marginal propensity to save. Assuming no change in autonomous expenditures this will tend to lower the equilibrium level of income compared with the initial position. The changes in the propensities to consume and import will lower the multiplier.

Essay questions

1 'The General Theory was a truly revolutionary work. In it, Keynes sought to demolish the then existing macroeconomics (what he terms classical economics) and replace it with a new theoretical structure for analysing macroeconomic questions.' (B. A. Corry) Explain and discuss. What were the policy implications of this new theoretical structure?

The main outline for the answer plan for this question readily suggests itself: it is about classical and Keynesian views. The basic material for this answer is in this chapter (particularly sections 7.2 to 7.3 and 7.7.1), though when you have read Chapters 8 and 11 you will be able to incorporate some additional points.

1 Introduction
Set the theoretical debate in its historical context.

2 The classical view
(a) Say's law – interest rate mechanism (use diagram – Figure 7.2);
(b) labour market – use labour market diagram to show classical view of unemployment; (c) policy implications.

3 The Keynesian view
Explanation of the Keynesian view with indications of how this differs from the classical view:
(a) Keynes's rejection of Say's law;
(b) Keynesian view of the labour market;
(c) policy implications.

4 Conclusion
Was it a revolution   (a) in theory? (b) for policy?

2 Explain the main economic effects of the OPEC oil price rises of the 1970s.

The question does not specify whether you should discuss micro- or macro-effects. Unless the context makes it clearer, a general interpretation should be given. The microeconomic effects were discussed in Chapter 5 and the supply and demand model should be used to explain the effects on the allocation of resources. The macroeconomic effects were outlined in section 7.7.4; the basic Keynesian model should be used to explain the effects on output and employment. The income–expenditure and withdrawals–injections diagrams would be highly appropriate. The imports–exports diagram could be used to illustrate the balance-of-payments aspects. You could also make reference to the UK's changing position in the 1970s from oil consumer to oil producer. Chapter 20 provides some discussion of this as part of a more detailed consideration of balance of payments, exchange rate and budgetary effects.

Chapter 8
Self-test questions

1 According to the accelerator relationship, will net investment increase (I), decrease (D), remain constant (C) or be zero (Z) in the following cases:

(a) income increases by successively larger amounts each year;

(b) income decreases by successively larger amounts each year;

(c) income increases by successively smaller amounts each year;

(d) income increases by the same amount each year;
(e) income remains the same each year.

2 In the following example the capital−output ratio is assumed to be 2 and replacement requirement to take account of worn out machines is 200 per year. Complete the table below:

Year	Output	Capital required (£)	Investment (£) Net	Replacement	Gross
1	1000	2000	0	200	200
2	1200			200	
3	1300			200	
4	1350			200	
5	1400			200	
6	1400			200	
7	1350			200	
8	1300			200	
9	1200			200	
10	1100			200	
11	1100			200	
12	1200			200	

3 A company is considering a new investment project and expects to receive a net cash flow (after allowance has been made for interest payments) of £200 a year for three years. The cost of the project is £520. Use the present value method to work out whether the project is profitable when interest rates are: (a) 10 per cent; (b) 5 per cent.

4 If an increase in government expenditure succeeded in stimulating output, what would you expect the effect to be on the main macreconomic objectives?

Answers

1 (a) I; (b) D; (c) D; (d) C; (e) Z.

2

Year	Output	Capital required (£)	Investment (£) Net	Replacement	Gross
1	1000	2000	0	200	200
2	1200	2400	400	200	600
3	1300	2600	200	200	400
4	1350	2700	100	200	300
5	1400	2800	100	200	300
6	1400	2800	0	200	200
7	1350	2700	−100	200	100
8	1300	2600	−100	200	100
9	1200	2400	−200	200	0
10	1100	2200	−200	200	0
11	1100	2200	0	200	200
12	1200	2400	200	200	400

3(a) The present value (PV) of these income flows when the interest rate is 10 per cent is £497.37, which is less than the cost of the project (£520), giving a net present value (NPV) of − £22.63, so the project is not profitable. This can be seen taking the internal rate of return approach (IRR) which at 7.5 per cent is less than the rate of interest (10 per cent).
(b) PV is £544.60 giving a NPV of +24.60, so the project is profitable. The IRR of 7.5 per cent now compares favourably with the rate of interest of 5 per cent.

4 The response of the major objectives to a change in output is not a subject on which there is universal agreement. The effect may differ, too, according to the state of the economy (e.g. depending on the amount of spare capacity). The following are the most commonly held views.
(a) Increased output will assist the achievement of full employment. Employment will increase unless the rise in output is insufficient to offset the improvements in productivity which tend to displace labour.
(b) Inflation is likely to increase as higher demand leads to greater pressure in goods and, particularly, labour markets. However this will depend on how much spare capacity there is initially.

(c) The balance of payments will tend to worsen as higher spending leads to an increase in imports. To the extent that inflation is higher and exchange rates do not alter, competitiveness will tend to deteriorate, so imports will increase and exporters will find it more difficult to sell abroad.
(d) It is far less certain how growth will respond (see section 8.6.1.1). In part this may depend on the type of government expenditure that is employed: certain public expenditure (e.g. on roads which reduce expensive traffic jams or training schemes which alleviate skill shortages) may raise the productivity and capacity of the economy.

Essay questions

1(a) What is the permanent income theory of consumption?
(b) How does the permanent income theory differ in its assumptions and policy implications from Keynesian consumption theory?   *ICA*

1 Introduction
2 Permanent income theory
Explain the permanent income theory (see section 8.2.2.2).
3 Difference from Keynesian consumption function
(a) Contrast absolute income and permanent income hypotheses.
(b) Policy implications:
 (i) Fiscal policy−permanent income theory implies lower multipliers because consumption is altered only to the extent that permanent income is affected, so the impact of tax changes is likely to be less than is suggested by the absolute income theory.
 (ii) Interest rates−implies that the rate of interest will affect consumption as it is used to discount future income in determining permanent income.
4 Conclusion

2 What effects will an increase in rates of interest be likely to have on the level of economic activity?   *ACCA*

1 Introduction
Indicate that the impact will depend upon the effect of interest rate changes on total spending or aggregate demand. A distinction could be made between nominal and real interest rates. The latter refers to interest rates adjusted for inflation.
2 Investment
(a) Marginalist neoclassical theory of investment suggests that interest rates are an important influence on investment.
(b) Other theories (e.g. accelerator and profits/liquidity theories) suggest different influences which imply that shifts of the investment schedule may be as, or more, important than movements along it in response to interest rate changes.
(c) For certain types of investment, particularly those which produce returns over a long period of time, e.g. housing, interest rates are likely to be more important.
3 Consumption
(a) The permanent income theory suggests that interest rates are important. (b) Interest rate changes affect the cost of credit, which will be important for certain consumer durable goods.
4 Exchange rates
Higher interest rates, *ceteris paribus*, will raise the exchange rate and this will make exports less competitive and make it easier for imports to compete, so reducing the demand for a country's domestic output.
5 Conclusion

Chapter 9

Self-test questions

1(a) What are the main functions of money?
(b) Indicate whether inflation tends to impair these functions.

2 Given the following (hypothetical) data what are the values of M0, M1, M2, M3, M3c, M4 and M5? (Data overleaf)

1 Notes and coins in circulation   10
2 Bankers' operational balances and till money   1
3 UK non-interest-bearing sterling sight deposits   30
4 UK interest bearing sterling sight deposits   40
5 Interest-bearing retail deposits   45
6 Building society retail deposits   90
7 UK sterling time deposits   100
8 Deposits in other currencies   25
9 Building society deposits   130
10 Building society holdings of M3   15
11 National savings deposits   10
12 Private sector holdings of money-market instruments   5

3 What would be the effect of the sale to the public of £100 of gilt-edged securities by the government on the balance sheet below? (Assume that the government does not spend the proceeds.) The desired reserve asset ratio is 10 per cent. Assume there is a zero cash drain in the process and that this is the only bank in the economy.

Liabilities		Assets	
Deposits	£10 000	: Reserves cash and	
		: balances at	
		: central bank	£1000
		: Loans	£9000
	£10 000	:	£10 000

4 Will the following tend to lead to an increase (I), decrease (D) or no change (NC) in the money supply:
(a) budget deficit financed by borrowing from the non-bank public;
(b) budget deficit financed by borrowing from the banks;
(c) balanced budget with overfunding;
(d) increase in bank lending.

Answers

1(a) Medium of exchange; store of wealth; unit of account; standard of deferred payment.

(b) Inflation reduces the purchasing power of money. Inflation impairs the store of wealth function. If the inflation rate is significant and variable then this will undermine the function of money as a medium of exchange – inflation poses problems for its use as a unit of account because the real value of £1 in one year is not the same as in another, thus comparisons cannot easily be made between different periods.

2 M0 11 (Row 1+2); M1 80 (1+3+4); M2 175 (1+3+5+6); M3 180 (1+3+4+7); M3c 205 (1+3+4+7+8); M4 320 (1+3+4+7+8+9−10); M5 335 (1+3+4+7+8+9−10+11+12).

3

Liabilities		Assets	
Deposits	£9000	: Reserves cash and balances at	
		: central bank	£900
		: Loans	£8100
	£9000	:	£9000

4(a) NC; **(b)** I; **(c)** D; **(d)** I.

Essay questions

1(a) List the main functions of the central bank of a country.
(b) Describe the means which are available to the central bank for regulating the demand for, and supply of, money and credit.

ACCA

Part (a)

Functions of the central bank (see section 9.4.7)
 (i) government's bank; (ii) bankers' bank;

(iii) managing exchange equalization account and intervening in exchange rate market;
(iv) conduct of monetary policy;
 (v) supervision of financial system;
(vi) issuer of bank notes.

Part (b)

Briefly indicate that there are a variety of definitions of money and that some components will be more susceptible to control than others. Generally the controls available may be fairly direct (e.g. directives) or indirect (e.g. interest rates). The framework for the operation of monetary policy is set by the Treasury with the PSBR.

 The means of regulation are:
 (i) Direct controls – the central bank could use quantitative controls, e.g. limits on bank lending. These were used extensively in the post-war period but have now been abandoned. There are problems with direct controls: one is the ability of institutions to innovate to bypass the controls and another is the difficulties posed by credit rationing.
 (ii) Requests to institutions to pursue particular policies are less formal than methods in (i).
(iii) The central bank could (though it does not do so in the UK) require banks to observe a certain reserve asset ratio. Varying this could affect the volume of bank deposits and advances.
(vi) The central bank may require banks to deposit a certain proportion of their liabilities as special deposits with it. These special deposits are not regarded as liquid assets so this will put pressure on banks to reduce deposits. This has a similar effect to varying the reserve asset ratio.
 (v) A means of regulation for all central banks, and an important one in the UK, is open-market operations. This involves the central bank buying and selling securities (bills and gilt-edged securities). This can alter the liquidity of the banking system and with it the volume of bank deposits.
(vi) The main thrust of open-market operations and other policies may be to affect interest rates. This will influence the demand for loans from banks, building societies and other institutions.
(vii) Intervention in the foreign exchange market can affect the money supply (see section 9.5.2 and Chapter 20 for an explanation of this point).

2(a) What is meant by the term 'Public Sector Borrowing Requirement' (PSBR)?
(b) Assuming the PSBR is zero, discuss the factors which could generate an increase in a country's money supply.
(c) Can credit creation be carried on indefinitely?

CII

Part (a)

The PSBR is the difference between public sector (central and local government and public corporations) expenditure and revenue which needs to be financed by borrowing.

Part (b)

The basic relationship between the money supply and the PSBR can be summarized as:

$$\Delta Money\ supply = PSBR - \begin{array}{c} Sales\ of \\ debt\ to \\ non\text{-}bank \end{array} + \begin{array}{c} Bank \\ lending \\ to\ private \\ sector \end{array} + \begin{array}{c} External \\ currency \\ flows \end{array}$$

If the PSBR is zero, the money supply could still increase for the following reasons:
 (i) Debt sales – if the government 'underfunds' each year, some part of the national debt will be due for repayment and the government could choose not to issue sufficient new gilts to cover the bonds that are repaid. This, *ceteris paribus*, will create a need to borrow from the banking system which will raise bank deposits and the money supply.

(ii) Bank lending–banks can increase the volume of bank deposits by making loans and in this way raise the money supply. This will apply to building societies too and will affect the M4 and M5 definitions of the money supply.

(iii) The balance of payments may affect the money supply. Surpluses will tend to raise the money supply as the increase in bank deposits resulting from exports and capital inflows is greater than the reduction in deposits from imports and capital outflows. This picture will be modified according to the exchange rate regime and intervention policy in the foreign exchange markets. If bank lending in sterling to overseas is spent on UK goods and services this will tend to expand the money supply.

Part (c)

Credit expansion will be limited by a number of factors:
(i) The quantity of reserves, given the reserve asset ratio, will limit the creation process because of banks' need to stay liquid.
(ii) Banks will be limited by customer demands for loans: if they do not wish to borrow then they cannot expand advances.
(iii) Government controls (e.g. directives or 'corset' type arrangements) may limit the process.
(iv) In the credit creation process there will be leakages: to government when gilts are bought from the central bank, to overseas, and cash leakages as the public will want to hold more cash as deposits rise.

Chapter 10

Self-test questions

1 Complete the following table and consider how far the data are consistent with the quantity theory of money.

	ΔMoney M3 (£b) M	Prices GDP deflator 1980 = 100 P	Output GDP (£b) 1980 prices O	Interest rate (Treasury bill rate)	Nominal GDP Y	Velocity of circulation V	Growth in money supply (ΔM%)	Inflation (ΔP%)	Growth in output (ΔO%)	ΔM−ΔO	Growth in nominal income (Y%)
1980	67	100.0	199.7	13.1			19.6	18.8	−1.9	21.5	21.6
1981	84	110.1	197.7	14.6							
1982	91	117.9	199.9	9.7							
1983	101	124.6	207.0	8.8							
1984	111	130.6	210.7	9.1							
1985	125	138.3	218.6	11.2							
1986	151	142.1	224.5	10.7							
1987	185	149.2	233.0	8.2							

(Economic Trends Annual Supplement, National Institute Economical Review)

2 Using the IS–LM model:

(a) explain the effect of an expansionary fiscal policy which involves a budget deficit which is financed:
(i) by borrowing from the public;
(ii) by borrowing from the banking system.
(b) If the deficit were maintained, how would the long-run effects differ from those you gave in answer to (a)?

3(a) What are the main motives for holding money?
(b) Why is the demand for money likely to be affected by a change in interest rates?

Answers

1

	Nominal GDP Y	Velocity of circulation V	Growth in money supply (ΔM%)	Inflation (ΔP%)	Growth in output (ΔO%)	ΔM−ΔO	Growth in nom. income (Y%)
1980	199.7	3.0	19.6	18.8	−1.9	21.5	21.6
1981	217.7	2.6	25.4	10.1	−1.0	26.4	9.0
1982	235.7	2.6	8.3	7.1	1.1	7.2	8.3
1983	257.9	2.6	11.0	5.7	3.6	7.4	9.4
1984	275.2	2.5	9.9	4.8	1.8	8.1	6.7
1985	302.3	2.4	12.6	5.9	3.7	8.9	9.8
1986	319.0	2.1	20.8	2.7	2.7	18.1	5.5
1987	347.6	1.9	22.5	5.0	3.8	18.7	9.0

Nominal income is calculated as follows:

Price index $\div$ 100 $\times$ *real output*, i.e. $P/100 \times O$.

Velocity is *Nominal income* $\div$ *Money stock*, i.e. $Y \div M$.

Consistency with the quantity theory can be viewed in a number of ways:

(a) $\Delta M\%$ and $\Delta P\%$: the correlation is not too impressive – although the two decline from the early 1980s to 1985, the rapid expansion in the money supply in 1981 did not coincide with, nor was it followed by, a period of particularly high inflation. The acceleration in money supply growth in 1986 and 1987 was not reflected in a rise in inflation rates. Time lags between money

supply changes and inflation may account for some of this discrepancy.

(b) Stable velocity: the quantity theory does assume that the velocity is predictable. This does not mean fixed and certainly the velocity in the 1980s has changed quite significantly. There is a clear downward trend in the data in the question but it is doubtful whether this was accurately predicted; certainly in the context of the previous 15 years the trend is less discernible.

(c) ΔM and ΔY: the quantity theory suggests there should be a close link between monetary growth (ΔM) and the growth in nominal income (ΔY). While there is some support for this, 1981 and the end period (1986–87) are not consistent with a close contemporaneous link. The relaxation of a number of controls on the banking system (e.g. abolition of the corset arrangement) accounts for some excessive growth.

(d) $\Delta M - \Delta O$: the view that it is monetary growth in excess of real output growth that causes inflation means that comparing $\Delta M - \Delta O$ with ΔP provides an indication of the performance of the quantity theory. The outcome again reveals 1981 and the mid-1980s as periods when the behaviour of the economy was not consistent with a simple quantity theory view.

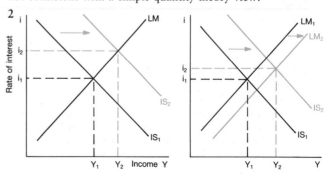

An expansionary fiscal policy will shift the IS schedule out to the right. In the case of (a)(i) the LM schedule will not shift because the money supply will not rise when the deficit is financed by borrowing from the public. This is not so in (a(ii)), so the LM schedule shifts out to the right as well.

(b) In the long run the deficit will involve:

(i) the issue of more bonds or gilt-edged securities each year to finance the deficit. With a fixed money supply the ratio of bonds to money will rise and we can expect an increase in the demand for money, causing the LM schedule to move inwards, leading to a rise in interest rates. The increase in the number of bonds will increase the financial wealth of the private sector and this will cause 'wealth effects' – private sector spending may rise because the sector is better off. This will shift the IS schedule outwards. The net effect of the IS and LM schedule shifts is an empirical matter – it may involve income rising or falling.

(ii) In the case where the deficit leads to increases in the money supply, the LM schedule will continue to shift outwards as long as there is a deficit. The wealth effects of an increased money stock could cause the IS schedule to shift out for the reasons stated above. The process is not likely to go on indefinitely because the higher income will raise tax revenues and at some point eliminate the budget deficit unless further expenditure increases or tax cuts are made. We have so far assumed that prices are constant; if they rise then the LM schedule will shift inwards, which will offset some or all of the income increase.

3(a) Transactions; precautionary and speculative.

(b) Transactions and precautionary balances are principally influenced by income levels; nevertheless high interest rates are likely to cause people to economize. The speculative demand is related to interest rates, with higher rates making bonds seem more attractive, so there is a lower demand for money.

Essay questions

What factors determine the demand for money? How are changes in the supply of money linked with the demand for goods and services

(a) from a Keynesian point of view

(b) from a monetarist viewpoint.   *ACCA*

1 Introduction
Indicate the problem in defining money.

2 Keynesian point of view

(a) Factors affecting the demand for money.

(i) transactions – income (but see answer to self-test question 10.2(b));

(ii) precautionary – income; (iii) speculative – interest rates.

So total demand is a function of interest rates and income. Keynesians tend to stress the large number of money substitutes which mean that demand for money is fairly interest elastic.

(b) Overall effect of changes in the money supply:

$$\Delta M \to \Delta i \to \Delta Exp \to \Delta Y \text{ (see Figure 10.5)}$$

where M = money supply, i = interest rate,
Exp = expenditure and Y = income.

(i) $\Delta M \to \Delta i$

Portfolio adjustment: increase in money supply will lead to the purchase of other financial assets which alter their price and the rate of interest;

(ii) $\Delta i \ \Delta Exp \to \Delta Y$

Effect on output will depend on interest elasticity of expenditure.

Those Keynesians who believe that money supply changes have little effect on the demand for goods and services tend to stress that the interest elasticity of demand for money is high while interest elasticity of expenditure is low. They also suggest that time lags between interest rate and expenditure changes may be considerable.

3 Monetarist viewpoint

(a) Factors affecting the demand for money: the simplest way of representing the monetarist position is sometimes presented as one where the demand for money is affected only by income, i.e.

the interest elasticity of demand is zero. A fuller picture would recognize that monetarists accept the portfolio adjustment referred to above but would stress that money does not have close substitutes in financial assets and adjustment back to equilibrium following an increase in the money supply involves increases in expenditure on goods and services as well as financial assets. In other words, the portfolio should be seen as embracing real (goods and services) expenditure as well as financial assets.

(b) Explaining the monetarist view of changes in the money supply involves an exposition of the quantity theory. A diagram could be used to illustrate the effect.

4 Conclusion
Point out that the Keynesians and monetarists have come closer together over the last 10 to 15 years on the relationship between money and demand. Many Keynesians have accepted that the earlier view (1950s and 1960s) that 'money does not matter' (i.e. has no effect on spending) is too extreme, while a number of monetarists have conceded that the stability of the demand for money, and therefore the relationship between M and Y, is not as strong or close as earlier monetarists claimed. Their differences now centre on how the effects of the change in spending are divided between prices and real output.

Chapter 11

Self-test questions

1 In the following cases will the aggregate demand curve shift outwards (DO) or inwards (DI) and/or the aggregate supply curve shift outwards (SO) or inwards (SI)?

(a) a fall in autonomous consumption;

(b) a rise in government expenditure;

(c) a cut in income tax;

(d) an increase in the money supply;

(e) a rise in real social security benefits;

(f) an appreciation of sterling.

2 Show the effect on an aggregate demand and supply diagram of an increase in the money supply. Distinguish between short- and long-run effects in the gradualist and new classical monetarist models.

3(a) What is meant by the 'natural rate of unemployment'?

(b) Which of the following would reduce the natural rate:

(i) a cut in real social security benefits;

(ii) an increase in aggregate demand;

(iii) a cut in income tax;

(iv) a reduction in trade union powers;

(v) an increase in the money supply.

4(a) Distinguish between the warranted and natural growth rate.

(b) If the two are not equal, what is consequence in the (i) Harrod–Domar and (ii) neoclassical growth models?

Answers

1(a) DI; (b) DO; (c) DO (demand effects) + SO (supply-side effects); (d) DO; (e) SI; (f) DI.

2 See Figure 11.2; The increase in the money supply shifts the demand schedule out to the right. In the case of the gradualist monetarist, the short-run supply schedule is upward sloping, so a short-run equilibrium position is B, compared with an initial position of A. As expectations are revised the short-run aggregate supply curve shifts upwards until a long-run position is achieved at C, where real income is unchanged and prices rise from P_1 to P_2. The long-run supply curve can be represented by the vertical line AS. The new classical economists believe the short-run supply curve will be vertical too. In their view expectations will be formed rationally, so unless the change in the money supply is a genuine surprise price setters will take this into account and equilibrium will alter directly from A to C.

3(a) Unemployment that exists at the equilibrium real wage

This position is one where expectations of price and wage inflation are correct.

(b) (i), (iii), (iv).

4 The warranted rate is the one which would fulfil the plans of households and firms. For example, it leaves firms feeling that they have invested the right amount; any other growth rate would leave them feeling they had over- or under-invested. The natural rate is the one that would allow full employment to be sustained. If the two are not equal then, according to the Harrod model, there will be growing unemployment or inflationary tendencies. In the neoclassical model, relative factor prices would alter to move the economy to a full employment path.

Essay questions

1 (a) What is meant by 'supply-side' policies?
(b) Why has there been so much emphasis on such policies in recent years? *ACCA*

Part (a)
Meaning of supply-side policies
(i) They are policies designed to shift the aggregate supply curve rather than aggregate demand. They are intended to increase the productive capacity of the country, i.e. shift the production possibility curve outwards. Great stress is laid on removing the disincentive effects of high income tax rates.
(ii) They tend to favour market solutions so that the approach embraces privatization, deregulation and the removal of impediments to factor mobility (e.g. housing policies). They seek to promote the 'enterprise culture'.
(iii) They are micro- rather than macro-orientated policies directed at improving the working of individual markets.

Part (b)
Reasons for greater reliance on supply-side policies
(i) Stagflation and the attack on Keynesian demand management: the poor performance of economies in the 1970s (slow growth, high unemployment and inflation) led to an attack on the Keynesian demand management policies which had dominated the post-war period, and a search for an alternative.
(ii) There was a revival of the (neo-)classical view on working of the economy. (Use the monetarist aggregate demand and supply model to illustrate that in the long run only shifts in aggregate supply can increase output; section 11.3.4.)
(iii) This alternative framework leads to the policy recommendation that aggregate demand policies (controlling the money supply) should be used to affect nominal values (prices) and supply-side policies should be directed at raising output and other real variables.
(iv) The appeal of supply-side policies, particularly their pro-market aspects, can be regarded as part of a wider disenchantment with the collectivist and state intervention approaches of the post-war period. This is broader than the macroeconomic arguments of (i). It stresses the importance of the individual initiatives and enterprise and as such not only includes matters of concern to economists (e.g. privatization, deregulation, etc) but also extends into the area of ideology and political philosophy.

2 To what extent is technological change likely to increase or decrease levels of employment? *ACCA*

Introduction
Nature of technological change
Technological change involves the application of new ideas to the production of goods and services. There are distinctions between invention (the discovery of new ideas) and innovation: product innovation (new products or services) and process innovation (new ways of producing existing goods and services). The rate of diffusion of innovation may well be important for its impact on employment.
Technical change and the firm

Technical change will lower costs and this can be expected to lead to lower prices and higher output levels. So although the change is likely to raise labour productivity (output per person), higher output will moderate or even outweigh the employment loss from the innovation. The employment impact will depend upon the elasticity of demand and the effect of the innovation of labour productivity.

4 Job creation and job destruction
Although a firm introducing an innovation may increase employment, it is quite likely that there will be a net reduction in jobs. However, there are likely to be job gains elsewhere in the economy. There will be some employment increases in the capital goods industry, and the technical change may well give rise to product innovation resulting in job gains.

5 Macroeconomic effects
Technical change which increases productivity will raise real income through lower prices and/or higher factor payments and this will stimulate demand and, *ceteris paribus*, the prospects for jobs.

6 Open-economy effects
The output and employment effects for open economies will depend on the rate at which the new technology is applied in different countries. The country that applies the new technology most rapidly can expect to gain a competitive advantage (as long as the exchange rate does not alter to compensate for this) bringing beneficial effects on output and employment.

7 Diffusion rates and market adjustments
The rate of diffusion and the ability of the market economy to reallocate resources according to price signals will to some extent determine the employment effects and how they are distributed between the short and the long run. For those who are critical of the ability of markets to cope with these adjustments, the prospects for employment may well depend upon an appropriate intervention, e.g. at the macro-level, to counteract a demand deficiency and retraining schemes to assist the mobility of labour.

Chapter 12

Self-test questions

1 The following monetarist model was discussed in 12.3.2:
$$U = U_N + f(\Delta P^e - \Delta P)$$

$$\uparrow\!\_\_\text{lag}\_\_|\uparrow$$
$$\Delta M$$

Assume the following specific values:
$$U = U_N + \quad f(\Delta P^e - \Delta P)$$
$$U = 5\% + 0.5\,(\Delta P^e - \Delta P)$$

and assume that the rate of inflation (ΔP^e) this year is equal to the rate of growth of the money supply (ΔM) last year:
$$\Delta P_t = \Delta M_{t-1}$$

and that the expected inflation rate (ΔP^e) this year is equal to last year's inflation rate:
$$\Delta P^e_t = \Delta P_{t-1}$$

The time lags are indicated by the arrows in the table.
(a) Complete the table below.

Year	ΔM	ΔP	ΔP^e	U
1	0	0	0	5
2	6	0	0	5
3	6	6	0	
4	8			
5	10			
6	12			
7	12			
8	9			
9	6			
10	3			
11	0			
12	0			
13	0			

(b) What is the relationship between inflation and expected inflation when unemployment is below the natural rate?
(c) Why did the same rate of monetary growth in years 2 and 3 produce different impacts on unemployment?
(d) What type of monetary policy is necessary if unemployment is to fall in successive years?
(e) If instead of a gradual reduction in the rate of monetary growth from year 8, the government had decided to stop the money supply from growing so that the rate of inflation in years 9 and 10 was zero per cent, what would have been the unemployment rate in year 9 and year 10?

Answers

1(a)

Year	ΔM	ΔP	ΔP^e	U
1	0	0	0	5
2	6	0	0	5
3	6	6	0	2
4	8	6	6	5
5	10	8	6	4
6	12	10	8	4
7	12	12	10	4
8	9	12	12	5
9	6	9	12	6.5
10	3	6	9	6.5
11	0	3	6	6.5
12	0	0	3	6.5
13	0	0	0	5

(b) $\Delta P > \Delta P^e$
(c) The impact of the 6 per cent monetary growth in years 2 and 3 is felt on unemployment in years 3 and 4. In year 3 unemployment falls dramatically because the monetary policy produces an inflation rate (6 per cent) significantly above the expected rate (0 per cent), but in year 4 expectations adapt to the 6 per cent rate of inflation and unemployment returns to the natural rate of 5 per cent.
(d) Accelerating monetary growth, i.e. where

$$(\Delta M_t - \Delta M_{t-1}) > (\Delta M_{t-1} - \Delta M_{t-2})$$

(e) 11 per cent in year 9 and 5 per cent in year 10.

Essay question

'Because of expectations it is easier to start an inflation than to stop it.' Explain this statement and discuss its applicability to the British economy.   *ICA*

1 Introduction
Indicate that there are differing views on the causes and cures of inflation which are often classified as monetarist and non-monetarist or Keynesian. Differences exist on the interpretation of the UK evidence.

2 Monetarist view
(a) Role of expectations – explain the monetarist interpretation of relationship between unemployment and inflation:

$$\Delta P = f(U) + \Delta P^e$$

So expectations play an important role in determining inflation.

(b) Gradualist view – adaptive expectations mean that people may wrongly predict expected inflation in the short run and that there will typically be a time delay before they adjust to a new situation. This means that there is a distinction between the short-run and long-run Phillips curves. Use a diagram like Figure 12.2 to illustrate this. In this view an increase in demand leads to a higher rate of inflation (e.g. *A* to *B* in Figure 12.2), but this causes a rise in the expected inflation rate as people adapt to higher inflation and the short-run Phillips curve shifts upwards (PC_1 to PC_2).

  If this process continues for some time the Phillips curve will have shifted out further so the unemployment cost of quickly eliminating inflation will be high; hence the gradualist

recommendation to take time over stopping inflation. This position is closest to the one in the question. Starting the process of inflation is relatively painless and is accompanied by unemployment below the natural rate as long as inflation is accelerating, whereas stopping it means allowing unemployment to rise above the natural rate.

(c) New classical view – in this model expectations are formed rationally and use will be made of available information on factors affecting inflation including policy changes. It means that the short-run as well as long-run Phillips curves can be regarded as vertical lines. The implication is that inflation can be stopped relatively easily, quickly and painlessly, i.e. there are no unemployment costs as long as the policy is widely understood and is credible. The statement in the question would not be accepted by those economists who hold this view.

3 The Keynesian view
Keynesians tend to explain inflation in terms of cost pressures where prices are based on costs, and wages (a major cost) will be influenced by prices. Expected inflation is likely to play a part in this process but stress is more often given to expectations of real wage increases. This can mean there is a strong upward pressure on wages and the asymmetry referred to above is likely to apply. Keynesians tend to be rather interventionist and many would advocate the use of an incomes policy to reduce inflation. In the short run this policy may be quite successful in bringing inflation down which means that the quote would not be fully accepted. However, the evidence seems to suggest that the reduction in inflation may only be temporary, as pressures build up and the incomes policy breaks down.

4 The UK economy experience
Reference here should be made to the relationship between unemployment and inflation – see Figure 12.10. Different interpretations can be given.

5 Conclusion

Chapter 13

Self test questions

1 The following data show the total utilities for two products *X* and *Y*:

Quantity	Total utility of X	Total utility of Y
1	6	28
2	10	48
3	13	60
4	15	68
5	16	72
6	16.5	74

(a) Calculate the marginal utilities of *X* and *Y*.
(b) If the price of *X* is £2 and the price of *Y* £4 and the consumer has £20 to spend, what quantities of *X* and *Y* will be bought?

2(a) Why do indifference curves not cross?
(b) Why do we normally expect indifference curves to be convex?
(c) What would the indifference map for prunes and apples look like for a person who disliked prunes but enjoyed apples?
(d) What would a policy maker's indifference curves look like for unemployment and inflation?

3 Complete the following table for a rise in the price of *X* indicating whether the quantity of *X* will increase (+) or fall (−).

Effect of a rise in the price of *X* on the quantity of *X*

Type of good	Substitution effect	Income effect	Total effect
Normal			
Inferior			
Giffen			

Answers

1 (a) The marginal utility (which is the additional utility derived from consuming an extra unit of a good) of each good is shown in the table below:

Quantity	Good X TU	Good X MU	Good X MU/P_X P_X=£2	Good X MU/P_X P_X=£1	Good Y TU	Good Y MU	Good Y MU/P_Y P_Y=£4
1	6	6	3	6	28	28	7
2	10	4	2	4	48	20	5
3	13	3	1.5	3	60	12	3
4	15	2	1	2	68	8	2
5	16	1	0.5	1	72	4	1
6	16.5	0.5	0.25	0.5	74	2	0.5

b) The consumer would buy 2 of X (spending £4) and 4 of Y spending £16). This would maximize her/his utility because it spends all his money and satisfies the condition for consumer equilibrium:

$$\frac{MU_X}{P_X} = \frac{MU_Y}{P_Y}$$

The ratios are equal to 2 in our example (see MU/P columns in the table above).

2(a) As indifference curves join points of equal utility and as one indifference curve to the right of another indicates combinations of higher utility it follows that the two cannot cross.

b) The marginal rate of substitution (which shows the rate at which one good will be substituted for another to maintain equal utility), which graphically is the slope of a tangent to the indifference curve, is not constant. The MRS_{YX} will decline as more of X is consumed, i.e. consumers are prepared to give up less and less of Y the greater the consumption of X.

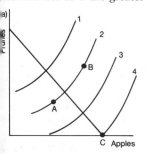 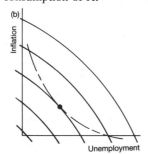

c) Unlike most indifference curve diagrams where we are considering two 'goods', here we are asked to illustrate a 'bad' (prunes) and a 'good' (apples). In these circumstances the indifference curves will have a positive gradient, i.e. slope up from left to right. Compare A and B on the indifference curve in figure (a) (above): as prunes are disliked the consumer will require more of the good, apples, to maintain equal satisfaction when more of the disliked prunes are consumed. The indifference curve will increase in utility as we go out to the right. Consumer equilibrium will be a 'corner solution', where all income is devoted to apples and none, not surprisingly, is spent on prunes. (See C on indifference curve 4).

d) Here we have two 'bads' and the indifference curves will look like those illustrated in Figure (b). In this case, curves nearer the origin indicate higher levels of satisfaction. The dotted line is the Phillips curve which is the constraint facing policy makers, so they will maximize utility at X.

3 Effect of a rise in price of X on the quantity of X

Type of good	Substitution effect	Income effect	Total effect
Normal	−	−	−
Inferior	−	+	−
Giffen	−	+	+

Essay question

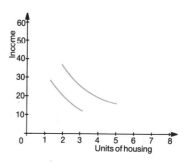

The diagram shows the preferences for units of housing compared with other goods that might be bought with income, which is measured on the vertical axis. If the rent is £10 per unit and income is £40, what is the consumer's equilibrium position? If the government decides to assist the poor by a 50 per cent subsidy on rents, what is the new equilibrium position? Consider an alternative of income support which would give the consumer the same utility as the rent subsidy scheme. How do the effects and costs differ? In the light of this is there a case for rent subsidies?

1 Original equilibrium position: consumers will purchase 2 units of housing spending £20 on this and £20 on other goods.

2 Rent subsidy – this will cause the budget line to swivel outwards so that it would be possible to purchase 8 units of housing if all income were spent on it. (Rents would be £80 but the 50 per cent subsidy would mean that households only pay £40.) The new equilbrium position will be where 4 units of housing are purchased, with households paying £20 after taking account of the subsidy and £20 will be spent on other goods. The cost of rent subsidies will be £20.

3 An income support scheme involves giving households sufficient income to place them on the same indifference curve as the rent subsidy scheme. In terms of the diagram, draw a budget line parallel to the original but at a tangent to the indifference curve associated with the rent subsidy. This involves giving households an extra £15 of income. The new equilibrium position is where they purchase 2.5 units of housing (spending £25) and spend £30 on other goods. The cost is clearly the £15 of income support.

4 The utility for households is the same for each scheme. The rent subsidy costs £20 and income support £15. So, why should rent subsidies be considered? There is one further effect to note: the quantity of housing consumed is higher with rent subsidies (4 units) than income support (2.5) – there is a substitution effect as well as an income effect. This leads to arguments in favour of rent subsidies which increase the consumption of housing:

(a) Externalities of housing, e.g. improved health.

(b) Society's responsibility for housing children decently means that decisions should not be left entirely to individuals.

(c) This leads on to the view that housing is a merit good and that, for example, the belief in equality of opportunity justifies subsidizing housing to ensure that poor housing does not set up a vicious circle of deprivation and poor performance in school and work.

(d) Society may be more prepared to pay taxes for targeted support on housing than general income support.

There are clearly counter arguments to these views. Externalities may be regarded as relatively small. Arguments (b) and (c) may be rejected on the grounds that individuals should be given the freedom to choose for themselves and that the paternalistic/maternalistic view is insulting and patronizing. (If households were given the £20 used in rent subsidy then they would get on to a higher indifference curve by consuming less housing – try drawing a budget line passing through the rent subsidy equilibrium point.) The emphasis on equality of opportunity is clearly an ethical position that not everybody would share. Subsidies will distort market prices so they do not reflect costs.

Chapter 14

Self-test questions

1 The following table represents the data on three isoquants for outputs of 5, 10 and 20 units of a good:

Output = 5		Output = 10		Output = 20	
Capital	Labour	Capital	Labour	Capital	Labour
10	6	10	8	10	14
7	8	7	9	7	16
4	12	5	13	5	24
3	16	4	16	4.5	32
2.5	24	3	24	4	64
2	32	2.5	32		

Plot the isoquants on graph paper and answer the following questions:

(a) Do these isoquants indicate increasing, decreasing or constant returns to scale?

(b) If the price of capital is £400 per unit, the wage for each worker is £100 and the total expenditure by the firm on factors is £3200, what output would the firm produce and what quantities of factors would be employed?

(c) If the price of capital halved and wages doubled, how must the employment of factors change to produce same output?

(d) Starting from the position described in (b), what would the effect on output and employment of factors be if the wages were halved to £50, with the price of capital (£400) and total outlay (£3200) unchanged?

2 Complete the following table by calculating the following costs: *TFC* total fixed costs; *TVC* total variable costs; *MC* marginal costs; *AVC* average variable costs; *AFC* average fixed costs; *ATC* average total costs.

Q	TC	TFC	TVC	MC	AFC	AVC	ATC
0	20						
1	42						
2	54						
3	64						
4	80						
5	104						
6	138						
7	182						
8	240						
9	315						
10	410						

3(a) Distinguish between long-run and short-run costs.

(b) Distinguish between increasing returns to a factor and increasing returns to scale.

(c) With reference to the data in question 2, would a firm continue to operate if it were selling 4 units at a price of £16 each? Would the same answer apply in the long run? If the firm sold 3 units at £10 would it shut down?

Answers

1

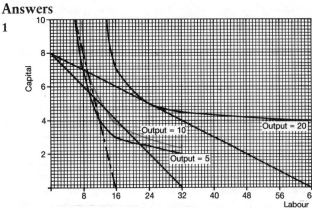

(a) Increasing returns: doubling of output does not require a doubling of inputs.

(b) The firm would produce 10 units of output and employ 4 units of capital and 16 of labour.

(c) 7 units of capital and 9 of labour.

(d) 20 units of output produced with 5 capital and 24 labour.

2

Q	TC	TFC	TVC	MC	AFC	AVC	ATC
0	20	20	0				
1	42	20	22	22	20.0	22.0	42.00
2	54	20	34	12	10.0	17.0	27.00
3	64	20	44	10	6.7	14.7	21.33
4	80	20	60	16	5.0	15.0	20.00
5	104	20	84	24	4.0	16.8	20.80
6	138	20	118	34	3.3	19.7	23.00
7	182	20	162	44	2.9	23.1	26.00
8	240	20	220	58	2.5	27.5	30.00
9	315	20	295	75	2.2	32.8	35.00
10	410	20	390	95	2.0	39.0	41.00

3(a) Short run refers to a period when some factors are fixed, hence fixed cost. In the long run all costs are variable because the use of all factors can be changed.

(b) Increasing returns to a factor refers to the additional output (or marginal product) that results from employing one more unit of a factor when some other factor(s) are fixed: it is a short-run phenomenon. In contrast, economies of scale are long-run because they refer to a period over which all factors, i.e. the scale of operations, can be changed. Increasing returns to scale occur when a doubling of inputs produces more than a doubling of output.

(c) In the short run it would stay open at a price of £16 because it is covering average variable costs, which are equal to £15, and making a contribution to fixed costs. In the long run, however, it would have to close. At a price of £10 and output of 3, not even *AVC* are being covered, so the firm will close down, even in the short run.

Essay question

John Smith previously earned £10 000 a year in employment and had £100 000 invested in government securities yielding 10 per cent per annum. He sold his securities for £100 000 and started his own business. Initially he rented a factory for £5000 per annum but subsequently purchased it for £20 000, leaving £80 000 as the financial capital within the firm.

John Smith's accountant's estimate that the total revenue of the firm in the past year was £100 000 and the total costs were £80 000, including a salary of £5000 paid to John Smith.

Estimate the profits of this firm from the viewpoint of (a) the accountant and (b) the economist, explaining clearly the reasons for any differences.   *ACCA*

1 Introduction

Outline the distinction between accountants and economists: the latter use opportunity costs, which is the amount lost by not using resources on the next best alternative use.

2 Accountant's view

The accountant will essentially take profits as the difference between revenue and costs:

Revenue	£100 000
Costs	£80 000
Profit	£20 000

3 The economist's view

Accountants do not generally attribute opportunity costs to a firm's use of its own resources unless cash transactions are made. For example, the owner's time will be valued at £5000 (the amount actually paid to John Smith) rather than the cost of this resource in terms of what he could have earned elsewhere, say £10 000. Similarly, the use of buildings, depreciated machinery and the use of the firm's own funds may not be costed in terms of their alternative uses. So the factory should not be regarded as 'costless' because it is owned by the firm, for it could be rented out for £5000. The firm is forgoing this sum by using the factory itself and this should be regarded as its cost.

Accountants may include items which inflate costs as compared with the economist's approach. Depreciation charges may not reflect the alternative use of machinery. If a machine has been bought and its second hand re-sale value is zero, then the machine should be regarded as costing nothing, no matter how much it originally cost: 'bygones are bygones'. We are not given any information on this item so we are not able to make any calculations on it.

The economist would calculate profits as follows:

Revenue		£100 000
Costs:		
Accountant's costs	£80 000	
Rent of factory (OC)	£5000	
Owner's time (OC – wage paid)	£5000	
Use of financial capital (OC)		
(£80 000 @ 10%)	£8000	
	£98 000	
Profit		£2000

Hence the economist's calculation of profit is only one-tenth of that of the accountant.

4 Conclusion
The economist's approach is particularly appropriate to the study of, and decisions about, resource allocation. It is especially useful for planning the use of a firm's scarce resources.

Chapter 15
Self-test questions

1 What conditions are necessary for perfect competition to exist? Which of the following markets meet or nearly meet these conditions?
(a) agriculture; (b) coal mining; (c) soap powders; (d) foreign exchange market; (e) stock exchange.

2 Explain why $MC = MR$ is a condition for profit maximization.

3 What effect would the following have on the output and profits of a perfectly competitive firm?
(a) an increase in local authority rates on business;
(b) an increase in electricity charges.

4 Explain the derivation of an industry supply curve for a perfectly competitive industry.

Answers

1 The main feature of perfect competition is that firms are price takers and are therefore faced by a perfectly elastic demand curve. There are several conditions that are necessary for this to be achieved: large number of producers; undifferentiated product; freedom to entry industry; well-informed consumers, etc. The following are close to being perfectly competitive: (a) though many sectors of agriculture are subject to government intervention, (d) and (e).

2 See Figure 15.2. If $MR > MC$ then firms are adding more to revenue than they are to costs so it will pay a profit-maximizing firm to expand as long as this is the case. When the expansion of output proceeds to a point where $MC > MR$, the firm is adding more to costs than to revenue and profits (if they are being made) will be reduced. Operating at point Q_2 will represent a point where profits cannot be increased any further.

3(a) Rates are a fixed cost and therefore an increase will affect AFC and ATC but not marginal cost. The profit-maximizing output is unaltered, though the rise in ATC will reduce profits and if the firms were in a long-run equilibrium position to start with losses would be made. In the long run, prices will rise to reflect increased costs. The industry contracts, although

individual firms that remain will increase their output in the long run because they will operate further up their MC curve.
(b) Electricity can be regarded as something that will enter variable costs (though part of the bill may be for fixed cost elements), so an increase in charges will raise MC as well as AVC, hence ATC) and so affect output even in the short term.

4 See section 15.3.5. A perfectly competitive industry's supply curve is the sum of firms' supply curves. The firm's supply curve is the MC curve because a profit-maximizing firm will produce where $MC = MR$ and this will be where $P = MC$ under perfect competition. However, it will not be the whole of the upward sloping part of the MC curve because firms will shut if price falls below AVC. So the industry supply curve is the sum of the firms' MC curves above the point where $MC = AVC$.

Essay question

What would be the effect on the egg industry of fears that eggs are infected with salmonella? Assume the industry is perfectly competitive and that there is no government intervention. Use diagrams to illustrate the impact on the individual egg producer.

1 Introduction
Health fears will affect the demand for eggs.
Short- and long-run effects can be distinguished.

2 Initial position – use of diagram
The basic diagram you require for this answer is Figure 15.6. Here we are going to use it to illustrate an inward shift of demand. The appropriate diagram is shown below. We assume a starting position, before the health scare, with firms in a long-run equilibrium position and price equal to P_1.

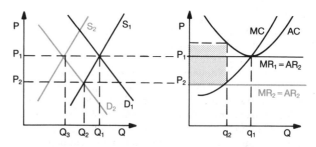

3 The short-run effects
The fears of salmonella will cause the demand curve to shift inwards, lowering the price to P_2. At this lower price firms still equate MC and MR, but this is now associated with a lower output, q_2 instead of q_1. It is this movement by all firms that lies behind the positive slope in the industry's supply curve. Firms are making losses as price (AR) is below average cost (AC). These losses will be sustained in the short run, as long as firms are operating above AVC.

4 The long-run effects
Losses cannot be endured in the long run, so firms leave the industry. This causes the supply curve to shift inwards which will raise prices. This process will continue until the industry has contracted sufficiently to eliminate losses so that firms that remain in the industry are earning normal profits. This will happen only when price returns to P_1.

5 Conclusion

Chapter 16
Self-test questions

1 Why does the marginal revenue schedule decline more rapidly than demand under conditions of imperfect competition?
2 Why does a sales maximizer operate at a higher output than a profit maximizer?
3 To what extent do you expect a monopoly to operate at a higher price and lower output level than perfectly competitive firms?

Answers

1 Firms facing a downward sloping curve will have to cut price in order to sell more output. However, although they gain the revenue from selling an additional good which is equal to its price, they suffer a loss of revenue by having to cut the price on all the other goods they sell.

2 The profit-maximizing monopolist will sell at a point where $MC = MR$. The sales maximizer will sell at a point where total revenue is maximized, i.e. will increase sales as long as revenue rises. This will be at a point where $MR = 0$. As long as $MC > 0$ then the profit maximizer produces at a lower output and a higher price.

3 The perfectly competitive industry will produce where $P = MC$, whereas the monopolist will produce where $MC = MR$ and as MR is less than price it follows that a monopolist will sell a lower output at a higher price (see Figure 16.5). This is on the assumption that costs are the same under monopoly as competition. It can be argued that they may be lower (economies of scale, monopoly profits providing the incentive to innovate) or higher (X-inefficiency).

Essay questions

1 A firm is operating in the short-run situation in conditions of monopolistic competition.
(a) How much will the firm produce? At what price will the good be sold? How much profit will the firm make?
(b) What will be the effect on output, price and profits of the firm of each of the following changes:
 (i) An increase in the rent of the factory;
 (ii) A fall in the price of raw materials.

1 Introduction
Monopolistic competition is a market structure where there are a large number of producers and there is freedom of entry and exit. It therefore has features in common with perfect competition; it is, however, faced by a downward sloping demand curve because it has a degree of monopoly either through its location (e.g. garage or take-away) or because of product differentiation.
2 The firm will maximize profits where $MC = MR$ and this will determine its output. The demand curve will show the price for which that output can be sold. The profit made will depend on whether the firm is in a long-run or short-run position. In the long run we expect any abnormal profits to attract new entrants (or losses to cause exits from the industry) as in perfect competition, so the equilibrium position will be the one shown in Figure 16.7. However, the question refers to a short-run position when abnormal profits could be earned. In this case the position could be illustrated by Figure 16.2.
3 The rent increase is a change in fixed costs in the short run, so it will affect the AFC and ATC but not the MC. The profit-maximizing output is therefore unaltered. The higher rent will simply reduce any abnormal profits that are being earned. If the firm was not earning normal profits then losses will be experienced and in the long run some firms will leave the industry. This will shift the demand outwards for existing firms (because survivors will benefit from the demand transferred from those exiting the industry) until the remaining firms can earn normal profits.

A fall in raw material prices will lower the MC curve as well as affecting AVC and ATC. The former will affect the profit-maximizing position, leading to an increase in output and a lowering of prices. Profits will increase in the short run but abnormal profits will, in the long run, attract new entrants.

2 State enterprises have lost favour in recent years. In the USA this has resulted in deregulation and in Britain it has resulted in privatization. With these developments in mind explain:
(a) the case for privatization; (b) the case against privatization.

1 Introduction
Define privatization: the transfer of ownership of publicly owned enterprises to the private sector. This can be distinguished from deregulation, which refers to the removal of statutory restraints on competition. Privatization is now widespread – Australia, New Zealand and the USA could be cited.
2 Case for privatization:
(a) There is a fairly widespread view that nationalized industries had a number of faults. They
 (i) were bureaucratic and insensitive to consumer demands;
 (ii) were monopolies, which led to inefficiencies;
 (iii) made losses: government underwriting meant they were not very efficient and presented the public with a sizable tax bill;
 (iv) were too subject to ministerial interference, which inhibited efficiency and long-term planning;
 (v) exhibited producer power, with overmanning and low productivity.
(b) If privatization means greater competition and exposure to market pressures then it is claimed that the usual benefits of the market can be enjoyed: there will be a drive to reduce costs and innovate and a more consumer-orientated approach.
(c) Private ownership, it is suggested, removes ministerial interference and allows more opportunity to plan. Freedom from Treasury controls on borrowing could permit a more rational approach to investment. Profit, it is argued, gives clear signals to management on performance.
(d) The proceeds of the sales provide revenue, so reducing the PSBR. To make the sale more attractive may involve limiting the amount of competition introduced on privatization, hence there may be a conflict between this advantage and (b) above.
(e) Wider share ownership is another possible objective.
3 Case against privatization:
(a) If the industry is monopolized then substituting a private monopoly may not improve efficiency and consumer consideration. If the controls are loosened then matters may deteriorate. One main argument for privatization rests upon being able to create a competitive environment.
(b) Competition may be wasteful in some circumstances, e.g. the natural monopolies.
(c) Basing allocative decisions on private costs and benefits may not be appropriate where there are significant externalities. Although there are various ways of responding to this some people argue that these can be better handled by state provision. The same argument may be used for merit goods, but it should be emphasized that public responsibility for delivering services does not necessarily require them to be produced by the public sector.
(d) There may be strategic/political arguments for public provision.
(e) Some critics of privatization would argue that public sector performance could be improved.
4 Conclusion
It would be desirable to resolve the arguments by an appeal to the empirical evidence. Unfortunately the evidence is far from clear cut.

Chapter 17

Self-test questions

1 The information below relates to a firm which has a perfectly elastic demand for its product (i.e. it is a price taker).

Number employed	Marginal physical product
1	30
2	45
3	50
4	45
5	35
6	25
7	20
8	15
9	10
10	5

a) What number would be employed if the wage were £350 and the price of the product were £10?
b) If the wage fell to £200, what number would be employed?
c) If the wage were £350 but the price of the product rose to £14, what number would be employed?

2 The table below relates to an industry:

Wage	Number of workers	Marginal revenue product (MRP)
100	0	
200	1	900
300	2	1000
400	3	900
500	4	800
600	5	750
700	6	700
800	7	650

a) What will the wage and employment levels be if:
(i) the industry is competitive and there is no union?
(ii) there is a monopsonist (sole buyer) and no unions?
b) If a union secures a monopoly supply of labour where there is a monopsonist buyer of labour and manages to negotiate a wage of £600, what will be the level of employment? What is the highest wage it can negotiate and maximize employment?

3(a) Plot Lorenz curves for original income and final income in 1985 from the table below.
b) Consider the final income for 1985 and 1976; would you expect the Gini coefficient to be larger or smaller in 1985 and what would it signify?

Distribution of original, disposable and final household income

Quintile groups of households	Original income 1985	Final income 1985	Final income 1976
Bottom fifth	0.3	6.7	7.4
Next fifth	6.0	11.8	12.7
Middle fifth	17.2	17.4	18.0
Next fifth	27.3	24.0	24.0
Top fifth	49.2	40.2	37.9

(Social Trends, 1988)

4 'Income tax cuts increase after tax income and will therefore encourage more work.' Do you agree?

Answers

1 (a) 5; (b) 7; (c) 6.
2 (a)(i) £700 wage with 6 people employed; (ii) £500 with 4 employed.
b) 5 will be employed and the highest wage that can be negotiated with maximum employment will be £700.

3(a)

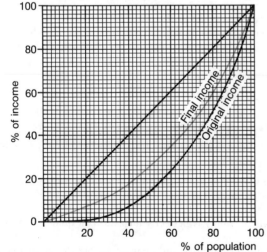

b) Larger, because the distribution of income is less equal.

4 This applies if the supply curve with respect to after tax income is upward sloping. More work will be substituted for leisure because this is relatively more attractive than before the tax cut. However, the supply curve may be backward sloping if people decide to take more leisure. This would happen if the income effect outweighed the substitution effect, i.e. higher income leads people to consume more leisure (the income effect) and this outweighs the increased attractiveness of work (substitution effect). On the individual level it has to be recognized that a number of people will be unable to alter their hours of work. For those who can, the evidence seems to suggest that some will work harder while others will choose more leisure.

Essay question

(a) Define and show the differences between transfer earnings, economic rent and quasi rent.
(b) What role do the rewards to factors of production play in the operation of the market economy? ACCA

Part (a)
Transfer earnings are what need to be paid to a factor to retain it in its present use and represent what the factor could earn elsewhere in the next best paid alternative use. Economic rent is the difference between the payment to the factor and transfer payments. It therefore represents payment over and above what is necessary to retain it in its present use. Figure 17.5 can be used to illustrate rent and transfer earnings and to make the point that the more inelastic the supply curve the greater will be the rent element in earnings. Quasi rent arises in the short run where a factor is immobile, and therefore inelastic in supply, so increasing the rent element. In the longer run, factors are more mobile so this aspect of rent is temporary.

Part (b)
Factor payments are part of the price signals of the market economy and a means of allocating resources. Prices are a way of rationing scarce factors of production; they also convey information. Changes in market conditions (for example a change in demand or technology) that alter the demand for factors will change factor prices. This acts as an indicator of the changed conditions and conveys the appropriate information. Prices provide incentives for factors to move between firms, occupations and regions.

Relative factor prices determine how factors are used in production: they affect factor intensity. A rise in the price of labour, ceteris paribus, will lead firms to use more capital-intensive methods. However, there may be market failure which means that factor prices do not fully carry out the functions indicated above; this can be caused by imperfect information and externalities.

Chapter 18

Self-test questions

1 From the information below,
(a) plot the Marginal Social Utility (MSU) and Marginal Social Cost (MSC) schedules. (b) What is the optimum output?
(c) What are the main conditions that are necessary for a market economy to achieve an optimum?

Quantity	MSU	MSC
10	10	2
20	8	4
30	6	6
40	4	8
50	2	10
60	0	12

2 Use the information in question 1 to represent the social costs and benefits of vaccination. Assume that the private marginal cost is equal to the social marginal cost. The following table gives the private benefits to those people who are vaccinated. We assume that the benefits received are reflected in the price that

people are prepared to pay, so we can regard this as the demand for vaccination.

Quantity	Private benefits
0	12
10	8
20	4
30	0

(a) What number of vaccinations would be purchased in an unregulated market?
(b) If the government were to intervene and supply vaccinations, what price would it charge to achieve the social optimum?

3 Using the data from question 1, suppose there is a situation where there are external costs, so that the private marginal costs are:

Quantity	Private marginal cost
10	1
20	2
30	4
40	6
50	8
60	10

(a) What output would be produced by an unregulated economy?
(b) If the government decided to impose a tax to achieve a social optimum position, what level of tax would be imposed?

4 The following information relates to costs of pollution and the costs of removing it:

Quantity of pollution	Costs of removing pollution	Costs of pollution
0	500	0
4	300	100
8	200	200
12	150	300
16	100	400

(a) What is the optimal amount of pollution?
(b) If a charge or tax for pollution is levied, at what level should the government set it?
(c) If the government decided to auction off pollution licences, what quantity should they issue?

Answers

1(a)

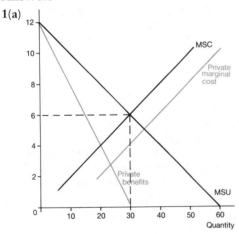

(b) 30; where $MSU = MSC$.
(c) If the condition $MSU = MSC$ is to be achieved by the market economy it requires that:
(i) $P = MC$; (ii) $P = MSU$ and $MC = MSC$; (iii) there are no public goods; (iv) information is perfect.

2(a) 20
(b) Zero price, so 30 vaccinations would be undertaken which would achieve the quantity associated with the optimum.

3(a) 35: competitive industries will produce where $P = MC$, where MC is private marginal cost.

(b) 2: this tax will mean that the equilibrium output will occur where $MSU = MSC$.

4(a) 8: this is where the costs of removing the pollution equal the costs to society of the pollution.
(b) 200; (c) 8.

Essay question

(a) Define an externality.
(b) What effects do externalities have on the allocation of resources?
(c) Explain briefly how the effects of externalities may be dealt with.   *ACCA*

Part (a)
An externality is a side effect of consumption or production which affects others (the utility of consumers and/or the costs of producers) and for which no payment is made. These externalities may be unwelcome external costs (e.g. pollution) or be beneficial (e.g. a drainage scheme by a farmer which benefits his neighbours or vaccination which reduces the incidence of a disease).

Part (b)
Externalities lead to a misallocation of resources. In a market economy resources are allocated according to private benefits and private costs; but the existence of externalities means that they diverge from social benefits and social costs. So, social cost = private cost + external cost.

An optimum allocation of resources requires MSU (marginal social utility, the marginal benefits to society) to equal MSC (marginal social cost, the extra costs to society of additional output); see Figure 18.1. The misallocation of resources caused by externalities can be illustrated by Figure 18.8, where the lefthand diagram shows the effect of external costs.

Part (c)
There are several ways of dealing with externalities:
(i) Market solution: the market may be able to respond to externalities where the number of parties involved is fairly limited. So a firm A that suffers a nuisance from firm B may pay B to desist. Alternatively, B may pay A compensation.
(ii) Taxes and subsidies may be used so that output is at the social optimum: for example, in the case of external costs in Figure 18.8, a tax of BC will move equilibrium output from Q_p to Q_s.
(iii) Regulation may be used to limit or prevent external costs.
(iv) Licences may be used to limit pollution – these could be auctioned off.
(v) State provision may be deemed appropriate where the externalities are regarded as large.

There may be problems associated with government intervention. Governments may wrongly estimate benefits and costs and administrative inefficiency may lead to 'government failure', which may outweigh the market failure the government is seeking to rectify.

Chapter 19

Self-test questions

1 The demand for a product is represented by the equation
$$Q = 600 - 100P$$
where Q is quantity and P is price, in pounds. A sales tax of £2 per unit is imposed. For the following cases:
(a) where supply is represented by the equation $Q = 100P$;
(b) where supply is perfectly inelastic at a quantity of 300; give
(i) equilibrium price and quantity before the tax is imposed;
(ii) equilibrium price and quantity after the tax is imposed;
(iii) tax revenue; (iv) share of tax paid by consumer;
(v) deadweight loss.

(a) Distinguish between the benefit and ability to pay principles of taxation.
b) Which principle best describes the following:
(i) income tax;
ii) community charge or poll tax;
ii) TV licences.

Answers

(a) **(i)** Price = £3; quantity = 300; **(ii)** price = £4; quantity = 00; **(iii)** £400; **(iv)** consumer pays half of the tax; **(v)** £100.
b) **(i)** Price = £3; quantity = 300; **(ii)** price = £3; quantity = 00; **(iii)** £600; **(iv)** producer pays all of the tax; **(v)** there is no eadweight loss.

(a) With the benefit principle, people pay taxes according to the enefits they receive, whereas the ability to pay principle involves ssessing tax payments on people's income or wealth rather than ie benefit they receive from state expenditure.
b) **(i)** Ability to pay principle; **(ii)** and **(iii)** benefit principle.

Essay question

Assess the case for the Community Charge (or Poll Tax).

Introduction

xplain that the Poll Tax is a locally determined tax which all dults will be expected to pay. A system of rebates for those eceiving benefits will be limited to 80 per cent of the tax so all dults will pay some poll tax. There will be a uniform business ax which will be determined by central government. Briefly idicate that the Poll Tax will replace the rates (a property tax) nd that other forms of local taxation such as sales and income ıx have been advocated and discussed.

The economic rationale for local government

riefly outline the economic rationale for local government, xplaining that linking local tax payments to local benefits is a vay of enabling voters to indicate preferences and a willingness o pay.

Criteria for assessing local taxes:
a) collection and compliance costs;
ɔ) economic efficiency
i) incidence should be confined to local authority so recipients of benefits pay the taxes;
i) taxes should not impede efficiency allocation of resources;
c) certainty of yield;
d) equity and ability to pay;
e) acceptability and fairness.

Poll Tax
ı) Collection and compliance costs are likely to be relatively igh compared with rates, as it will be difficult to compile an p-to-date register of all adults in a locality.
ɔ) **(i)** Incidence should be confined to the local authority so recipients of benefits will pay the taxes. This is deemed to be one of the main advantages of the tax. The limited system of rebates will mean that all adults pay some tax. The uniform business tax will mean that all businesses pay the same even though some may receive different benefits.
i) The Poll Tax will not have disincentive effects because the same will be paid irrespective of income. However, for those who lose benefits the marginal rate will be high. Poll Tax increases the incentive to purchase housing which will be taxed at a lower rate than most other goods and services; it also increases the tax advantage of housing as a use of savings. A uniform business tax means that location decisions should not be affected.
c) The yield is less certain than rates but more predictable than or other local taxes.
d) The Poll Tax is highly regressive.
e) Advocates of Poll Tax suggest it is fairer than rates in rcumstances where large families living in the same type of roperty pay the same rates as a single retired person. Against

this, the regressive element of the tax gives rise to much bitterness and resentment and does not accord with many peoples' notion of fairness.

5 Domestic Rates
(a) These have low collection and compliance costs.
(b) **(i)** Incidence is confined to the local authority so recipients of benefits pay tax. This does not apply to the business rate.
(ii) The domestic rate system broadly taxed housing in line with VAT.
(c) There is certainty of yield.
(d) Higher value properties were subject to higher rates but rates were regressive, forming a lower proportion of income as incomes rise.
(e) Rates aroused mixed feelings.

6 Other local taxes: sales and income taxes
(a) The collection and compliance costs would depend on the form of tax.
(b) **(i)** Incidence might not be confined to the local authority – people will travel to avoid higher sales taxes and there are difficulties for income tax, which is presently assessed on where people work, not where they live.
(ii) Taxes should not impede efficient allocation of resources.
(c) Yield is less certain because it depends on the state of the economy.
(d) National income tax is widely regarded as equitable.
(e) Views differ as to whether other forms of local tax would be fair and acceptable.

Chapter 20
Self-test questions

1 The following table shows the output per worker of producing products A and B in three different situations. Ignore the contribution of other factors.

	Situation 1		Situation 2		Situation 3	
	A	B	A	B	A	B
West Germany	120	60	120	60	120	60
UK	80	20	80	40	80	60

(a) Will there be benefits from trade in each of these situations? Briefly explain your answer.
(b) If so, in which product will each country specialize and trade?

2 Assume the equilibrium exchange rate for sterling is $2:£1.
(a) If exchange rates are fixed, consider the exchange rates £1 : $1, £1 : $2, and £1 : $3 and explain:
 (i) the balance of payments position;
 (ii) the intervention required to maintain the exchange rate in the short run;
(iii) the long-run policy required to maintain exchange rates.
(b) If exchange rates are freely floating, what is the effect of a deterioration in competitiveness resulting from the country experiencing a faster rate of inflation than its competitors?

Answers

1 In answering the question you should calculate the opportunity costs of producing the goods A and B in each of the countries; see the table below:

	Situation 1		Situation 2		Situation 3	
	A	B	A	B	A	B
West Germany	0.5	2	0.5	2	0.5	2
UK	0.25	4	0.5	2	0.75	1.33

(a) There will be benefits from trade in situations 1 and 3 but not in 2. In 2 there are no differences in opportunity costs so it does not benefit countries to trade.
(b) UK will export A and West Germany will specialize in and export B in situation 1. This will be reversed in situation 3.

2(a) (i) £1 : $3 deficit; £1 : $2 equilibrium; £1 : $1 surplus.

(ii) £1 : $3 buy £; £1 : $2 no intervention required; £1 : $1 sell £.

(iii) £1 : $3: deflationary policies, designed to reduce the demand for imports (shift supply of £ inwards) and inflation, which will improve competitiveness, *ceteris paribus*, and will shift the demand for £ outwards and the supply curve inwards.

£1 : $2: none required.

£1 : $1: opposite of (i). In addition it is possible to allow reserves of foreign currency to be acquired.

(b) The loss of competitiveness would shift the supply schedule out to the right, as more goods and services are imported at a given exchange rate and the demand schedule for £ would shift inwards as UK exports become less attractive.

Essay questions

1 One consequence of the world recession has been a renewed call by some writers for a period of 'protectionism', in respect of their own economies. With this in mind explain:

(a) the case for protectionism;

(b) the case against protectionism. *ACCA*

1 Introduction

Define protectionism: the restriction of free trade. It may take many forms: tariffs, quotas, imposing standards or taxes which are designed to discriminate against imports. The discussion here largely concentrates on tariffs, but most of the arguments apply to other forms of protection.

2 The case for protectionism

(a) Sectional interests (e.g. certain industries and groups of employees) will gain because output and employment will be higher, at least in the short run. However, there will be losers, as consumers will have to pay higher prices.

(b) Tariffs could be justified where an industry requires a temporary period of protection whilst it becomes established. Thereafter, because it has a comparative advantage it will survive without protection. Critics of this argument would ask why, if the industry is profitable in the long run, the market would not invest in it and suffer any short-term losses.

(c) There is a case for imposing a tariff or other restriction where one country is dumping goods at prices below costs of production in another. This argument really applies only where this is done to destroy competition and allow the dumper to acquire a monopoly position which it will exploit by subsequently raising prices.

(d) Tariffs may be justified where they are effectively being used as a means of indirect taxation because an undeveloped tax system limits the imposition of taxes on domestically produced goods.

(e) Tariffs may be justifiable to protect an industry for strategic purposes (defence of a country) or to retain a way of life (e.g. craft or agricultural industries). This means sacrificing some of the gains from trade for these socio-political objectives.

(f) There is a macroeconomic argument that tariffs are a means of reducing unemployment, as domestic firms produce goods that otherwise would be imported. Against this must be set the loss to the consumer (see 1 above) and the possibility that this protection may induce inefficiencies and slow productivity improvements so damaging growth.

3 The case against protectionism

(a) Protectionism would prevent a country from achieving the gains from trade (the theory of comparative advantage).

(b) If there was a widespread retaliation against a country imposing tariffs this could lead to a trade war between nations and considerable loss of the benefits of trade.

(c) One major objection to protectionism is that it tends to induce inefficient practices because the reduction in competition of low cost rivals reduces the pressure on domestic firms.

(d) Tariffs or quotas will tend to raise the prices of imported goods; so if they are applied on a widespread scale, inflation will rise in the year of their introduction. This should be a once and for all effect; however if it gives rise to a price–wage spiral then the effect may be more long lasting.

2 In April 1987 the Chancellor of the Exchequer indicated a policy of keeping the pound near its then existing level (approximately $1.60 and DM2.90).

(a) What are the advantages of keeping a stable exchange rate?

(b) How could this be achieved:

(i) in the short term; (ii) in the long term?

(c) Has the Chancellor's objective of keeping the pound stable been achieved? *CIE*

Part (a)

Advantages of a stable exchange rate:

(i) It encourages trade because it means that traders (exporters and importers) have a reasonable idea of prices they can charge and they will have to pay. But note that stable nominal exchange rates may conflict with a stable real rate implying that competitiveness is changing.

(ii) It will tend to moderate inflation if competing countries have low rates of inflation.

Part (b)

Policies to maintain stable exchange rates

(i) in the short term:

– intervention in foreign exchange market (buying/selling sterling)

– interest rate adjustments; raising interest rates may be used to prevent a fall in the exchange rate;

– policy 'news': the foreign exchange market reacts immediately to a wide range of news, e.g. trade and inflation statistics.

(ii) in the long term:

– appropriate monetary and fiscal policies would have to be pursued so that inflation rates are broadly in line with foreign countries.

– long-term changes and the balance of payments may pose difficulties for maintaining the exchange rate.

Part (c)

This part of the question (which only accounts for 4 out of a possible 20 marks) is a reminder that it is important in many areas of economics to read newspapers and keep up to date. When this particular examination was taken both rates were substantially above those mentioned in the question.

Index